Workshop on Creating Speech and Language Data with Amazons Mechanical Turk 2010

Held at NAACL HLT 2010

Los Angeles, California, USA
6 June 2010

ISBN: 978-1-61738-676-3

Printed from e-media with permission by:

Curran Associates, Inc.
57 Morehouse Lane
Red Hook, NY 12571

CURRAN ASSOCIATES INC. proceedings.com

Some format issues inherent in the e-media version may also appear in this print version.

Printed by Curran Associates, Inc. (2010)

Association for Computational Linguistics
209 N. Eighth Street
Stroudsburg, Pennsylvania 18360

Phone: 1-570-476-8006
Fax: 1-570-476-0860

acl@aclweb.org

Additional copies of this publication are available from:

Curran Associates, Inc.
57 Morehouse Lane
Red Hook, NY 12571 USA
Phone: 845-758-0400
Fax: 845-758-2634
Email: curran@proceedings.com
Web: www.proceedings.com

Preface

The NAACL-2010 Workshop on Creating Speech and Language Data With Amazon's Mechanical Turk explores applications of crowdsourcing technologies for the creation and study of language data. Recent work has evaluated the effectiveness of using crowdsourcing platforms, such as Amazon's Mechanical Turk, to create annotated data for natural language processing applications. This workshop further explores this area and these proceedings contain 34 papers and an overview paper that each experiment with applications of Mechanical Turk. The diversity of applications showcases the new possibilities for annotating speech and text, and has the potential to dramatically change how we create data for human language technologies.

Papers in the workshop also looked at best practices in creating data using Mechanical Turk. Experiments evaluated how to design Human Intelligence Tasks (HITs), how to attract users to the task, how to price annotation tasks, and how to ensure data quality. Applications include the creation of data sets for standard NLP tasks, developing entirely new tasks, and investigating new ways of integrating user feedback in the learning process.

The workshop featured an open-ended shared task in which 35 teams were awarded $100 of credit on Amazon Mechanical Turk to spend on an annotation task of their choosing. Results of the shared task are described in short papers and all collected data is publicly available. Shared task participants focused on data collection questions, such as how to convey complex tasks to non-experts, how to evaluate and ensure quality and annotation cost and speed.

The organizers thank the workshop participants who contributed to an incredibly strong workshop program. We also thank the program committee for quickly reviewing the large number of submissions. Special thanks go to Sharon Chiarella, vice president of Amazon Mechanical Turk, for funding the shared task, Ted Sandler of Amazon for assistance in organizing the shared task, Stephanie Geerlings and Lukas Biewald of CrowdFlower for making their service available to shared task participants, and to Jonny Weese for editing and compiling the final proceedings.

Organizers:

Chris Callison-Burch, Johns Hopkins University
Mark Dredze, Johns Hopkins University

Program Committee:

Breck Baldwin, Alias-i, Inc.
Jordan Boyd-Graber, University of Maryland
Michael Bloodgood, Johns Hopkins University
Bob Carpenter, Alias-i, Inc.
David Chen, University of Texas, Austin
Maxine Eskenazi, Carnegie Mellon University
Nikesh Garera, Kosmix Corporation
Jim Glass, Massachusetts Institute of Technology
Alex Gruenstein, Google, Inc.
Janna Hamaker, Amazon.com, Inc.
Jon Hamaker, Microsoft Corporation
Samer Hassan, University of North Texas
Alexandre Klementiev, Johns Hopkins University
Benjamin Lambert, Carnegie Mellon University
Ben Leong, University of North Texas
Ian McGraw, Massachusetts Institute of Technology
Scott Novotney, Johns Hopkins University
Brendan O'Connor, Carnegie Mellon University
Gabriel Parent, Carnegie Mellon University
Massimo Poesio, University of Essex
Joe Polifroni, Nokia Research Labs
Joseph Reisinger, University of Texas, Austin
Ted Sandler, Amazon.com, Inc.
Stephanie Seneff, Massachusetts Institute of Technology
Kevin Small, Tufts University
Rion Snow, Stanford University / Twitter, Inc.

Table of Contents

Workshop Program

Sunday, June 6, 2010

9:00	**Morning Session**
	Creating Speech and Language Data With Amazon's Mechanical Turk Chris Callison-Burch and Mark Dredze
9:10	Invited Talk
10:10	*Corpus Creation for New Genres: A Crowdsourced Approach to PP Attachment* Mukund Jha, Jacob Andreas, Kapil Thadani, Sara Rosenthal and Kathleen McKeown
10:30	**Coffee Break**
11:00	**Poster Session 1**
	Clustering dictionary definitions using Amazon Mechanical Turk Gabriel Parent and Maxine Eskenazi
	Semi-supervised Word Alignment with Mechanical Turk Qin Gao and Stephan Vogel
	Rating Computer-Generated Questions with Mechanical Turk Michael Heilman and Noah A. Smith
	Crowdsourced Accessibility: Elicitation of Wikipedia Articles Scott Novotney and Chris Callison-Burch
	Document Image Collection Using Amazon's Mechanical Turk Audrey Le, Jerome Ajot, Mark Przybocki and Stephanie Strassel
	Using Amazon Mechanical Turk for Transcription of Non-Native Speech Keelan Evanini, Derrick Higgins and Klaus Zechner
	Exploring Normalization Techniques for Human Judgments of Machine Translation Adequacy Collected Using Amazon Mechanical Turk Michael Denkowski and Alon Lavie

Sunday, June 6, 2010 (continued)

Can Crowds Build parallel corpora for Machine Translation Systems?
Vamshi Ambati and Stephan Vogel

Turker-Assisted Paraphrasing for English-Arabic Machine Translation
Michael Denkowski, Hassan Al-Haj and Alon Lavie

Annotating Large Email Datasets for Named Entity Recognition with Mechanical Turk
Nolan Lawson, Kevin Eustice, Mike Perkowitz and Meliha Yetisgen-Yildiz

Annotating Named Entities in Twitter Data with Crowdsourcing
Tim Finin, William Murnane, Anand Karandikar, Nicholas Keller, Justin Martineau and Mark Dredze

MTurk Crowdsourcing: A Viable Method for Rapid Discovery of Arabic Nicknames?
Chiara Higgins, Elizabeth McGrath and Laila Moretto

An Enriched MT Grammar for Under $100
Omar F. Zaidan and Juri Ganitkevitch

12:30 **Lunch**

1:30 **Afternoon Session 1**

Using the Amazon Mechanical Turk to Transcribe and Annotate Meeting Speech for Extractive Summarization
Matthew Marge, Satanjeev Banerjee and Alexander Rudnicky

Using Mechanical Turk to Annotate Lexicons for Less Commonly Used Languages
Ann Irvine and Alexandre Klementiev

Opinion Mining of Spanish Customer Comments with Non-Expert Annotations on Mechanical Turk
Bart Mellebeek, Francesc Benavent, Jens Grivolla, Joan Codina, Marta R. Costa-Jussà and Rafael Banchs

Crowdsourcing and language studies: the new generation of linguistic data
Robert Munro, Steven Bethard, Victor Kuperman, Vicky Tzuyin Lai, Robin Melnick, Christopher Potts, Tyler Schnoebelen and Harry Tily

Not-So-Latent Dirichlet Allocation: Collapsed Gibbs Sampling Using Human Judgments
Jonathan Chang

Sunday, June 6, 2010 (continued)

3:10 **Coffee Break**

3:30 **Afternoon Session 2**

Collecting Image Annotations Using Amazon's Mechanical Turk
Cyrus Rashtchian, Peter Young, Micah Hodosh and Julia Hockenmaier

Non-Expert Evaluation of Summarization Systems is Risky
Dan Gillick and Yang Liu

Shedding (a Thousand Points of) Light on Biased Language
Tae Yano, Philip Resnik and Noah A. Smith

4:30 **Poster Session 2**

Evaluation of Commonsense Knowledge with Mechanical Turk
Jonathan Gordon, Benjamin Van Durme and Lenhart Schubert

Cheap Facts and Counter-Facts
Rui Wang and Chris Callison-Burch

The Wisdom of the Crowds Ear: Speech Accent Rating and Annotation with Amazon Mechanical Turk
Stephen Kunath and Steven Weinberger

Crowdsourcing Document Relevance Assessment with Mechanical Turk
Catherine Grady and Matthew Lease

Preliminary Experiments with Amazon's Mechanical Turk for Annotating Medical Named Entities
Meliha Yetisgen-Yildiz, Imre Solti, Fei Xia and Scott Halgrim

Tools for Collecting Speech Corpora via Mechanical-Turk
Ian Lane, Matthias Eck, Kay Rottmann and Alex Waibel

Measuring Transitivity Using Untrained Annotators
Nitin Madnani, Jordan Boyd-Graber and Philip Resnik

Sunday, June 6, 2010 (continued)

Creating Speech and Language Data With Amazon's Mechanical Turk

Chris Callison-Burch and **Mark Dredze**
Human Language Technology Center of Excellence
& Center for Language and Speech Processing
Johns Hopkins University
ccb,mdredze@cs.jhu.edu

Abstract

In this paper we give an introduction to using Amazon's Mechanical Turk crowdsourcing platform for the purpose of collecting data for human language technologies. We survey the papers published in the NAACL-2010 Workshop. 24 researchers participated in the workshop's shared task to create data for speech and language applications with $100.

1 Introduction

This paper gives an overview of the NAACL-2010 Workshop on Creating Speech and Language Data With Amazon's Mechanical Turk. A number of recent papers have evaluated the effectiveness of using Mechanical Turk to create annotated data for natural language processing applications. The low cost, scalable workforce available through Mechanical Turk (MTurk) and other crowdsourcing sites opens new possibilities for annotating speech and text, and has the potential to dramatically change how we create data for human language technologies. Open questions include: What kind of research is possible when the cost of creating annotated training data is dramatically reduced? What new tasks should we try to solve if we do not limit ourselves to reusing existing training and test sets? Can complex annotation be done by untrained annotators? How can we ensure high quality annotations from crowd-sourced contributors?

To begin addressing these questions, we organized an open-ended $100 shared task. Researchers were given $100 of credit on Amazon Mechanical Turk to spend on an annotation task of their choosing. They were required to write a short paper describing their experience, and to distribute the data that they created. They were encouraged to address the following questions: How did you convey the task in terms that were simple enough for non-experts to understand? Were non-experts as good as experts? What did you do to ensure quality? How quickly did the data get annotated? What is the cost per label? Researchers submitted a 1 page proposal to the workshop organizers that described their intended experiments and expected outcomes. The organizers selected proposals based on merit, and awarded $100 credits that were generously provided by Amazon Mechanical Turk. In total, 35 credits were awarded to researchers.

Shared task participants were given 10 days to run experiments between the distribution of the credit and the initial submission deadline. 30 papers were submitted to the shared task track, of which 24 were accepted. 14 papers were submitted to the general track of which 10 were accepted, giving a 77% acceptance rate and a total of 34 papers. Shared task participants were required to provide the data collected as part of their experiments. All of the shared task data is available on the workshop website.

2 Mechanical Turk

Amazon's Mechanical Turk[1] is an online marketplace for work. Amazon's tag line for Mechanical Turk is *artificial* artificial intelligence, and the name refers to a historical hoax from the 18th cen-

[1] http://www.mturk.com/

Proceedings of the NAACL HLT 2010 Workshop on Creating Speech and Language Data with Amazon's Mechanical Turk, pages 1–12,
Los Angeles, California, June 2010.

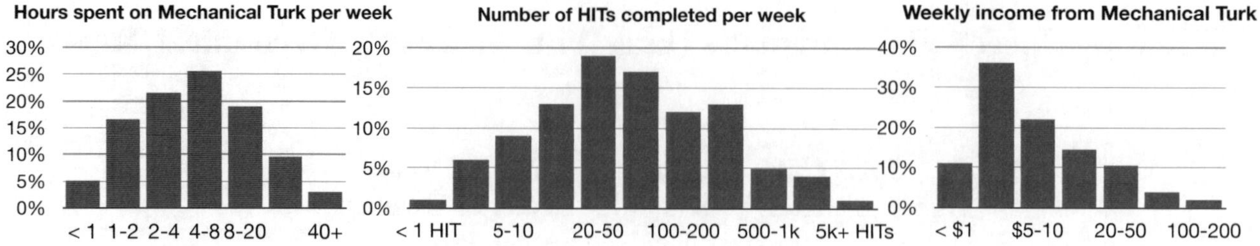

Figure 1: Time spent, HITs completed, and amount earned from a survey of 1,000 Turkers by Ipeirotis (2010).

tury where a chess-playing automaton appeared to be able to beat human opponents using a mechanism, but was, in fact, controlled by a person hiding inside the machine. These hint at the the primary focus of the web service, which is to get people to perform tasks that are simple for humans but difficult for computers. The basic unit of work on MTurk is even called a Human Intelligence Task (HIT).

Amazon's web service provides an easy way to pay people small amounts of money to perform HITs. Anyone with an Amazon account can either submit HITs or work on HITs that were submitted by others. Workers are referred to as "Turkers" and people designing the HITs are called "Requesters." Requesters set the amount that they will pay for each item that is completed. Payments are frequently as low as $0.01. Turkers are free to select whichever HITs interest them.], and to disregard HITs that they find uninteresting or which they deem pay too little.

Because of its focus on tasks requiring human intelligence, Mechanical Turk is obviously applicable to the field of natural language processing. Snow et al. (2008) used Mechanical Turk to inexpensively collect labels for several NLP tasks including word sense disambiguation, word similarity, textual entailment, and temporal ordering of events. Snow et al. had two exciting findings. First, they showed that a strong correlation between non-expert and expert annotators can be achieved by combining the judgments of multiple non-experts, for instance by voting on each label using 10 different Turkers. Correlation and accuracy of labeling could be further improved by weighting each Turker's vote by calibrating them on a small amount of gold standard data created by expert annotators. Second, they collected a staggering number of labels for a very small amount of money. They collected 21,000 labels for just over $25. Turkers put in over 140+ hours worth of human effort to generate the labels. The amount of participation is surprisingly high, given the small payment.

Why do you complete tasks in MTurk?	US	India
To spend free time fruitfully and get cash (e.g., instead of watching TV)	70%	60%
For "primary" income purposes (e.g., gas, bills, groceries, credit cards)	15%	27%
For "secondary" income purposes, pocket change (for hobbies, gadgets)	60%	37%
To kill time	33%	5%
The tasks are fun	40%	20%
Currently unemployed or part time work	30%	27%

Table 1: Motivations for participating on Mechanical Turk from a survey of 1,000 Turkers by Ipeirotis (2010).

Turker demographics

Given the amount of work that can get done for so little, it is natural to ask: who would contribute so much work for so little pay, and why? The answers to these questions are often mysterious because Amazon does not provide any personal information about Turkers (each Turker is identifiable only through a serial number like A23KO2TP7I4KK2). Ipeirotis (2010) elucidates some of the reasons by presenting a demographic analysis of Turkers. He built a profile of 1000 Turkers by posting a survey to MTurk and paying $0.10 for people to answer questions about their reasons for participating on Mechanical Turk, the amount that they earn each week, and how much time they spend, as well as demographic information like country of origin, gender, age, education level, and household income.

One suspicion that people often have when they first hear about MTurk is that it is some sort of digital sweatshop that exploits workers in third world countries. However, Ipeirotis reports that nearly half

(47%) of the Turkers who answered his survey were from the United States, with the next largest group (34%) coming from India, and the remaining 19% spread between 66 other countries.

Table 1 gives the survey results for questions relating to why people participate on Mechanical Turk. It shows that most US-based workers use Mechanical Turk for secondary income purposes (to have spending money for hobbies or going out), but that the overwhelming majority of them use it to spend their time more fruitfully (i.e., instead of watching TV). The economic downturn may have increased participation, with 30% of the US-based Turkers reporting that they are unemployed or underemployed. The public radio show Marketplace recently interviewed unemployed Turkers (Rose, 2010). It reports that they earn a little income, but that they do not earn enough to make a living. Figure 1 confirms this, giving a break down of how much time people spend on Mechanical Turk each week, how many HITs they complete, and how much money they earn. Most Turkers spend less than 8 hours per week on Mechanical Turk, and earn less than $10 per week through the site.

3 Quality Control

Ipeirotis (2010) reports that just over half of Turkers have a college education. Despite being reasonably well educated, it is important to keep in mind that Turkers do not have training in specialized subjects like NLP. Because the Turkers are non-experts, and because the payments are generally so low, quality control is an important consideration when creating data with MTurk.

Amazon provides three mechanisms to help ensure quality:

- Requesters have the option of rejecting the work of individual Turkers, in which case they are not paid.[2] Turkers can also be blocked from doing future work for a requester.

- Requesters can specify that each HIT should be redundantly completed by several different Turkers. This allows higher quality labels to be selected, for instance, by taking the majority label.

- Requesters can require that all workers meet a particular set of qualifications, such as sufficient accuracy on a small test set or a minimum percentage of previously accepted submissions.

Amazon provides two qualifications that a Requester can use by default. These are past HIT Approval Rate and Location. The location qualification allows the Requester to have HITs done only by residents of a certain country (or to exclude Turkers from certain regions). Additionally, Requesters can design custom Qualification Tests that Turkers must complete before working on a particular HIT. These can be created through the MTurk API, and can either be graded manually or automatically. An important qualification that isn't among Amazon's default qualifications is language skills. One might design a qualification test to determine a Turker's ability to speak Arabic or Farsi before allowing them to do part of speech tagging in those languages, for instance.

There are several reasons that poor quality data might be generated. The task may be too complex or the instructions might not be clear enough for Turkers to follow. The financial incentives may be too low for Turkers to act conscientiously, and certain HIT designs may allow them to simply randomly click instead of thinking about the task. Mason and Watts (2009) present a study of financial incentives on Mechanical Turk and find, counterintuitively, that increasing the amount of compensation for a particular task does not tend to improve the quality of the results. Anecdotally, we have observed that sometimes there is an inverse relationship between the amount of payment and the quality of work, because it is more tempting to cheat on high-paying HITs if you don't have the skills to complete them. For example, a number of Turkers tried to cheat on an Urdu to English translation HIT by cutting-and-pasting the Urdu text into an online machine translation system (expressly forbidden in the instructions) because we were paying the comparatively high amount of $1.

[2]Since the results are downloadable even if they are rejected, this could allow unscrupulous Requesters to abuse Turkers by rejecting all of their work, even if it was done well. Turkers have message boards at `http://www.turkernation.com/`, where they discuss Requesters. They even have a Firefox plugin called Turkopticon that lets them see ratings of how good the Requesters are in terms of communicating with Turkers, being generous and fair, and paying promptly.

3.1 Designing HITs for quality control

We suggest designing your HITs in a way that will deter cheating or that will make cheating obvious. HIT design is part of the art of using MTurk. It can't be easily quantified, but it has a large impact on the outcome. For instance, we reduced cheating on our translation HIT by changing the design so that we displayed images of the Urdu sentences instead of text, which made it impossible to copy-and-paste into an MT system for anyone who could not type in Arabic script.

Another suggestion is to include information within the data that you upload to MTurk that will not be displayed to the Turkers, but will be useful to you when reviewing the HITs. For example, we include machine translation output along with the source sentences. Although this is not displayed to Turkers, when we review the Turkers' translations we compare them to the MT output. This allows us to reject translations that are identical to the MT, or which are just random sentences that are unrelated to the original Urdu. We also use a javascript[3] to gather the IP addresses of the Turkers and do geolocation to look up their location. Turkers in Pakistan require less careful scrutiny since they are more likely to be bilingual Urdu speakers than those in Romania, for instance.

CrowdFlower[4] provides an interface for designing HITs that includes a phase for the Requester to input gold standard data with known labels. Inserting items with known labels alongside items which need labels allows a Requester to see which Turkers are correctly replicating the gold standard labels and which are not. This is an excellent idea. If it is possible to include positive and negative controls in your HITs, then do so. Turkers who fail the controls can be blocked and their labels can be excluded from the final data set. CrowdFlower-generated HITs even display a score to the Turkers to give them feedback on how well they are doing. This provides training for Turkers, and discourages cheating.

[3] http://wiki.github.com/callison-burch/mechanical_turk_workshop/geolocation

[4] http://crowdflower.com/

3.2 Iterative improvements on MTurk

Another class of quality control on Mechanical Turk is through iterative HITs that build on the output of previous HITs. This could be used to have Turkers judge whether the results from a previous HIT conformed to the instructions, and whether it is of high quality. Alternately, the second set of Turkers could be used to improve the quality of what the first Turkers created. For instance, in a translation task, a second set of US-based Turkers could edit the English produced by non-native speakers.

CastingWords,[5] a transcription company that uses Turker labor, employs this strategy by having a first-pass transcription graded and iteratively improved in subsequent passes. Little et al. (2009) even designed an API specifically for running iterative tasks on MTurk.[6]

4 Recommended Practices

Although it is hard to define a set of "best practices" that applies to all HITs, or even to all NLP HITs, we recommend the following guidelines to Requesters. First and foremost, it is critical to convey instructions appropriately for non-experts. The instructions should be clear and concise. To calibrate whether the HIT is doable, you should first try the task yourself, and then have a friend from outside the field try it. This will help to ensure that the instructions are clear, and to calibrate how long each HIT will take (which ought to allow you to price the HITs fairly).

If possible, you should insert positive and negative controls so that you can quickly screen out bad Turkers. This is especially important for HITs that only require clicking buttons to complete. If possible, you should include a small amount of gold standard data in each HIT. This will allow you to determine which Turkers are good, but will also allow you weight the Turkers if you are combining the judgments of multiple Turkers. If you are having Turkers evaluate the output of systems, then randomize the order that the systems are shown in.

When publishing papers that use Mechanical Turk as a source of training data or to evaluate the output of an NLP system, report how you ensured the quality of your data. You can do this by measuring the

[5] http://castingwords.com/

[6] http://groups.csail.mit.edu/uid/turkit/

inter-annotator agreement of the Turkers against experts on small amounts of gold standard data, or by stating what controls you used and what criteria you used to block bad Turkers. Finally, whenever possible you should publish the data that you generate on Mechanical Turk (and your analysis scripts and HIT templates) alongside your paper so that other people can verify it.

5 Related work

In the past two years, several papers have published about applying Mechanical Turk to a diverse set of natural language processing tasks, including: creating question-answer sentence pairs (Kaisser and Lowe, 2008), evaluating machine translation quality and crowdsouring translations (Callison-Burch, 2009), paraphrasing noun-noun compouds for SemEval (Butnariu et al., 2009), human evaluation of topic models (Chang et al., 2009), and speech transcription (McGraw et al., 2010; Marge et al., 2010a; Novotney and Callison-Burch, 2010a). Others have used MTurk for novel research directions like non-simulated active learning for NLP tasks such as sentiment classification (Hsueh et al., 2009) or doing quixotic things like doing human-in-the-loop minimum error rate training for machine translation (Zaidan and Callison-Burch, 2009).

Some projects have demonstrated the super-scalability of crowdsourced efforts. Deng et al. (2009) used MTurk to construct ImageNet, an annotated image database containing 3.2 million that are hierarchically categorized using the WordNet ontology (Fellbaum, 1998). Because Mechanical Turk allows researchers to experiment with crowdsourcing by providing small incentives to Turkers, other successful crowdsourcing efforts like Wikipedia or Games with a Purpose (von Ahn and Dabbish, 2008) also share something in common with MTurk.

6 Shared Task

The workshop included a shared task in which participants were provided with $100 to spend on Mechanical Turk experiments. Participants submitted a 1 page proposal in advance describing their intended use of the funds. Selected proposals were provided $100 seed money, to which many participants added their own funds. As part of their participation, each team submitted a workshop paper describing their experiments as well as the data collected and described in the paper. Data for the shared papers is available at the workshop website.[7]

This section describes the variety of data types explored and collected in the shared task. Of the 24 participating teams, most did not exceed the $100 that they were awarded by a significant amount. Therefore, the variety and extent of data described in this section is the result of a minimal $2,400 investment. This achievement demonstrates the potential for MTurk's impact on the creation and curation of speech and language corpora.

6.1 Traditional NLP Tasks

An established core set of computational linguistic tasks have received considerable attention in the natural language processing community. These include knowledge extraction, textual entailment and word sense disambiguation. Each of these tasks requires a large and carefully curated annotated corpus to train and evaluate statistical models. Many of the shared task teams attempted to create new corpora for these tasks at substantially reduced costs using MTurk.

Parent and Eskenazi (2010) produce new corpora for the task of word sense disambiguation. The study used MTurk to create unique word definitions for 50 words, which Turkers then also mapped onto existing definitions. Sentences containing these 50 words were then assigned to unique definitions according to word sense.

Madnani and Boyd-Graber (2010) measured the concept of transitivity of verbs in the style of Hopper and Thompson (1980), a theory that goes beyond simple grammatical transitivity – whether verbs take objects (transitive) or not – to capture the amount of action indicated by a sentence. Videos that portrayed verbs were shown to Turkers who described the actions shown in the video. Additionally, sentences containing the verbs were rated for aspect, affirmation, benefit, harm, kinesis, punctuality, and volition. The authors investigated several approaches for eliciting descriptions of transitivity from Turkers.

Two teams explored textual entailment tasks. Wang and Callison-Burch (2010) created data for

[7] `http://sites.google.com/site/amtworkshop2010/`

recognizing textual entailment (RTE). They submitted 600 text segments and asked Turkers to identify facts and counter-facts (unsupported facts and contradictions) given the provided text. The resulting collection includes 790 facts and 203 counter-facts. Negri and Mehdad (2010) created a bi-lingual entailment corpus using English and Spanish entailment pairs, where the hypothesis and text come from different languages. The authors took a publicly available English RTE data set (the PASCAL-RTE3 dataset1) and created an English-Spanish equivalent by having Turkers translating the hypotheses into Spanish. The authors include a timeline of their progress, complete with total cost over the 10 days that they ran the experiments.

In the area of natural language generation, Heilman and Smith (2010) explored the potential of MTurk for ranking of computer generated questions about provided texts. These questions can be used to test reading comprehension and understanding. 60 Wikipedia articles were selected, for each of which 20 questions were generated. Turkers provided 5 ratings for each of the 1,200 questions, creating a significant corpus of scored questions.

Finally, Gordon et al. (2010) relied on MTurk to evaluate the quality and accuracy of automatically extracted common sense knowledge (factoids) from news and Wikipedia articles. Factoids were provided by the KNEXT knowledge extraction system.

6.2 Speech and Vision

While MTurk naturally lends itself to text tasks, several teams explored annotation and collection of speech and image data. We note that one of the papers in the main track described tools for collecting such data (Lane et al., 2010).

Two teams used MTurk to collect text annotations on speech data. Marge et al. (2010b) identified easy and hard sections of meeting speech to transcribe and focused data collection on difficult segments. Transcripts were collected on 48 audio clips from 4 different speakers, as well as other types of annotations. Kunath and Weinberger (2010) collected ratings of accented English speech, in which non-native speakers were rated as either Arabic, Mandarin or Russian native speakers. The authors obtained multiple annotations for each speech sample, and tracked the native language of each annotator, allowing for an analysis of rating accuracy between native English and non-native English annotators.

Novotney and Callison-Burch (2010b) used MTurk to elicit new speech samples. As part of an effort to increase the accessibility of public knowledge, such as Wikipedia, the team prompted Turkers to narrate Wikipedia articles. This required Turkers to record audio files and upload them. An additional HIT was used to evaluate the quality of the narrations.

A particularly creative data collection approach asked Turkers to create handwriting samples and then to submit images of their writing (Tong et al., 2010). Turkers were asked to submit handwritten shopping lists (large vocabulary) or weather descriptions (small vocabulary) in either Arabic or Spanish. Subsequent Turkers provided a transcription and a translation. The team collected 18 images per language, 2 transcripts per image and 1 translation per transcript.

6.3 Sentiment, Polarity and Bias

Two papers investigated the topics of sentiment, polarity and bias. Mellebeek et al. (2010) used several methods to obtain polarity scores for Spanish sentences expressing opinions about automative topics. They evaluated three HITs for collecting such data and compared results for quality and expressiveness. Yano et al. (2010) evaluated the political bias of blog posts. Annotators labeled 1000 sentences to determine biased phrases in political blogs from the 2008 election season. Knowledge of the annotators own biases allowed the authors to study how bias differs on the different ends of the political spectrum.

6.4 Information Retrieval

Large scale evaluations requiring significant human labor for evaluation have a long history in the information retrieval community (TREC). Grady and Lease (2010) study four factors that influence Turker performance on a document relevance search task. The authors present some negative results on how these factors influence data collection. For further work on MTurk and information retrieval, readers are encouraged to see the SIGIR 2010 Workshop on Crowdsourcing for Search Evaluation.[8]

[8]http://www.ischool.utexas.edu/~cse2010/call.htm

6.5 Information Extraction

Information extraction (IE) seeks to identify specific types of information in natural languages. The IE papers in the shared tasks focused on new domains and genres as well as new relation types.

The goal of relation extraction is to identify relations between entities or terms in a sentence, such as *born in* or *religion*. Gormley et al. (2010) automatically generate potential relation pairs in sentences by finding relation pairs appearing in news articles as given by a knowledge base. They ask Turkers if a sentence supports a relation, does not support a relation, or whether the relation makes sense. They collected close to 2500 annotations for 17 different person relation types.

The other IE papers explored new genres and domains. Finin et al. (2010) obtained named entity annotations (person, organization, geopolitical entity) for several hundred Twitter messages. They conducted experiments using both MTurk and CrowdFlower. Yetisgen-Yildiz et al. (2010) explored medical named entity recognition. They selected 100 clinical trial announcements from ClinicalTrials.gov. 4 annotators for each of the 100 announcements identified 3 types of medical entities: medical conditions, medications, and laboratory test.

6.6 Machine Translation

The most popular shared task topic was Machine Translation (MT). MT is a data hungry task that relies on huge corpora of parallel texts between two languages. Performance of MT systems depends on the size of training corpora, so there is a constant search for new and larger data sets. Such data sets are traditionally expensive to produce, requiring skilled translators. One of the advantages to MTurk is the diversity of the Turker population, making it an especially attractive source of MT data. Shared task papers in MT explored the full range of MT tasks, including alignments, parallel corpus creation, paraphrases and bilingual lexicons.

Gao and Vogel (2010) create alignments in a 300 sentence Chinese-English corpus (Chinese aligned to English). Both Ambati and Vogel (2010) and Bloodgood and Callison-Burch (2010) explore the potential of MTurk in the creation of MT parallel corpora for evaluation and training. Bloodgood and Callison-Burch replicate the NIST 2009 Urdu-English test set of 1792 sentences, paying only \$0.10 a sentence, a substantially reduced price than the typical annotator cost. The result is a data set that is still effective for comparing MT systems in an evaluation. Ambati and Vogel create corpora with 100 sentences and 3 translations per sentence for all the language pairs between English, Spanish, Urdu and Telugu. This demonstrates the feasibility of creating cheap corpora for high and low resource languages.

Two papers focused on the creation and evaluation of paraphrases. Denkowski et al. (2010) generated and evaluated 728 paraphrases for Arabic-English translation. MTurk was used to identify correct and fix incorrect paraphrases. Over 1200 high quality paraphrases were created. Buzek et al. (2010) evaluated error driven paraphrases for MT. In this setting, paraphrases are used to simplify potentially difficult to translate segments of text. Turkers identified 1780 error regions in 1006 English/Chinese sentences. Turkers provided 4821 paraphrases for these regions.

External resources can be an important part of an MT system. Irvine and Klementiev (2010) created lexicons for low resource languages. They evaluated translation candidates for 100 English words in 32 languages and solicited translations for 10 additional languages. Higgins et al. (2010) expanded name lists in Arabic by soliciting common Arabic nicknames. The 332 collected nicknames were primarily provided by Turkers in Arab speaking countries (35%), India (46%), and the United States (13%).

Finally, Zaidan and Ganitkevitch (2010) explored how MTurk could be used to directly improve an MT grammar. Each rule in an Urdu to English translation system was characterized by 12 features. Turkers were provided examples for which their feedback was used to rescore grammar productions directly. This approach shows the potential of fine tuning an MT system with targeted feedback from annotators.

7 Future Directions

Looking ahead, we can't help but wonder what impact MTurk and crowdsourcing will have on the speech and language research community. Keeping in mind Niels Bohr's famous exhortation "Prediction is very difficult, especially if it's about the future," we attempt to draw some conclusions and predict future directions and impact on the field.

Some have predicted that access to low cost, highly scalable methods for creating language and speech annotations means the end of work on unsupervised learning. Many a researcher has advocated his or her unsupervised learning approach because of annotation costs. However, if 100 examples for any task are obtainable for less than $100, why spend the time and effort developing often inferior unsupervised methods? Such a radical change is highly debatable, in fact, one of this paper's authors is a strong advocate of such a position while the other disagrees, perhaps because he himself works on unsupervised methods. Certainly, we can agree that the potential exists for a change in focus in a number of ways.

In natural language processing, data drives research. The introduction of new large and widely accessible data sets creates whole new areas of research. There are many examples of such impact, the most famous of which is the Penn Treebank (Marcus. et al., 1994), which has 2910 citations in Google scholar and is the single most cited paper on the ACL anthology network (Radev et al., 2009). Other examples include the CoNLL named entity corpus (Sang and Meulder (2003) with 348 citations on Google Scholar), the IMDB movie reviews sentiment data (Pang et al. (2002) with 894 citations) and the Amazon sentiment multi-domain data (Blitzer et al. (2007) with 109 citations) . MTurk means that creating similar data sets is now much cheaper and easier than ever before. It is highly likely that new MTurk produced data sets will achieve prominence and have significant impact. Additionally, the creation of shared data means more comparison and evaluation against previous work. Progress is made when it can be demonstrated against previous approaches on the same data. The reduction of data cost and the rise of independent corpus producers likely means more accessible data.

More than a new source for *cheap* data, MTurk is a source for *new types* of data. Several of the papers in this workshop collected information about the annotators in addition to their annotations. This creates potential for studying how different user demographics understand language and allow for targeting specific demographics in data creation. Beyond efficiencies in cost, MTurk provides access to a global user population far more diverse than those provided by more professional annotation settings. This will have a significant impact on low resource languages as corpora can be cheaply built for a much wider array of languages. As one example, Irvine and Klementiev (2010) collected data for 42 languages without worrying about how to find speakers of such a wide variety of languages. Additionally, the collection of Arabic nicknames requires a diverse and numerous Arabic speaking population (Higgins et al., 2010). In addition to extending into new languages, MTurk also allows for the creation of evaluation sets in new genres and domains, which was the focus of two papers in this workshop (Finin et al., 2010; Yetisgen-Yildiz et al., 2010). We expect to see new research emphasis on low resource languages and new domains and genres.

Another factor is the change of data type and its impact on machine learning algorithms. With professional annotators, great time and care are paid to annotation guidelines and annotator training. These are difficult tasks with MTurk, which favors simple intuitive annotations and little training. Many papers applied creative methods of using simpler annotation tasks to create more complex data sets. This process can impact machine learning in a number of ways. Rather than a single gold standard, annotations are now available for many users. Learning across multiple annotations may improve systems (Dredze et al., 2009). Additionally, even with efforts to clean up MTurk annotations, we can expect an increase in noisy examples in data. This will push for new more robust learning algorithms that are less sensitive to noise. If we increase the size of the data ten-fold but also increase the noise, can learning still be successful? Another learning area of great interest is active learning, which has long relied on simulated user experiments. New work evaluated active learning methods with real users using MTurk (Baker et al., 2009; Ambati et al., 2010; Hsueh et al., 2009; **?**). Finally, the composition of complex data set annotations from simple user inputs can transform the method by which we learn complex outputs. Current approaches expect examples of labels that exactly match the expectation of the system. Can we instead provide lower level simpler user annotations and teach systems how to learn from these to construct complex output? This would open more complex annotation tasks to MTurk.

A general trend in research is that good ideas come from unexpected places. Major transformations in the field have come from creative new approaches. Consider the Penn Treebank, an ambitious and difficult project of unknown potential. Such large changes can be uncommon since they are often associated with high cost, as was the Penn Treebank. However, MTurk greatly reduces these costs, encouraging researchers to try creative new tasks. For example, in this workshop Tong et al. (2010) collected handwriting samples in multiple languages. Their creative data collection may or may not have a significant impact, but it is unlikely that it would have been tried had the cost been very high.

Finally, while obtaining new data annotations from MTurk is cheap, it is not trivial. Workshop participants struggled with how to attract Turkers, how to price HITs, HIT design, instructions, cheating detection, etc. No doubt that as work progresses, so will a communal knowledge and experience of how to use MTurk. There can be great benefit in new toolkits for collecting language data using MTurk, and indeed some of these have already started to emerge (Lane et al., 2010)[9].

Acknowledgements

Thanks to Sharon Chiarella of Amazon's Mechanical Turk for providing $100 credits for the shared task, and to CrowdFlower for allowing free use of their tool to workshop participants.

Research funding was provided by the NSF under grant IIS-0713448, by the European Commission through the EuroMatrixPlus project, and by the DARPA GALE program under Contract No. HR0011-06-2-0001. The views and findings are the authors' alone.

References

Cem Akkaya, Alexander Conrad, Janyce Wiebe, and Rada Mihalcea. 2010. Amazon Mechanical Turk for subjectivity word sense disambiguation. In *NAACL Workshop on Creating Speech and Language Data With Amazon's Mechanical Turk.*

Vamshi Ambati and Stephan Vogel. 2010. Can crowds build parallel corpora for machine translation systems? In *NAACL Workshop on Creating Speech and Language Data With Amazon's Mechanical Turk.*

Vamshi Ambati, Stephan Vogel, and Jamie Carbonell. 2010. Active learning and crowd-sourcing for machine translation. *Language Resources and Evaluation (LREC).*

Kathy Baker, Steven Bethard, Michael Bloodgood, Ralf Brown, Chris Callison-Burch, Glen Coppersmith, Bonnie Dorr, Wes Filardo, Kendall Giles, Ann Irvine, Mike Kayser, Lori Levin, Justin Martineau, Jim Mayfield, Scott Miller, Aaron Phillips, Andrew Philpot, Christine Piatko, Lane Schwartz, and David Zajic. 2009. Semantically-informed machine translation. Technical Report 002, Johns Hopkins Human Language Technology Center of Excellence, Summer Camp for Applied Language Exploration, Johns Hopkins University, Baltimore, MD.

John Blitzer, Mark Dredze, and Fernando Pereira. 2007. Biographies, bollywood, boom-boxes and blenders: Domain adaptation for sentiment classification. In *Association for Computational Linguistics (ACL).*

Michael Bloodgood and Chris Callison-Burch. 2010a. Bucking the trend: Large-scale cost-focused active learning for statistical machine translation. In *48th Annual Meeting of the Association for Computational Linguistics*, Uppsala, Sweden.

Michael Bloodgood and Chris Callison-Burch. 2010b. Using Mechanical Turk to build machine translation evaluation sets. In *NAACL Workshop on Creating Speech and Language Data With Amazon's Mechanical Turk.*

Cristina Butnariu, Su Nam Kim, Preslav Nakov, Diarmuid Ó Séaghdha, Stan Szpakowicz, and Tony Veale. 2009. Semeval-2010 Task 9: The interpretation of noun compounds using paraphrasing verbs and prepositions. In *Workshop on Semantic Evaluations.*

Olivia Buzek, Philip Resnik, and Ben Bederson. 2010. Error driven paraphrase annotation using Mechanical Turk. In *NAACL Workshop on Creating Speech and Language Data With Amazon's Mechanical Turk.*

Chris Callison-Burch. 2009. Fast, cheap, and creative: Evaluating translation quality using amazon's mechanical turk. In *Proceedings of the 2009 Conference on Empirical Methods in Natural Language Processing (EMNLP-2009)*, Singapore.

Jonathan Chang, Jordan Boyd-Graber, Chong Wang, Sean Gerrish, and David M. Blei. 2009. Reading tea leaves: How humans interpret topic models. In *Neural Information Processing Systems.*

[9] `http://wiki.github.com/callison-burch/mechanical_turk_workshop/`

Jonathan Chang. 2010. Not-so-Latent Dirichlet Allocation: Collapsed Gibbs sampling using human judgments. In *NAACL Workshop on Creating Speech and Language Data With Amazon's Mechanical Turk*.

Jia Deng, Wei Dong, Richard Socher, Li-Jia Li, Kai Li, and Li Fei-Fei. 2009. Imagenet: A large-scale hierarchical image database. In *Proceedings of the IEEE Conference on Computer Vision and Pattern Recognition (CVPR*, Miami Beach, Floriday.

Michael Denkowski and Alon Lavie. 2010. Exploring normalization techniques for human judgments of machine translation adequacy collected using Amazon Mechanical Turk. In *NAACL Workshop on Creating Speech and Language Data With Amazon's Mechanical Turk*.

Michael Denkowski, Hassan Al-Haj, and Alon Lavie. 2010. Turker-assisted paraphrasing for English-Arabic machine translation. In *NAACL Workshop on Creating Speech and Language Data With Amazon's Mechanical Turk*.

Mark Dredze, Partha Pratim Talukdar, and Koby Crammer. 2009. Sequence learning from data with multiple labels. In *ECML/PKDD Workshop on Learning from Multi-Label Data (MLD)*.

Keelan Evanini, Derrick Higgins, and Klaus Zechner. 2010. Using Amazon Mechanical Turk for transcription of non-native speech. In *NAACL Workshop on Creating Speech and Language Data With Amazon's Mechanical Turk*.

Christiane Fellbaum. 1998. *WordNet: An Electronic Lexical Database*. Bradford Books.

Tim Finin, William Murnane, Anand Karandikar, Nicholas Keller, Justin Martineau, and Mark Dredze. 2010. Touring PER, ORG and LOC on $100 a day. In *NAACL Workshop on Creating Speech and Language Data With Amazon's Mechanical Turk*.

Qin Gao and Stephan Vogel. 2010. Semi-supervised word alignment with Mechanical Turk. In *NAACL Workshop on Creating Speech and Language Data With Amazon's Mechanical Turk*.

Dan Gillick and Yang Liu. 2010. Non-expert evaluation of summarization systems is risky. In *NAACL Workshop on Creating Speech and Language Data With Amazon's Mechanical Turk*.

Jonathan Gordon, Benjamin Van Durme, and Lenhart Schubert. 2010. Evaluation of commonsense knowledge with Mechanical Turk. In *NAACL Workshop on Creating Speech and Language Data With Amazon's Mechanical Turk*.

Matthew R. Gormley, Adam Gerber, Mary Harper, and Mark Dredze. 2010. Non-expert correction of automatically generated relation annotations. In *NAACL Workshop on Creating Speech and Language Data With Amazon's Mechanical Turk*.

Catherine Grady and Matthew Lease. 2010. Crowdsourcing document relevance assessment with Mechanical Turk. In *NAACL Workshop on Creating Speech and Language Data With Amazon's Mechanical Turk*.

Michael Heilman and Noah A. Smith. 2010. Rating computer-generated questions with Mechanical Turk. In *NAACL Workshop on Creating Speech and Language Data With Amazon's Mechanical Turk*.

Chiara Higgins, Elizabeth McGrath, and Laila Moretto. 2010. AMT crowdsourcing: A viable method for rapid discovery of Arabic nicknames? In *NAACL Workshop on Creating Speech and Language Data With Amazon's Mechanical Turk*.

Paul J. Hopper and Sandra A. Thompson. 1980. Transitivity in grammar and discourse. *Language*, 56:251–299.

Pei-Yun Hsueh, Prem Melville, and Vikas Sindhwani. 2009. Data quality from crowdsourcing: A study of annotation selection criteria. In *Proceedings of the NAACL HLT 2009 Workshop on Active Learning for Natural Language Processing*, pages 27–35, Boulder, Colorado, June. Association for Computational Linguistics.

Panos Ipeirotis. 2010. New demographics of Mechanical Turk. `http://behind-the-enemy-lines.blogspot.com/2010/03/new-demographics-of-mechanical-turk.html`.

Ann Irvine and Alexandre Klementiev. 2010. Using Mechanical Turk to annotate lexicons for less commonly used languages. In *NAACL Workshop on Creating Speech and Language Data With Amazon's Mechanical Turk*.

Mukund Jha, Jacob Andreas, Kapil Thadani, Sara Rosenthal, and Kathleen McKeown. 2010. Corpus creation for new genres: A crowdsourced approach to PP attachment. In *NAACL Workshop on Creating Speech and Language Data With Amazon's Mechanical Turk*.

Michael Kaisser and John Lowe. 2008. Creating a research collection of question answer sentence pairs with Amazons Mechanical Turk. In *Proceedings of the Sixth International Language Resources and Evaluation (LREC'08)*, Marrakech, Morocco.

Stephen Kunath and Steven Weinberger. 2010. The wisdom of the crowd's ear: Speech accent rating and annotation with Amazon Mechanical Turk. In *NAACL Workshop on Creating Speech and Language Data With Amazon's Mechanical Turk*.

Ian Lane, Matthias Eck, Kay Rottmann, and Alex Waibel. 2010. Tools for collecting speech corpora via Mechanical-Turk. In *NAACL Workshop on Creating Speech and Language Data With Amazon's Mechanical Turk*.

Nolan Lawson, Kevin Eustice, Mike Perkowitz, and Meliha Yetisgen Yildiz. 2010. Annotating large email datasets for named entity recognition with Mechanical Turk. In *NAACL Workshop on Creating Speech and Language Data With Amazon's Mechanical Turk*.

Greg Little, Lydia B. Chilton, Rob Miller, and Max Goldman. 2009. Turkit: Tools for iterative tasks on mechanical turk. In *Proceedings of the Workshop on Human Computation at the International Conference on Knowledge Discovery and Data Mining (KDD-HCOMP '09)*, Paris.

Nitin Madnani and Jordan Boyd-Graber. 2010. Measuring transitivity using untrained annotators. In *NAACL Workshop on Creating Speech and Language Data With Amazon's Mechanical Turk*.

Mitch Marcus., Beatrice Santorini, and Mary Ann Marcinkiewicz. 1994. Building a large annotated corpus of english: The penn treebank. *Computational linguistics*, 19(2):313–330.

Matthew Marge, Satanjeev Banerjee, and Alexander Rudnicky. 2010a. Using the Amazon Mechanical Turk for transcription of spoken language. *ICASSP*, March.

Matthew Marge, Satanjeev Banerjee, and Alexander Rudnicky. 2010b. Using the Amazon Mechanical Turk to transcribe and annotate meeting speech for extractive summarization. In *NAACL Workshop on Creating Speech and Language Data With Amazon's Mechanical Turk*.

Winter Mason and Duncan J. Watts. 2009. Financial incentives and the "performance of crowds". In *Proceedings of the Workshop on Human Computation at the International Conference on Knowledge Discovery and Data Mining (KDD-HCOMP '09)*, Paris.

Ian McGraw, Chia ying Lee, Lee Hetherington, and Jim Glass. 2010. Collecting voices from the crowd. *LREC*, May.

Bart Mellebeek, Francesc Benavent, Jens Grivolla, Joan Codina, Marta R. Costa-Jussà, and Rafael Banchs. 2010. Opinion mining of spanish customer comments with non-expert annotations on Mechanical Turk. In *NAACL Workshop on Creating Speech and Language Data With Amazon's Mechanical Turk*.

Robert Munro, Steven Bethard, Victor Kuperman, Vicky Tzuyin Lai, Robin Melnick, Christopher Potts, Tyler Schnoebelen, and Harry Tily. 2010. Crowdsourcing and language studies: the new generation of linguistic data. In *NAACL Workshop on Creating Speech and Language Data With Amazon's Mechanical Turk*.

Matteo Negri and Yashar Mehdad. 2010. Creating a bi-lingual entailment corpus through translations with Mechanical Turk: $100 for a 10 days rush. In *NAACL Workshop on Creating Speech and Language Data With Amazon's Mechanical Turk*.

Scott Novotney and Chris Callison-Burch. 2010a. Cheap, fast and good enough: Automatic speech recognition with non-expert transcription. *NAACL*, June.

Scott Novotney and Chris Callison-Burch. 2010b. Crowdsourced accessibility: Elicitation of Wikipedia articles. In *NAACL Workshop on Creating Speech and Language Data With Amazon's Mechanical Turk*.

Bo Pang, Lillian Lee, and Shivakumar Vaithyanathan. 2002. Thumbs up?: sentiment classification using machine learning techniques. In *Empirical Methods in Natural Language Processing (EMNLP)*.

Gabriel Parent and Maxine Eskenazi. 2010. Clustering dictionary definitions using Amazon Mechanical Turk. In *NAACL Workshop on Creating Speech and Language Data With Amazon's Mechanical Turk*.

Dragomir R. Radev, Pradeep Muthukrishnan, and Vahed Qazvinian. 2009. The acl anthology network. In *Proceedings of the 2009 Workshop on Text and Citation Analysis for Scholarly Digital Libraries*, pages 54–61, Suntec City, Singapore, August. Association for Computational Linguistics.

Cyrus Rashtchian, Peter Young, Micah Hodosh, and Julia Hockenmaier. 2010. Collecting image annotations using Amazon's Mechanical Turk. In *NAACL Workshop on Creating Speech and Language Data With Amazon's Mechanical Turk*.

Joel Rose. 2010. Some turn to 'Mechanical' job search. `http://marketplace.publicradio.org/display/web/2009/06/30/pm_turking/`. Marketplace public radio. Air date: June 30, 2009.

Erik Tjong Kim Sang and Fien De Meulder. 2003. Introduction to the conll-2003 shared task: Language-independent named entity recognition. In *CoNLL-2003*.

Rion Snow, Brendan O'Connor, Daniel Jurafsky, and Andrew Y. Ng. 2008. Cheap and fast - but is it good? Evaluating non-expert annotations for natural language tasks. In *Proceedings of the 2008 Conference on Empirical Methods in Natural Language Processing (EMNLP-2008)*, Honolulu, Hawaii.

Audrey Tong, Jerome Ajot, Mark Przybocki, and Stephanie Strassel. 2010. Document image collection using Amazon's Mechanical Turk. In *NAACL Workshop on Creating Speech and Language Data With Amazon's Mechanical Turk*.

Luis von Ahn and Laura Dabbish. 2008. General techniques for designing games with a purpose. *Communications of the ACM*.

Rui Wang and Chris Callison-Burch. 2010. Cheap facts and counter-facts. In *NAACL Workshop on Creating*

Speech and Language Data With Amazon's Mechanical Turk.

Tae Yano, Philip Resnik, and Noah A Smith. 2010. Shedding (a thousand points of) light on biased language. In *NAACL Workshop on Creating Speech and Language Data With Amazon's Mechanical Turk.*

Meliha Yetisgen-Yildiz, Imre Solti, Scott Halgrim, and Fei Xia. 2010. Preliminary experiments with Amazon's Mechanical Turk for annotating medical named entities. In *NAACL Workshop on Creating Speech and Language Data With Amazon's Mechanical Turk.*

Omar F. Zaidan and Chris Callison-Burch. 2009. Feasibility of human-in-the-loop minimum error rate training. In *Proceedings of EMNLP 2009*, pages 52–61, August.

Omar Zaidan and Juri Ganitkevitch. 2010. An enriched MT grammar for under $100. In *NAACL Workshop on Creating Speech and Language Data With Amazon's Mechanical Turk.*

Corpus Creation for New Genres: A Crowdsourced Approach to PP Attachment

Mukund Jha, Jacob Andreas, Kapil Thadani, Sara Rosenthal and **Kathleen McKeown**
Department of Computer Science
Columbia University
New York, NY 10027, USA
{mj2472, jda2129}@columbia.edu, {kapil, sara, kathy}@cs.columbia.edu

Abstract

This paper explores the task of building an accurate prepositional phrase attachment corpus for new genres while avoiding a large investment in terms of time and money by crowdsourcing judgments. We develop and present a system to extract prepositional phrases and their potential attachments from ungrammatical and informal sentences and pose the subsequent disambiguation tasks as multiple choice questions to workers from Amazon's Mechanical Turk service. Our analysis shows that this two-step approach is capable of producing reliable annotations on informal and potentially noisy blog text, and this semi-automated strategy holds promise for similar annotation projects in new genres.

1 Introduction

Recent decades have seen rapid development in natural language processing tools for parsing, semantic role-labeling, machine translation, etc., and much of this success can be attributed to the study of statistical techniques and the availability of large annotated corpora for training. However, the performance of these systems is heavily dependent on the domain and genre of their training data, i.e. systems trained on data from a particular domain tend to perform poorly when applied to other domains and adaptation techniques are not always able to compensate (Dredze et al., 2007). For this reason, achieving high performance on new domains and genres frequently necessitates the collection of annotated training data from those domains and genres, a time-consuming and frequently expensive process.

This paper examines the problem of collecting high-quality annotations for new genres with a focus on time and cost efficiency. We explore the well-studied but non-trivial task of prepositional phrase (PP) attachment and describe a semi-automated system for identifying accurate attachments in blog data, which is frequently noisy and difficult to parse. PP attachment disambiguation involves finding a correct attachment for a prepositional phrase in a sentence. For example, in the sentence "*We went to John's house on Saturday*", the phrase *"on Saturday"* attaches to the verb *"went"*. In another example, *"We went to John's house on 12th Street"*, the PP *"on 12th street"* attaches to the noun *"John's house"*. This sort of disambiguation requires semantic knowledge about sentences that is difficult to glean from their surface form, a problem which is compounded by the informal nature and irregular vocabulary of blog text.

In this work, we investigate whether crowdsourced human judgments are capable of distinguishing appropriate attachments. We present a system that simplifies the attachment problem and represents it in a format that can be intuitively tackled by humans.

Our approach to this task makes use of a heuristic-based system built on a shallow parser that identifies the likely words or phrases to which a PP can attach. To subsequently select the correct attachment, we leverage human judgments from multiple untrained annotators (referred to here as *workers*) through Amazon's Mechanical Turk [1], an online marketplace for work. This two-step approach of-

[1] http://www.mturk.amazon.com

Proceedings of the NAACL HLT 2010 Workshop on Creating Speech and Language Data with Amazon's Mechanical Turk, pages 13–20,
Los Angeles, California, June 2010.

fers distinct advantages: the automated system cuts down the space of potential attachments effectively with little error, and the disambiguation task can be reduced to small multiple choice questions which can be tackled quickly and aggregated reliably.

The remainder of this paper focuses on the PP attachment task over blog text and our analysis of the resulting aggregate annotations. We note, however, that this type of semi-automated approach is potentially applicable to any task which can be reliably decomposed into independent judgments that untrained annotators can tackle (e.g., quantifier scoping, conjunction scope). This work is intended as an initial step towards the development of efficient hybrid annotation tools that seamlessly incorporate aggregate human wisdom alongside effective algorithms.

2 Related Work

Identifying PP attachments is an essential task for building syntactic parse trees. While this task has been studied using fully-automated systems, many of them rely on parse tree output for predicting potential attachments (Ratnaparkhi et al., 1994; Yeh and Vilain, 1998; Stetina and Nagao, 1997; Zavrel et al., 1997). However, systems that rely on good parses are unlikely to perform well on new genres such as blogs and machine translated texts for which parse tree training data is not readily available.

Furthermore, the predominant dataset for evaluating PP attachment is the RRR dataset (Ratnaparkhi et al., 1994) which consists of PP attachment cases from the Wall Street Journal portion of the Penn Treebank. Instead of complete sentences, this dataset consists of sets of the form $\{V,N_1,P,N_2\}$ where $\{P,N_2\}$ is the PP and $\{V,N_1\}$ are the potential attachments. This simplification of the PP attachment task to a choice between two alternatives is unrealistic when considering the potential long-distance attachments encountered in real-world text.

While blogs and other web text, such as discussion forums and emails, have been studied for a variety of tasks such as information extraction (Hong and Davison, 2009), social networking (Gruhl et al., 2004), and sentiment analysis (Leshed and Kaye, 2006), we are not aware of any previous efforts to gather syntactic data (such as PP attachments) in the genre. Syntactic methods such as POS tagging, parsing and structural disambiguation are commonly used when analyzing well-structured text. Including the use of syntactic information has yielded improvements in accuracy in speech recognition (Chelba and Jelenik, 1998; Collins et al., 2005) and machine translation (DeNeefe and Knight, 2009; Carreras and Collins, 2009). We anticipate that datasets such as ours could be useful for such tasks as well.

Amazon's Mechanical Turk (MTurk) has become very popular for manual annotation tasks and has been shown to perform equally well over labeling tasks such as affect recognition, word similarity, recognizing textual entailment, event temporal ordering and word sense disambiguation, when compared to annotations from experts (Snow et al., 2008). While these tasks were small in scale and intended to demonstrate the viability of annotation via MTurk, it has also proved effective in large-scale tasks including the collection of accurate speech transcriptions (Gruenstein et al., 2009). In this paper we explore a method for corpus building on a large scale in order to extend annotation into new domains and genres.

We previously evaluated crowdsourced PP attachment annotation by using MTurk workers to reproduce PP attachments from the Wall Street Journal corpus (Rosenthal et al., 2010). The results demonstrated that MTurk workers are capable of identifying PP attachments in newswire text, but the approach used to generate attachment options is dependent on the existing gold-standard parse trees and cannot be used on corpora where parse trees are not available. In this paper, we build on the semi-automated annotation principle while avoiding the dependency on parsers, allowing us to apply this technique to the noisy and informal text found in blogs.

3 System Description

Our system must both identify PPs and generate a list of potential attachments for each PP in this section. Figure 1 illustrates the structure of the system.

First, the system extracts sentences from scraped blog data. Text is preprocessed by stripping HTML tags, advertisements, non-Latin and non-printable

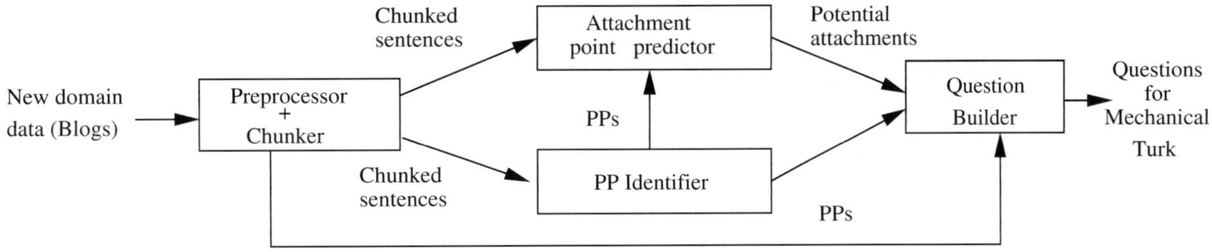

Figure 1: Overview of question generation system

characters. Emoticon symbols are removed using a standard list. [2]

The cleaned data is then partitioned into sentences using the NLTK sentence splitter. [3] In order to compensate for the common occurrence of informal punctuation and web-specific symbols in blog text, we replace all punctuation symbols between quotation marks and parentheses with placeholder tags (e.g. ⟨QuestionMark⟩) during the sentence splitting process and do the same for website names, time markers and referring phrases (e.g. *@John*). Additionally, we attempt to re-split sentences at ellipsis boundaries if they are longer than 80 words and discard them if this fails.

As parsers trained on news corpora tend to perform poorly on unstructured texts like blogs, we rely on a chunker to partition sentences into phrases. Choosing a good chunker is essential to this approach: around 35% of the cases in which the correct attachment is not predicted by the system are due to chunker error. We experimented with different chunkers over a random sample of 50 sentences before selecting a CRF-based chunker (Phan, 2006) for its robust performance.

The chunker output is initially processed by fusing together chunks in order to ensure that a single chunk represents a complete attachment point. Two consecutive NP chunks are fused if the first contains an element with a possessive part of speech tag (e.g. *John's book*), while particle chunks (PRT) are fused with the VP chunks that precede them (e.g. *pack up*). These chunked sentences are then processed to identify PPs and potential attachment points for them, which can then be used to generate questions for MTurk workers.

3.1 PP Extraction

PPs can be classified into two broad categories based on the number of chunks they contain. A *simple PP* consists of only two chunks: a preposition and one noun phrase, while a *compound PP* has multiple simple PPs attached to its primary noun phrase. For example, in the sentence "*I just made some last-minute changes to the latest issue of our newsletter*", the PP with preposition "*to*" can be considered to be either the simple PP "*to the latest issue*" or the compound PP "*to the latest issue of our newsletter*".

We handle compound PPs by breaking them down into multiple simple PPs; compound PPs can be recovered by identifying the attachments of their constituent simple PPs. Our simple PP extraction algorithm identifies PPs as a sequence of chunks that consist of one or more prepositions terminating in a noun phrase or gerund.

3.2 Attachment Point Prediction

A PP usually attaches to the noun or verb phrase preceding it or, in some cases, can modify a following clause by attaching to the head verb. We build a set of rules based on this intuition to pick out the potential attachments in the sentence; these rules are described in Table 1. The rules are applied separately for each PP in a sentence and in the same sequence as mentioned in the table (except for rule 4, which is applied while choosing a chunk using any of the other rules).

[2] `http://www.astro.umd.edu/~marshall/smileys.html`

[3] `http://www.nltk.org`

	Rule	Example
1	Choose closest NP and VP preceding the PP.	I made modifications **to our newsletter**.
2	Choose next closest VP preceding the PP if the VP selected in (1) contains a VBG.	He snatched the disk flying away **with one hand**.
3	Choose first VP following the PP.	**On his desk** he has a photograph.
4	All chunks inside parentheses are skipped, unless the PP falls within parentheses.	Please refer to the new book (second edition) **for more notes**.
5	Choose anything immediately preceding the PP that is not out of chunk and has not already been picked.	She is full **of excitement**.
6	If a selected NP contains the word *and*, expand it into two options, one with the full expression and one with only the terms following *and*.	He is president and chairman **of the board**.
7	For PPs in chains of the form P-NP-P-NP (PP-PP), choose all the NPs in the chain preceding the PP and apply all the above rules considering the whole chain as a single PP.	They found my pictures of them **from the concert**.
8	If there are fewer than four options after applying the above rules, also select the VP preceding the last VP selected, the NP preceding the last NP selected, and the VP following the last VP picked.	

Table 1: List of rules for attachment point predictor. In the examples, PPs are denoted by boldfaced text and potential attachment options are underlined.

4 Experiments

An experimental study was undertaken to test our hypothesis that we could obtain reliable annotations on informal genres using MTurk workers. Here we describe the dataset and our methods.

4.1 Dataset and Interface

We used a corpus of blog posts made on LiveJournal [4] for system development and evaluation. Only posts from English-speaking countries (i.e. USA, Canada, UK, Australia and New Zealand) were considered for this study.

The interface provided to MTurk workers showed the sentence on a plain background with the PP highlighted and a statement prompting them to pick the phrase in the sentence that the given PP modified. The question was followed by a list of options. In addition, we provided MTurk workers the option to indicate problems with the given PP or the listed options. Workers could write in the correct attachment if they determined that it wasn't present in the list of options, or the correct PP if the one they were presented with was malformed. This allowed them to correct errors made by the chunker and automated attachment point predictor. In all cases, workers were forced to pick the best answer among the options regardless of errors. We also supplied a number of examples covering both well-formed and erroneous cases to aid them in identifying appropriate attachments.

[4] `http://www.livejournal.com`

4.2 Experimental Setup

For our experiment, we randomly selected 1000 questions from the output produced by the system and provided each question to five different MTurk workers, thereby obtaining five different judgments for each PP attachment case. Workers were paid four cents per question and the average completion time per task was 48 seconds. In total $225 was spent on the full study with $200 spent on the workers and $25 on MTurk fees.The total time taken for the study was approximately 16 hours.

A pilot study was carried out with 50 sentences before the full study to test the annotation interface and experiment with different ways of presenting the PP and attachment options to workers. During this study, we observed that while workers were willing to suggest correct answers or PPs when faced with erroneous questions, they often opted to not pick any of the options provided unless the question was well-formed. This was problematic because, in many cases, expert annotators *were* able to identify the most appropriate attachment option. Therefore, in the final study we forced them to pick the most suitable option from the given choices before indicating errors and writing in alternatives.

Workers in agreement	Number of questions	Accuracy	Coverage
5 (unanimity)	389	97.43%	41.33%
$\geq$ 4 (majority)	689	94.63%	73.22%
$\geq$ 3 (majority)	887	88.61%	94.26%
$\geq$ 2 (plurality)	906	87.75%	96.28%
Total	**941**	**84.48%**	**100%**

Table 2: Accuracy and coverage over agreement thresholds

5 Evaluation corpus

In order to determine if the MTurk results were reliable, worker responses had to be validated by having expert annotators perform the same task. For this purpose, two of the authors annotated the 1000 questions used for the experiment independently and compared their judgments. Disagreements were observed in 127 cases; these were then resolved by a pool of non-author annotators. If all three annotators on a case disagreed with each other the question was discarded; this situation occured 43 times. An additional 16 questions were discarded because they did not have a valid PP. For example, "*I am painting with my blanket on today*". Here "*on today*" is incorrectly extracted as a PP because the particle "on" is tagged as a preposition. The rest of the analysis presented in this section was performed on the remaining 941 sentences.

The annotators' judgments were compared to the answers provided by the MTurk workers and, in the case of disagreement between the experts and the majority of workers, the sentences were manually inspected to determine the reason. In five cases, more than one valid attachment was possible; for example, in the sentence "*The video below is of my favourite song on the album - A Real Woman*", the PP "*of my favourite song*" could attach to either the noun phrase "*the video*" or the verb "*is*" and conveys the same meaning. In such cases, both the experts and the workers were considered to have chosen the correct answer.

In 149 cases, the workers also augmented their choices by providing corrections to incomplete answers and badly constructed PPs. For example, the PP "*of the Rings and Mikey*" in the sentence "*Samwise from Lord of the Rings and Mikey from The Goonies are the same actor ?*" was corrected to "*of the Rings*". In 34/39 of the cases where the correct answer was not present in the options provided, at least one worker indicated correct attachment for the PP.

5.1 Attachment Prediction Evaluation

We measure the recall for our attachment point predictor as the number of questions for which the correct attachment appeared among the generated options divided by the total number of questions. The system achieves a recall of 95.85% (902/941 questions). We observed that in many cases where the correct attachment point was not predicted, it was due to a chunker error. For example, in the following sentence, "*Stop all the clocks , cut off the telephone , Prevent the dog from barking with a juicy bone...*", the PP "*from barking*" attaches to the verb "*Prevent*"; however, due to an error in chunking "*Prevent*" is tagged as a noun phrase and hence is not picked by our system. The correct attachment was also occasionally missed when the attachment point was too far from the PP. For example, in the sentence "*Fitting as many people as possible on one sofa and under many many covers and getting intimate*", the correct attachment for the PP "*under many many covers*" is the verb "*Fitting*" but it is not picked by our system.

Even though the correct attachment was not always given, the workers could still provide their own correct answer. In the first example above, 3/5 workers indicated that the correct attachment was not in the list of options and wrote it in.

6 Results

Table 2 summarizes the results of the experiment. We assess both the coverage and reliability of worker predictions at various levels of worker agreement. This serves as an indicator of the effectiveness of the MTurk results: the accuracy can be taken

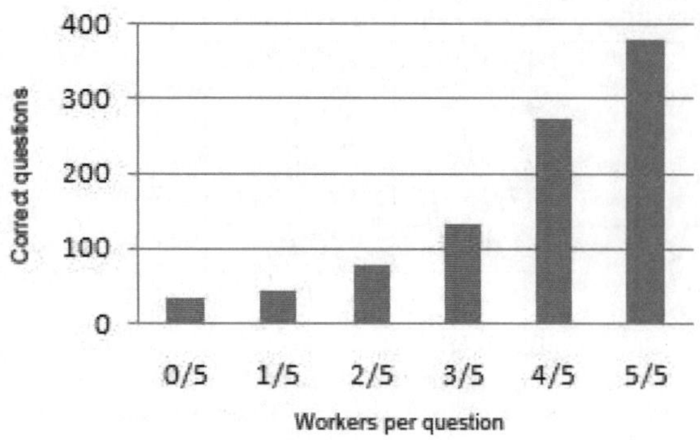

Figure 2: The number of questions in which exactly x workers provided the correct answer

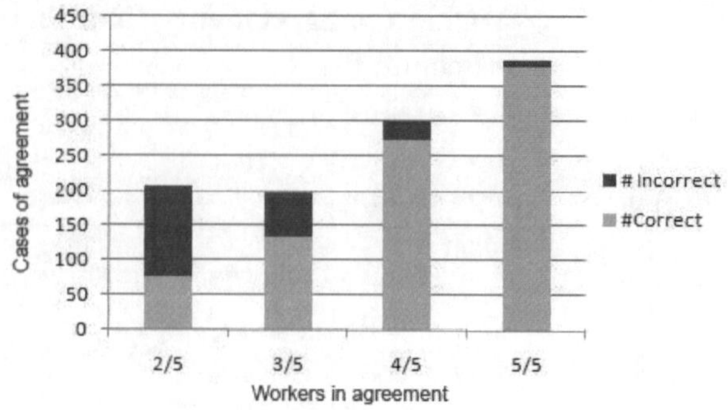

Figure 3: The number of cases in which exactly x workers agreed on an answer

as a general confidence measure for worker predictions; when five workers agree we can be 97.43% confident in the correctness of their prediction, when at least four workers agree we can be 94.63% confident, etc. *Unanimity* indicates that all workers agreed on an answer, *majority* indicates that more than half of workers agreed on an answer, and *plurality* indicates that two workers agreed on a single answer, while the remaining three workers each selected different answers. We observe that at high levels of worker agreement, we get extremely high accuracy but limited coverage of the data set; as we decrease our standard for agreement, coverage increases rapidly while accuracy remains relatively high.

Figure 2 shows the number of workers providing the correct answer on a per-question basis. This illustrates the distribution of worker agreements across questions. Note that in the majority of cases (69.2%), at least four workers provided the correct answer; in only 3.6% of cases were no workers able to select the correct attachment.

Figure 3 shows the distribution of worker agreements. Unlike Table 2, these figures are not cumulative and include non-plurality two-worker agreements. Note that the number of agreements discussed in this figure is greater than the 941 evaluated because in some cases there were multiple agreements on a single question. As an example, three workers may choose one answer while the remaining two workers choose another; this question then produces both a three-worker agreement as well as a two-worker agreement.

No. of options	No. of cases	Accuracy
< 4	179	86.59%
4	718	84.26%
> 4	44	79.55%

Table 3: Variation in worker performance with the number of attachment options presented

All questions on which there is agreement also produce a majority vote, with one exception: the 2/2/1 agreement. Although the correct answer was selected by one set of two workers in every case of 2/2/1 agreement, this is not particularly useful for corpus-building as we have no way to identify *a priori* which set is correct. Fortunately, 2/2/1 agreements were also quite rare and occurred in only 3% of cases.

Figure 3 appears to indicate that instances of agreement between two workers are unlikely to produce good attachments; they have a an average accuracy of 37.2%. However, this is due in large part to cases of 3/2 agreement, in which the two workers in the minority are usually wrong, as well as cases of 2/2/1 agreement which contain at least one incorrect instance of two-worker agreement. However, if we only consider cases in which the two-worker agreement forms a plurality (i.e. all other workers disagree amongst themselves), we observe an average accuracy of 64.3% which is similar to that of cases of three-worker agreement (67.7%).

We also attempted to study the variation in worker performance based on the complexity of the task; specifically looking at how response accuracy varied depending on the number of options that workers were presented with. Although our system aimed to

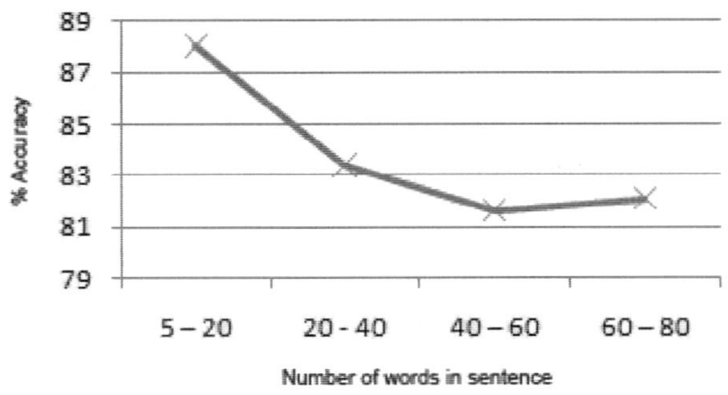

Figure 4: Variation in accuracy with sentence length.

generate four attachment options per case, fewer options were produced for small sentences and opening PPs while additional options were generated in sentences containing PP-NP chains (see Table 1 for the complete list of rules). Table 3 shows the variation in accuracy with the number of options provided to the workers. We might expect that an increased number of options may be correlated with decreased accuracy and the data does indeed seem to suggest this trend; however, we do not have enough datapoints for the cases with fewer or more than four options to verify whether this effect is significant.

We also analyzed the relationship between the length of the sentence (in terms of number of words) and the accuracy. Figure 4 indicates that as the length of the sentence increases, the average accuracy decreases. This is not entirely unexpected as lengthy sentences tend to be more complicated and therefore harder for human readers to parse.

7 Conclusions and Future Work

We have shown that by working in conjunction with automated attachment point prediction systems, MTurk workers are capable of annotating PP attachment problems with high accuracy, even when working with unstructured and informal blog text. This work provides an immediate framework for the building of PP attachment corpora for new genres without a dependency on full parsing.

More broadly, the semi-automated framework outlined in this paper is not limited to the task of annotating PP attachments; indeed, it is suitable for almost any syntactic or semantic annotation task where untrained human workers can be presented with a limited number of options for selection. By dividing the desired annotation task into smaller sub-tasks that can be tackled independently or in a pipelined manner, we anticipate that more syntactic information can be extracted from unstructured text in new domains and genres without the sizable investment of time and money normally associated with hiring trained linguists to build new corpora. To this end, we intend to further leverage the advent of crowdsourcing resources in order to tackle more sophisticated annotation tasks.

Acknowledgements

The authors would like to thank Kevin Lerman for his help in formulating the original ideas for this work. This material is based on research supported in part by the U.S. National Science Foundation (NSF) under IIS-05-34871. Any opinions, findings and conclusions or recommendations expressed in this material are those of the authors and do not necessarily reflect the views of the NSF.

References

Xavier Carreras and Michael Collins. 2009. Non-projective parsing for statistical machine translation. In *Proceedings of EMNLP*, pages 200–209.

Ciprian Chelba and Frederick Jelenik. 1998. Structured language modeling for speech recognition. In *Proceedings of NLDB*.

Michael Collins, Brian Roark, and Murat Saraclar. 2005. Discriminative syntactic language modeling for speech recognition. In *Proceedings of ACL*, pages 507–514.

Steve DeNeefe and Kevin Knight. 2009. Synchronous tree adjoining machine translation. In *Proceedings of EMNLP*, pages 727–736.

Mark Dredze, John Blitzer, Partha Pratim Talukdar, Kuzman Ganchev, João Graca, and Fernando Pereira. 2007. Frustratingly hard domain adaptation for dependency parsing. In *Proceedings of the CoNLL Shared Task Session of EMNLP-CoNLL*, pages 1051–1055, Prague, Czech Republic, June. Association for Computational Linguistics.

Alex Gruenstein, Ian McGraw, and Andrew Sutherland. 2009. A self-transcribing speech corpus: collecting continuous speech with an online educational game. In *Proceedings of the Speech and Language Technology in Education (SLaTE) Workshop*.

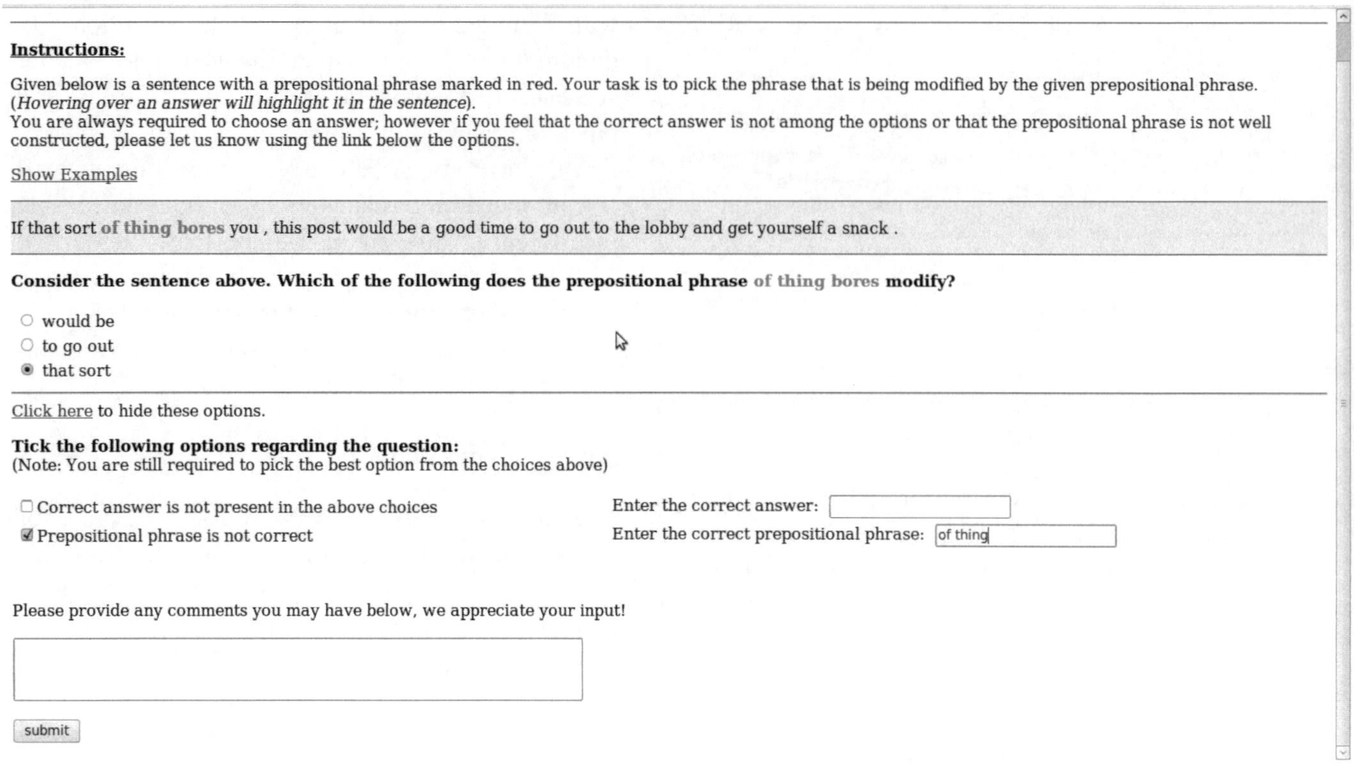

Figure 5: HIT Interface for PP attachment task

Daniel Gruhl, R. Guha, David Liben-Nowell, and Andrew Tomkins. 2004. Information diffusion through blogspace. In *Proceedings of WWW*, pages 491–501.

Liangjie Hong and Brian D. Davison. 2009. A classification-based approach to question answering in discussion boards. In *Proceedings of SIGIR*, pages 171–178.

Gilly Leshed and Joseph 'Jofish' Kaye. 2006. Understanding how bloggers feel: recognizing affect in blog posts. In *CHI '06 extended abstracts on Human factors in computing systems*, pages 1019–1024.

Xuan-Hieu Phan. 2006. CRFChunker: CRF English phrase chunker. `http://crfchunker.sourceforge.net`.

Adwait Ratnaparkhi, Jeff Reynar, and Salim Roukos. 1994. A maximum entropy model for prepositional phrase attachment. In *Proceedings of HLT*, pages 250–255.

Sara Rosenthal, William J. Lipovsky, Kathleen McKeown, Kapil Thadani, and Jacob Andreas. 2010. Semi-automated annotation for prepositional phrase attachment. In *Proceedings of LREC*, Valletta, Malta.

Rion Snow, Brendan O'Connor, Daniel Jurafsky, and Andrew Y. Ng. 2008. Cheap and fast—but is it good?: evaluating non-expert annotations for natural language tasks. In *Proceedings of EMNLP*, pages 254–263.

Jiri Stetina and Makoto Nagao. 1997. Corpus based PP attachment ambiguity resolution with a semantic dictionary. In *Proceedings of the Workshop on Very Large Corpora*, pages 66–80.

Alexander S. Yeh and Marc B. Vilain. 1998. Some properties of preposition and subordinate conjunction attachments. In *Proceedings of COLING*, pages 1436–1442.

Jakub Zavrel, Walter Daelemans, and Jorn Veenstra. 1997. Resolving PP attachment ambiguities with memory-based learning. In *Proceedings of the Workshop on Computational Language Learning (CoNLL)*, pages 136–144.

Appendix A: Mechanical Turk Interface

Figure 5 shows a screenshot of the interface provided to the Mechanical Turk workers for the PP attachment task. By default, examples and additional options are hidden but can be viewed using the links provided. The screenshot illustrates a case in which a worker is confronted with an incorrect PP and uses the additional options to correct it.

Clustering dictionary definitions using Amazon Mechanical Turk

Gabriel Parent **Maxine Eskenazi**

Language Technologies Institute
Carnegie Mellon University
5000 Forbes Avenue
15213 Pittsburgh, USA

{gparent,max}@cs.cmu.edu

Abstract

Vocabulary tutors need word sense disambiguation (WSD) in order to provide exercises and assessments that match the sense of words being taught. Using expert annotators to build a WSD training set for all the words supported would be too expensive. Crowdsourcing that task seems to be a good solution. However, a first required step is to define what the possible sense labels to assign to word occurrence are. This can be viewed as a clustering task on dictionary definitions. This paper evaluates the possibility of using Amazon Mechanical Turk (MTurk) to carry out that prerequisite step to WSD. We propose two different approaches to using a crowd to accomplish clustering: one where the worker has a global view of the task, and one where only a local view is available. We discuss how we can aggregate multiple workers' clusters together, as well as pros and cons of our two approaches. We show that either approach has an interannotator agreement with experts that corresponds to the agreement between experts, and so using MTurk to cluster dictionary definitions appears to be a reliable approach.

1 Introduction

For some applications it is useful to disambiguate the meanings of a polysemous word. For example, if we show a student a text containing a word like "bank" and then automatically generate questions about the meaning of that word as it appeared in the text (say as the bank of a river), we would like to have the meaning of the word in the questions match the text meaning. Teachers do this each time they assess a student on vocabulary knowledge. For intelligent tutoring systems, two options are available. The first one is to ask a teacher to go through all the material and label each appearance of a polysemous word with its sense. This option is used only if there is a relatively small quantity of material. Beyond that, automatic processing, known as Word Sense Disambiguation (WSD) is essential. Most approaches are supervised and need large amounts of data to train the classifier for each and every word that is to be taught and assessed.

Amazon Mechanical Turk (MTurk) has been used for the purpose of word sense disambiguation (Snow et al, 2008). The results show that non-experts do very well (100% accuracy) when asked to identify the correct sense of a word out of a finite set of labels created by an expert. It is therefore possible to use MTurk to build a training corpus for WSD. In order to extend the Snow et al crowdsourced disambiguation to a large number of words, we need an efficient way to create the set of senses of a word. Asking an expert to do this is costly in time and money. Thus it is necessary to have an efficient Word Sense Induction (WSI) system. A WSI system induces the different senses of a word and provides the corresponding sense labels. This is the first step to crowdsourcing WSD on a large scale.

While many studies have shown that MTurk can be used for labeling tasks (Snow et al, 2008), to rate automatically constructed artifacts (Callison-Burch, 2009, Alonso et al, 2008) and to transcribe speech (Ledlie et al, 2009, Gruenstein et al, 2009), to our knowledge, there has not been much work on evaluating the use of MTurk for

Proceedings of the NAACL HLT 2010 Workshop on Creating Speech and Language Data with Amazon's Mechanical Turk, pages 21–29,
Los Angeles, California, June 2010.

clustering tasks. The goal of this paper is to investigate different options available to crowdsource a clustering task and evaluate their efficiency in the concrete application of word sense induction.

2 Background

2.1 WSD for vocabulary tutoring

Our interest in the use of MTurk for disambiguation comes from work on a vocabulary tutor; REAP (Heilman et al, 2006). The tutor searches for documents from the Web that are appropriate for a student to use to learn vocabulary from context (appropriate reading level, for example). Since the system finds a large number of documents, making a rich repository of learning material, it is impossible to process all the documents manually. When a document for vocabulary learning is presented to a student, the system should show the definition of the words to be learned (focus words). In some cases a word has several meanings for the same part of speech and thus it has several definitions. Hence the need for WSD to be included in vocabulary tutors.

2.2 WSI and WSD

The identification of a list of senses for a given word in a corpus of documents is called word sense induction (WSI). SemEval 2007 and 2010 (SigLex, 2008) both evaluate WSI systems. The I2R system achieved the best results in 2007 with an F-score of 81.6% (I2R by Niu (2007)). Snow et al (2007) have a good description of the inherent problem of WSI where the appropriate granularity of the clusters varies for each application. They try to solve this problem by building hierarchical-like word sense structures. In our case, each dictionary definition for a word could be considered as a unique sense for that word. Then, when using MTurk as a platform for WSD, we could simply ask the workers to select which of the dictionary definitions best expresses the meaning of the words in a document. The problem here is that most dictionaries give quite several definitions for a word. Defining one sense label per dictionary definition would result in too many labels, which would, in turn, make the MTurk WSD less efficient and our dataset sparser, thus decreasing the quality of the classifier. Another option, investigated by Chklovski and Mihalcea (2003), is to use WordNet sense definitions as the possible labels. They obtained more than 100,000 labeled instances from a crowd of volunteers. They conclude that WordNet senses are not coarse enough to provide high interannotator agreement, and exploit workers disagreement on the WSD task to derive coarser senses.

The granularity of the senses for each word is a parameter that is dependent on the application. In our case, we want to be able to assess a student on the sense of a word that the student has just been taught. Learners have the ability to generalize the context in which a word is learned. For example, if a student learns the meaning of the word "bark" as the sound of a dog, they can generalize that this can also apply to human shouting. Hence, there is no need for two separate senses here. However, a student could not generalize the meaning "hard cover of a tree" from that first meaning of "bark". This implies that students should be able to distinguish coarse word senses. (Kulkarni et al., 2007) have looked at automatic clustering of dictionary definitions. They compared K-Means clustering with Spectral Clustering. Various features were investigated: raw, normalized word overlap with and without stop words. The best combination results in 74% of the clusters having no misclassified definitions. If those misclassified definitions end up being used to represent possible sense labels in WSD, wrong labels might decrease the quality of the disambiguation stage. If a student is shown a definition that does not match the sense of a word in a particular context, they are likely to build the wrong conceptual link. Our application requires higher accuracy than that achieved by automatic approaches, since students' learning can be directly affected by the error rate.

2.3 Clustering with MTurk

The possible interaction between users and clustering algorithms has been explored in the past. Huang and Mitchell (2006) present an example of how user feedback can be used to improve clustering results. In this study, the users were not asked to provide clustering solutions. Instead, they fine tuned the automatically generated solution.

With the advent of MTurk, we can use human judgment to build clustering solutions. There are multiple approaches for combining workforce: parallel with aggregation (Snow et al, 2008), iterative

(Little et al, 2009) and collaboration between workers (Horton, Turker Talk, 2009). These strategies have been investigated for many applications, most of which are for labeling, a few for clustering. The Deneme blog presents an experiment where website clustering is carried out using MTurk (Little, Website Clustering, 2009). The workers' judgments on the similarity between two websites are used to build a distance matrix for the distance between websites. Jagadeesan and others (2009) asked workers to identify similar objects in a pool of 3D CAD models. They then used frequently co-occurring objects to build a distance matrix, upon which they then applied hierarchical clustering. Those two approaches are different: the first gives the worker only two items of the set (a local view of the task), while the latter offers the worker a global view of the task. In the next sections we will measure the accuracy of these approaches and their advantages and disadvantages.

3 Obtaining clusters from a crowd

REAP is used to teach English vocabulary and to conduct learning studies in a real setting, in a local ESL school. The vocabulary tutor provides instructions for the 270 words on the school's core vocabulary list, which has been built using the Academic Word List (Coxhead, 2000). In order to investigate how WSI could be accomplished using Amazon Mechanical Turk, 50 words were randomly sampled from the 270, and their definitions were extracted from the Longman Dictionary of Contemporary English (LDOCE) and the Cambridge Advanced Learner's Dictionary (CALD). There was an average of 6.3 definitions per word.

The problem of clustering dictionary definitions involves solving two sub-problems: how many clusters there are, and which definitions belong to which clusters. We could have asked workers to solve both problems at the same time by having them dynamically change the number of clusters in our interface. We decided not to do this due to the fact that some words have more than 12 definitions. Since the worker already needs to keep track of the semantics of each cluster, we felt that having them modify the number of sense boxes would increase their cognitive load to the point that we would see a decrease in the accuracy of the results.

Thus the first task involved determining the number of general meanings (which in our case determines the number of clusters) that there are in a list of definitions. The workers were shown the word and a list of its definitions, for example, for the word "clarify":

- *to make something clearer and easier to understand*
- *to make something clear or easier to understand by giving more details or a simpler explanation*
- *to remove water and unwanted substances from fat, such as butter, by heating it*

They were then asked: "How many general meanings of the word *clarify* are there in the following definitions?" We gave a definition of what we meant by general versus specific meanings, along with several examples. The worker was asked to enter a number in a text box (in the above example the majority answered 2). This 2-cent HIT was completed 13 times for every 50 words, for a total of 650 assignments and $13.00. A majority vote was used to aggregate the workers' results, giving us the number of clusters in which the definitions were grouped. In case of a tie, the lowest number of clusters was retained, since our application requires coarse-grained senses.

The number of "general meanings" we obtained in this first HIT[1] was then used in two different HITs. We use these two HITs to determine which definitions should be clustered together. In the first setup, which we called "global-view" the workers had a view of the entire task. They were shown the word and **all of its definitions**. They were then prompted to drag-and-drop the definitions into different sense boxes, making sure to group the definitions that belong to the same general meaning together (Figure 3, Appendix). Once again, an explicit definition of what was expected for "general meaning" along with examples was given. Also, a flash demo of how to use the interface was provided. The worker got 3 cents for this HIT. It was completed 5 times for each of the 50 words, for a total cost of $7.50. We created another HIT where the workers were not given all of the definitions; we called this setup "local-view". The worker was asked to indicate if **two definitions** of a word were related to the same meaning or different meanings

[1] The code and data used for the different HITs are available at http://www.cs.cmu.edu/~gparent/amt/wsi/

(Figure 4, Appendix). For each word, we created all possible pairs of definitions. This accounts for an average of 21 pairs for all of the 50 words. For each pair, 5 different workers voted on whether it contained the same or different meanings, earning 1 cent for each answer. The total cost here was $52.50. The agreement between workers was used to build a distance matrix: if the 5 workers agreed that the two definitions concerned the same sense, the distance was set to 0. Otherwise, it was set to the number of workers who thought they concerned different senses, up to a distance of 5. Hierarchical clustering was then used to build clustering solutions from the distance matrices. We used complete linkage clustering, with Ward's criterion.

4 Evaluation of global-view vs. local-view approaches

In order to evaluate our two approaches, we created a gold-standard (GS). Since the task of WSI is strongly influenced by an annotator's grain size preference for the senses, four expert annotators were asked to create the GS. The literature offers many metrics to compare two annotators' clustering solutions (Purity and Entropy (Zhao and Karypis, 2001), clustering F-Measure (Fung et al., 2003) and many others). SemEval-2 includes a WSI task where V-Measure (Rosenberg and Hirschberg, 2007) is used to evaluate the clustering solutions. V-Measure involves two metrics, homogeneity and completeness, that can be thought of as precision and recall. Perfect homogeneity is obtained if the solutions have clusters whose data points belong to a single cluster in the GS. Perfect completeness is obtained if the clusters in the GS contain data points that belong to a single cluster in the evaluated solution. The V-Measure is a (weighted) harmonic mean of the homogeneity and of the completeness metrics. Table 1 shows inter-annotator agreement (ITA) among four experts on the test dataset, using the average V-Measure over all the 50 sense clusters.

	GS #1	GS #2	GS #3	GS #4
GS #1	1,000	0,850	0,766	0,770
GS #2	0,850	1,000	0,763	0,796
GS #3	0,766	0,763	1,000	0,689
GS #4	0,770	0,796	0,689	1,000

Table 1 - ITA on WSI task for four annotators

We can obtain the agreement between one expert and the three others by averaging the three V-Measures. We finally obtain an "Experts vs. Experts" ITA of 0.772 by averaging this value for all of our experts. The standard deviation for this ITA is 0.031.To be considered reliable, non-expert clustering would have to agree with the 4 experts with a similar result.

5 Aggregating clustering solutions from multiple workers

Using a majority vote with the local-view HIT is an easy way of taking advantage of the "wisdom of crowd" principle. In order to address clustering from a local-view perspective, we need to build all possible pairs of elements. The number of those pairs is $O(n^2)$ on the number of elements to cluster. Thus the cost grows quickly for large clustering problems. For 100 elements to cluster there are 4950 pairs of elements to show to workers. For large problems, a better approach would be to give the problem to multiple workers through global-view, and then find a way to merge all of the clustering solutions to benefit from the wisdom of crowd. Consensus clustering (Topchy et al, 2005) has emerged as a way of combining multiple weak clusterings into a better one. The cluster-based similarity partitioning algorithm (CSPA) (Strehl and Ghosh, 2002) uses the idea that elements that are frequently clustered together have high similarity. With MTurk, this involves asking multiple workers to provide full clusterings, and then, for each pair of elements, counting the number of times they co-occur in the same clusters. This count is used as a similarity measure between elements, which then is used to build a distance matrix. We can then use it to recluster elements. The results from this technique on our word sense induction problem are shown in the next section.

	Random	K-Means	*local*	*global* CSPA	*global* centroid
GS #1	0,387	0,586	0,737	0,741	0,741
GS #2	0,415	0,613	0,765	0,777	0,777
GS #3	0,385	0,609	0,794	0,805	0,809
GS #4	0,399	0,606	0,768	0,776	0,776
Avg. ITA	0.396 ± 0.014	0.603 ± 0.012	**0.766 ± 0.023**	**0.775 ± 0.026**	**0.776 ± 0.028**

Table 2 - Interannotator agreement for our different approaches (bold numbers are within one standard deviation of the Expert vs. Expert ITA of 0.772 ± 0.031 described in section 4)

Another possibility is to determine which clustering solution is the centroid of the set of clusterings obtained from the worker. Finding centroid clustering (Hu and Sung, 2006) requires a between-cluster distance metric. We decided to use the entropy-based V-Measure for this purpose. For every pair of workers' solutions, we obtain their relative distance by calculating

1-VMeasure(cluster #1,cluster #2).

Then, for each candidate's clusters, we average the distance with every other candidate's. The candidate with the lowest average distance, the centroid, is picked as the "crowd solution". Results from this technique are also shown in the next section.

6 Results

For the first HIT the goal was to determine the number of distinct senses in a list of definitions. The Pearson correlation between the four annotators on the number of clusters they used for the 50 words was computed. These correlations can be viewed as how much the different annotators had the same idea of the grain size to be used to define senses. While experts 1, 2 and 4 seem to agree on grain size (correlation between 0.71 and 0.75), expert 3 had a different opinion. Correlations between that expert and the three others are between 0.53 and 0.58. The average correlation between experts is 0.63. On the other hand, the crowd solution does not agree as well with experts #1,#2 and #4 (Pearson correlation of 0.64, 0.68, 0.66), while it better approaches expert 3, with a correlation of 0.68. The average correlation between the non-expert solution and the experts' solutions is 0.67.

	GS #1	GS #2	GS #3	GS #4	N-E
GS #1	0	24	26	29	26
GS #2	24	0	30	27	26
GS #3	26	30	0	37	20
GS #4	29	27	37	0	27
N-E	26	26	20	27	0
Average	**26.25**	**26.75**	**28.25**	**30**	**24.75**

Table 3 - Absolute difference of number of clusters

Another way to analyze the agreement on grain size of the word sense between annotators is to sum the absolute difference of number of clusters for the 50 words (Table 3). In this way, we can specifically examine the results for the four annotators and for the non-expert crowd (N-E) solution, averaging that difference for each annotator versus all of the others (including the N-E solution).

To determine how a clustering solution compared to our GS, we computed the V-Measure for all 50 words between the solution and each GS. By averaging the score on the four GSs, we get an averaged ITA score between the clustering solution and the experts. For the sake of comparison, we first computed the score of a random solution, where definitions are randomly assigned to any one cluster. We also implemented K-means clustering using normalized word-overlap (Kulkarni et al., 2007), which has the best score on their test set.

The resulting averaged ITA of our local-view approaches that of all 4 experts. We did the same with the global-view after applying CSPA and our centroid identification algorithm to the 5 clustering solutions the workers submitted. Table 2 shows the agreement between each expert and those approaches, as well as the averaged ITA.

For the local-view and global-view "centroid", we looked at how the crowd size would affect the accuracy. We first computed the averaged ITA by considering the answers from the first worker. Then, step by step, we added the answers from the second, third, fourth and fifth workers, each time computing the averaged ITA. Figure 1 shows the ITA as a function of the workers.

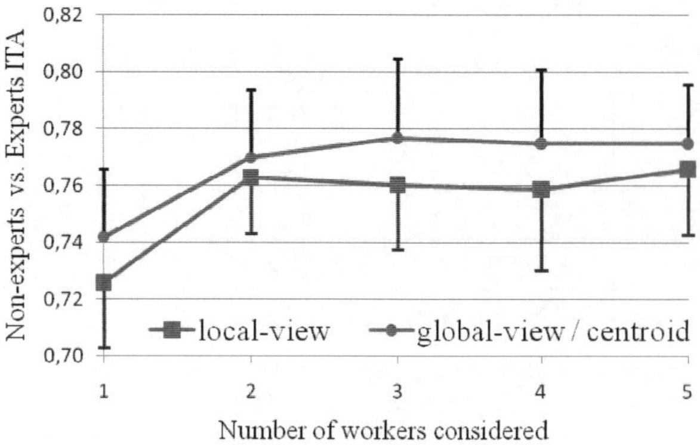

Figure 1 - Impact of the crowd size on the ITA of the local and global approaches

7 Discussion

Since our two approaches are based on the result of the first HIT, which determines the number of clusters, the accuracy of that first task is extremely important. It turns out that the correlation between the crowd solution and the experts (0.67) is actually higher than the average correlation between experts (0.63). One way to explain this is that of the 4 experts, 3 had a similar opinion on what the grain size should be, while the other one had a different opinion. The crowd picked a grain size that was actually between those two opinions, thus resulting in a higher correlation. This hypothesis is also supported by Table 3. The average difference in the number of clusters is lower for the N-E solution than for any expert solution. The crowd of 13 was able to come up with a grain size that could be seen as a good consensus of the four annotators' grain size. This allows us to believe that using the crowd to determine the number of clusters for our two approaches is a reliable technique.

As expected, Table 3 indicates that our two setups behave better than randomly assigning definitions to clusters. This is a good indication that the workers did not complete our tasks randomly. The automatic approach (K-Means) clearly behaves better than the random baseline. However, the clusters obtained with this approach agree less with the experts than any of our crowdsourced approaches. This confirms the intuition that humans are better at distinguishing word senses than an automatic approach like K-Means.

Our first hypothesis was that global-view would give us the best results: since the worker completing a global-view HIT has an overall view of the task, they should be able to provide a better solution. The results indicate that the local-view and global-view approaches give similar results in terms of ITA. Both of those approaches have closer agreement with the experts, than the experts have with each other (all ITAs are around 77%).

Here is an example of a solution that the crowd provided through local-view for the verb 'tape' with the definitions;

A. To record something on tape
B. To use strips of sticky material, especially to fix two things together or to fasten a parcel
C. To record sound or picture onto a tape
D. To tie a bandage firmly around an injured part of someone's body, strap
E. To fasten a package, box etc with tape

The crowd created two clusters: one by grouping A and C to create a "record audio/video" sense, and another one by grouping B,D and E to create a "fasten" sense. This solution was also chosen by two of the four experts. One of the other experts grouped definitions E with A and C, which is clearly an error since there is no shared meaning. The last expert created three clusters, by assigning D to a different cluster than B and E. This decision can be considered valid since there is a small semantic distinction between D and B/E from the fact that D is "fasten" for the specific case of injured body parts. However, a student could generalize D from B and E. So that expert's grain size does not correspond to our specifications.

We investigated two different aggregation techniques for clustering solutions, CSPA and centroid identification. In this application, both techniques give very similar results with only 2 clusters out of 50 words differing between the two techniques. Centroid identification is easier to implement, and doesn't require reclustering the elements. Figure 1 shows the impact of adding more workers to the crowd. While it seems advantageous to use 3 workers' opinions rather than only 1, (gain of 0.04), adding a fourth and fifth worker does not improve the average ITA.

Local-view is more tolerant to errors than global-view. If a chaotic worker randomly answers one pair of elements, the entire final clustering will not be affected. If a chaotic (or cheating) worker answers randomly in global-view, the entire clustering solution will be random. Thus, while a policy of using only one worker's answer for a local-view

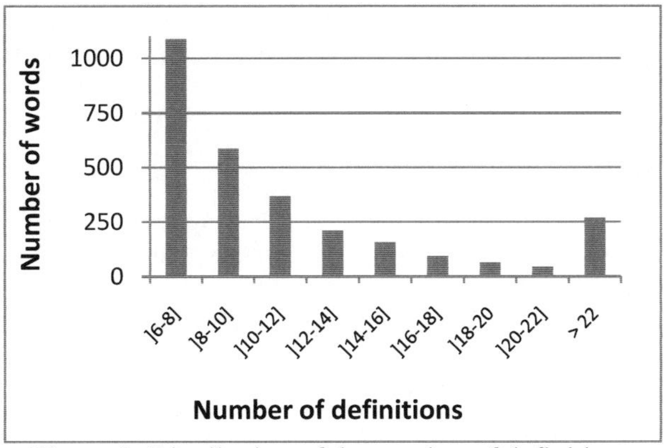

Figure 2- Distribution of the number of definitions

HIT could be adopted, the same policy might result in poor clustering if used for the global-view HIT.

However, global-view has the advantage over local-view of being cheaper. Figure 2 shows the distribution of the number of definitions extracted from both LDOCE and CALD per word (starting at word with more than 6 definitions). Since the local-view cost increases in a quadratic manner as the number of elements to cluster increases it would cost more than $275,000 to group the definitions of 30,000 words coming from the two dictionaries (using the parameters described in 3). It would be possible to modify it to only ask workers for the similarity of a subset of pairs of elements and then reconstruct the incomplete distance matrix (Hathaway and Bezdek, 2002). A better option for clustering a very large amount of elements is to use global-view. For the same 30,000 words above, the cost of grouping definitions using this technique would be around $4,500. This would imply that worker would have to create clusters from set of over 22 definitions. Keeping the cost constant while increasing the number of elements to cluster might decrease the workers' motivation. Thus scaling up a global-view HIT requires increasing the reward. It also requires vigilance on how much cognitive load the workers have to handle. Cognitive load can be seen as a function of the number of elements to cluster and of the number of clusters that a new element can be assigned to. If a worker only has to decide if an element should be in A or B, the cognitive load is low. But if the worker has to decide among many more classes, the cognitive load may increase to a point where the worker is hampered from providing a correct answer.

8 Conclusion

We evaluated two different approaches for crowdsourcing dictionary definition clustering as a means of achieving WSI. Global-view provides an interface to the worker where all the elements to be clustered are displayed, while local-view displays only two elements at a time and prompts the worker for their similarity. Both approaches show as much agreement with experts as the experts do with one another. Applying either CSPA or centroid identification allows the solution to benefit from the wisdom of crowd effect, and shows similar results. While global-view is cheaper than local-view, it is also strongly affected by worker error, and sensitive to the effect of increased cognitive load.

It appears that the task of clustering definitions to form word senses is a subjective one, due to different ideas of what the grain size of the senses should be. Thus, even though it seems that our two approaches provide results that are as good as those of an expert, it would be interesting to try crowdsourced clustering on a clustering problem where an objective ground truth exists. For example, we could take several audio recordings from each of several different persons. After mixing up the recordings from the different speakers, we could ask workers to clusters all the recordings from the same person. This would provide an even stronger evaluation of local-view against global-view since we could compare them to the true solution, the real identity of the speaker.

There are several interesting modifications that could also be attempted. The local-view task could ask for similarity on a scale of 1 to 5, instead of a binary choice of same/different meaning. Also, since using global-view with one large problem causes high cognitive load, we could partition a bigger problem, e.g., with 30 definitions, into 3 problems including 10 definitions. Using the same interface as global-view, the workers could cluster the sub-problems. We could then use CSPA to merge local clusters into a final cluster with the 30 definitions.

In this paper we have examined clustering word sense definitions. Two approaches were studied, and their advantages and disadvantages were described. We have shown that the use of human computation for WSI, with an appropriate crowd size and mean of aggregation, is as reliable as using expert judgments.

Acknowledgements

Funding for this research is provided by the National Science Foundation, Grant Number SBE-0836012 to the Pittsburgh Science of Learning Center (PSLC, http://www.learnlab.org).

References

Alonso, O., Rose, D. E., & Stewart, B. (2008). Crowdsourcing for relevance evaluation. ACM SIGIR Forum , 42 (2), pp. 9-15.

Callison-Burch, C. (2009). Fast, Cheap, and Creative: Evaluating Translation Quality Using Amazon's Mechanical Turk. Proceedings of EMNLP 2009.

Coxhead, A. (2000). A new academic word list. TESOL quarterly , 34 (2), 213-238.

Chklovski, T. & Mihalcea, R. (2003). Exploiting agreement and disagreement of human annotators for word sense disambiguation. Proceedings of RANLP 2003.

Fung, B. C., Wang, K., & Ester, M. (2003). Hierarchical document clustering using frequent itemsets. Proc. of the SIAM International Conference on Data Mining.

Gruenstein, A., McGraw, I., & Sutherland, A. (2009). "A self-transcribing speech corpus: collecting continuous speech with an online educational game". SLaTE Workshop.

Hathaway, R. J., & Bezdek, J. C. (2001). Fuzzy c-means clustering of incomplete data. IEEE Transactions on Systems, Man, and Cybernetics, Part B , 31 (5), 735-744.

Heilman, M. Collins-Thompson, K., Callan, J. & Eskenazi M. (2006). Classroom success of an Intelligent Tutoring System for lexical practice and reading comprehension. Proceedings of the Ninth International Conference on Spoken Language.

Horton, J. (2009, 12 11). Turker Talk. Retrieved 01 2010, from Deneme: http://groups.csail.mit.edu/uid/deneme/?p=436

Hu, T., & Sung, S. Y. (2006). Finding centroid clusterings with entropy-based criteria. Knowledge and Information Systems , 10 (4), 505-514.

Huang, Y., & Mitchell, T. M. (2006). Text clustering with extended user feedback. Proceedings of the 29th annual international ACM SIGIR conference on Research and development in information retrieval (p. 420). ACM.

Jagadeesan, A., Lynn, A., Corney, J., Yan, X., Wenzel, J., Sherlock, A., et al. (2009). Geometric reasoning via internet CrowdSourcing. 2009 SIAM/ACM Joint Conference on Geometric and Physical Modeling (pp. 313-318). ACM.

Kulkarni, A., Callan, J., & Eskenazi, M. (2007). Dictionary Definitions: The Likes and the Unlikes. Proceedings of the SLaTE Workshop on Speech and Language Technology in Education. Farmington, PA, USA.

Ledlie, J., Odero, B., Minkow, E., Kiss, I., & Polifroni, J. (2009). Crowd Translator: On Building Localized Speech Recognizers through Micropayments. Nokia Research Center.

Little, G. (2009, 08 22). Website Clustering. Retrieved 01 2010, from Deneme: http://groups.csail.mit.edu/uid/deneme/?p=244

Little, G., Chilton, L. B., Goldman, M., & Miller, R. C. (2009). TurKit: tools for iterative tasks on mechanical Turk. Proceedings of the ACM SIGKDD Workshop on Human Computation (pp. 29-30). ACM.

Niu, Z.-Y., Dong-Hong, J., & Chew-Lim, T. (2007). I2r: Three systems for word sense discrimination, chinese word sense disambiguation, and english word sense disambiguation. Proceedings of the Fourth International Workshop on Semantic Evaluations (SemEval-2007) (pp. 177-182). Prague, Czech Republic: Association for Computational Linguistics.

Rosenberg, A., & Hirschberg, J. (2007). V-measure: A conditional entropy-based external cluster evaluation measure. Proceedings of the 2007 Joint Conference EMNLP-CoNLL, (pp. 410-420).

SigLex, A. (2008). Retrieved 01 2010, from SemEval-2, Evaluation Exercises on Semantic Evaluation: http://semeval2.fbk.eu/semeval2.php

Snow, R., O'Connor, B., Jurafsky, D., & Ng, A. Y. (2008). Cheap and fast---but is it good? Evaluating non-expert annotations for natural language tasks. Proceedings of the Conference on Empirical Methods in Natural Language Processing (pp. 254-263). Association for Computational Linguistics.

Snow, R., Prakash, S., Jurafsky, D., & Ng, A. Y. (2007). Learning to Merge Word Senses. Proceedings of the 2007 Joint Conference on Empirical Methods in Natural Language Processing and Computational Natural Language Learning (EMNLP-CoNLL) (pp. 1005-1014). Prague, Czech Republic: Association for Computational Linguistics.

Strehl, A., & Ghosh, J. (2003). Cluster ensembles---a knowledge reuse framework for combining multiple partitions. The Journal of Machine Learning Research , 3, 583-617.

Topchy, A., Jain, A. K., & Punch, W. (2005). Clustering ensembles: Models of consensus and weak partitions. IEEE Transactions on Pattern Analysis and Machine Intelligence , 27 (12), 1866-1881.

Zhao, Y., & Karypis, G. (2001). Criterion functions for document clustering: Experiments and analysis. Report TR 01–40, Department of Computer Science, University of Minnesota.

Appendix

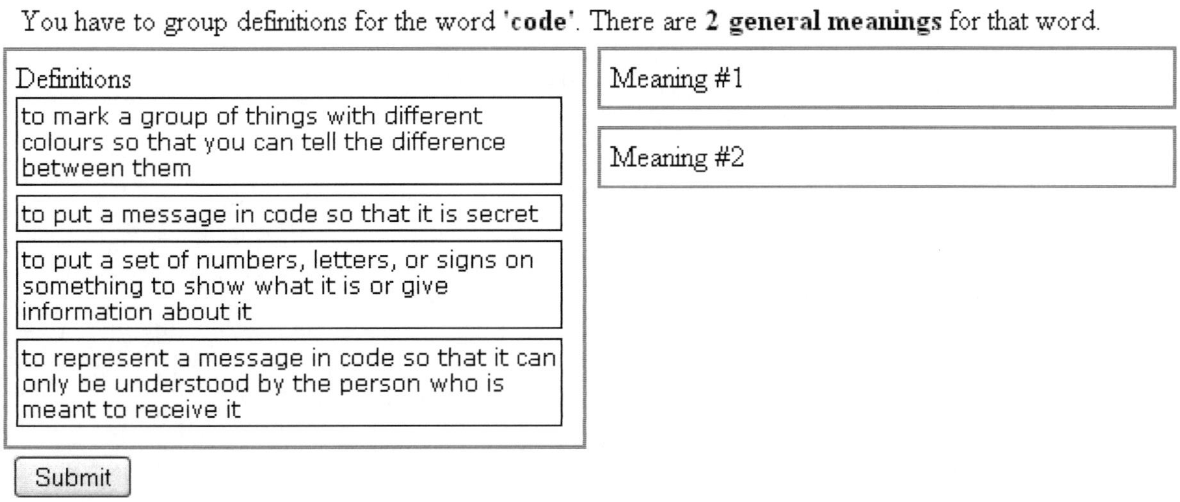

Figure 3: Example of a *global-view* HIT for the word "code" (not all of the instructions are shown)

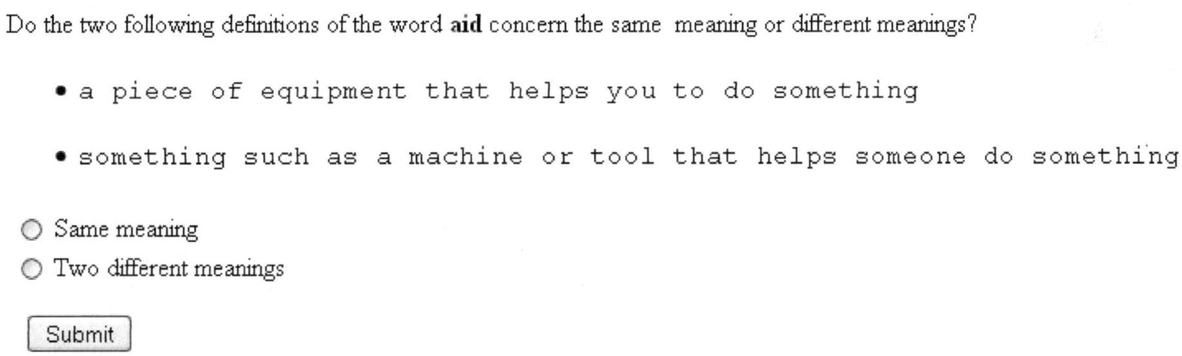

Figure 4: Example of a *local-view* HIT for the word "aid" (not all of the instructions are shown)

Consensus versus Expertise : A Case Study of Word Alignment with Mechanical Turk

Qin Gao and **Stephan Vogel**
Language Technologies Institute
Carnegie Mellon University
5000 Forbes Avenue, Pittsburgh PA, 15213
{qing,stephan.vogel}@cs.cmu.edu

Abstract

Word alignment is an important preprocessing step for machine translation. The project aims at incorporating manual alignments from Amazon Mechanical Turk (MTurk) to help improve word alignment quality. As a global crowdsourcing service, MTurk can provide flexible and abundant labor force and therefore reduce the cost of obtaining labels. An easy-to-use interface is developed to simplify the labeling process. We compare the alignment results by Turkers to that by experts, and incorporate the alignments in a semi-supervised word alignment tool to improve the quality of the labels. We also compared two pricing strategies for word alignment task. Experimental results show high precision of the alignments provided by Turkers and the semi-supervised approach achieved 0.5% absolute reduction on alignment error rate.

1 Introduction

Word alignment is used in various natural language processing tasks. Most state-of-the-art statistical machine translation systems rely on word alignment as a preprocessing step. The quality of word alignment is usually measured by AER, which is loosely related to BLEU score (Lopez and Resnik, 2006). There has been research on utilizing manually aligned corpus to assist automatic word alignment, and obtains encouraging results on alignment error rate. (Callison-Burch et al., 2004; Blunsom and Cohn, 2006; Fraser and Marcu, 2006; Niehues and Vogel, 2008; Taskar et al., 2005; Liu et al., 2005; Moore, 2005). However, how to obtain large amount of alignments with good quality is problematic. Labeling word-aligned parallel corpora requires significant amount of labor. In this paper we explore the possibility of using Amazon Mechanical Turk (MTurk) to obtain manual word alignment faster, cheaper, with high quality.

Crowdsourcing is a way of getting random labor force on-line with low cost. MTurk is one of the leading providers for crowdsourcing marketplace. There have been several research papers on using MTurk to help natural language processing tasks, Callison-Burch (2009) used MTurk to evaluate machine translation results. Kittur et al. (2008) showed the importance of validation data set, the task is evaluating quality of Wikipedia articles. There are also experiments use the annotation from MTurk in place of training data. For example (Kaisser et al., 2008) and (Kaisser and Lowe, 2008) used MTurk to build question answering datasets and choose summary lengths that suite the need of the users.

Word alignment is a relatively complicate task for inexperienced workers. The fact puts us in a dilemma, we can either provide lengthy instructions and train the workers, or we must face the problem that workers may have their own standards. The former solution is impractical in the context of crowdsourcing because heavily trained workers will expect higher payment, which defeats economical nature of crowdsourcing. Therefore we are forced to face the uncertainty, and ask ourselves the following questions: First, how consistent would the labels from random labelers be, given minimal or no instructions? Second, how consistent would these intuitive labels be consistent with the labels from expert labelers? Third, if there is certain level of consistency between the intuitive labels and the labels from experts, can we extract most reliable links from the former? Last but not least, given the alignment links, can we utilize them to help automatic word alignment without further human efforts?

The statistics on the data we get shows the internal consistency among multiple MTurk alignments is greater than 70%, and the precision is greater than 84% when consider all the links. By applying majority vote and consensus strategies, we can select links that have greater than 95% accuracy. When applying the alignment links on a new aligner that can perform constrained EM algorithm for IBM models we observe 0.5% absolute improvements on alignment error rate. The average per-word cost is about 2 cent per word.

The paper will be organized as follows, first we will discuss the design principle of the task and the implementation of the application for word alignment in section 2. Section 3 describes the algorithm used in utilizing the manual alignments. Section 4 presents the analysis on the harvested data and the expert labels, and the the experiment results of semi-supervised word alignment. Section 5 concludes the paper.

Proceedings of the NAACL HLT 2010 Workshop on Creating Speech and Language Data with Amazon's Mechanical Turk, pages 30–34,
Los Angeles, California, June 2010.

2 Design of the task

In this task, we want to collect manual word alignment data from MTurk workers, Figure 2 shows an example of word alignment. There are two sentences which are translation of each other. There are links between words in two sentences, indicating the words are translation pairs. Notice that one word can be aligned to zero or more words, if a word is aligned to zero word, we can assume it is aligned to a virtual empty word. Therefore, given a sentence pair, we want workers to link words in source sentence to one or more target words or the empty word.

In our experiment, we use a Chinese-English parallel corpus and ask workers to alignment the words in Chinese sentence to the words in English sentence. We do not provide any alignment links from automatic aligner.

2.1 Guidelines of design

MTurk represents a new pattern of market that has yet be thoroughly studied. Mason and Watts (2009) shows that higher payment does not guarantee results with higher quality. Also, one should be aware that the web-based interface is vulnerable to automatic scripts that generate highly consistent yet meaningless results. To ensure a better result, several measures must be combined: 1) Require workers to take qualifications before they can accept the tasks. 2) Implement an interface less vulnerable to automatic scripts. 3) Build quality control mechanism that filters inaccurate results, and finally 4) Redesign the interface so that the time spent by careful and careless workers does not differ too much, so there is less incentives for workers to submit random results. With these guidelines in mind, we put together several elements into the HIT.

Qualifications

We require the workers to take qualifications, which requires them to pick correct translation of five Chinese words. The Chinese word is rendered in bitmap.

Interface implementation

We implemented the word alignment interface on top of Google Web Toolkit, which enables developing `Javascript` based Web application in `Java`. Because all the content of the interface, including the content in the final result, is generated dynamically in the run time, it is much more difficult to hack than plain HTML forms. Figure 1 shows a snapshot of the interface[1]. The labeling procedure requires only mouse click. The worker need to label all the words with a golden background[2]. To complete the task, the worker needs to: 1) Click on the Chinese word he want to label. 2) Click on the English words he want the Chinese word to be linked, or click on the empty word to the end of the sentence. 3) If he want to delete a link, he need to click on the English word again, otherwise he can move on to next unlabeled word, or to modify links on another labeled word. 4) Only when all required words are labeled, the user would be allowed to click on submit button.

The interface has two more functionalities, first, it allows to specify a subset of words in the sentence for user to label, as shown in the snapshot, words with white background are not required to label. Secondly it supports providing initial alignment on the sentence.

Quality control

Quality control is a crucial component of the system. For problems that have clear gold standard answers to a portion of data, the quality control can be done by mingling the known into the unknown, and rejecting the submissions with low qualities on known samples. However in our situation it is not easy to do so because although we have fully manual aligned sentences, we do not have corpus in which the sentences are partially aligned, therefore if we want to use the method we have to let worker label an additional sentence, which may double the effort for the workers. Also we do not provide thorough standard for users, therefore before we know the divergence of the alignments, we actually do not know how to set the threshold, even with given gold standard labels. In addition, if the method will be applied on languages with low resource, we cannot assume availability of gold standard answers. Therefore, we only try to filter out answers base on the consensus. The quality control works as follows. Firstly we assign an alignment task to $2n + 1$ workers. For these submissions, we first try to build a majority answer from these assignments. For each alignment *link*, if it appears in more than n submissions. Then every individual assignments will be compared to the majority alignment, so we can get the precision and recall rates. If either precision or recall rate is lower than a threshold, we will reject the submission.

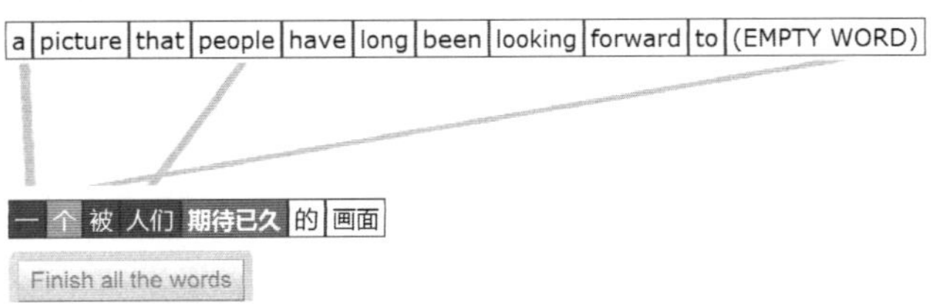

Figure 1: A snapshot of the labeling interface.

2.2 Pricing and worker base

We tried two pricing strategies. The first one fixes the number of words that a worker need to label for each HIT, and fix the rate for each HIT. The second one always

[1] A demo of the latest version can be found at `http://alt-aligner.appspot.com`, the source code of the aligner is distributed under Apache License 2.0 on `http://code.google.com/p/alt-aligner/`

[2] If the document is printed in greyscale, the lightest background (except the white one) is actually golden, the second lightest one is red and the darkest one is dark blue.

asks workers to label every word in the sentence, in the mean time we vary the rate for each HIT according to the lengths of source sentences. For each strategy we tried different rates, starting from 10 words per cent. However we did not get enough workers even after the price raised to 2 words per cent. The result indicates a limited worker base of Chinese speakers.

3 Utilizing the manual alignments

As we can expect, given no explicit guideline for word alignments, the variance of different assignments can be fairly large, a question will raise what can we do with the disagreements? As we will see later in the experiment part, the labels are more likely to be consistent with expert labels if more workers agree on it. Therefore, a simple strategy is to use only the links that more workers have consensus on them.

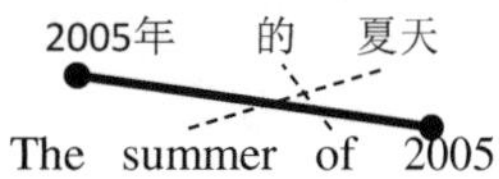

Figure 2: Partial and full alignments

However the method instantly gives rise to a problem. Now the alignment is not "full alignments", instead, they are "partial". The claim seems to be trivial but they have completely different underlying assumptions. Figure 2 shows the comparison of partial alignments (the bold link) and full alignments (the dashed and the bold links). In the example, if full alignment is given, we can assert *2005* is only aligned to 2005年, not to 的or 夏天, but we cannot do that if only partial alignment is given. In this paper we experiment with a novel method which uses the partial alignment to constraint the EM algorithm in the parameter estimation of IBM models.

IBM Models (Brown et. al., 1993) are a series of generative models for word alignment. GIZA++ (Och and Ney, 2003) is the most widely used implementation of IBM models and HMM (Vogel et al., 1996) where EM algorithm is employed to estimate the model parameters. In the E-step, it is possible to obtain sufficient statistics from all possible alignments for simple models such as Model 1 and Model 2. Meanwhile for fertility-based models such as Model 3, 4, 5, enumerating all possible alignments is NP-complete. In practice, we use simpler models such as HMM or Model 2 to generate a "center alignment" and then try to find better alignments among the neighbors of it. The neighbors of an alignment $a_1^J = [a_1, a_2, \cdots, a_J], a_j \in [0, I]$ is defined as alignments that can be generated from a_1^J by one of the operators: 1) Move operator $m_{[i,j]}$, that changes $a_j := i$, i.e. arbitrarily set word f_j in source sentence to align to word e_i in target sentence; 2) Swap operator $s_{[j_1,j_2]}$ that exchanges a_{j_1} and a_{j_2}. The algorithm will update the center alignment as long as a better alignment can be found, and finally outputs a local optimal alignment. The neighbor alignments of the alignment are then used in collecting the counts for the M Step.

In order to use partial manual alignments to constrain the search space, we separate the algorithm into two stages, first the seed alignment will be optimized towards the constraints. Each iteration we only pick a new center alignment with less inconsistent links than the original one, until the alignment is consistent with all constraints. After that, in each iteration we pick the alignment with highest likelihood but does not introduce any inconsistent links. The algorithm will output a local optimal alignment consistent with the partial alignment. When collecting the counts for M-step, we also need to exclude all alignments that are not consistent with the partial manual alignment. The task can also be done by skipping the inconsistent alignments in the neighborhood of the local optimal alignment.

4 Experiment and analysis

In this section we will show the analysis of the harvested MTurk alignments and the results of the semi-supervised word alignment experiments.

4.1 Consistency of the manual alignments

We first examine the internal consistency of the MTurk alignments. We calculate the internal consistency rate in both results. Because we requested three assignments for every question, we classify the links in two different ways. First, if a link appear in all three submissions, we classify it as "consensus link". Second, if a link appear in more than one submissions, we classify it as "majority", otherwise it is classified as "minority". Table 1 presents the statistics of partial alignment and full alignment tasks. Note that by spending the same amount of money, we get more sentences aligned because for fixed rate partial sentence alignment tasks, sometimes we may have overlaps between tasks. Therefore we also calculate a subset of full alignment tasks that consists of all the sentences in partial alignment tasks. The statistics shows that although generally full alignment tasks generates more links, the partial alignment tasks gives denser alignments. It is interesting to know whether the denser alignments lead to higher recall rate or lower precision.

4.2 Comparing MTurk and expert alignments

To exam the quality of alignments, we compared them with expert alignments. Table 2 lists the precision, recall and F-1 scores for partial and full alignment tasks. We compare the consistency of all links, the links in majority group and the consensus links.

As we can observe from the results, the Turkers tend to label less links than the experts, Interestingly, the overall quality of partial alignment tasks is significantly better than full alignment tasks. Despite the lower recall rate, it is encouraging that the majority vote and consensus links

	Partial	Full	Full-Int
Number of sentences	135	239	135
Number of words	2,008	3,241	2,008
Consensus words	13,03	2,299	1,426
Consensus rate(%)	64.89	70.93	71.02
Total Links	7,508	9,767	6,114
Consensus Links	5,625	7,755	4,854
Consensus Rate(%)	74.92	79.40	79.39
Total Unique Links	3,186	3,989	2,506
Consensus Links	1,875	2,585	1,618
Consensus Rate(%)	58.85	64.80	64.54
In majority group	2,447	3,193	1,426
Majority rate(%)	76.80	80.04	71.06

Table 1: Internal consistency of manual alignments, here Full-Int means statistics of full alignment tasks on the sentences that also aligned using partial alignment task

	All Links			Majority Links			Consensus Links		
	P.	R.	F.	P.	R.	F.	P.	R.	F.
P	0.84	0.88	0.86	0.95	0.76	0.84	0.98	0.60	0.74
F	0.88	0.70	0.78	0.96	0.61	0.75	0.99	0.51	0.68
I	0.87	0.71	0.79	0.95	0.62	0.75	0.98	0.52	0.68

Table 2: Consistency of MTurk alignments with expert alignments, showing precision (P), recall (R) and F1 (F) between MTurk and expert alignments. P, F, and I correspond to Partial, Full and Full-Int in Table 1

yield very high precisions against expert alignments. Table 3 lists the words with most errors. Most errors occur on function words. A manual review shows that more than 85% errors have function words on either Chinese side or English side. The result, however, is as expected because these words are hard to label and we did not provide clear rule for function words.

4.3 Results of semi-supervised word alignment

In this experiment we try to use the alignment links in the semi-supervised word alignment algorithm. We use Chinese-English manually aligned corpus in the experiments, which contains 21,863 sentence pairs, 424,683 Chinese words and 524,882 English words. First, we use the parallel corpus to train IBM models without any manual alignments, we run 5 iterations of model 1 and HMM,

Chinese				English			
FN		FP		FN		FP	
64	的	16	，	122	the	15	,
26	是	11	个	67	NULL	11	a
19	，	9	是	43	of	6	the
17	个	3	被	36	to	6	is
16	公园	3	有	24	a	4	to

Table 3: Words that most errors occur, FN means a false negative error occurred on the word, i.e. a link to this word or from this word is missing. FP means false positive, accordingly. The manual alignment links comes from majority vote.

3 iterations of model 3 and 6 iterations of model 4. Then we resume the training procedure from the third iterations of model 4. This time we load the manual alignment links and perform 3 iterations of constrained EM. We also experiment with 3 different sets of alignments. Table 4 presents the improvements on the alignment quality.

Unsupervised						
	Ch-En			En-Ch		
	Prec.	Recall	AER	Prec.	Recall	AER
	68.22	46.88	44.43	65.35	55.05	40.24
All Links						
Partial	68.28	47.09	44.26	65.86	55.63	39.68
Full-Int	68.28	47.09	44.26	65.85	55.63	39.69
Full	68.37	47.15	44.19	65.90	55.67	39.65
Majority Links						
Partial	68.28	47.08	44.27	65.84	55.62	39.70
Full-Int	68.28	47.08	44.27	65.84	55.61	39.71
Full	68.37	47.13	44.20	65.88	55.65	39.67
Consensus Links						
Partial	68.24	47.06	44.30	65.83	55.60	39.71
Full-Int	68.25	47.06	44.29	65.83	55.60	39.72
Full	68.31	47.10	44.25	65.86	55.63	39.68

Table 4: The performance of using manual alignments in semi-supervised word alignment

From the result we can see that given the same amount of links the improvement of alignment error rate is generally the same for partial and full alignment tasks, however, if we consider the amount of money spent on the task, the full alignment task collect much more data than partial alignments, we consider full sentence alignment more cost efficient in this sense.

5 Conclusion

In this pilot experiment, we explore the possibility of using Amazon Mechanical Turk (MTurk) to collect bilingual word alignment data to assist automatic word alignment. We develop a system including a word alignment interface based on Javascript and a quality control scheme. To utilize the manual alignments, we develop a semi-supervised word alignment algorithm that can perform constrained EM with partial alignments. The algorithm enables us to use only the most reliable links by majority vote or consensus. The effectiveness of these methods is proven by small-scale experiments. The results show the manual alignments from MTurk have high precision with expert word alignment, especially when filtered by majority vote or consensus. We get small improvement on semi-supervised word alignment. Given the promising results, it is interesting to see if the tendency will carry on when we scale up the experiments.

However the experiment also shows some problems, first the coverage of worker base on MTurk is limited. Given small worker base for specific languages, the cost efficiency for NLP tasks in those languages is questionable.

References

P. Blunsom and T. Cohn. 2006. Discriminative word alignment with conditional random fields. In *Proceedings of the 21st International Conference on Computational Linguistics and the 44th annual meeting of the Association for Computational Linguistics*, pages 65–72.

P. F. Brown et. al. 1993. The mathematics of statistical machine translation: Parameter estimation. In *Computational Linguistics*, volume 19(2), pages 263–331.

C. Callison-Burch, D. Talbot, and D. Osborne. 2004. Statistical machine translation with word- and sentence-aligned parallel corpora. In *Proceedings of the 42nd Annual Meeting of the Association for Computational Linguistics (ACL-2004).*

C. Callison-Burch. 2009. Fast, cheap, and creative: Evaluating translation quality using Amazon's Mechanical Turk. In *Proceedings of the 2009 Conference on Empirical Methods in Natural Language Processing*, pages 286–295. Association for Computational Linguistics.

A. Fraser and D. Marcu. 2006. Semi-supervised training for statistical word alignment. In *ACL-44: Proceedings of the 21st International Conference on Computational Linguistics and the 44th annual meeting of the Association for Computational Linguistics*, pages 769–776.

M. Kaisser and J. B. Lowe. 2008. A research collection of question answer sentence pairs. In *Proceedings of The 6th Language Resources and Evaluation Conference.*

M. Kaisser, M. Hearst, and J.B. Lowe. 2008. Evidence for varying search results summary lengths. In *Proceedings of the 46th Annual Meeting of the Association for Computational Linguistics.*

A. Kittur, E. H. Chi, and B Suh. 2008. Crowdsourcing user studies with mechanical turk. In *CHI '08: Proceeding of the twenty-sixth annual SIGCHI conference on Human factors in computing systems*, pages 453–456.

Y. Liu, Q. Liu, and S. Lin. 2005. Log-linear models for word alignment. In *ACL '05: Proceedings of the 43rd Annual Meeting on Association for Computational Linguistics*, pages 459–466.

A. Lopez and P. Resnik. 2006. Word-based alignment, phrase-based translation: What's the link? with philip resnik. In *Proceedings of the 7th Biennial Conference of the Association for Machine Translation in the Americas (AMTA-2006).*

W. Mason and D. J. Watts. 2009. Financial incentives and the "performance of crowds". In *HCOMP '09: Proceedings of the ACM SIGKDD Workshop on Human Computation*, pages 77–85.

R. C Moore. 2005. A discriminative framework for bilingual word alignment. In *Proceedings of the conference on Human Language Technology and Empirical Methods in Natural Language Processing*, pages 81–88.

J. Niehues and S. Vogel. 2008. Discriminative word alignment via alignment matrix modeling. In *Proceedings of the Third Workshop on Statistical Machine Translation*, pages 18–25.

F. J. Och and H. Ney. 2003. A systematic comparison of various statistical alignment models. In *Computational Linguistics*, volume 1:29, pages 19–51.

B. Taskar, S. Lacoste-Julien, and D. Klein. 2005. A discriminative matching approach to word alignment. In *Proceedings of the conference on Human Language Technology and Empirical Methods in Natural Language Processing*, pages 73–80.

S. Vogel, H. Ney, and C. Tillmann. 1996. HMM based word alignment in statistical machine translation. In *Proceedings of 16th International Conference on Computational Linguistics)*, pages 836–841.

Rating Computer-Generated Questions with Mechanical Turk

Michael Heilman
Language Technologies Institute
Carnegie Mellon University
Pittsburgh, PA 15213, USA
mheilman@cs.cmu.edu

Noah A. Smith
Language Technologies Institute
Carnegie Mellon University
Pittsburgh, PA 15213, USA
nasmith@cs.cmu.edu

Abstract

We use Amazon Mechanical Turk to rate computer-generated reading comprehension questions about Wikipedia articles. Such application-specific ratings can be used to train statistical rankers to improve systems' final output, or to evaluate technologies that generate natural language. We discuss the question rating scheme we developed, assess the quality of the ratings that we gathered through Amazon Mechanical Turk, and show evidence that these ratings can be used to improve question generation.

1 Introduction

This paper discusses the use of Amazon Mechanical Turk (MTurk) to rate computer-generated reading comprehension questions about Wikipedia articles.

We have developed a question generation system (Heilman and Smith, 2009; Heilman and Smith, 2010) that uses the overgenerate-and-rank paradigm (Langkilde and Knight, 1998). In the the overgenerate-and-rank approach, many system-generated outputs are ranked in order to select higher quality outputs. While the approach has had considerable success in natural language generation (Langkilde and Knight, 1998; Walker et al., 2001), it often requires human labels on system output for the purpose of learning to rank. We employ MTurk to reduce the time and cost of acquiring these labels.

For many problems, large labeled datasets do not exist. One alternative is to build rule-based systems, but it is often difficult and time-consuming to accurately encode relevant linguistic knowledge in rules. Another alternative, unsupervised or semi-supervised learning, usually requires clever formulations of bias that guide the learning process (Carroll and Charniak, 1992; Yarowsky, 1995); such intuitions are not always available. Thus, small, application-specific labeled datasets, which can be cheaply constructed using MTurk, may provide considerable benefits by enabling the use of supervised learning.

In addition to using MTurk ratings to train a learned ranking component, we could also use MTurk ratings to evaluate the final top-ranked output of our system. More generally, MTurk can be a useful evaluation tool for systems that output natural language (e.g., systems for natural language generation, summarization, translation). For example, Callison-Burch (2009) used MTurk to evaluate machine translations. MTurk facilitates the efficient measurement and understanding of errors made by such technologies, and could be used to complement automatic evaluation metrics such as BLEU (Papineni et al., 2002) and ROUGE (Lin, 2004).

It is true that, for our task, MTurk workers annotate computer-generated rather than human-generated natural language. Thus, the data will not be as generally useful as other types of annotations, such as parse trees, which could be used to build general purpose syntactic parsers. However, for the reasons described above, we believe the use of MTurk to rate computer-generated output can be useful for the training, development, and evaluation of language technologies.

The remainder of the paper is organized as follows: §2 and §3 briefly describe the question generation system and corpora used in our experiments. §4 provides the details of our rating scheme. §5 discusses the quantity, cost, speed, and quality of the ratings we gathered. §6 presents preliminary experiments showing that the MTurk ratings improve question ranking. Finally, in §7, we conclude.

Proceedings of the NAACL HLT 2010 Workshop on Creating Speech and Language Data with Amazon's Mechanical Turk, pages 35–40,
Los Angeles, California, June 2010.

2 Question Generation System

We use MTurk to improve and evaluate a system for automatic question generation (QG). In our QG approach, hand-crafted rules transform declarative sentences from an input text into a large set of questions (i.e., hundreds per page). This rule system is complemented by a statistical ranker, which ranks questions according to their quality. Currently, we focus on basic linguistic issues and the goal of producing *acceptable* questions—that is, questions that are grammatical, make sense, and are not vague. We believe an educator could select and revise output from the system in order to produce a final set of high-quality, challenging questions.

Our system is described by Heilman and Smith (2010). In that work, we employed a different scheme involving binary judgments of question quality according to various factors such as grammaticality, vagueness, and others. We also employed university students as novice annotators. For the training dataset, only one human rated each question. See Heilman and Smith (2009) for more details.[1]

3 Corpora

In our experiments, we generated questions from 60 articles sampled from the "featured" articles in the English Wikipedia[2] that have between 250 and 2,000 word tokens. This collection provides expository texts written at an adult reading level from a variety of domains, which roughly approximates the prose that a secondary or post-secondary level student would encounter. By choosing from the featured articles, we intended to select well-edited articles about topics of general interest. We then randomly selected 20 questions from each of 60 articles for labeling with MTurk.[3]

[1]We also generated some questions using a technique that replaces pronouns and underspecified noun phrases with antecedent mentions identified by a coreference resolver. We will not provide details about this component here because they are not relevant to our use of MTurk to rate questions. A forthcoming paper will describe these additions.

[2]The English Wikipedia data were downloaded on December 16, 2008 from `http://en.wikipedia.org`

[3]Five questions were later eliminated from this set due to minor implementation changes, the details of which are uninteresting. The final set contained 1,195 questions.

	Rating	Details
1	Bad	The question has major problems.
2	Unacceptable	The question definitely has a minor problem.
3	Borderline	The question might have a problem, but I'm not sure.
4	Acceptable	The question does not have problems.
5	Good	The question is as good as one that a human teacher might write for a reading quiz.

Table 1: The five-point question rating scale.

4 Rating Scheme

This section describes the rating scheme we developed for evaluating the quality of computer-generated questions on MTurk.

Questions were presented independently as single human intelligence tasks (HITs). At the top of the page, raters were given the instructions shown in Figure 1 along with 7 examples of good and bad questions with their appropriate ratings. Below the instructions and examples was an excerpt from the source text consisting of up to 5 sentences of context, ending with the primary sentence that the question was generated from. The question to be rated then followed.

Below each question was the five-point rating scale shown in Table 1. Workers were required to select a single rating by clicking a radio button. At the bottom of the page, the entire source article text was given, in case the worker felt it was necessary to refer back to more context.

We paid 5 cents per rating,[4] and each question was rated by five workers. With the 10% commission charge by Amazon, each question cost 27.5 cents.

The final rating value was computed by taking the arithmetic mean of the ratings. Table 2 provides some examples of questions and their mean ratings.

4.1 Monitoring Turker Ratings

During some pilot tests, we found that it was particularly important to set some qualification criteria for workers. Specifically, we only allowed workers

[4]Given the average time spent per HIT, the pay rate can be extrapolated to $5–10 per hour.

Rate computer-generated reading questions

Rate computer-generated questions with respect to whether they would be acceptable quiz questions. The questions are meant to assess whether a student has read a text and understands the literal meaning of it. Acceptable questions should be grammatical and have a clear answer. However, acceptable questions need not be "deep," challenging, or interesting questions. Please ignore any text formatting problems (e.g., capitalization, punctuation, spelling errors, extra spaces between words).

If you are not a native speaker of English, please do not complete this task.

Instructions

1. Read the **Context**, which is taken from a longer article. Pay particular attention to the last sentence.
2. Read the **Question** that a computer generated from the last sentence of the context.
3. Rate the quality of the question on a five-point scale (see below).
4. If necessary, refer to the **Full Article** from which the context was taken.

Reasons that questions can be unacceptable.

(Un)grammaticality	The question is ungrammatical, does not make sense, or uses the wrong question word (e.g., who, what, which, etc.).
Incorrect Information	The question implies something that is obviously incorrect, according to the given context.
Vagueness	The question has no simple and clear answer (even a good reader would not know the answer).
Awkwardness/Other	The question is very awkwardly phrased., or has some other problem (e.g., no native speaker of English would say it this way).

Figure 1: A screenshot of the instructions given to workers.

who had completed at least 50 previously accepted HITs. We also required that at least 95% of workers' previous submissions had been accepted.

We also submitted HITs in batches of 100 to 500 so that we could more closely monitor the process.

In addition, we performed a limited amount of semi-automated monitoring of the ratings, and rejected work from workers who were clearly randomly clicking on answers or not following the rating scheme properly. We tried to err on the side of accepting bad work. After all ratings for a batch of questions were received, we calculated for each worker the number of ratings submitted, the average time spent on each question, the average rating, and the correlation of the worker's rating with the mean of the other 4 ratings. We used a combination of these statistics to identify extremely bad workers (e.g., ones who had negative correlations with other workers and spent less than 10 seconds per question). If some of the ratings for a question were rejected, then the HIT was "extended" in order to receive 5 ratings.

5 Quantity, Cost, Speed, and Quality

This section discusses the quantity and quality of the question ratings we received from MTurk.

5.1 Quantity and Cost of Ratings

We received 5 ratings each for 1,200 questions, costing a total of $330. 178 workers participated. Workers submitted 33.9 ratings on average (s.d. = 58.0). The distribution of ratings per worker was highly skewed, such that a handful of workers submitted 100 or more ratings (max = 395). The ratings from these who submitted more than 100 ratings seemed to be slightly lower in quality but still acceptable. The median number of ratings per worker was 11.

5.2 Speed of Ratings

Ratings were received very quickly once the HITs were submitted. Figure 2 shows the cumulative number of ratings received for a batch of questions,

Source Text Excerpt	Question	Rating
MD 36 serves as the main road through the Georges Creek Valley, a region which is historically known for coal mining, and has been designated by MDSHA as part of the Coal Heritage Scenic Byway.	*Which part has MD 36 been designated by MDSHA as?*	1.4
He worked further on the story with the Soviet author Isaac Babel, but no material was ever published or released from their collaboration, and the production of Bezhin Meadow came to an end.	*What did the production of Bezhin Meadow come to?*	2.0
The design was lethal, successful and much imitated, and remains one of the definitive weapons of World War II.	*Does the design remain one of the definitive weapons of World War II?*	2.8
Francium was discovered by Marguerite Perey in France (from which the element takes its name) in 1939.	*Where was Francium discovered by Marguerite Perey in 1939?*	3.8
Lazare Ponticelli was the longest-surviving officially recognized veteran... Although he attempted to remain with his French regiment, he eventually enlisted in...	*Did Lazare Ponticelli attempt to remain with his French regiment?*	4.4

Table 2: Example computer-generated questions, along with their mean ratings from Mechanical Turk.

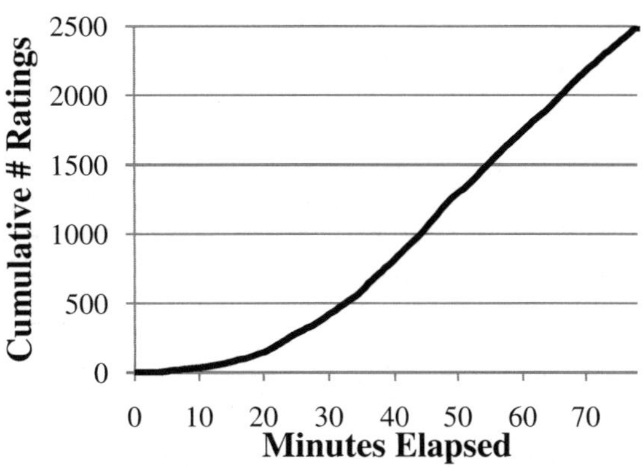

Figure 2: The cumulative number of ratings submitted by MTurk workers over time, for a batch of 497 questions posted simultaneously (there are 5 ratings per question).

indicating that more than 1,000 ratings were received per hour.

5.3 Quality of Ratings

We evaluated inter-rater agreement by having the first author and an independent judge rate a random sample of 40 questions from 4 articles. The independent judge was a computational linguist. The Pearson correlation coefficient between the first author's ratings and the mean ratings from MTurk workers was $r = 0.79$, which is fairly strong though not ideal. The correlation between the independent judge's ratings and the MTurk workers was $r = 0.74$. These fairly strong positive correlations between the MTurk ratings and the two human judges provide evidence that the rating scheme is consistent and well-defined. The results also agree with Snow et al. (2008), who found that aggregating labels from 3 to 7 workers often provides expert levels of agreement. Interestingly, the agreement between the two human raters was somewhat lower ($r = 0.65$), suggesting that aggregated labels from a crowd of MTurk workers can be more reliable than individual humans.[5]

6 Using Labeled Data to Improve Question Ranking

In this section, we provide some preliminary results to demonstrate that MTurk ratings can be used for learning to rank QG output.

First, we briefly characterize the quality of *unranked* output. Figure 3 shows a histogram of the mean MTurk ratings for the 1,195 questions, showing that only a relatively small fraction of the questions created by the overgenerating steps of our system are acceptable: 12.9% when using 3.5 as the threshold for acceptability.

However, ranking can lead to substantially higher levels of quality in the top-ranked questions, which

[5]We also converted the ratings into binary values based on whether they exceeded a threshold of 3.5. After this conversion to a nominal scale, we computed a Cohen's κ of 0.54, which indicates "moderate" agreement (Landis and Koch, 1977).

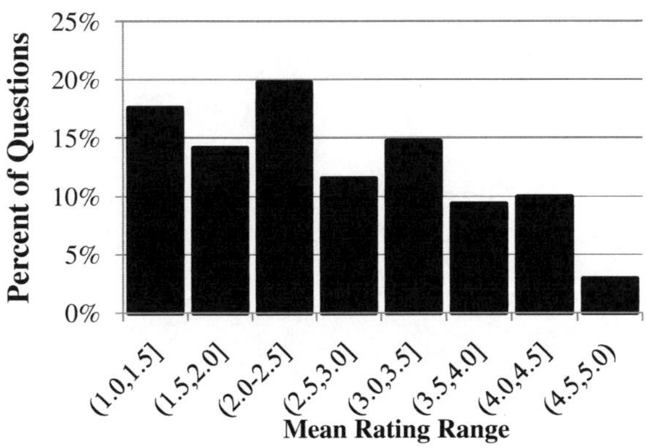

Figure 3: The distribution of the 1,195 question ratings.

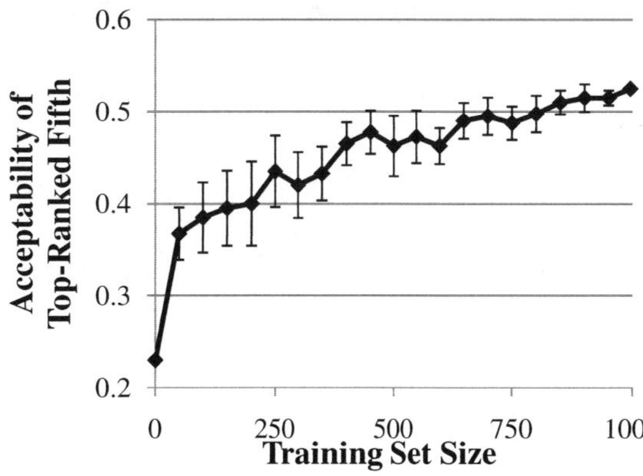

Figure 4: A graph of the acceptability of top-ranked questions when datasets of increasing size are used to train a statistical question ranker. Error bars show 95% confidence intervals computed from the 10 runs of the sampling process.

might be presented first in a user interface. Therefore, we investigated how many MTurk-rated questions are needed to train an effective statistical question ranker. Our ranking model is essentially the same as the one used by Heilman and Smith (2010). Rather than logistic regression, which we used previously, here we use a linear regression with ℓ_2 regularization to account for the ordinal scale of the averaged question ratings. We set the regularization parameter through cross-validation with the training data.

The regression includes all of the features described by Heilman and Smith (2010). It includes features for sentence lengths, whether the question includes various WH words, whether certain syntactic transformations performed during QG, whether negation words are present in questions, how many times various parts of speech appeared, and others. It also includes some additional coreference features for parts of speech and lengths of noun phrase mentions and their antecedents.[6] In all, the ranker includes 326 features.

For our experiments, we set aside a randomly chosen 200 of the 1,195 rated questions as a test set. We then trained statistical rankers on randomly sampled subsets of the remaining questions, from size $N = 50$ up to $N = 995$. For each value of N, we used the ranker trained on that amount of data to rank the 200 test questions. We then computed the percentage of the top fifth of the ranked test set questions with a mean rating above 3.5. For each N less than 995, we repeated the entire sampling, training, and ranking process 10 times and averaged the results. (We used the same 200 question test set throughout the process.)

Figure 4 presents the results, with the acceptability of unranked questions (23%) included at $N = 0$ for comparison. We see that ranking more than doubles the acceptability of the top-ranked questions, consistent with findings from Heilman and Smith (2010). It appears that ranking performance improves as more training data are used. When 650 examples were used, 49% of the top-ranked questions were acceptable. Ranking performance appears to level off somewhat when more than 650 training examples are used. However, we speculate that if the model included more fine-grained features, the value of additional labeled data might increase.[7]

7 Conclusion

In this paper, we used MTurk to gather quality ratings for computer-generated questions. We pre-

[6]Since these additional coreference features are not immediately relevant to this work, we will not describe them fully here. A forthcoming paper will describe them in more detail.

[7]To directly compare the ranker's predictions to the correlations presented in §5.3, we computed a correlation coefficient between the test set ratings from MTurk and the ratings predicted by the ranker when it was trained on all 995 training examples. The coefficient was $r = 0.36$, which is statistically significant ($p < .001$) but suggests that there is substantial room for improvement in the ranking model.

sented a question rating scheme, and found high levels of inter-rater agreement ($r \geq 0.74$) between ratings from reliable humans and ratings from MTurk. We also showed that ratings can be gathered from MTurk quickly (more than 1,000 per hour) and cheaply (less than 30 cents per question).

While ratings of computer-generated language are not as generally useful as, for example, annotations of the syntactic structure of human-generated language, many research paradigms involving the automatic generation of language may be able to benefit from using MTurk to quickly and cheaply evaluate ongoing work. Also, we demonstrated that such ratings can be used in an overgenerate-and-rank strategy to greatly improve the quality of a system's top-ranked output.

References

C. Callison-Burch. 2009. Fast, cheap, and creative: Evaluating translation quality using Amazon's Mechanical Turk. In *Proc. of EMNLP*.

G. Carroll and E. Charniak. 1992. Two experiments on learning probabilistic dependency grammars from corpora. Technical report, Brown University.

M. Heilman and N. A. Smith. 2009. Question generation via overgenerating transformations and ranking. Technical Report CMU-LTI-09-013, Language Technologies Institute, Carnegie Mellon University.

M. Heilman and N. A. Smith. 2010. Good question! statistical ranking for question generation. In *Proc. of NAACL-HLT*.

J. R. Landis and G. G. Koch. 1977. The measurement of observer agreement for categorical data. *Biometrics*, 33.

I. Langkilde and Kevin Knight. 1998. Generation that exploits corpus-based statistical knowledge. In *Proc. of ACL*.

C. Lin. 2004. ROUGE: a package for automatic evaluation of summaries. In *Proc. of Workshop on Text Summarization*.

K. Papineni, S. Roukos, T. Ward, and W.-J. Zhu. 2002. BLEU: a method for automatic evaluation of machine translation. In *Proc. of ACL*.

R. Snow, B. O'Connor, D. Jurafsky, and A. Ng. 2008. Cheap and fast – but is it good? evaluating non-expert annotations for natural language tasks. In *Proc. of EMNLP*.

M. A. Walker, O. Rambow, and M. Rogati. 2001. Spot: a trainable sentence planner. In *Proc. of NAACL*.

D. Yarowsky. 1995. Unsupervised word sense disambiguation rivaling supervised methods. In *Proc. of ACL*.

Shared Task: Crowdsourced Accessibility Elicitation of Wikipedia Articles

Scott Novotney and **Chris Callison-Burch**
Center for Language and Speech Processing
Johns Hopkins University
3400 North Charles Street
Baltimore, MD, USA
snovotne@bbn.com ccb@jhu.edu

Abstract

Mechanical Turk is useful for generating complex speech resources like conversational speech transcription. In this work, we explore the next step of eliciting narrations of Wikipedia articles to improve accessibility for low-literacy users. This task proves a useful test-bed to implement qualitative vetting of workers based on difficult to define metrics like narrative quality. Working with the Mechanical Turk API, we collected sample narrations, had other Turkers rate these samples and then granted access to full narration HITs depending on aggregate quality. While narrating full articles proved too onerous a task to be viable, using other Turkers to perform vetting was very successful. Elicitation is possible on Mechanical Turk, but it should conform to suggested best practices of simple tasks that can be completed in a streamlined workflow.

1 Introduction

The rise of Mechanical Turk publications in the NLP community leaves no doubt that non-experts can provide useful annotations for low cost. Emerging best practices suggest designing short, simple tasks that require little amount of upfront effort to most effectively use Mechanical Turk's labor pool. Suitable tasks are best limited to those easily accomplished in 'short bites' requiring little context switching. For instance, most annotation tasks in prior work (Snow et al., 2008) required selection from an enumerated list, allowing for easy automated quality control and data collection.

More recent work to collect speech transcription (Novotney and Callison-Burch, 2010) or parallel text translations (Callison-Burch, 2009) demonstrated that Turkers can provide useful free-form annotation.

In this paper, we extend open ended collection even further by eliciting narrations of English Wikipedia articles. To vet prospective narrators, we use *qualitative* qualifications by aggregating the opinions of other Turkers on narrative style, thus avoiding quantification of qualitative tasks.

The Spoken Wikipedia Project[1] aims to increase the accessibility of Wikipedia by recording articles for use by blind or illiterate users. Since 2008, over 1600 English articles covering topics from art to technology have been narrated by volunteers. The charitable nature of this work should provide additional incentive for Turkers to complete this task. We use Wikipedia narrations as an initial proof-of-concept for other more challenging elicitation tasks such as spontaneous or conversational speech.

While previous work used other Turkers in second-pass filtering for quality control, we flip this process and instead require that narrators be judged favorably before working on full narration tasks. Relying on human opinion sidesteps the difficult task of automatically judging narrative quality. This requires a multi-pass workflow to manage potential narrators and grant them access to the full narration HITs through Mechanical Turk's Qualifications.

In this paper, we make the following points:

- Vetting based on qualitative criteria like narration quality can be effectively implemented through Turker-provided ratings.

[1] http://en.wikipedia.org/wiki/Wikipedia:WikiProject_Spoken_Wikipedia

Proceedings of the NAACL HLT 2010 Workshop on Creating Speech and Language Data with Amazon's Mechanical Turk, pages 41–44,
Los Angeles, California, June 2010.

- Narrating full articles is too complex and time-consuming for timely task throughput - best practices are worth following.
- HITs should be streamlined as much as possible. Requiring Turkers to perform work outside of the web interface seemingly hurt task completion rate.

2 Prior Work

The research community has demonstrated that complex annotations (like speech transcription and elicitation) can be provided through Mechanical Turk.

Callison-Burch (2009) showed that Turkers could accomplish complex tasks like translating Urdu or creating reading comprehension tests.

McGraw et al. (2009) used Mechanical Turk to improve an English isolated word speech recognizer by having Turkers listen to a word and select from a list of probable words at a cost of $20 per hour of transcription.

Marge et al. (2010) collected transcriptions of clean speech and demonstrated that duplicate transcription of non-experts can match expert transcription.

Novotney and Callison-Burch (2010) collected transcriptions of conversational speech for as little as $5 / hour of transcription and demonstrated that resources are better spent annotating more data than improving data quality.

McGraw et al. (2010) elicited short snippets of English street addresses through a web interface. 103 hours were elicted in just over three days.

3 Narration Task

Using a python library for parsing Wikipedia[2], we extracted all text under the `<p>` tag as a heuristic for readable content. We ignored all other content like lists, info boxes or headings. Since we wanted to preserve narrative flow, each article was posted as one HIT, paying $0.05 per paragraph. Articles averaged 40 paragraphs, so each HIT averaged $2 in payment - some as little as $0.25.

We provided instructions for using recording software and asked Turkers to record one paragraph at a time. Using Mechanical Turk's API, we generated an XML template for each paragraph and let the Turker upload a file through the `FileUploadAnswer` form. The API supports constraints on file extensions, so we were able to require that all files be in mp3 format before the Turker could submit the work.

Mechanical Turk's API supports file requests through the `GetFileUploadURL` call. A URL is dynamically generated on Amazon's servers which stays active for one minute. We then fetched each audio file and stored them locally on our own servers for later processing.

Since these narrations are meant for public consumption and are difficult to quality control, we required prospective Turkers first qualify.

4 Granting Qualitative Qualifications

Qualifications are prerequisites that limit which Turkers can work on a HIT. A common qualification provided by Mechanical Turk is a minimum approval rating for a Turker, indicating what percentage of submitted work was approved. We created a qualification for our narration tasks since we wanted to ensure only those turkers with a good speaking voice would complete our tasks.

However, the definition of a "good speaking voice" is not easy to quantify. Luckily, this task is well suited to Mechanical Turk's concept of *artificial* artificial intelligence. Humans can easily decide a narrator's quality while automatic methods would be impractical. Additionally, we never define what a 'good' narration voice is, relying instead on public opinion.

4.1 Workflow

We implemented the qualification ratings using the API with three different steps. Turkers who wish to complete the full narration HITs are first directed to a 'qualification' HIT with one sample paragraph paying $0.05. We then use other Turkers to rate the quality of the narrator, asking them to judge based on speaking style, audio clarity and pronunciation.

Post Qualification The narration qualification and full narration HITs are posted.

Sample HIT A prospective narrator uploads a recording of a sample paragraph earning $0.05.

[2]http://github.com/j2labs/wikipydia

The audio is downloaded and hosted on our web host.

Rating HIT A HIT is created to be completed ten times. Turkers make a binary decision as to whether they would listen to a full article by the narrator and optionally suggest feedback.

Grant Qualification The ten ratings are collected and if five or more are positive we grant the qualification. The narrator is then automatically contacted with the decision and provided with any feedback from the rating Turkers.

Although not straightforward, the API made it possible to dynamically create HITs, approve assignments, sync audio files and ratings,notify workers and grant qualifications. It does not, however, manage state across HITs, requiring us to implement our own control logic for associating workers with narration and rating HITs. Once implemented, managing the process was as simple as invoking three perl scripts a few times a day. These could easily be rolled into one background process automatically controlling the entire workflow.

4.2 Effectiveness of Turker Ratings

Thirteen Turkers submitted sample audio files over the course of a week. Collecting the ten ratings took a few hours per Turker. The average rating for the narrators was 7.5, with three of the thirteen being rejected for having a score less than 5. The authors agreed with the sentiment of the raters and feel that the qualification process correctly filtered out the poor narrators.

Below is a sample of the comments for an approved narrator and a rejected narrator.

This Turker was approved with 9/10 votes.

- The narration was very easy to understand. The speaker's tone was even, well-paced, and clear. Great narration.
- Very good voice, good pace and modulation.
- Very nice voice and pleasant to listen to. I would have guessed that this was a professional voice actor.

This Turker was rejected with 3/10 votes.

- Monotone voice, uninterested and barely literate. I would never listen to this voice for any length of time.
- muddy audio quality; narrator has a tired and a very low tone quality.
- Very solemn voice - didn't like listening to it.

5 Data Analysis

Of the thirteen qualified Turkers, only two went on to complete full narrations. This happened only after we shortened the articles to the initial five paragraphs and raised payment to $0.25 per paragraph. While the audio was clear, both authors exhibited mispronunciations of domain-specific terms. For instance, one author narrating Isaac Newton mispronounced *Principia* with a soft *c* (/prɪn**s**ɪpiə/) instead of a hard *c* (/prɪn**k**ɪpiə/) and *indices* as /ɪndaɪsɛz/. Since the text is known ahead of time, one could include a pronunciation guide for rare words to assist the narrator.

The more disapointing result, however, is the very slow return of the narration task. Contrasting with the successful elicitation of (McGraw et al., 2010), two reasons clearly stand out.

First, these tasks were much too long in length. This was due to constraints we placed on collection to improve data quality. We assumed that multiple narrators for a single article would ruin the narrative flow. Since few workers were willing to complete five recordings, future work could chop each article into smaller chunks to be completed by multiple narrators. In contrast, eliciting spoken addresses has no need for continuity across samples, thus the individual HITs in (McGraw et al., 2010) could be much smaller.

Second, and more importantly, our HITs required much more effort on the part of the Turker. We chose to fully use Mechanical Turk's API to manage data and did not implement audio recording or data transmission through the browser. Turkers were required to record audio in a separate program and then upload the files. We thought the added ability to re-record and review audio would be a plus compared to in-browser recording. In contrast, (McGraw et al., 2010) used a javascript package to record narrations directly in the browser window. While it was simple to use the API, it raised too much of a barrier for Turkers to complete the task.

5.1 Feasability for Full Narration

Regardless of the task effectiveness, it is not clear that Mechanical Turk is cost effective for large scale narration. A reasonable first task would be to narrate the 2500 featured articles on Wikipedia's home page. They average 44 paragraphs in length with around 4311 words per article. Narrating this corpus would cost $5500 at the rate of $0.05 per paragraph - if workers would be willing to complete at that rate.

6 Conclusion

Our experiments with Mechanical Turk attempted to find the limits of data collection and nebulous task definitions. Long-form narration was unsuccessful due to the length of the tasks and the lack of a streamlined workflow for the Turkers. However, assigning qualifications based upon aggregating qualitative opinions was very successful. This task exploited the strenghts of Mechanical Turk by quickly gathering judgements that are easy for humans to make but near impossible to reliably automate.

The contrast between the failure of this narration task and the success of previous elicitation is due to the nature of the underlying task. Our desire to have one narrator per article prevented elicitation in short bites of a few seconds long. Additionally, our efforts to solely use Mechanical Turk's API limited the simplicity of the workflow. While our backend work was greatly simplified since we relied on existing data management code, the lack of in-browser recording placed too much burden on the Turkers.

We would make the following changes if we were to reimplement this task:

1. Integrate the workflow into the browser.

2. Perform post-process quality control to block bad narrators from completing more HITs.

3. Drop the requirement of one narrator per article. A successful compromise might be one section, averaging around five paragraphs.

4. Only narrate the lead in to an article (first pargagraph) first. If a user requests a full narration, then seek out the rest of the article.

5. Place qualification as a much larger set of assignments. Turkers often sort HITs by available assignments, so the qualification HIT was rarely seen.

References

Chris Callison-Burch. 2009. Fast, Cheap, and Creative: Evaluating Translation Quality Using Amazons Mechanical Turk. *EMNLP*.

Matthew Marge, Satanjeev Banerjee, and Alexander Rudnicky. 2010. Using the amazon mechanical turk for transcription of spoken language. *ICASSP*, March.

Ian McGraw, Alexander Gruenstein, and Andrew Sutherland. 2009. A self-labeling speech corpus: Collecting spoken words with an online educational game. In *INTERSPEECH*.

Ian McGraw, Chia ying Lee, Lee Hetherington, and Jim Glass. 2010. Collecting Voices from the Crowd. *LREC*, May.

Scott Novotney and Chris Callison-Burch. 2010. Cheap, Fast and Good Enough: Automatic Speech Recognition with Non-Expert Transcription . *NAACL*, June.

Rion Snow, Brendan O'Connor, Daniel Jurafsky, and Andrew Y. Ng. 2008. Cheap and fast—but is it good?: evaluating non-expert annotations for natural language tasks. In *EMNLP*.

Document Image Collection Using Amazon's Mechanical Turk

Audrey Le, Jerome Ajot, Mark Przybocki
National Institute of Standards and Technology
100 Bureau Drive, Stop 8940
Gaithersburg, MD 20876, USA
{audrey.le|jerome.ajot|mark.przybocki}
@nist.gov

Stephanie Strassel
Linguistic Data Consortium
3600 Market Street, Suite 810
Philadelphia, PA 19104, USA
strassel@ldc.upenn.edu

Abstract

We present findings from a collaborative effort aimed at testing the feasibility of using Amazon's Mechanical Turk as a data collection platform to build a corpus of document images. Experimental design and implementation workflow are described. Preliminary findings and directions for future work are also discussed.

1 Introduction

The National Institute of Standards and Technology (NIST) and Linguistic Data Consortium (LDC) at the University of Pennsylvania have a strong collaborative history of providing evaluation and linguistic resources for the Human Language Technology (HLT) community[1]. The NAACL 2010 Workshop on Creating Speech and Language Data with Amazon's Mechanical Turk[2] presents an interesting opportunity to extend this collaboration in a novel data collection task. This collaborative experiment will occur in the context of the NIST Open Handwriting Recognition and Translation Evaluation (OpenHaRT) (NIST, 2010), which requires a collection of Arabic handwritten document images. While some Arabic handwritten document collections do exist (Combating Terrorism Center, 2006, 2007; University of Colorado at Boulder, 1998) these resources are inadequate to support an open technology evaluation. Some existing corpora are not publicly accessible, while others are very small or limited in scope/content, or contain features (e.g. Personal Identifying Information) that prevent their use in a NIST evaluation. New data collection for OpenHaRT using traditional methods of recruiting human subjects is cost-prohibitive and time consuming.

Recent studies (Callison-Burch, 2009) have demonstrated the viability of Amazon's Mechanical Turk as a data collection platform for tasks including English translations for foreign text sources. We propose to build on the success of previous studies, and expand data collection to target highly variable samples of foreign handwritten texts along with their English translations. While data collected from this effort will be donated to the workshop and larger research community, our hope is that this collaboration will also provide a means to explore the feasibility of this approach more generally, and that it will result in protocols that can be used to collect substantial volumes of handwritten text to support the NIST OpenHaRT evaluation. The remainder of this paper documents this pilot study, describing both the experimental design and implementation workflow followed by our findings and hypotheses.

2 Data Collection Experimental Design

Our data collection targets images of handwritten foreign language text, prepared according to a pre-defined set of characteristics. Text from the images is transcribed verbatim. English translations of the text are provided. Collected data is verified for accuracy[3] and image quality.

2.1 Collection Approach

[1] Since 1987 NIST has conducted public evaluations of human language technologies and has collaborated with LDC to collects much of the data used in support for these evaluations.

[2] http://sites.google.com/site/amtworkshop2010

[3] Due to time constraints, transcript and translation verification was conducted offline by LDC staff.

Proceedings of the NAACL HLT 2010 Workshop on Creating Speech and Language Data with Amazon's Mechanical Turk, pages 45–52,
Los Angeles, California, June 2010.

For this pilot study we collected data in two primary languages, Arabic and Spanish[4]. These languages are of interest for a number of reasons. Linguistically, they show large typological and orthographic differences. Strategically, Arabic is of high interest to a number of ongoing HLT evaluations, while Spanish is important to U.S. commercial interests. Practically, we also hoped to take advantage of a likely pool of Spanish-speaking Turkers[5] whose facility with the written language may vary. We defined two categories or genres for collection – *shopping list* and *description of the current weather*. The rationale for selecting the general shopping list was to elicit text with a potentially large set of vocabularies while the description of the current weather was included to elicit text with a narrow set of vocabularies.

To simplify the collection process and to make the tasks as natural as possible, we placed no artificial constraints on the writers. That is, we do not regulate writing implements (e.g., pen, pencil, crayon, marker, etc.), paper types (e.g., lined, unlined, graphed, colored, etc.), orientation of the handwriting (e.g., straight, curved, etc.), handwriting speed, etc. To sample naturally-occurring variation in digital images, we placed no constraints on image quality (resolution, lighting, orientation, etc.) Many of these features could be labeled as subsequent Mechanical Turk HITs[6].

2.2 Collection Tasks

The collection has three types of tasks:

- *Image Collection* – This task requires the Turker to perform a writing assignment given a specified topic and source language. The writing assignment is electronically scanned or photographed and uploaded to our repository.
- *Image Transcription* – For each handwritten image, the corresponding text is transcribed verbatim.
- *Image Translation* – For each transcribed foreign language text, an accurate and fluent English translation is provided.

2.3 Task Implementation and Quality Control

Each task listed above corresponds to a single HIT. Initial payment rates for each HIT type were established after reviewing comparable HITs available between 2/19/10 – 2/23/10. Payment rates were finalized after additional review of comparable HITs in mid-March; HIT payments were also adjusted to encourage rapid completion for some tasks. Arabic HITs were priced higher than Spanish HITs because we wanted to investigate the price dimension when we compared Arabic to a language that is more widely spoken by the population at large[7].

Image Collection

We targeted collection of 18 images per language (Spanish, Arabic) per genre (weather report, shopping list) for a total of 36 per language. Three English shopping list images were also collected as a control set for comparison of Turker performance. HIT instructions were brief:

> 1. Take a piece of paper, and write down {a brief description of today's weather | a shopping list} in {Spanish | Arabic}. You can use any type of paper and writing implement (pen, pencil, etc.) you have handy, but only write on the front of the page. Use your normal handwriting.
> 2. Using a digital camera or scanner, take a picture or scan a copy of the {weather report | list} you just created. Make sure you don't cut off any of the handwriting.
> 3. Upload the image file[8].

[4] A very small English collection was undertaken to provide a baseline control set for comparison.

[5] "Turkers" is the term used to refer to people who perform tasks for money at the online marketplace Amazon's Mechanical Turk.

[6] Coined by Amazon, HIT stands for Human Intelligence Task and refers to a task that a person can work on and be compensated for completing the work.

[7] http://www.nationsonline.org/oneworld/most_spoken_languages.htm

[8] Turkers were not given instructions about how to name the uploaded file; such instructions could have facilitated task/workflow management and should be implemented in future efforts.

HIT instructions were written in English for the Spanish-language task; a note at the top of the HIT specified that the task should be performed by Spanish speakers. For the Arabic-language task, initial instructions were also written in English; this was later revised to use instructions written in Arabic to better target Arabic-speaking Turkers. We did not require Turkers to take a language qualification test. The HITs remained open for one week, and time allocated per HIT was 30 minutes. Payment for the image collection task was set at $0.11 per image for Spanish and $0.15 for Arabic.

Quality control for the image collection task involved annotators at LDC reviewing each submitted image and determining whether it was in fact in the targeted language and genre (weather report or shopping list).

Image Transcription

Each image was then transcribed. We targeted two unique transcripts per collected, approved image[9]. HIT instructions were as follows:

> •The image below contains {Spanish | Arabic} handwriting. Your job is to transcribe exactly what you see. Type out all the words and punctuation you see, exactly as they are written. Do not correct any spelling mistakes or other errors in the handwriting. If the image contains any punctuation, copy that exactly using the punctuation character on your keyboard that is closest to what was written.
>
> •If the handwritten image is a list on multiple lines, transcribe one line at a time, inserting a line break (by hitting the "Enter" key) after each new line.
>
> •For any words that you cannot read, or if you're just not sure what the writing says, just do the best you can and transcribe as much of the word as you can make out. Add ?? to the beginning of any word you are not sure of.
>
> •Before submitting your transcript, please double check to make sure you have transcribed every line in the image, without leaving anything out or adding anything that isn't in the image.

Instructions for the Spanish transcription task were provided in English, whereas the Arabic instructions were written in Arabic. For this task we required Turkers to have an approval rating of 95% or higher. The HITs remained open for four days for Spanish and one week for Arabic; time allocated per HIT was 30 minutes. Payment for the transcription task was set at $0.20 per image for Spanish and $0.25 for Arabic.

Quality control on the transcription task involved fluent Spanish or Arabic annotators at LDC reviewing the transcripts against the image and making a three-level accuracy judgment: perfect transcript (no errors); acceptable transcript (minor errors in transcription or punctuation); unacceptable transcript (major errors). Transcripts judged as "perfect" or "acceptable" were passed on to the final translation task.

Image Translation

We targeted one unique translation per collected, approved transcript. HIT instructions were as follows:

> Below is a brief shopping list or weather report in {Spanish | Arabic}. Your job is to provide an English translation of this document. Your translation should be accurate, and should use fluent English.
>
> •Translate every sentence, phrase or word, without leaving anything out or adding any information.
>
> •If there are spelling mistakes or other errors in the {Spanish | Arabic} text, just translate what you think the intended word is.
>
> •If there is any punctuation in the {Spanish | Arabic} text, copy that over exactly into the English translation.
>
> •Try to follow the same document layout and line breaks as in the original {Spanish | Arabic} text.
>
> •Some {Spanish | Arabic} words may have ?? at the beginning. You should copy the ?? over onto the beginning of the corresponding English translated word.
>
> •Put !! at the beginning of any English word whose translation you're not sure of.

[9] The total number of images assigned for transcription was lower than the number collected in some cases, due to timeline and task staging constraints.

•NOTE: Do not use automatic translations from the web for this task. Such submissions will be rejected.

Because this task targeted fluent English translations, instructions were written in English for both the Spanish and Arabic translation HITs. For this task we required Turkers to have an approval rating of 95% or higher. The HITs remained open for two days for Spanish and four days for Arabic; time allocated per HIT was 1 hour. Payment for the translation task was set at \$1.25 per image for Spanish and \$1.50 for Arabic[10].

Quality control on this task involved LDC bilingual annotators checking the translation against the transcript, and making a judgment of "acceptable" or "unacceptable". Perfect translation was not required but the translation had to be a generally adequate and fluent rendering of the foreign language text. Translation QC annotators were permitted to consult the image file for context, but were not permitted to penalize a Turker based on information only available in the image file, since Turkers working on translation HITs did not have access to the image file.

3 Collection Yield and Results

Table 1 summarizes the total number of image, transcription and translation HITs made available, submitted and approved for each language and genre. As originally planned, our study would have produced a total of 36 images per language, with two transcripts per image (for a total of 72 per language) and one translation per transcript (72 per language). Actual yields for the image collection task were considerably lower, and targets for the subsequent tasks were adjusted.

In the case of Arabic, all approved images were made available for transcription. For Spanish some images were submitted and approved after the transcription HITs had been assigned; time constraints did not permit creating additional transcription HITs for these later images. For both languages, all approved transcription HITs were made available for subsequent translation.

Note too that the number of submitted HITs actually exceeds the number of available HITs in some cases; this is because rejected HITs were made available for completion by new Turkers.

		Avail. HITs	**Submtd**	**Aprvd**
Spanish Shopping List	*Images*	18	13	10
	Transcripts	14	16	14
	Translations	14	21	12
Spanish Weather Report	*Images*	18	7	5
	Transcripts	6	6	6
	Translations	6	13	5
Arabic Shopping List	*Images*	18	11	3
	Transcripts	6	9	6
	Translations	6	7	0
Arabic Weather Report	*Images*	18	6	2
	Transcripts	4	5	4
	Translations	4	5	1
English Shopping List	*Images*	3	3	3
	Transcripts	6	6	6
	Translations	n/a		

Table 1: Collection Summary

Proof of Concept: English Control Set

Collection of the small English-language control set was entirely successful: Turkers quickly completed the image collection task and provided accurate transcripts of each English image. Though small in number, the submitted images show considerable variation in image quality (lighting, rotation, resolution, scan versus photo) and handwriting quality (paper type and writing implement).

All images were approved during the quality control pass. Transcript collection was extremely fast: all six transcripts (two copies per image) were collected within minutes of posting the HITs. Transcript quality was uniformly acceptable. As a baseline, the English control task demonstrates the feasibility of using MTurk for at least some kinds of image collection and transcription.

[10] These rates were set in part based on need for rapid completion of these HITs.

Figure 1: Handwritten English shopping list

Spanish Results

The Spanish language collection was largely successful. The first challenge was finding fluent Spanish speaking Turkers. No special effort was made to advertise the task to Spanish speakers beyond posting the hits on MTurk. Each HIT's title, description and associated keywords included the term "Spanish" but did not contain any Spanish language content.

While we targeted a total of 36 Spanish images, only 20 were submitted, of which 15 were approved. Images were rejected largely because of fraud, principally stemming from duplicate copies of the same handwritten image being submitted under different Worker IDs. Image and handwriting quality showed a great deal of variation. Turkers used plain unlined paper, lined paper and graph paper with a variety of writing implements. Some submitted printed handwriting while others used cursive. We observed some interesting document formatting issues; for instance some Turkers provided multi-column shopping lists. Image quality ranged from a clean, high resolution scan with the image perfectly centered, to low-quality bitmap files with edges of the paper bent or wrinkled and the page skewed off-center. Other image artifacts included lighting variation within a single image due to the use of a flash while photographing the image.

The transcription task was completed largely as planned, with two transcripts acquired for all images. Two transcripts HITs were rejected, in both cases because the Turker provided a translation instead of a transcript; these images were made available for re-assignment to other Turkers and accurate transcripts were eventually obtained. The transcription task presented several difficulties that, while anticipated, were not fully addressed in this limited pilot study. While Spanish handwriting contains numerous diacritics (e.g., the tilde in piñata) these were variably rendered in the transcription task. Some transcribers tried to incorporate the diacritics directly, whereas others used plain ascii for transcription resulting in either missing diacritics, or non-standard symbols standing in for diacritics. For instance, "piñata" might be alternately transcribed as "piñata", "pinata", "pin~ata" or something else. The issue of input and rendering for non-English characters is a well-known problem in corpus creation, but in this pilot study no special effort was made to control for it. Similarly, special formatting characters (e.g. for bullet-pointed shopping lists) were variably rendered by Turkers and did not always display as intended in the resulting output file. During transcription QC, LDC annotators made an effort to standardize rendering of such characters to facilitate the translation task. Future MTurk data collection efforts will need to devote more attention to character encoding, input and rendering issues.

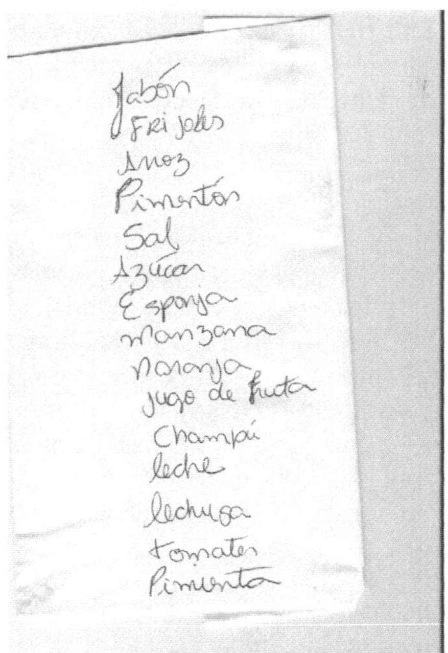

Figure 2: Handwritten Spanish shopping list

Translation proved to be the most difficult of the three tasks. We targeted collection of one translation per approved transcript, for a planned total of two translations per image. We fell somewhat short of this collection goal, in part because timeline constraints meant the batch of translation HITs was only available for a few days. The rejection rate on translation HITs was also much higher than the rate for images or transcripts. Rejected translation HITs fell into two categories: an obvious machine translation from the web (typically Google Translate)[15]; or an apparent human translation that did not constitute fluent English.

Because the collected images were short and simple with little or no formatting or document structure, and because transcripts were QC'd prior to translation, it was believed that Turkers could create an accurate translation without making reference to the original image file. Therefore, the image was not displayed during translation; instead Turkers were given only a plain text version of the transcript. This approach did contribute to some translation difficulties especially for special characters (like the Celsius symbol, °C, frequently used in the weather reports).

Based on the rejection rate for individual HITs, some images proved harder to translate than others. This appears to be largely an issue of translation difficulty due to specialized terminology (e.g. brand names and abbreviations in a shopping list) rather than influence from errors in transcription.

Arabic Results

Not surprisingly, data collection for Arabic proved quite challenging. Locating fluent Arabic speakers among Turkers was extremely difficult. As noted elsewhere our pilot study was limited to using Amazon's default MTurk infrastructure and so we did not undertake any special efforts to direct Turkers to our HITs beyond posting them on MTurk. Instructions for the image collection and transcription HITs were written in Arabic, and keywords for all tasks contained the words "Arabic", written in both Arabic and English. The HIT titles also contained the word "Arabic" written in both languages.

As with Spanish we targeted a total of 36 Arabic images (18 per genre). While nearly as many images were submitted as in the corresponding Spanish task (17 compared to 20 for Spanish), only 5 Arabic images were approved. Reasons for rejection included the image being in English rather than Arabic; the image being typed instead of handwritten; and several cases of identical images being submitted under multiple WorkerIDs. Among the approved images we again observed an exciting range of image and handwriting variation, including several cases of out-of-focus photos; an example is provided in Figure 3.

The Arabic transcription task proved to be fairly straightforward, and we successfully collected two independent transcripts for each approved image. A handful of transcripts were rejected because they were grossly inaccurate (the Turker simply copied the instructions or image URL into the transcript rather than providing an actual transcript).

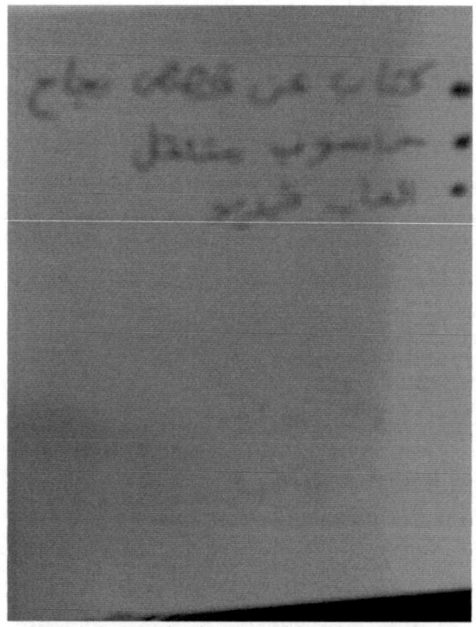

Image 3: Handwritten Arabic shopping list

There was an initial concern about whether Turkers would encounter difficulties inputting Arabic text into the transcription HIT interface but this did not seem to affect performance. One unanticipated difficulty was creation of the HITs themselves; the Amazon HIT management interface had some difficulties rendering bi-directional text. This is a common problem in

[15] Each suspect translation was submitted to Google Translate during the QC/review process.

annotation tool design, and is especially problematic when left-to-right and right-to-left reading order is required in a single line, for instance when characters like parenthesis or ascii numbers are interspersed with Arabic text. A similar difficulty emerged when viewing batch-wide results of the transcription task. The default file output format (.csv) is intended for viewing in a tool like Excel. However, the output does not appear to be natively Unicode-compliant and therefore Arabic characters are not rendered correctly. No straightforward solution presented itself within the Amazon HIT management interface, and the scope of this pilot project did not permit exploration of solutions using third-party APIs. Instead, results were extracted individually for each HIT using the GUI, which proved to be very time consuming and resulted in a loss of some formatting information (like line wrapping).

Unsurprisingly, the Arabic translation task proved to be the most difficult. Of twelve submitted translation HITs, only one resulted in an acceptable translation. The low success rate is likely due to a number of factors. As discussed, there appear to be few Arabic speakers (and even fewer fluent Arabic-English bilinguals) among the Turker population at large. Second, the translation task was available for only a few days. To offset this, the payment per HIT for Arabic (and Spanish) was quite high, though this may have contributed to the final challenge: fraudulent submissions. Rejected HITs followed the normal pattern. Most were machine translations from the web (again, primarily from Google Translate) while others appeared to be highly disfluent human translations, of the type that might be expected from a first year Arabic student working without a dictionary.

4 Discussion and Future Plans

As a feasibility study, our experiment can be called a qualified success. With respect to image collection MTurk seems to be a viable option at least for some languages and genres. While there was some "fraud", most submitted images were usable and the image properties were highly variable, suggesting that this task is well-suited to MTurk and that the HIT instructions were adequate. A wide range of writing surfaces emerged including lined, unlined and graph paper, as well as colored paper. Less variation was observed in writing implements (for instance it appears that no one used pencil, crayon or fat marker). There were some surprising features of the handwriting itself beyond the expected quality variation; for instance someone writing perpendicular to the lines on ruled paper. Image quality ranged along the expected dimensions of resolution, skew and slant, and scanning artifacts like bent corners or wrinkled pages. There were also unexpected artifacts of image photography including uneven lighting due to a flash going off and out-of-focus images. The content submitted for each genre showed considerable variation as well. For instance, Turkers submitted shopping lists for not just groceries, but also electronics and a combined shopping/to-do list for an upcoming vacation or trip. The results are promising for future image collection efforts at least for English or other languages for which Turkers are readily accessible.

The transcription task was moderately successful. Apart from finding Turkers with appropriate language skills, the primary challenges are technical, in terms of character encoding for input and display/rendering. The basic Amazon MTurk interface does not provide adequate support to fully resolve this and future efforts will need to explore other options. Quality control is a bigger issue for the transcription task, and adequate resources must be devoted to addressing this in any future collection. Multiple transcripts were generated for each image to facilitate using MTurk to collect comparative judgments on transcription quality, although time constraints prevented this from being implemented. In future we envision incorporating three kinds of MTurk QC for transcription: simple judgment of transcript accuracy; comparison of multiple transcripts for a single image; and correction of transcripts judged inadequate. It is expected that project staff (as opposed to Turkers) will still need to be involved in some degree of QC. We anticipate that the transcription task would be substantially harder for images collected in other genres, particularly in cases where reading order is not obvious or explicit in the image. For instance in a collection of images of complex multi-column forms that have been completed by hand, one transcriber might work from top to bottom in column 1 then proceed to column 2, whereas another transcriber might proceed left to right (or right-to-left for Arabic) without respect to columns. It is unclear whether MTurk could be productively used for these more complex transcription tasks that typically require a customized user interface and significant annotator training.

Unsurprisingly, translation was the most difficult and least successful task, largely because of the shortage of Arabic and Spanish Turkers and the compressed timeline for translation. Still, translation of general content is a feasible task for MTurk given appropriate quality control measures. Future efforts will need to explore other options for locating appropriate Turkers. As with the transcription task, we also anticipate adding more quality control steps to the MTurk pipeline including acquisition of multiple translations with staged quality judgments, comparision and correction. We will also revisit the question of whether translation HITs should include both the transcript and the image file. While this adds complexity to the translation task, it may also help to improve the overall translation quality, and for more complex types of handwritten images translation may be impossible without reference to the image.

In future efforts we also anticipate needing to have dedicated project staff to facilitate HIT construction and approval, data processing, and interactions with either the Amazon or third party APIs. We encountered some practical challenges in this pilot study with respect management of the results across tasks. As noted earlier, naming conventions were not specified in the HIT instructions for image collection, so images had to be manually renamed to make them unique and readily identifiable by genre and language. Extracting transcription output from the results table and presenting it for the translation HIT with document formatting and character encoding intact was another challenge that requires additional exploration.

Future efforts should also revisit the cost model, using information about actual time required to complete each type of HIT. In all cases, HITs were completed in just a few minutes. We also need to further explore cost/quality tradeoffs, since high-paying tasks (like translation) are also the most prone to fraud and therefore require additional QC measures.

In conclusion, we have used MTurk to produce a small pilot corpus of handwritten, transcribed and translated images in three languages and two genres. This study has provided evidence that MTurk is a viable option for image corpus creation at least for some languages, and has suggested avenues for task refinement and future work in this area. The data collected in this study will be distributed to workshop participants, and portions will be selected for use in the NIST Open HaRT evaluation.

Disclaimer

Certain commercial products and software are identified in this paper in order to explain our research. Such identification does not imply recommendation or endorsement by NIST, nor does it imply that the products and software identified are necessarily the best available for the purpose.

References

Chris Callison-Burch. 2009. *Fast, Cheap and Creative: Evaluating Translation Quality with Amazon's Mechanical Turk,* in Proceedings of Empirical Methods in Natural Language Processing 2009.

Combating Terrorism Center at West Point, United States Military Academy. 2007. *CTC's Harmony Reports*, http://ctc.usma.edu/harmony/harmony_menu.asp (accessed March 2, 2010).

Combating Terrorism Center at West Point, United States Military Academy. 2006. *The Islamic Imagery Project: Visual Motifs in Jihadi Internet Propaganda,* Combating Terrorism Center at West Point, West Point, NY.

NIST. 2010. *NIST 2010 Open Handwriting Recognition and Translation Evaluation Plan*, http://www.nist.gov/itl/iad/mig/upload/Open HaRT2010_EvalPlan_v2-7.pdf (accessed February 25, 2010).

University of Colorado at Boulder Office of News Services. 1998. *CU-Boulder Archives Acquires Iraqi Secret Police Files*, http://www.colorado.edu/news/releases/1998/33.html (accessed March 2, 2010).

Using Amazon Mechanical Turk for Transcription of Non-Native Speech

Keelan Evanini, Derrick Higgins, and Klaus Zechner
Educational Testing Service
{KEvanini, DHiggins, KZechner}@ets.org

Abstract

This study investigates the use of Amazon Mechanical Turk for the transcription of non-native speech. Multiple transcriptions were obtained from several distinct MTurk workers and were combined to produce merged transcriptions that had higher levels of agreement with a gold standard transcription than the individual transcriptions. Three different methods for merging transcriptions were compared across two types of responses (spontaneous and read-aloud). The results show that the merged MTurk transcriptions are as accurate as an individual expert transcriber for the read-aloud responses, and are only slightly less accurate for the spontaneous responses.

1 Introduction

Orthographic transcription of large amounts of speech is necessary for improving speech recognition results. Transcription, however, is a time consuming and costly procedure. Typical transcription speeds for spontaneous, conversational speech are around 7 to 10 times real-time (Glenn and Strassel, 2008). The transcription of non-native speech is an even more difficult task–one study reports an average transcription time of 12 times real-time for spontaneous non-native speech (Zechner, 2009).

In addition to being more costly and time consuming, transcription of non-native speech results in a higher level of disagreement among transcribers in comparison to native speech. This is especially true when the speaker's proficiency is low and the speech contains large numbers of grammatical errors, incorrect collocations, and disfluencies. For example, one study involving highly predictable speech shows a decline in transcriber agreement (measured using Word Error Rate, WER) from 3.6% for native speech to 6.4% for non-native speech (Marge et al., to appear). Another study involving spontaneous non-native speech showed a range of WER between 15% and 20% (Zechner, 2009).

This study uses the Amazon Mechanical Turk (MTurk) resource to obtain multiple transcriptions for non-native speech. We then investigate several methods for combining these multiple sources of information from individual MTurk workers (turkers) in an attempt to obtain a final merged transcription that is more accurate than the individual transcriptions. This methodology results in transcriptions that approach the level of expert transcribers on this difficult task. Furthermore, a substantial savings in cost can be achieved.

2 Previous Work

Due to its ability to provide multiple sources of information for a given task in a cost-effective way, several recent studies have combined multiple MTurk outputs for NLP annotation tasks. For example, one study involving annotation of emotions in text used average scores from up to 10 turkers to show the minimum number of MTurk annotations required to achieve performance comparable to experts (Snow et al., 2008). Another study used preference voting to combine up to 5 MTurk rankings of machine translation quality and showed that the resulting judgments approached expert inter-annotator agreement (Callison-Burch, 2009). These

Proceedings of the NAACL HLT 2010 Workshop on Creating Speech and Language Data with Amazon's Mechanical Turk, pages 53–56,
Los Angeles, California, June 2010.

tasks, however, are much simpler than transcription.

MTurk has been used extensively as a transcription provider, as is apparent from the success of a middleman site that act as an interface to MTurk for transcription tasks.[1] However, to our knowledge, only one previous study has systematically evaluated the quality of MTurk transcriptions (Marge et al., to appear). This recent study also combined multiple MTurk transcriptions using the ROVER method (Fiscus, 1997) to produce merged transcriptions that approached the accuracy of expert transcribers. Our study is similar to that study, except that the speech data used in our study is much more difficult to transcribe–the utterances used in that study were relatively predictable (providing route instructions for robots), and contained speech from native speakers and high-proficiency non-native speakers. Furthermore, we investigate two additional merging algorithms in an attempt to improve over the performance of ROVER.

3 Experimental Design

3.1 Audio

The audio files used in this experiment consist of responses to an assessment of English proficiency for non-native speakers. Two different types of responses are examined: spontaneous and read-aloud. In the spontaneous task, the speakers were asked to respond with their opinion about a topic described in the prompt. The speech in these responses is thus highly unpredictable. In the read-aloud task, on the other hand, the speakers were asked to read a paragraph out loud. For these responses, the speech is highly predictable; any deviations from the target script are due to reading errors or disfluencies.

For this experiment, one set of 10 spontaneous (SP) responses (30 seconds in duration) and two sets of 10 read-aloud (RA) responses (60 seconds in duration) were used. Table 1 displays the characteristics of the responses in the three batches.

3.2 Transcription Procedure

The tasks were submitted to the MTurk interface in batches of 10, and a turker was required to complete the entire batch in order to receive payment. Turkers received $3 for a complete batch of transcriptions ($0.30 per transcription).

[1] http://castingwords.com/

Batch	Duration	# of Words (Mean)	# of Words (Std. Dev.)
SP	30 sec.	33	14
RA1	60 sec.	97	4
RA2	60 sec.	93	10

Table 1: Characteristics of the responses used in the study

Different interfaces were used for transcribing the two types of responses. For the spontaneous responses, the task was a standard transcription task: the turkers were instructed to enter the words that they heard in the audio file into a text box. For the read-aloud responses, on the other hand, they were provided with the target text of the prompt, one word per line. They were instructed to make annotations next to words in cases where the speaker deviated from the target text (indicating substitutions, deletions, and insertions). For both types of transcription task, the turkers were required to successfully complete a short training task before proceeding onto the batch of 10 responses.

4 Methods for Merging Transcriptions

4.1 ROVER

The ROVER method was originally developed for combining the results from multiple ASR systems to produce a more accurate hypothesis (Fiscus, 1997). This method iteratively aligns pairs of transcriptions to produce a word transition network. A voting procedure is then used to produce the merged transcription by selecting the most frequent word (including NULL) in each correspondence set; ties are broken by a random choice.

4.2 Longest Common Subsequence

In this method, the Longest Common Subsequence (LCS) among the set of transcriptions is found by first finding the LCS between two transcriptions, comparing this output with the next transcription to find their LCS, and iterating over all transcriptions in this manner. Then, each transcription is compared to the LCS, and any portions of the transcription that are missing between words of the LCS are tallied. Finally, words are interpolated into the LCS by selecting the most frequent missing sequence from the set of transcriptions (including the empty sequence); as with the ROVER method, ties are broken by a random choice among the most frequent candidates.

4.3 Lattice

In this method, a word lattice is formed from the individual transcriptions by iteratively adding transcriptions into the lattice to optimize the match between the transcription and the lattice. New nodes are only added to the graph when necessary. Then, to produce the merged transcription, the optimal path through the lattice is determined. Three different configurations for computing the optimal path through the lattice method were compared. In the first configuration, "Lattice (TW)," the weight of a path through the lattice is determined simply by adding up the total of the weights of each edge in the path. Note that this method tends to favor longer paths over shorter ones, assuming equal edge weights. In the next configuration, "Lattice (AEW)," a cost for each node based on the average edge weight is subtracted as each edge of the lattice is traversed, in order to ameliorate the preference for longer paths. Finally, in the third configuration, "Lattice (TWPN)," the weight of a path through the lattice is defined as the total path weight in the "Lattice (TW)" method, normalized by the number of nodes in the path (again, to offset the preference for longer paths).

4.4 WER calculation

All three of the methods for merging transcriptions are sensitive to the order in which the individual transcriptions are considered. Thus, in order to accurately evaluate the methods, for each number of transcriptions used to create the merged transcription, $N \in \{3, 4, 5\}$, all possible permutations of all possible combinations were considered. This resulted in a total of $\frac{5!}{(5-N)!}$ merged transcriptions to be evaluated. For each N, the overall WER was computed from this set of merged transcriptions.

5 Results

Tables 2 - 4 present the WER results for different merging algorithms for the two batches of read-aloud responses and the batch of spontaneous responses. In each table, the merging methods are ordered according to their performance when all transcriptions were used (N=5). In addition, the overall WER results for the individual turkers and an expert transcriber are provided for each set of responses. In each case, the WER is computed by comparison with a gold standard transcription that was created by having an expert transcriber edit the transcription of a different expert transcriber.

Method	N=3	N=4	N=5
Individual Turkers		7.0%	
Lattice (TWPN)	6.4%	6.4%	6.4%
Lattice (TW)	6.4%	6.4%	6.4%
LCS	6.0%	5.6%	5.6%
Lattice (AEW)	6.1%	6.0%	5.5%
ROVER	5.5%	5.2%	5.1%
Expert		4.7%	

Table 2: WER results 10 read-aloud responses (RA1)

Method	N=3	N=4	N=5
Individual Turkers		9.7%	
Lattice (TW)	9.5%	9.5%	9.4%
Lattice (TWPN)	8.3%	8.0%	8.0%
Lattice (AEW)	8.2%	7.4%	7.8%
ROVER	7.9%	7.9%	7.6%
LCS	8.3%	8.0%	7.5%
Expert		8.1%	

Table 3: WER results for 10 read-aloud responses (RA2)

In all cases, the merged transcriptions have a lower WER than the overall WER for the individual turkers. Furthermore, for all methods, the merged output using all 5 transcriptions has a lower (or equal) WER to the output using 3 transcriptions. For the first batch of read-aloud responses, the ROVER method performed best, and reduced the WER in the set of individual transcriptions by 27.1% (relative) to 5.1%. For the second batch of read-aloud responses, the LCS method performed best, and reduced the WER by 22.6% to 7.5%. Finally, for the batch of spontaneous responses, the Lattice (TW) method performed best, and reduced the WER by 25.6% to 22.1%.

Method	N=3	N=4	N=5
Individual Turkers		29.7%	
Lattice (TWPN)	29.1%	28.9%	28.3%
LCS	29.2%	28.4%	27.0%
Lattice (AEW)	28.1%	25.8%	25.1%
ROVER	25.4%	24.5%	24.9%
Lattice (TW)	25.5%	23.5%	22.1%
Expert		18.3%	

Table 4: WER results for 10 spontaneous responses

6 Conclusions

As is clear from the levels of disagreement between the expert transcriber and the gold standard transcription for all three tasks, these responses are much more difficult to transcribe accurately than native spontaneous speech. For native speech, expert transcribers can usually reach agreement levels over 95% (Deshmukh et al., 1996). For these responses, however, the WER for the expert transcriber was worse than this even for the read-aloud speech. These low levels of agreement can be attributed to the fact that the speech is drawn from a wide range of English proficiency levels among test-takers. Most of the responses contain disfluencies, grammatical errors, and mispronunciations, leading to increased transcriber uncertainty.

The results of merging multiple MTurk transcriptions of this non-native speech showed an improvement over the performance of the individual transcribers for all methods considered. For the read-aloud speech, the agreement level of the merged transcriptions approached that of the expert transcription when only three MTurk transcriptions were used. For the spontaneous responses, the performance of the best methods still lagged behind the expert transcription, even when five MTurk transcriptions were used. Due to the consistent increase in performance, and the low cost of adding additional transcribers (in this study the cost was $0.30 per audio minute for read-aloud speech and $0.60 per audio minute for spontaneous speech), the approach of combining multiple transcriptions should always be considered when MTurk is used for transcription. It is also possible that lower payments per task could be provided without a decrease in transcription quality, as demonstrated by Marge et al. (to appear). Additional experiments will address the practicality of producing more accurate merged transcriptions for an ASR system—simply collecting larger amounts of non-expert transcriptions may be a better investment than producing higher quality data (Novotney and Callison-Burch, 2010).

It is interesting that the Lattice (TW) method of merging transcriptions clearly outperformed all other methods for the spontaneous responses, but was less beneficial than the LCS and ROVER methods for read-aloud speech. It is likely that this is caused by the preference of the Lattice (TW) method for longer paths through the word lattice, since individual transcribers of spontaneous speech may mark different words as unitelligible, even though these words exist in the gold standard transcription. Further studies with a larger number of responses will be needed to test this hypothesis.

References

Chris Callison-Burch. 2009. Fast, cheap and creative: Evaluating translation quality using Amazon's Mechanical Turk. In *Proc. EMNLP*.

Neeraj Deshmukh, Richard Jennings Duncan, Aravind Ganapathiraju, and Joseph Picone. 1996. Benchmarking human performance for continuous speech recognition. In *Proc. ICSLP*.

Jonathan G. Fiscus. 1997. A post-processing system to yield word error rates: Recognizer Ooutput Voting Error Reduction (ROVER). In *Proc. ASRU*.

Meghan Lammie Glenn and Stephanie Strassel. 2008. Shared linguistic resources for the meeting domain. In *Lecture Notes in Computer Science*, volume 4625, pages 401–413. Springer.

Matthew Marge, Satanjeev Banerjee, and Alexander I. Rudnicky. to appear. Using the Amazon Mechanical Turk for transcription of spoken language. In *Proc. ICASSP*.

Scott Novotney and Chris Callison-Burch. 2010. Cheap, fast, and good enough: Automatic speech recognition with non-expert transcription. In *Proc. NAACL*.

Rion Snow, Brendan O'Connor, Daniel Jurafsky, and Andrew Y. Ng. 2008. Cheap and fast – But is it good? Evaluating non-expert annotations for natural language tasks. In *Proc. EMNLP*.

Klaus Zechner. 2009. What did they actually say? Agreement and disagreement among transcribers of non-native spontaneous speech responses in an English proficiency test. In *Proc. ISCA-SLaTE*.

Exploring Normalization Techniques for Human Judgments of Machine Translation Adequacy Collected Using Amazon Mechanical Turk

Michael Denkowski and **Alon Lavie**
Language Technologies Institute
School of Computer Science
Carnegie Mellon University
Pittsburgh, PA 15232, USA
{mdenkows,alavie}@cs.cmu.edu

Abstract

This paper discusses a machine translation evaluation task conducted using Amazon Mechanical Turk. We present a translation adequacy assessment task for untrained Arabic-speaking annotators and discuss several techniques for normalizing the resulting data. We present a novel 2-stage normalization technique shown to have the best performance on this task and further discuss the results of all techniques and the usability of the resulting adequacy scores.

1 Introduction

Human judgments of translation quality play a vital role in the development of effective machine translation (MT) systems. Such judgments can be used to measure system quality in evaluations (Callison-Burch et al., 2009) and to tune automatic metrics such as METEOR (Banerjee and Lavie, 2005) which act as stand-ins for human evaluators. However, collecting reliable human judgments often requires significant time commitments from expert annotators, leading to a general scarcity of judgments and a significant time lag when seeking judgments for new tasks or languages.

Amazon's Mechanical Turk (MTurk) service facilitates inexpensive collection of large amounts of data from users around the world. However, Turkers are not trained to provide reliable annotations for natural language processing (NLP) tasks, and some Turkers attempt to game the system by submitting random answers. For these reasons, NLP tasks must be designed to be accessible to untrained users and data normalization techniques must be employed to ensure that the data collected is usable.

This paper describes a MT evaluation task for translations of English into Arabic conducted using MTurk and compares several data normalization techniques. A novel 2-stage normalization technique is demonstrated to produce the highest agreement between Turkers and experts while retaining enough judgments to provide a robust tuning set for automatic evaluation metrics.

2 Data Set

Our data set consists of human adequacy judgments for automatic translations of 1314 English sentences into Arabic. The English source sentences and Arabic reference translations are taken from the Arabic-English sections of the NIST Open Machine Translation Evaluation (Garofolo, 2001) data sets for 2002 through 2005. Selected sentences are between 10 and 20 words in length on the Arabic side. Arabic machine translation (MT) hypotheses are obtained by passing the English sentences through Google's free online translation service.

2.1 Data Collection

Human judgments of translation adequacy are collected for each of the 1314 Arabic MT output hypotheses. Given a translation hypothesis and the corresponding reference translation, annotators are asked to assign an adequacy score according to the following scale:

4 – Hypothesis is completely meaning equivalent with the reference translation.

Proceedings of the NAACL HLT 2010 Workshop on Creating Speech and Language Data with Amazon's Mechanical Turk, pages 57–61,
Los Angeles, California, June 2010.

3 – Hypothesis captures more than half of meaning of the reference translation.

2 – Hypothesis captures less than half of meaning of the reference translation.

1 – Hypothesis captures no meaning of the reference translation.

Adequacy judgments are collected from untrained Arabic-speaking annotators using Amazon's Mechanical Turk (MTurk) service. We create a human intelligence task (HIT) type that presents Turkers with a MT hypothesis/reference pair and asks for an adequacy judgment. To make this task accessible to non-experts, the traditional definitions of adequacy scores are replaced with the following: (4) excellent, (3) good, (2) bad, (1) very bad. Each rating is accompanied by an example from the data set which fits the corresponding criteria from the traditional scale. To make this task accessible to the Arabic speakers we would like to complete the HITs, the instructions are provided in Arabic as well as English.

To allow experimentation with various data normalization techniques, we collect judgments from 10 unique Turkers for each of the translations. We also ask an expert to provide "gold standard" judgments for 101 translations drawn uniformly from the data. These 101 translations are recombined with the data and repeated such that every 6th translation has a gold standard judgment, resulting in a total of 1455 HITs. We pay Turkers \$0.01 per HIT and Amazon fees of \$0.005 per HIT, leading to a total cost of \$218.25 for data collection and an effective cost of \$0.015 per judgment. Despite requiring Arabic speakers, our HITs are completed at a rate of 1000-3000 per day. It should be noted that the vast majority of Turkers working on our HITs are located in India, with fewer in Arabic-speaking countries such as Egypt and Syria.

3 Normalization Techniques

We apply multiple normalization techniques to the data set and evaluate their relative performance. Several techniques use the following measures:

- Δ: For judgments ($J = j_1 ... j_n$) and gold standard ($G = g_1 ... g_n$), we define average distance:

$$\Delta(J, G) = \frac{\sum_{i=1}^{n} |g_i - j_i|}{n}$$

- K: For two annotators, Cohen's kappa coefficient (Smeeton, 1985) is defined:

$$K = \frac{P(A) - P(E)}{1 - P(E)}$$

where $P(A)$ is the proportion of times that annotators agree and $P(E)$ is the proportion of times that agreement is expected by chance.

3.1 Straight Average

The baseline approach consists of keeping all judgments and taking the straight average on a per-translation basis without additional normalization.

3.2 Removing Low-Agreement Judges

Following Callison-Burch et al. (2009), we calculate pairwise inter-annotator agreement ($P(A)$) of each annotator with all others and remove judgments from annotators with $P(A)$ below some threshold. We set this threshold such that the highest overall agreement can be achieved while retaining at least one judgment for each translation.

3.3 Removing Outlying Judgments

For a given translation and human judgments ($j_1 ... j_n$), we calculate the distance (δ) of each judgment from the mean ($\bar{j}$):

$$\delta(j_i) = |j_i - \bar{j}|$$

We then remove outlying judgments with $\delta(j_i)$ exceeding some threshold. This threshold is also set such that the highest agreement is achieved while retaining at least one judgment per translation.

3.4 Weighted Voting

Following Callison-Burch (2009), we treat evaluation as a weighted voting problem where each annotator's contribution is weighted by agreement with either a gold standard or with other annotators. For this evaluation, we weigh contribution by $P(A)$ with the 101 gold standard judgments.

3.5 Scaling Judgments

To account for the notion that some annotators judge translations more harshly than others, we apply per-annotator scaling to the adequacy judgments based on annotators' signed distance from gold standard judgments. For judgments ($J = j_1...j_n$) and gold standard ($G = g_1...g_n$), an additive scaling factor is calculated:

$$\lambda_+(J, G) = \frac{\sum_{i=1}^{n} g_i - j_i}{n}$$

Adding this scaling factor to each judgment has the effect of shifting the judgments' center of mass to match that of the gold standard.

3.6 2-Stage Technique

We combine judgment scaling with weighted voting to produce a 2-stage normalization technique addressing two types of divergence in Turker judgments from the gold standard. Divergence can be either consistent, where Turkers regularly assign higher or lower scores than experts, or random, where Turkers guess blindly or do not understand the task.

Stage 1: Given a gold standard ($G = g_1...g_n$), consistent divergences are corrected by calculating $\lambda_+(J, G)$ for each annotator's judgments ($J = j_i...j_n$) and applying $\lambda_+(J, G)$ to each j_i to produce adjusted judgment set J'. If $\Delta(J', G) < \Delta(J, G)$, where $\Delta(J, G)$ is defined in Section 3, the annotator is considered consistently divergent and J' is used in place of J. Inconsistently divergent annotators' judgments are unaffected by this stage.

Stage 2: All annotators are considered in a weighted voting scenario. In this case, annotator contribution is determined by a distance measure similar to the kappa coefficient. For judgments ($J = j_1...j_n$) and gold standard ($G = g_1...g_n$), we define:

$$K_\Delta(J, G) = \frac{(\max \Delta - \Delta(J, G)) - E(\Delta)}{\max \Delta - E(\Delta)}$$

where $\max \Delta$ is the average maximum distance between judgments and $E(\Delta)$ is the expected distance between judgments. Perfect agreement with the gold standard produces $K_\Delta = 1$ while chance agreement produces $K_\Delta = 0$. Annotators with $K_\Delta \leq 0$ are removed from the voting pool and final scores are calculated as the weighted averages of judgments from all remaining annotators.

Type	Δ	K_Δ
Uniform-a	1.02	0.184
Uniform-b	1.317	-0.053
Gaussian-2	1.069	0.145
Gaussian-2.5	0.96	0.232
Gaussian-3	1.228	0.018

Table 2: Weights assigned to random data

4 Results

Table 1 outlines the performance of all normalization techniques. To calculate $P(A)$ and K with the gold standard, final adequacy scores are rounded to the nearest whole number. As shown in the table, removing low-agreement annotators or outlying judgments greatly improves Turker agreement and, in the case of removing judgments, decreases distance from the gold standard. However, these approaches remove a large portion of the judgments, leaving a skewed data set. When removing judgments, 1172 of the 1314 translations receive a score of 3, making tasks such as tuning automatic metrics infeasible.

Weighing votes by agreement with the gold standard retains most judgments, though neither Turker agreement nor agreement with the gold standard improves. The scaling approach retains all judgments and slightly improves correlation and Δ, though K decreases. As scaled judgments are not whole numbers, Turker $P(A)$ and K are not applicable.

The 2-stage approach outperforms all other techniques when compared against the gold standard, being the only technique to significantly raise correlation. Over 90% of the judgments are used, as shown in Figure 1. Further, the distribution of final adequacy scores (shown in Figure 2) resembles a normal distribution, allowing this data to be used for tuning automatic evaluation metrics.

4.1 Resistance to Randomness

To verify that our 2-stage technique handles problematic data properly, we simulate user data from 5 unreliable Turkers. Turkers "Uniform-a" and "Uniform-b" draw answers randomly from a uniform distribution. "Gaussian" Turkers draw answers randomly from Gaussian distributions with $\sigma = 1$ and μ according to name. Each "Turker" contributes one judgment for each translation. As shown in Ta-

Technique	Retained	Gold Standard Correlation	Δ	$P(A)$	K	Turker $P(A)$	K
Straight Average	**14550**	0.078	0.988	0.356	0.142	0.484	0.312
Remove Judges	6627	-0.152	1.002	0.347	0.129	0.664	0.552
Remove Judgments	9250	0	0.891	0.356	0.142	**0.944**	**0.925**
Weighted Voting	14021	0.152	0.968	0.356	0.142	0.484	0.312
Scale Judgments	**14550**	0.24	0.89	0.317	0.089	N/A	N/A
2-Stage Technique	13621	**0.487**	**0.836**	**0.366**	**0.155**	N/A	N/A

Table 1: Performance of normalization techniques

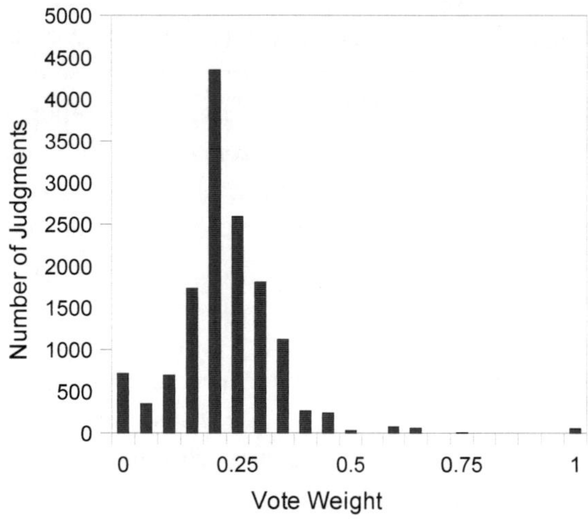

Figure 1: Distribution of weights for judgments

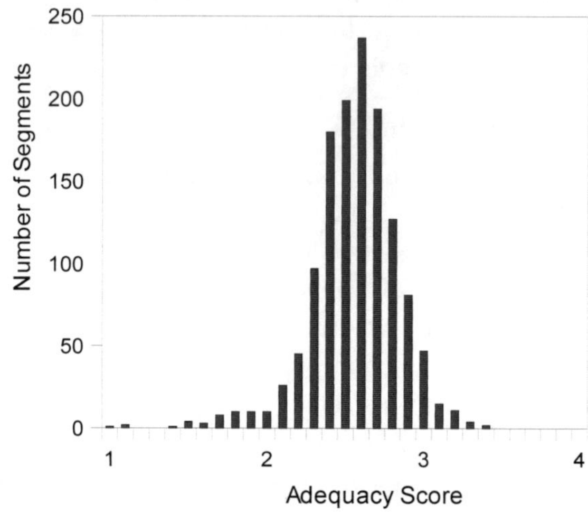

Figure 2: Distribution of adequacy scores after 2-stage normalization

ble 2, only Gaussian-2.5 receives substantial weight while the others receive low or zero weight. This follows from the fact that the actual data follows a similar distribution, and thus the random Turkers have negligible impact on the final distribution of scores.

5 Conclusions and Future Work

We have presented an Arabic MT evaluation task conducted using Amazon MTurk and discussed several possibilities for normalizing the collected data. Our 2-stage normalization technique has been shown to provide the highest agreement between Turkers and experts while retaining enough judgments to avoid problems of data sparsity and appropriately down-weighting random data. As we currently have a single set of expert judgments, our future work involves collecting additional judgments from multiple experts against which to further test our techniques. We then plan to use normalized Turker adequacy judgments to tune an Arabic version of the METEOR (Banerjee and Lavie, 2005) MT evaluation metric.

References

Satanjeev Banerjee and Alon Lavie. 2005. METEOR: An Automatic Metric for MT Evaluation with Improved Correlation with Human Judgments. In *Proc. ACL WIEEMMTS*.

Chris Callison-Burch, Philipp Koehn, Christof Monz, and Josh Schroeder. 2009. Findings of WMT09. In *Proc. WMT09*.

Chris Callison-Burch. 2009. Fast, cheap, and creative: Evaluating translation quality using Amazon's Mechanical Turk. In *Proc. EMNLP09*.

John Garofolo. 2001. NIST Open Machine Translation Evaluation. http://www.itl.nist.gov/iad/mig/tests/mt/.

N. C. Smeeton. 1985. Early History of the Kappa Statistic. In *Biometrics*, volume 41.

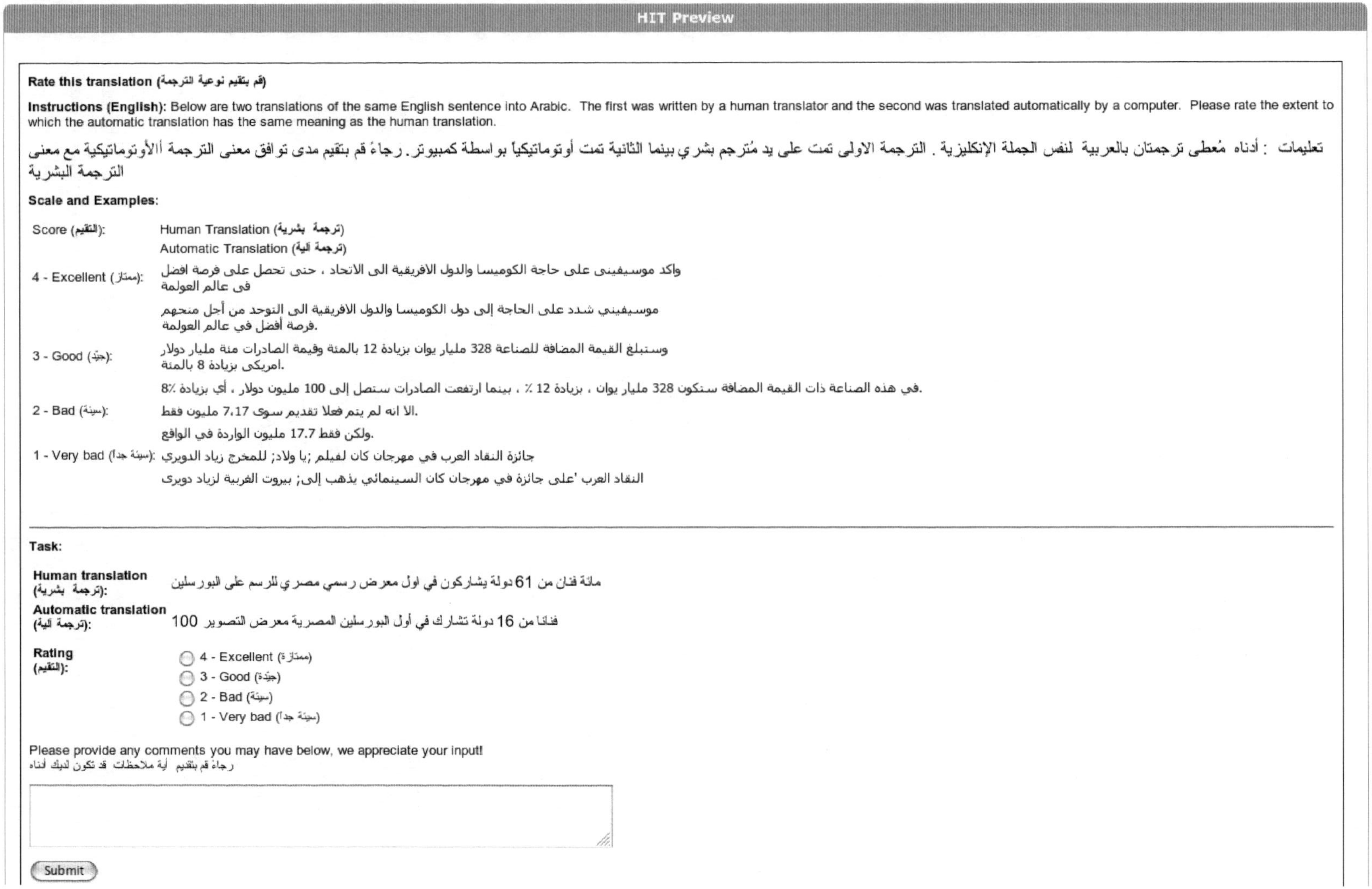

Figure 3: Example HIT as seen by Turkers

Can Crowds Build Parallel Corpora for Machine Translation Systems?

Vamshi Ambati and Stephan Vogel
{vamshi,vogel}@cs.cmu.edu
Language Technologies Institute, Carnegie Mellon University
5000 Forbes Avenue, Pittsburgh, PA 15213, USA

Abstract

Corpus based approaches to machine translation (MT) rely on the availability of parallel corpora. In this paper we explore the effectiveness of Mechanical Turk for creating parallel corpora. We explore the task of sentence translation, both into and out of a language. We also perform preliminary experiments for the task of phrase translation, where ambiguous phrases are provided to the turker for translation in isolation and in the context of the sentence it originated from.

1 Introduction

Large scale parallel data generation for new language pairs requires intensive human effort and availability of bilingual speakers. Only a few languages in the world enjoy sustained research interest and continuous financial support for development of automatic translation systems. For most remaining languages there is very little interest or funding available and limited or expensive access to experts for data elicitation. Crowd-sourcing compensates for the lack of experts with a large pool of expert/non-expert crowd. However, crowd-sourcing has thus far been explored in the context of eliciting annotations for a supervised classification task, typically monolingual in nature (Snow et al., 2008). In this shared task we test the feasibility of eliciting parallel data for Machine Translation (MT) using Mechanical Turk (MTurk). MT poses an interesting challenge as we require turkers to have understanding/writing skills in both the languages. Our work is similar to some recent work on crowd-sourcing and machine translation (Ambati et al., 2010; Callison-Burch, 2009), but focuses primarily on the setup and design of translation tasks on MTurk with varying granularity levels, both at sentence- and phrase-level translation.

2 Language Landscape on MTurk

We first conduct a pilot study by posting 25 sentences each from a variety of language pairs and probing to see the reception on MTurk. Language-pair selection was based on number of speakers in the language and Internet presence of the population. Languages like Spanish, Chinese, English, Arabic are spoken by many and have a large presence of users on the Internet. Those like Urdu, Tamil, Telugu although spoken by many are not well represented on the Web. Languages like Swahili, Zulu, Haiti are neither spoken by many nor have a great presence on the Web. For this pilot study we selected Spanish, Chinese, English, Urdu, Telugu, Hindi, Haitian Creole languages. We do not select German, French and other language pairs as they have already been explored by Callison-Burch (2009). Our pilot study helped us calibrate the costs for different language pairs as well as helped us select the languages to pursue further experiments. We found that at lower pay rates like 1 cent, it is difficult to find a sufficient number of translators to complete the task. For example, we could not find turkers to complete the translation from English to Haitian-Creole even after a period of 10 days. Haitian creole is spoken by a small population and it seems that only a very small portion of that was on MTurk. For a few other languages pairs, while we could find a

Proceedings of the NAACL HLT 2010 Workshop on Creating Speech and Language Data with Amazon's Mechanical Turk, pages 62–65,
Los Angeles, California, June 2010.

Pair	Cost per sen	Days
Spanish-Eng	\$0.01	1
Telugu-Eng	\$0.02	2
Eng-Creole	\$0.06	-
Urdu-Eng	\$0.03	1
Hindi-Eng	\$0.03	1
Chinese-Eng	\$0.02	1

Table 1: Cost vs. Completion for Language pairs

few turkers attempting the task, the price had to be increased to attract any attention. Table 1 shows the findings of our pilot study. We show the minimum cost at which we could start getting turkers to provide translations and the number of days they took to complete the task. MTurk has so far been a suppliers' market, and translation of rare-languages shows how a limited supply of turkers leads to a buyer's market; only fair.

3 Challenges for Crowd-Sourcing and Machine Translation

We use MTurk for all our crowd-sourcing experiments. In case of MT, a HIT on MTurk is one or more sentences in the source language that need to be translated to a target language. Making sure that the workers understand the task is the first step towards a successful elicitation using the crowd. We provide detailed instructions on the HIT for both completion of the task and its evaluation. Mechanical turk also has a provision to seek annotations from qualified workers, from a specific location with a specific success rate in their past HITs. For all our HITs we set the worker qualification threshold to 90%. We use the terms HIT vs. task and turker vs. translator interchangeably.

3.1 Quality Assurance

Quality assurance is a concern with an online crowd where the expertise of the turkers is unknown. We also notice from the datasets we receive that consistently poor and noisy translators exist. Problems like blank annotations, mis-spelling, copy-pasting of input are prevalent, but easy to identify. Turkers who do not understand the task but attempt it anyway are the more difficult ones to identify, but this is to be expected with non-experts. Redundancy of translations for the input and computing majority consensus translation is agreed to be an effective solution to identify and prune low quality translation. We discuss in following section computation of majority vote using fuzzy matching.

For a language pair like Urdu-English, we noticed a strange scenario, where the translations from two turkers were significantly worse in quality, but consistently matched each other, there by falsely boosting the majority vote. We suspect this to be a case of cheating, but this exposes a loop in majority voting which needs to be addressed, perhaps by also using gold standard data.

Turking Machines: We also have the problem of machines posing as turkers – 'Turking machine' problem. With the availability of online translation systems like Google translate, Yahoo translate (Babelfish) and Babylon, translation tasks on MTurk become easy targets to this problem. Turkers either use automatic scripts to get/post data from automatic MT systems, or make slight modifications to disguise the fact. This defeats the purpose of the task, as the resulting corpus would then be biased towards some existing automatic MT system. It is extremely important to keep gamers in check; not only do they pollute the quality of the crowd data, but their completion of a HIT means it becomes unavailable to genuine turkers who are willing to provide valuable translations. We, therefore, collect translations from existing automatic MT services and use them to match and block submissions from gamers. We rely on some gold-standard to identify genuine matches with automatic translation services.

3.2 Output Space and Fuzzy Matching

Due to the natural variability in style of turkers, there could be multiple different, but perfectly valid translations for a given sentence. Therefore it is difficult to match translation outputs from two turkers or even with gold standard data. We therefore need a fuzzy matching algorithm to account for lexical choices, synonymy, word ordering and morphological variations. This problem is similar to the task of automatic translation output evaluation and so we use METEOR (Lavie and Agarwal, 2007), an automatic MT evaluation metric for comparing two sentences. METEOR has an internal aligner that matches words in the sentences given and scores them separately based on whether the match was supported by synonymy, exact match or fuzzy match. The scores are then combined to provide a global matching score. If the score is above a threshold δ, we treat the sentences to be equivalent translations of the source sentence. We can set the δ parameter to different values, based on what is acceptable to the application. In our experiments, we set $\delta = 0.7$. We did not choose BLEU scoring metric as it is strongly oriented towards exact matching and high precision, than towards robust matching for high recall.

4 Sentence Translation

The first task we setup on MTurk was to translate full sentences from a source language into a target language. The population we were interested in was native speakers of one of the languages. We worked with four languages - English, Spanish, Telugu and Urdu. We chose 100 sentences for each language-pair and requested three different translations for each sentence. The Spanish data was taken from BTEC (Takezawa et al., 2002) corpus, consisting of short sentences in the travel domain. Telugu data was taken from the sports and politics section of a regional newspaper. For Urdu, we used the NIST-Urdu Evaluation 2008 data. We report results in Table 2. Both Spanish and Urdu had gold standard translations, as they were taken from parallel corpora created by language experts. As the data sets are small, we chose to perform manual inspection rather than use automatic metrics like BLEU to score match against gold-standard data.

4.1 Translating into English

The first batch of HITs were posted to collect translations into English. We noticed from manual inspection of the quality of translations that most of our translators were non-native speakers of English. This calls for adept and adequate methods for evaluating the translation quality. For example more than 50% of the Spanish-English tasks were completed in India, and in some cases a direct output of automatic translation services.

4.2 Translating out of English

The second set of experiments were to test the effectiveness of translating out of English. The ideal target population for this task were native speakers of the target language who also understood English. Most participant turkers who provided Urdu and Telugu translations, were from India and USA and were non-native speakers of English. However, one problem with enabling this task was the writing system. Most turkers do not have the tools to create content in their native language. We used 'Google Transliterate' API [1] to enable production of non-English content. This turned out to be an interesting HIT for the turkers, as they were excited to create their native language content. This is evident from the increased number of participant turkers. Manual inspection of translations revealed that this direction resulted in higher quality translations for both Urdu and Telugu and slightly lower quality for Spanish.

Language Pair	Cost	#Days	#Turkers
Spanish-English	\$0.01	1	16
Telugu-English	\$0.02	4	12
Urdu-English	\$0.03	2	13
English-Spanish	\$0.01	1	19
English-Telugu	\$0.02	3	35
English-Urdu	\$0.03	2	21

Table 2: Sentence translation data

5 Phrase Translation

Phrase translation is useful in reducing the cost and effort of eliciting translations by focusing on those parts of the sentence that are difficult to translate. It fits well into the paradigm of crowdsourcing where small tasks can be provided to a lot of translators. For this task, we were interested in understanding how well non-experts translate sub-sentential segments, and whether exposure to 'context' was helpful. For this set of experiments we use the Spanish-English language pair, where the turkers were presented with Spanish phrases to translate. The phrases were selected from the standard phrase tables produced by statistical phrase-based MT (Koehn et al., 2007), that was trained on the entire 128K BTEC corpus for Spanish-English. We computed an entropy score for each entry in the phrase table under the translation probability distributions in both directions and picked the set of 50

[1] http://www.google.com/transliterate/

Type	%Agreement	%Gold match
Out of Context	64%	32%
In Context	68%	33%

Table 3: Phrase Translation: Spanish-English

Length	Count	Example
1	2	cierras
2	11	vienes aqu
3	26	hay una en
4	8	a conocer su decisin
5	4	viene bien a esa hora

Table 4: Details of Spanish-English phrases used

most ambiguous phrases according to this metric. Table 4 shows sample and the length distribution of the phrases selected for this task.

5.1 In Context vs. Out of Context

We performed two kinds of experiments to study phrase translation and role of context. In the first case, the task was designed to be as simple as possible with each phrase to be translated as an individual HIT. We provided a source phrase and request turkers to translate a phrase under any hypothesized context. For the second task, we gave a phrase associated with the sentence that it originated from and requested the turkers to translate the phrase only in the context of the sentence. For both cases, we analyzed the data for inter-translator agreement;% of cases where there was a consensus translation), and agreement with the gold standard; % of times the translated phrase was present in the gold standard translation of the source sentence it came from. As shown in Table 3, translating in-context produced a better match with gold standard data and scored slightly better on the inter-translator agreement. We think that when translating out of context, most translators choose as appropriate for a context in their mind and so the inter-translator agreement could be lower, but when translating within the context of a sentence, they make translation choices to suit the sentence which could lead to better agreement scores. In future, we will extend these experiments to other language pairs and choose phrases not by entropy metric, but to study specific language phenomenon.

6 Conclusion

Our experiments helped us better understand the formulation of translation tasks on MTurk and its challenges. We experimented with both translating into and out of English and use transliteration for addressing the writing system issue. We also experiment with in-context and out-of-context phrase translation task. While working with non-expert translators it is important to address quality concerns alongside keeping in check any usage of automatic translation services. At the end of the shared task we have sampled the 'language landscape' on MTurk and have a better understanding of what to expect when building MT systems for different language pairs.

References

Vamshi Ambati, Stephan Vogel, and Jaime Carbonell. 2010. Active learning and crowd-sourcing for machine translation. In *Proceedings of the LREC 2010*, Malta, May.

Chris Callison-Burch. 2009. Fast, cheap, and creative: Evaluating translation quality using Amazon's Mechanical Turk. In *EMNLP 2009*, pages 286–295, Singapore, August. Association for Computational Linguistics.

Philipp Koehn, Hieu Hoang, Alexandra Birch Mayne, Christopher Callison-Burch, Marcello Federico, Nicola Bertoldi, Brooke Cowan, Wade Shen, Christine Moran, Richard Zens, Chris Dyer, Ondrej Bojar, Alexandra Constantin, and Evan Herbst. 2007. Moses: Open source toolkit for statistical machine translation. In *ACL Demonstration Session*.

Alon Lavie and Abhaya Agarwal. 2007. Meteor: an automatic metric for mt evaluation with high levels of correlation with human judgments. In *WMT 2007*, pages 228–231, Morristown, NJ, USA.

Rion Snow, Brendan O'Connor, Daniel Jurafsky, and Andrew Ng. 2008. Cheap and fast – but is it good? evaluating non-expert annotations for natural language tasks. In *Proceedings of the EMNLP 2008*, pages 254–263, Honolulu, Hawaii, October.

Toshiyuki Takezawa, Eiichiro Sumita, Fumiaki Sugaya, Hirofumi Yamamoto, and Seiichi Yamamoto. 2002. Towards a broad-coverage bilingual corpus for speech translation of travel conversation in the real world. In *Proceedings of LREC 2002, Las Palmas, Spain.*

Turker-Assisted Paraphrasing for English-Arabic Machine Translation

Michael Denkowski and **Hassan Al-Haj** and **Alon Lavie**
Language Technologies Institute
School of Computer Science
Carnegie Mellon University
Pittsburgh, PA 15232, USA
{mdenkows,hhaj,alavie}@cs.cmu.edu

Abstract

This paper describes a semi-automatic paraphrasing task for English-Arabic machine translation conducted using Amazon Mechanical Turk. The method for automatically extracting paraphrases is described, as are several human judgment tasks completed by Turkers. An ideal task type, revised specifically to address feedback from Turkers, is shown to be sophisticated enough to identify and filter problem Turkers while remaining simple enough for non-experts to complete. The results of this task are discussed along with the viability of using this data to combat data sparsity in MT.

1 Introduction

Many language pairs have large amounts of parallel text that can be used to build statistical machine translation (MT) systems. For such language pairs, resources for system tuning and evaluation tend to be disproportionately abundant in the language typically used as the target. For example, the NIST Open Machine Translation Evaluation (OpenMT) 2009 (Garofolo, 2009) constrained Arabic-English development and evaluation data includes four English translations for each Arabic source sentence, as English is the usual target language. However, when considering this data to tune and evaluate an English-to-Arabic system, each English sentence has a single Arabic translation and such translations are often identical. With at most one reference translation for each source sentence, standard minimum error rate training (Och, 2003) to the BLEU metric (Papineni et al., 2002) becomes problematic, as BLEU relies on the availability of multiple references.

We describe a semi-automatic paraphrasing technique that addresses this problem by identifying paraphrases that can be used to create new reference translations based on valid phrase substitutions on existing references. Paraphrases are automatically extracted from a large parallel corpus and filtered by quality judgments collected from human annotators using Amazon Mechanical Turk. As Turkers are not trained to complete natural language processing (NLP) tasks and can dishonestly submit random judgments, we develop a task type that is able to catch problem Turkers while remaining simple enough for untrained annotators to understand.

2 Data Set

The parallel corpus used for paraphrasing consists of all Arabic-English sentence pairs in the NIST OpenMT Evaluation 2009 (Garofolo, 2009) constrained training data. The target corpus to be paraphrased consists of the 728 Arabic sentences from the OpenMT 2002 (Garofolo, 2002) development data.

2.1 Paraphrase Extraction

We conduct word alignment and phrase extraction on the parallel data to produce a phrase table containing Arabic-English phrase pairs (a, e) with translation probabilities $P(a|e)$ and $P(e|a)$. Follow-

Proceedings of the NAACL HLT 2010 Workshop on Creating Speech and Language Data with Amazon's Mechanical Turk, pages 66–70,
Los Angeles, California, June 2010.

ing Bannard and Callison-Burch (2005), we identify Arabic phrases (a_1) in the target corpus that are translated by at least one English phrase (e). We identify paraphrase candidates as alternate Arabic phrases (a_2) that translate e. The probability of a_2 being a paraphrase of a_1 given foreign phrases e is defined:

$$P(a_2|a_1) = \sum_e P(e|a_1)P(a_2|e)$$

A language model trained on the Arabic side of the parallel corpus is used to further score the possible paraphrases. As each original phrase (a_1) occurs in some sentence (s_1) in the target corpus, a paraphrased sentence (s_2) can be created by replacing a_1 with one of its paraphrases (a_2). The final paraphrase score considers context, scaling the paraphrase probability proportionally to the change in log-probability of the sentence:

$$F(a_2, s_2|a_1, s_1) = P(a_2|a_1)\frac{\log P(s_1)}{\log P(s_2)}$$

These scores can be combined for each pair (a_1, a_2) to obtain overall paraphrase scores, however we use the F scores directly as our task considers the sentences in which paraphrases occur.

3 Turker Paraphrase Assessment

To determine which paraphrases to use to transform the development set references, we elicit binary judgments of quality from human annotators. While collecting this data from experts would be expensive and time consuming, Amazon's Mechanical Turk (MTurk) service facilitates the rapid collection of large amounts of inexpensive data from users around the world. As these users are not trained to work on natural language processing tasks, any work posted on MTurk must be designed such that it can be understood and completed successfully by untrained annotators. Further, some Turkers attempt to dishonestly profit from entering random answers, creating a need for tasks to have built-in measures for identifying and filtering out problem Turkers.

Our original evaluation task consists of eliciting two yes/no judgments for each paraphrase and corresponding sentence. Shown the original phrase (a_1) and the paraphrase (a_2), annotators are asked whether or not these two phrases could have the same meaning in some possible context. Annotators are then shown the original sentence (s_1) and the paraphrased sentence (s_2) and asked whether these two sentences have the same meaning. This task has the attractive property that if s_1 and s_2 have the same meaning, a_1 and a_2 *can* have the same meaning. Annotators assigning "yes" to the sentence pair should always assign "yes" to the phrase pair.

To collect these judgments from MTurk, we design a human intelligence task (HIT) that presents Turkers with two instances of the above task along with a text area for optional feedback. The task description asks skilled Arabic speakers to evaluate paraphrases of Arabic text. For each HIT, we pay Turkers \$0.01 and Amazon fees of \$0.005 for a total label cost of \$0.015. For our initial test, we ask Turkers to evaluate the 400 highest-scoring paraphrases, collecting 3 unique judgments for each paraphrase in and out of context. These HITs were completed at a rate of 200 per day.

Examining the results, we notice that most Turkers assign "yes" to the sentence pairs more often than to the phrase pairs, which should not be possible. To determine whether quality of Turkers might be an issue, we run another test for the same 400 paraphrases, this time paying Turkers \$0.02 per HIT and requiring a worker approval rate of 98% to work on this task. These HITs, completed by high quality Turkers at a rate of 100 per day, resulted in similarly impossible data. However, we also received valuable feedback from one of the Turkers.

3.1 Turker Feedback

We received a comment from one Turker that our evaluation task was causing confusion. The Turker would select "no" for some paraphrase in isolation due to missing information. However, the Turker would then select "yes" for the paraphrased sentence, as the context surrounding the phrase rendered the missing information unnecessary. This illustrates the point that untrained annotators understand the idea of "possible context" differently from experts and allows us to restructure our HITs to be ideal for untrained Turkers.

3.2 Revised Main Task

We simplify our task to eliminate as many sources of ambiguity as possible. Our revised task simply presents annotators with the original sentence labeled "sentence 1" and the paraphrased sentence labeled "sentence 2", and asks whether or not the two sentences have the same meaning. Each HIT, titled "Evaluate Arabic Sentences", presents Turkers with 2 such tasks, pays \$0.02, and costs \$0.005 in Amazon fees.

Without additional consideration, this task remains highly susceptible to random answers from dishonest or unreliable Turkers. To ensure that such Turkers are identified and removed, we intersperse absolute positive and negative examples with the sentence pairs from our data set. Absolute positives consist of the same original sentence s_1 repeated twice and should always receive a "yes" judgment. Absolute negatives consist of some original s_1 and a different, randomly selected original sentence s'_1 with several words dropped to obscure meaning. Absolute negatives should always receive a "no" judgment. Positive and negative control cases can be inserted with a frequency based either on desired confidence that enough cases are encountered for normalization or on the availability of funds.

Inserting either a positive or negative control case every 5th task increases the per-label cost to \$0.0156. We use this task type to collect 3 unique judgments for each of the 1280 highest-scoring paraphrases at a total cost of \$60.00 for 2400 HITs. These HITs were completed substantially faster at a rate of 500-1000 per day. The results of this task are discussed in section 4.

3.3 Editing Task

We conduct an additional experiment to see if Turkers will fix paraphrases judged to be incorrect. The task extends the sentence evaluation task described in the previous section by asking Turkers who select "no" to edit the paraphrase text in the second sentence such that the sentences have the same meaning. While the binary judgment task is used for filtering only, this editing task ensures a usable data point for every HIT completed. As such, fewer total HITs are required and high quality Turkers can be

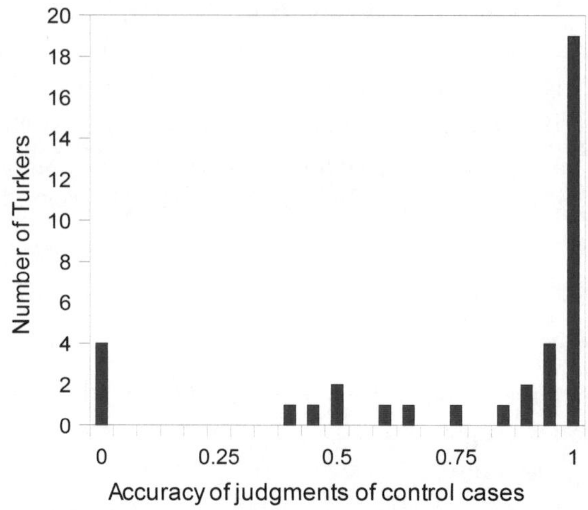

Figure 1: Turker accuracy classifying control cases

paid more for each HIT. We run 3 sequential tests for this task, offering \$0.02, \$0.04, and \$0.10 per paraphrase approved or edited.

Examining the results, we found that regardless of price, very few paraphrases were actually edited, even when Turkers selected "no" for sentence equality. While this allows us to easily identify and remove problem Turkers, it does not solve the issue that honest Turkers either cannot or will not provide usable paraphrase edits for this price range. A brief examination by an expert indicates that the \$0.02 per HIT edits are actually better than the \$0.10 per HIT edits.

4 Results

Our main task of 2400 HITs was completed through the combined effort of 47 unique Turkers. As shown Figure 1, these Turkers have varying degrees of accuracy classifying the control cases. The two most common classes of Turkers include (1) those spending 15 or more seconds per judgment and scoring above 0.9 accuracy on the control cases and (2) those spending 5-10 seconds per judgment and scoring between 0.4 and 0.6 accuracy as would be expected by chance. As such, we accept but do not consider the judgments of Turkers scoring between 0.7 and 0.9 accuracy on the control set, and reject all HITs for Turkers scoring below 0.7, republishing them to be completed by other workers.

Decision	Confirm	Reject	Undec.
Paraphrases	726	423	131

Table 1: Turker judgments of top 1280 paraphrases

لسلاح	الطيران	الكيني
to-weapon	the-aviation	the-Kenyan
For the Kenyan air force		
للقوات	الجوية	الكينية
for-the-forces	Air	the-Kenyan
For the Kenyan air force		
يلي	اهم	العناوين
following	most-important	headlines
Following are the most important headlines		
يلي	اهم	الانباء
following	most-important	news
Following are the most important headlines		

Figure 2: Paraphrases confirmed by Turkers

After removing judgments from below-threshold annotators, all remaining judgments are used to confirm or reject the covered paraphrases. If a paraphrase has at least 2 remaining judgments, it is confirmed if at least 2 annotators judge it positively and rejected otherwise. Paraphrases with fewer than 2 remaining judgments are considered undecidable. Table 1 shows the distribution of results for the 1280 top-scoring paraphrases. As shown in the table, 726 paraphrases are confirmed as legitimate phrase substitutions on reference translations, providing an average of almost one paraphrase per reference. Figures 2 and 3 show example Arabic paraphrases filtered by Turkers.

5 Conclusions

We have presented a semi-automatic paraphrasing technique for creating additional reference translations. The paraphrase extraction technique provides a ranked list of paraphrases and their contexts which can be incrementally filtered by human judgments. Our judgment task is designed to address specific Turker feedback, remaining simple enough for non-experts while successfully catching problem users. The $60.00 worth of judgments collected produces enough paraphrases to apply an average of one phrase substitution to each reference. Our future work includes collecting sufficient data to substitute multiple paraphrases into each Arabic reference in our development set, producing a full additional set of reference translations for use tuning our English-to-Arabic MT system. The resulting individual paraphrases can also be used for other tasks in MT and NLP.

النمسا	باسم		
Austria	in-the-name		
Austria on behalf			
من	الرئاسة	النمساوية	
from	the-presidency	the-Austrian	
From the Austrian presidency			
الدفاع	وزير		
the-defense	minister		
The minister of defense			
الماضي	صرح	وزير	الدفاع
the-past	stated	minister	the-defense
the past the minister of defense stated			

Figure 3: Paraphrases rejected by Turkers

Acknowledgements

This work was supported by a $100 credit from Amazon.com, Inc. as part of a shared task for the NAACL 2010 workshop "Creating Speech and Language Data With Amazon's Mechanical Turk".

References

Colin Bannard and Chris Callison-Burch. 2005. Paraphrasing with Bilingual Parallel Corpora. In *Proc. of ACL*.

John Garofolo. 2002. NIST OpenMT Eval. 2002. http://www.itl.nist.gov/iad/mig/tests/mt/2002/.

John Garofolo. 2009. NIST OpenMT Eval. 2009. http://www.itl.nist.gov/iad/mig/tests/mt/2009/.

Franz Josef Och. 2003. Minimum Error Rate Training for Statistical Machine Translation. In *Proc. of ACL*.

Kishore Papineni, Salim Roukos, Todd Ward, and Wei-Jing Zhu. 2002. BLEU: a Method for Automatic Evaluation of Machine Translation. In *Proc. of ACL*.

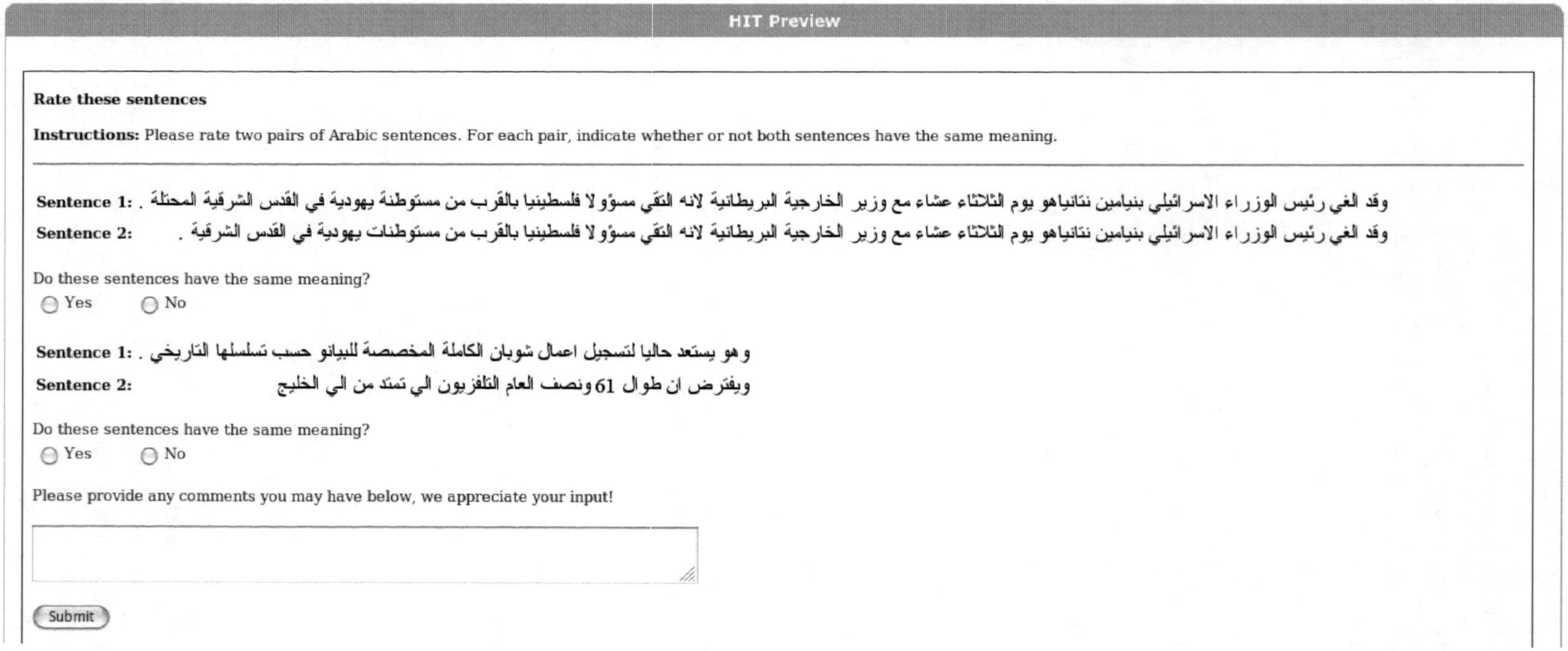

Figure 4: Example HIT as seen by Turkers

Annotating Large Email Datasets for Named Entity Recognition with Mechanical Turk

Nolan Lawson, Kevin Eustice, Mike Perkowitz
Kiha Software
100 South King Street, Suite 320
Seattle, WA 98104
{nolan,kevin,mikep}@kiha.com

Meliha Yetisgen-Yildiz
Biomedical and Health Informatics
University of Washington
Seattle, WA 98101
melihay@u.washington.edu

Abstract

Amazon's Mechanical Turk service has been successfully applied to many natural language processing tasks. However, the task of named entity recognition presents unique challenges. In a large annotation task involving over 20,000 emails, we demonstrate that a competitive bonus system and inter-annotator agreement can be used to improve the quality of named entity annotations from Mechanical Turk. We also build several statistical named entity recognition models trained with these annotations, which compare favorably to similar models trained on expert annotations.

1 Introduction

It is well known that the performance of many machine learning systems is heavily determined by the size and quality of the data used as input to the training algorithms. Additionally, for certain applications in natural language processing (NLP), it has been noted that the particular algorithms or feature sets used tend to become irrelevant as the size of the corpus increases (Banko and Brill 2001). It is therefore not surprising that obtaining large annotated datasets is an issue of great practical importance for the working researcher. Traditionally, annotated training data have been provided by experts in the field or the researchers themselves, often at great costs in terms of time and money. Recently, however, attempts have been made to leverage non-expert annotations provided by Amazon's Mechanical Turk (MTurk) service to create large training corpora at a fraction of the usual costs (Snow *et al.* 2008). The initial results seem promising, and a new avenue for enhancing existing sources of annotated data appears to have been opened.

Named entity recognition (NER) is one of the many fields of NLP that rely on machine learning methods, and therefore large training corpora. Indeed, it is a field where more is almost always better, as indicated by the traditional use of named entity gazetteers (often culled from external sources) to simulate data that would have been inferred from a larger training set (Minkov *et al.* 2005; Mikheev *et al.* 1999). Therefore, it appears to be a field that could profit from the enormous bargain-price workforce available through MTurk.

It is not immediately obvious, though, that MTurk is well-suited for the task of NER annotation. Commonly, MTurk has been used for the classification task (Snow *et al.* 2008) or for straightforward data entry. However, NER does not fit well into either of these formats. As pointed out by Kozareva (2006), NER can be thought of as a composition of two subtasks: 1) determining the start and end boundaries of a textual entity, and 2) determining the label of the identified span. The second task is the well-understood classification task, but the first task presents subtler problems. One is that MTurk's form-based user interface is inappropriate for the task of identifying textual spans. Another problem is that MTurk's fixed-fee payment system encourages low recall on the part of the annotators, since they receive the same pay no matter how many entities they identify.

This paper addresses both of these problems by describing a custom user interface and competitive payment system that together create a fluid user experience while encouraging high-quality annotations. Further, we demonstrate that MTurk successfully scales to the task of annotating a very large set of documents (over 20,000), with each document annotated by multiple workers. We also present a system for resolving inter-annotator conflicts to create the final training corpus, and determine the ideal agreement threshold to maximize precision and recall of a statistical named entity recognition model. Finally, we demonstrate that a model

Proceedings of the NAACL HLT 2010 Workshop on Creating Speech and Language Data with Amazon's Mechanical Turk, pages 71–79,
Los Angeles, California, June 2010.

trained on our corpus is on par with one trained from expert annotations, when applied to a labeled test set.

2 Related Work

Mechanical Turk is a virtual market in which any requester can post tasks that are simple for humans but difficult for computers. MTurk has been adopted for a variety of uses both in industry and academia from user studies (Kittur *et al.* 2008) to image labeling (Sorokin and Forsyth 2008). In March 2007, Amazon claimed the user base of MTurk consisted of over 100,000 users from 100 countries (Pontin 2007).

In the scope of this paper, we examine the feasibility of MTurk in creating large-scale corpora for training statistical named entity recognition models. However, our work was not the first application of MTurk in the NLP domain. Snow *et al.* (2008) examined the quality of labels created by MTurk workers for various NLP tasks including word sense disambiguation, word similarity, text entailment, and temporal ordering. Since the publication of Snow *et al.*'s paper, MTurk has become increasingly popular as an annotation tool for NLP research. Examples include Nakov's work on creating a manually annotated resource for noun-noun compound interpretation based on paraphrasing verbs by MTurk (Nakov 2008) and Callison-Burch's machine translation evaluation study with MTurk (Callison-Burch 2009). In contrast to the existing research, we both evaluated the quality of corpora generated by MTurk in different named entity recognition tasks and explored ways to motivate the workers to do higher quality work. We believe the experiences we present in this paper will contribute greatly to other researchers as they design similar large-scale annotation tasks.

3 General Problem Definition

Named entity recognition (NER) is a well-known subtask of information extraction. Traditionally, the task has been based on identifying words and phrases that refer to various entities of interest, including persons, locations, and organizations, (Nadeau and Sekine 2007). The problem is usually posed as a sequence labeling task similar to the part-of-speech (POS) tagging or phrase-chunking tasks, where each token in the input text corresponds to a label in the output, and is solved with sequential classification algorithms (such as CRF, SVMCMM, or MEMM).

Previous works have tackled NER within the biomedical domain (Settles 2004), newswire domain (Grishman and Sundheim 1996), and email domain (Minkov *et al.* 2005). In this paper, we focus on extracting entities from email text.

It should be noted that email text has many distinctive features that create a unique challenge when applying NER. For one, email text tends to be more informal than either newswire or biomedical text, which reduces the usefulness of learned features that depend on patterns of capitalization and spelling. Also, the choice of corpora in email text is particularly important. As email corpora tend to come from either a single company (e.g., the Enron Email Dataset[1]) or a small group of people (e.g., the Sarah Palin email set[2]), it is easy to build a classifier that overfits the data. For instance, a classifier trained to extract personal names from Enron emails might show an especially high preference to words such as "White," "Lay," and "Germany," because they correspond to the names of Enron employees.

Within the newswire and biomedical domains, such overfitting may be benign or actually beneficial, since documents in those domains tend to deal with a relatively small and pre-determined set of named entities (e.g., politicians and large corporations for newswire text, gene and protein names for biomedical text). For NER in the email domain, however, such overfitting is unacceptable. The personal nature of emails ensures that they will almost always contain references to people, places, and organizations not covered by the training data. Therefore, for the classifier to be useful on any spontaneous piece of email text, a large, heterogeneous training set is desired.

To achieve this effect, we chose four different sources of unlabeled email text to be annotated by the Mechanical Turk workers for input into the training algorithms:

1. The Enron Email Dataset.
2. The 2005 TREC Public Spam Corpus (non-spam only).[3]
3. The 20 Newsgroups Dataset.[4]
4. A private mailing list for synthesizer aficionados called "Analogue Heaven."

4 Mechanical Turk for NER

As described previously, MTurk is not explicitly designed for NER tasks. Because of this, we de-

[1] http://www.cs.cmu.edu/~enron/

[2] http://palinemail.crivellawest.net/

[3] http://plg.uwaterloo.ca/~gvcormac/treccorpus/

[4] http://people.csail.mit.edu/jrennie/20Newsgroups/

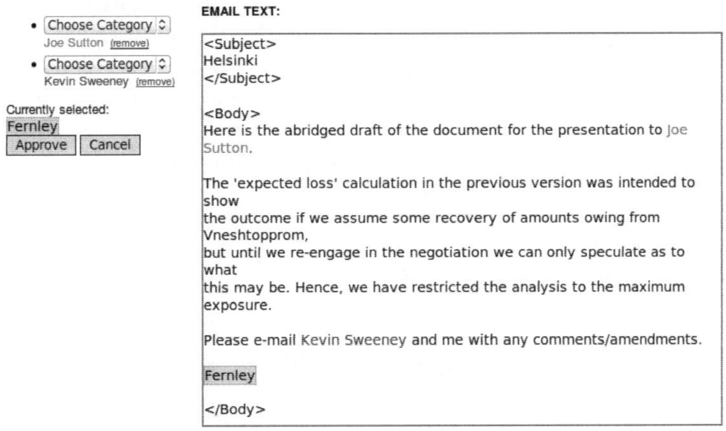

Fig. 1: Sample of the interface presented to workers.

cided to build a custom user interface and bonus payment system that largely circumvents the default MTurk web interface and instead performs its operations through the MTurk Command Line Tools.[5] Additionally, we built a separate set of tools designed to determine the ideal number of workers to assign per email.

4.1 User Interface

In order to adapt the task of NER annotation to the Mechanical Turk format, we developed a web-based graphical user interface using JavaScript that allowed the user to select a span of text with the mouse cursor and choose different categories of entities from a dropdown menu. The interface also used simple tokenization heuristics to divide the text into highlightable spans and resolve partial overlaps or double-clicks into the next largest span. For instance, highlighting the word "Mary" from "M" to "r" would result in the entire word being selected.

Each Human Intelligence Task (or HIT, a unit of payable work in the Mechanical Turk system) presented the entire subject and body of an email from one of the four corpora. To keep the HITs at a reasonable size, emails with bodies having less than 60 characters or more than 900 characters were omitted. The average email length, including both subject and body, was 405.39 characters.

For the labeling task, we chose three distinct entity types to identify: PERSON, LOCATION, and ORGANIZATION. To reduce potential worker confusion and make the task size smaller, we also broke up each individual HIT by entity type, so the user only had to concentrate on one at a time.

For the PERSON and LOCATION entity types, we noticed during initial tests that there was a user tendency to conflate unnamed references (such as "my mom" and "your house") with true named references. Because NER is intended to be limited only to named entities (i.e., references that contain proper nouns), we asked the users to distinguish between "named" and "unnamed" persons and locations, and to tag both separately. The inclusion of unnamed entities was intended to keep their named counterparts pure and undiluted; the unnamed entities were discarded after the annotation process was complete. The same mechanism could have been used for the ORGANIZATION entity type, but the risk of unnamed references seemed smaller.

Initially, we ran a small trial with a base rate of $0.03 for each HIT. However, after compiling the results we noticed that there was a general tendency for the workers to under-tag the entities. Besides outright freeloaders (i.e., workers who simply clicked "no entities" each time), there were also many who would highlight the first one or two entities, and then ignore the rest of the email.

This may have been due to a misunderstanding of the HIT instructions, but we conjectured that a deeper reason was that we were paying a base rate regardless of the number of entities identified. Ideally, a HIT with many entities to highlight should pay more than a HIT with fewer. However, the default fixed-rate system was paying the same for both, and the workers were responding to such an inflexible incentive system accordingly. To remedy this situation, we set about to create a payment system that would motivate higher recall on entity-rich emails, while still discouraging the opposite extreme of random over-tagging.

5 http://mturkclt.sourceforge.net

4.2 Bonus Payment System

Mechanical Turk provides two methods for paying workers: fixed rates on each HIT and bonuses to individual workers for especially good work. We chose to leverage these bonuses to form the core of our payment system. Each HIT would pay a base rate of $0.01, but each tagged entity could elicit a bonus of $0.01-$0.02. PERSON entities paid $0.01, while LOCATION and ORGANIZATION entities paid $0.02 (since they were rarer).

To ensure quality and discourage over-tagging, bonuses for each highlighted entity were limited based on an agreement threshold with other workers. This threshold was usually set such that a majority agreement was required, which was an arbitrary decision we made in order to control costs. The terms of the bonuses were explained in detail in the instructions page for each HIT.

Additionally, we decided to leverage this bonus system to encourage improvements in worker performance over time. Since the agreed-upon spans that elicited bonuses were assumed to be mostly correct, we realized we could give feedback to the workers on these entities to encourage similar performance in the future.

In general, worker bonuses are a mysterious and poorly understood motivational mechanism. Our feedback system attempted to make these bonuses more predictable and transparent. The system we built uses Amazon's "NotifyWorkers" REST API to send messages directly to the workers' email accounts. Bonuses were batched on a daily basis, and the notification emails gave a summary description of the day's bonuses.

```
In recognition of your performance, you
were awarded a bonus of $0.5 ($0.02x25)
for catching the following span(s): ['ve-
gas', 'Mt. Hood', 'Holland', [...]
```

Fig. 2: Example bonus notification.

Both the UI and the bonus/notification system were works in progress that were continually refined based on comments from the worker community. We were pleasantly surprised to find that, throughout the annotation process, the Mechanical Turk workers were generally enthusiastic about the HITs, and also interested in improving the quality of their annotations. Out of 169,156 total HITs, we received 702 comments from 140 different workers, as well as over 50 email responses and a dedicated thread at TurkerNation.com[6]. Most of the feedback was positive, and negative feedback was almost solely directed at the UI. Based on their comments, we continually tweaked and debugged the UI and HIT instructions, but kept the basic structure of the bonus system.

4.3 Worker Distribution

With the bonus system in place, it was still necessary to determine the ideal number of workers to assign per email. Previously, Snow *et al.* (2008) used expert annotations to find how many Mechanical Turk workers could "equal" an expert in terms of annotation quality. Because we lacked expert annotations, we developed an alternative system to determine the ideal number of workers based purely on inter-annotator agreement.

As described in the previous section, the most significant problem faced with our HITs was that of low recall. Low precision was generally not considered to be a problem, since, with enough annotators, inter-annotator agreement could always be set arbitrarily high in order to weed out false positives. Recall, on the other hand, could be consistently expected to improve as more annotators were added to the worker pool. Therefore, the only problem that remained was to calculate the marginal utility (in terms of recall) of each additional annotator assigned to an email.

In order to estimate this marginal recall gain for each entity type, we first ran small initial tests with a relatively large number of workers. From these results, we took all the entities identified by at least two workers and set those aside as the gold standard annotations; any overlapping annotations were collapsed into the larger one. Next, for each *n* number of workers between 2 and the size of the entire worker pool, we randomly sampled *n* workers from the pool, re-calculated the entities based on agreement from at least two workers within that group, and calculated the recall relative to the gold standard annotation. The threshold of 2 was chosen arbitrarily for the purpose of this experiment.

From this data we generated a marginal recall curve for each entity type, which roughly approximates how many workers are required per email before recall starts to drop off significantly. As expected, each graph shows a plateau-like behavior as the number of workers increases, but some entity types reach their plateau earlier

[6] http://turkers.proboards.com/index.cgi?action=display&board=everyoneelse&thread=3177

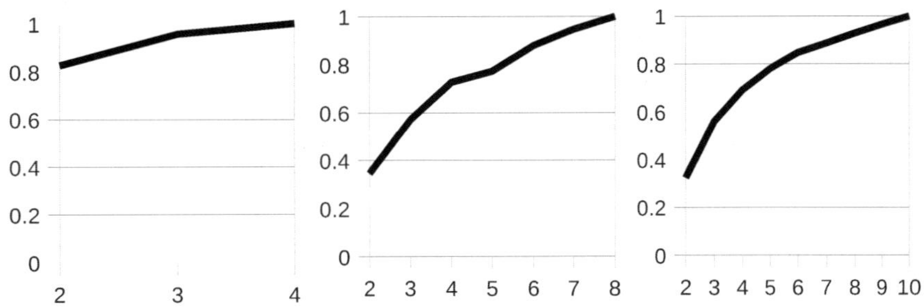

Fig. 3: Marginal recall curves for PERSON, LOCATION, and ORGANIZATION entity types, from a trial run of 900-1,000 emails. Recall is plotted on the y-axis, the number of annotators on the x-axis.

than others. Most saliently, Person entities seem to require only a few workers to reach a relatively high recall, compared to LOCATION or ORGANIZATION entities.

Based on the expected diminishing returns for each entity type, we determined some number of workers to assign per email that we felt would maximize entity recall while staying within our budgetary limits. After some tinkering and experimentation with marginal recall curves, we ultimately settled on 4 assignments for PERSON entities, 6 for LOCATION entities, and 7 for ORGANIZATION entities.

5 Corpora and Experiments

We ran our Mechanical Turk tasks over a period of about three months, from August 2008 to November 2008. We typically processed 500-1,500 documents per day. In the end, the workers annotated 20,609 unique emails which totaled 7.9 megabytes, including both subject and body.

All in all, we were pleasantly surprised by the speed at which each HIT series was completed. Out of 39 total HIT series, the average completion time (i.e. from when the HITs were first posted to MTurk.com until the last HIT was completed) was 3.13 hours, with an average of 715.34 emails per HIT series. The fastest completion time per number of emails was 1.9 hours for a 1,000-email task, and the slowest was 5.13 hours for a 100-email task. We noticed, that, paradoxically, larger HIT series were often completed more quickly – most likely because Amazon promotes the larger tasks to the front page.

5.1 Corpora Annotation

In Table 1, we present several statistics regarding the annotation tasks, grouped by corpus and entity type. Here, "Cost" is the sum of all bonuses and base rates for the HITs, "Avg. Cost" is the average amount we paid in bonuses and base rates per email, "Avg. # Workers" is the average number of workers assigned per email, "Avg. Bonus" is the average bonus per HIT, "Avg. # Spans" is the average number of entities highlighted per HIT, and "Avg. Time" is the average time of completion per HIT in seconds. Precision and recall are reported relative to the "gold standards" determined by the bonus agreement thresholds. None of the reported costs include fees paid to Amazon, which varied based on how the bonuses were batched.

A few interesting observations emerge from these data. For one, the average bonus was usually a bit more than the base rate of $0.01. The implication is that bonuses actually comprised the majority of the compensation, somewhat calling into question their role as a "bonus."

Also noteworthy is that ORGANIZATION entities took less time per identified span to complete than either location or person entities. However, we suspect that this is due to the fact that we ran the ORGANIZATION tasks last (after PERSON and LOCATION), and by that time we had ironed out several bugs in the UI, and our workers had become more adept at using it.

5.2 Worker Performance

In the end, we had 798 unique workers complete 169,156 total HITs. The average number of HITs per worker was 211.97, but the median was only 30. Ten workers who tagged no entities were blocked, and the 1,029 HITs they completed were rejected without payment.

For the most part, a small number of dedicated workers completed the majority of the tasks. Out of all non-rejected HITs, the top 10 most prolific workers completed 22.51%, the top 25 completed 38.59%, the top 50 completed 55.39%, and the top 100 completed 74.93%.

Callison-Burch (2009) found in their own Mechanical Turk system that the workers who contributed more tended to show lower quality,

Corpus	Entity	Cost	#Emails	Avg. Cost	Avg. #Workers	Avg. Bonus	Avg. #Spans	Avg. Precision	Avg. Recall	Avg. Time
20N.	Loc.	315.68	1999	0.1579	6	0.0163	1.6885	0.5036	0.7993	144.34
A.H.	Loc.	412.2	2500	0.1649	6.4	0.0158	1.1924	0.6881	0.8092	105.34
Enron	Loc.	323.54	3000	0.1078	6.23	0.0073	1.0832	0.3813	0.7889	105.25
TREC	Loc.	274.88	2500	0.1100	6	0.0083	1.1847	0.3794	0.7864	122.97
20N.	Org.	438.44	3500	0.1253	7	0.0079	1.2396	0.3274	0.6277	105.68
A.H.	Org.	396.48	2500	0.1586	7	0.0127	1.2769	0.4997	0.7062	92.01
Enron	Org.	539.19	2500	0.2157	8.6	0.0151	1.3454	0.5590	0.7415	80.55
TREC	Org.	179.94	1500	0.1200	7	0.0071	0.8923	0.4414	0.6992	84.23
20N.	Per.	282.51	2500	0.1130	4	0.0183	2.8693	0.7267	0.9297	152.77
A.H.	Per.	208.78	2500	0.0835	4	0.0109	1.6529	0.7459	0.9308	112.4
Enron	Per.	54.11	400	0.1353	6.14	0.0120	2.7360	0.8343	0.8841	111.23
TREC	Per.	214.37	2500	0.0857	4	0.0114	1.5918	0.7950	0.9406	103.73

Table 1: Statistics by corpus and entity type (omitting rejected work).

as measured by agreement with an expert. We had hoped that our bonus system, by rewarding quality work with higher pay, would yield the opposite effect, and in practice, our most prolific workers did indeed tend to show the highest entity recall.

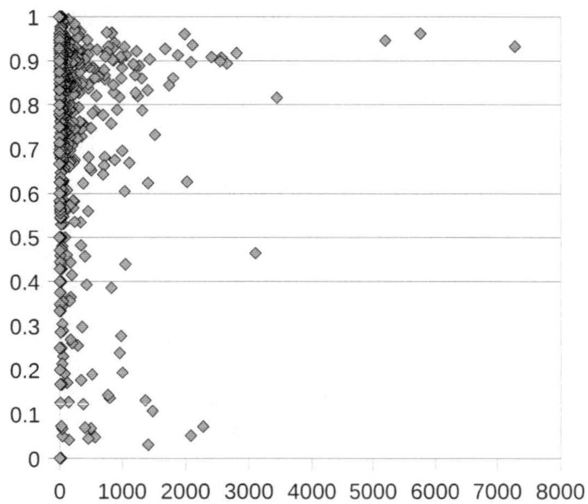

Fig. 4: # HITs Completed vs. Recall

Figure 4 shows how each of the non-rejected workers fared in terms of entity recall (relative to the "gold standard" determined by the bonus agreement threshold), compared to the number of HITs completed. As the chart shows, out of the 10 most productive workers, only one had an average recall score below 60%, and the rest all had scores above 80%. While there are still quite a few underperforming workers within the core group of high-throughput annotators, the general trend seemed to be that the more HITs a worker completes, the more likely he/she is to agree with the other annotators. This chart may be directly compared to a similar one in Callison-Burch (2009), where the curve takes largely the opposite shape. One interpretation of this is that our bonus system had the desired effect on annotator quality.

5.3 Annotation Quality Experiments

To evaluate the quality of the worker annotations, one would ideally like to have at least a subset annotated by an expert, and then compare the expert's judgments with the Mechanical Turk workers'. However, in our case we lacked expert annotations for any of the annotated emails. Thus, we devised an alternative method to evaluate the annotation quality, using the NER system built into the open-source MinorThird toolkit.[7]

MinorThird is a popular machine learning and natural language processing library that has previously been applied to the problem of NER with some success (Downey *et al.* 2007). For our purposes, we wanted to minimize the irregularity introduced by deviating from the core features and algorithms available in MinorThird, and therefore did not apply any feature selection or feature engineering in our experiments. We chose to use MinorThird's default "CRFLearner," which is a module that learns feature weights using the IITB CRF library[8] and then applies them to a conditional Markov model-based extractor. All of the parameters were set to their default value, including the built-in "TokenFE" feature extractor, which extracts features for the lowercase value of each token and its capitalization pattern. The version of MinorThird used was 13.7.10.8.

In order to convert the Mechanical Turk annotations to a format that could be input as training data to the NER system, we had to resolve the conflicting annotations of the multiple workers into a unified set of labeled documents. Similarly to the bonus system, we achieved this using a simple voting scheme. In contrast to the bonus system, though, we experimented with multiple inter-annotator agreement thresholds between 1 and 4. For the PERSON corpora this meant a relatively stricter threshold than for the LOCATION or

[7] http://minorthird.sourceforge.net
[8] http://crf.sourceforge.net

ORGANIZATION corpora, since the PERSON corpora typically had only 4 annotations per document. Mail subjects and bodies were split into separate documents.

Four separate experiments were run with these corpora. The first was a 5-fold cross-evaluation (i.e., a 80%/20% split) train/test experiment on each of the twelve corpora. Because this test did not rely on any expert annotations in the gold standard, our goal here was only to roughly measure the "cohesiveness" of the corpus. Low precision and recall scores should indicate a messy corpus, where annotations in the training portion do not necessarily help the extractor to discover annotations in the test portion. Conversely, high precision and recall scores should indicate a more cohesive corpus – one that is at least somewhat internally consistent across the training and test portions.

The second test was another train/test experiment, but with the entire Mechanical Turk corpus as training data, and with a small set of 182 emails, of which 99 were from the W3C Email Corpus[9] and 83 were from emails belonging to various Kiha Software employees, as test data. These 182 test emails were hand-annotated for the three entity types by the authors. Although this test data was small, our goal here was to demonstrate how well the trained extractors could fare against email text from a completely different source than the training data.

The third test was similar to the second, but used as its test data 3,116 Enron emails annotated for PERSON entities.[10] The labels were manually corrected by the authors before testing. The goal here was the same as with the second test, although it must be acknowledged that the PERSON training data did make use of 400 Enron emails, and therefore the test data was not from a completely separate domain.

The fourth test was intended to increase the comparability of our own results with those that others have shown in NER on email text. For the test data, we chose two subsets of the Enron Email Corpus used in Minkov *et al.* (2005).[11] The first, "Enron-Meetings," contains 244 training documents, 242 tuning documents, and 247 test documents. The second, "Enron-Random," contains 89 training documents, 82 tuning documents, and 83 test documents. For each, we tested our statistical recognizers against all three divisions combined as well as the test set alone.

6 Results

The results from these four tests are presented in Tables 2-5. In these tables, "Agr." refers to inter-annotator agreement, "TP" to token precision, "SP" to span precision, "TR" to token recall, "SR" to span recall, "TF" to token F-measure, and "SF" to span F-measure. "Span" scores do not award partial credit for entities, and are therefore a stricter measure than "token" scores.

Entity	Agr.	TP	TR	TF
Loc.	1	60.07%	54.65%	57.23%
	2	**75.47%**	**70.51%**	**72.90%**
	3	71.59%	60.99%	65.86%
	4	59.50%	41.40%	48.83%
Org.	1	70.79%	49.34%	58.15%
	2	**77.98%**	55.97%	**65.16%**
	3	38.96%	**57.87%**	46.57%
	4	64.68%	50.19%	56.52%
Per.	1	86.67%	68.27%	76.38%
	2	**89.97%**	**77.36%**	**83.19%**
	3	87.58%	76.19%	81.49%
	4	75.19%	63.76%	69.00%

Table 2: Cross-validation test results.

Entity	Agr.	TP	TR	TF
Loc.	1	65.90%	37.52%	47.82%
	2	**83.33%**	**56.28%**	**67.19%**
	3	84.05%	48.12%	61.20%
	4	84.21%	26.10%	39.85%
Org.	1	41.03%	35.54%	38.09%
	2	62.89%	**30.77%**	**41.32%**
	3	**66.00%**	15.23%	24.75%
	4	84.21%	9.85%	17.63%
Per.	1	85.48%	**70.81%**	**77.45%**
	2	69.93%	69.72%	69.83%
	3	86.95%	64.40%	73.99%
	4	**95.02%**	43.29%	59.49%

Table 3: Results from the second test.

The cross-validation test results seem to indicate that, in general, an inter-annotator agreement threshold of 2 produces the most cohesive corpora regardless of the number of workers assigned per email. In all cases, the F-measure peaks at 2 and then begins to drop afterwards.

The results from the second test, using the W3C and Kiha emails as test data, tell a slightly different story, however. One predictable observation from these data is that precision tends to increase as more inter-annotator agreement is required, while recall decreases. We believe that

[9] http://tides.umiacs.umd.edu/webtrec/trecent/parsed_w3c_corpus.html

[10] http://www.cs.cmu.edu/~wcohen/repository.tgz and http://www.cs.cmu.edu/~einat/datasets.html.

[11] http://www.cs.cmu.edu/~einat/datasets.html.

this is due to the fact that entities that were confirmed by more workers tended to be less controversial or ambiguous than those confirmed by fewer. Most surprising about these results is that, although F-measure peaks with the 2-agreement corpora for both LOCATION and ORGANIZATION entities, PERSON entities actually show the worst precision when using the 2-agreement corpus. In the case of PERSON entities, the corpus generated using no inter-annotator agreement at all, i.e., annotator agreement of 1, actually performs the best in terms of F-measure.

Agr.	TP	TR	TF
1	80.56%	62.55%	70.42%
2	85.08%	**67.66%**	**75.37%**
3	93.25%	57.13%	70.86%
4	**95.61%**	39.67%	56.08%

Table 4: Results from the third test.

Data	Agr.	TP	TR	TF	SP	SR	SF
E-M	1	**100%**	57.16%	72.74%	**100%**	50.10%	66.75%
(All)	2	**100%**	**64.31%**	**78.28%**	**100%**	**56.11%**	**71.88%**
	3	**100%**	50.44%	67.06%	**100%**	45.11%	62.18%
	4	**100%**	31.41%	47.81%	**100%**	27.91%	43.64%
E-M	1	**100%**	62.17%	76.68%	**100%**	51.30%	67.81%
(Test)	2	**100%**	**66.36%**	**79.78%**	**100%**	**54.28%**	**70.36%**
	3	**100%**	55.72%	71.56%	**100%**	45.72%	62.76%
	4	**100%**	42.24%	59.39%	**100%**	36.06%	53.01%
E-R	1	36.36%	59.91%	45.25%	40.30%	53.75%	46.07%
(All)	2	70.83%	**65.32%**	67.96%	67.64%	**57.68%**	62.26%
	3	88.69%	58.63%	**70.60%**	82.93%	54.38%	**65.68%**
	4	**93.59%**	43.68%	59.56%	**89.33%**	41.22%	56.41%
E-R	1	**100%**	60.87%	75.68%	**100%**	54.82%	70.82%
(Test)	2	**100%**	**64.70%**	**78.56%**	**100%**	**59.05%**	**74.26%**
	3	**100%**	63.06%	77.34%	**100%**	58.38%	73.72%
	4	**100%**	43.04%	60.18%	**100%**	40.10%	57.25%

Table 5: Results from the fourth test.

With the third test, however, the results are more in line with those from the cross-validation tests: F-measure peaks with the 2-agreement corpus and drops off as the threshold increases. Most likely these results can be considered more significant than those from the second test, since this test corpus contains almost 20 times the number of documents.

For the fourth test, we report both token-level statistics and span-level statistics (i.e., where credit for partially correct entity boundaries is not awarded) in order to increase comparability with Minkov *et al.* (2005). With one exception, these tests seem to show again that the highest F-measure comes from the annotator created using an agreement level of 2, confirming results from the first and third tests.

The fourth test may also be directly compared to the results in Minkov *et al.* (2005), which report span F-measure scores of 59.0% on Enron-Meetings and 68.1% on Enron-Random, for a CRF-based recognizer using the "Basic" feature set (which is identical to ours) and using the "train" division for training and the "test" division for testing. In both cases, our best-performing annotators exceed these scores – an 11.5% improvement on Enron-Meetings and a 6.16% improvement on Enron-Random. This is an encouraging result, given that our training data largely come from a different source than the test data, and that the labels come from non-experts. We see this as confirmation that very large corpora annotated by Mechanical Turk workers can surpass the quality of smaller corpora annotated by experts.

7 Conclusion

In order to quickly and economically build a large annotated dataset for NER, we leveraged Amazon's Mechanical Turk. MTurk allowed us to build a dataset of 20,609 unique emails with 169,156 total annotations in less than four months. The MTurk worker population responded well to NER tasks, and in particular responded well to the bonus and feedback scheme we put into place to improve annotation quality. The bonus feedback system was designed to improve the transparency of the compensation system and motivate higher quality work over time. Encouragingly, our results indicate that the workers who completed the most documents also had consistently high entity recall, i.e., agreement with other workers, indicating that the system achieved the desired effect.

Given a large body of MTurk annotated documents, we were able to leverage inter-annotator agreement to control the precision and recall of a CRF-based recognizer trained on the data. Importantly, we also showed that inter-annotator agreement can be used to predict the appropriate number of workers to assign to a given email in order to maximize entity recall and reduce costs.

Finally, a direct comparison of the entity recognizers generated from MTurk annotations to those generated from expert annotations was very promising, suggesting that Mechanical Turk is appropriate for NER annotation tasks, when care is taken to manage annotator error.

Acknowledgments

Thanks to Dolores Labs for the initial version of the UI, and thanks to Amazon and the 798 Mechanical Turk workers for making this work possible.

References

Michele Banko and Eric Brill. 2001. Scaling to very very large corpora for natural language disambiguation. In *ACL '01*:26-33.

Chris Callison-Burch. 2009. Fast, cheap, and creative: evaluating translation quality using Amazon's Mechanical Turk. In *EMNLP '09:*286-295.

Doug Downey, Matthew Broadhead, and Oren Etzioni. 2007. Locating complex named entities in web text. In *IJCAI '07*.

Ralph Grishman and Beth Sundheim. 1996. Message Understanding Conference-6: a brief history. In *Proceedings of the 16th conference on Computational Linguistics*:466-471.

Aniket Kittur, Ed H. Chi, and Bongwon Suh. 2008. Crowdsourcing user studies with Mechanical Turk. In *Proceedings of CHI 2008*.

Zornitsa Kozareva. 2006. Bootstrapping named entity recognition with automatically generated gazetteer lists. In *Proceedings of the Eleventh Conference of the European Chapter of the Association for Computational Linguistics*:15-21.

Andrei Mikheev, Marc Moens, and Claire Grover. 1999. Named entity recognition without gazetteers. In *Proceedings of the Ninth Conference of the European chapter of the Association for Computational Linguistics*:1-8.

Einat Minkov, Richard C. Wang, and William W. Cohen. 2005. Extracting personal names from email: applying named entity recognition to informal text. In *HTL '05*:443-450.

David Nadeau and Satoshi Sekine. 2007. A survey of named entity recognition and classification. *Linguisticae Investigationes*, 30(1):3-26.

Preslav Nakov. 2008. Noun compound interpretation using paraphrasing verbs: Feasibility study. In *Proceedings of the 13th international conference on Artificial Intelligence: Methodology, Systems and Applications* (*AIMSA 2008*):103–117.

Jason Pontin. 2007. Artificial Intelligence, With Help From the Humans. In *New York Times* (March 25, 2007).

Burr Settles. 2004. Biomedical named entity recognition using conditional random fields and rich feature sets. In *Proceedings of the COLING 2004 International Joint Workshop on Natural Language Processing in Biomedicine and its Applications*.

Rion Snow, Brendan O'Connor, Daniel Jurafsky, and Andrew Y. Ng. 2008. Cheap and fast – but is it good?: evaluating non-expert annotations for natural language tasks. In *EMNLP '08*:254-263.

Alexander Sorokin and David Forsyth. Utility data annotation with Amazon MTurk. In *Proceedings of Computer Vision and Pattern Recognition Workshop at CVPR'08*.

Annotating Named Entities in Twitter Data with Crowdsourcing

Tim Finin, Will Murnane, Anand Karandikar, Nicholas Keller and Justin Martineau
Computer Science and Electrical Engineering
University of Maryland, Baltimore County
Baltimore MD 21250
(finin,willm1,anandk1,nick6,jm1)@umbc.edu

Mark Dredze
Human Language Technology Center of Excellence
Johns Hopkins University
Baltimore MD 21211
mdredze@cs.jhu.edu

Abstract

We describe our experience using both Amazon Mechanical Turk (MTurk) and CrowdFlower to collect simple named entity annotations for Twitter status updates. Unlike most genres that have traditionally been the focus of named entity experiments, Twitter is far more informal and abbreviated. The collected annotations and annotation techniques will provide a first step towards the full study of named entity recognition in domains like Facebook and Twitter. We also briefly describe how to use MTurk to collect judgements on the quality of "word clouds."

1 Introduction and Dataset Description

Information extraction researchers commonly work on popular formal domains, such as news articles. More diverse studies have included broadcast news transcripts, blogs and emails (Strassel et al., 2008). However, extremely informal domains, such as Facebook, Twitter, YouTube or Flickr are starting to receive more attention. Any effort aimed at studying these informal genres will require at least a minimal amount of labeled data for evaluation purposes.

This work details how to efficiently annotate large volumes of data, for information extraction tasks, at low cost using MTurk (Snow et al., 2008; Callison-Burch, 2009). This paper describes a case study for information extraction tasks involving short, informal messages from Twitter. Twitter is a large multi-user site for broadcasting short informal messages. Twitter is an extreme example of an informal genre (Java et al., 2007) as users frequently abbreviate their posts to fit within the specified limit. Twitter is a good choice because it is very popular: Twitter users generate a tremendous number of status updates (tweets) every day[1]. This is a good genre to work on named entity extraction since many tweets refer to and contain updates about named entities.

Our Twitter data set has over 150 million tweets from 1.5 million users collected over a period of three years. Tweets are unlike formal text. They are limited to a maximum of 140 characters, a limit originally set to allow them to fit into an SMS message. Consequently, the use of acronyms and both standard and non-standard abbreviations (e.g., *b4* for before and *ur* for your) are very common. Tweets tend to be telegraphic and often consist of sentence fragments or other ungrammatical sequences. Normal capitalization rules (e.g., for proper names, book titles, etc.) are commonly ignored.

Furthermore, users have adopted numerous conventions including hashtags, user mentions, and retweet markers. A hashtag (e.g., #earthquake) is a token beginning with a '#' character that denotes one of the topic of a status. Hashtags can be used as pure metadata or serve both as a word and as metadata, as the following two examples show.

- EvanEcullen: #chile #earthquake #tsunami They heard nothing of a tsunami until it slammed into their house with an unearthly http://tl.gd/d798d
- LarsVonD: Know how to help #Chile after the #Earthquake

[1]Pingdom estimated that there were nearly 40 million tweets a day in January 2010 (pingdom.com, 2010).

Proceedings of the NAACL HLT 2010 Workshop on Creating Speech and Language Data with Amazon's Mechanical Turk, pages 80–88,
Los Angeles, California, June 2010.

(1) *report from the economist: #chile counts the cost of a devastating earthquake and makes plans for recovery. http://bit.ly/dwoQMD* Note: "the economist" was not recognized as an ORG.
(2) *how come when george bush wanted to take out millions for the war congress had no problem...but whe obama wants money for healthcare the ...* Note: Both "george bush" and "obama" were missed as PERs.
(3) *RT @woodmuffin: jay leno interviewing sarah palin: the seventh seal starts to show a few cracks* Note: RT (code for a re-tweet) was mistaken as a position and sarah palin missed as a person.

Table 1: Standard named entity systems trained on text from newswire articles and other well formed documents lose accuracy when applied to short status updates.

The Twitter community also has a convention where user names preceded by an @ character (known as "mentions") at the beginning of a status indicate that it is a message directed at that user. A user mention in the middle of a message is interpreted as a general reference to that user. Both uses are shown in this status:

- paulasword: @obama quit calling @johnboener a liar, you liar

The token RT is used as a marker that a person is forwarding a tweet originally sent by another user. Normally the re-tweet symbol begins the message and is immediately followed by the user mention of the original author or sometimes a chain of re-tweeters ending with the original author, as in

- politicsiswar: RT @KatyinIndy @SamiShamieh: Ghost towns on rise under Obama http://j.mp/cwJSUg #tcot #gop (Deindustrialization of U.S.- Generation Zero)

Finally, "smileys" are common in Twitter statuses to signal the users' sentiment, as in the following.

- sallytherose: Just wrote a 4-page paper in an hour and a half. BOiiiiii I'm getting good at this. :) Leftover Noodles for dinner as a reward. :D

The Twitter search service also uses these to retrieve tweets matching a query with positive or negative sentiment.

Typical named entity recognition systems have been trained on formal documents, such as news wire articles. Their performance on text from very different sources, especially informal genres such as Twitter tweets or Facebook status updates, is poor. In fact, "Systems analyzing correctly about 90% of the sequences from a journalistic corpus can have a decrease of performance of up to 50% on more informal texts." (Poibeau and Kosseim, 2001) However, many large scale information extraction systems require extracting and integrating useful information from online social networking sources that are informal such as Twitter, Facebook, Blogs, YouTube and Flickr.

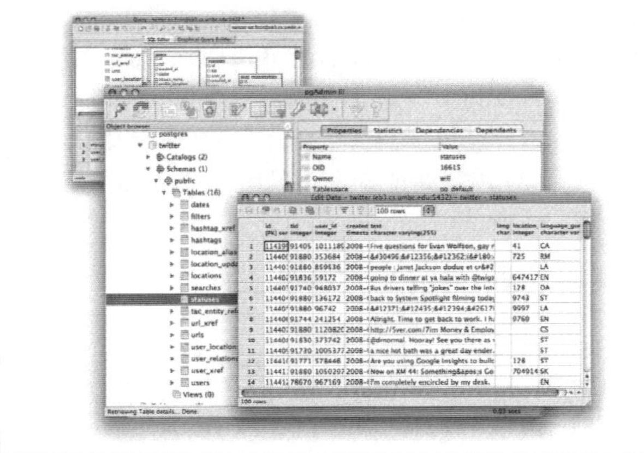

Figure 1: Our Twitter collection is stored in a relational database and also in the Lucene information retrieval system.

To illustrate the problem we applied both the NLTK (Bird et al., 2009) and the Stanford named entity recognizers (Finkel et al., 2005) without retraining to a sample Twitter dataset with mixed results. We have observed many failures, both false positives and false negatives. Table 1 shows some examples of these.

2 Task design

We developed separate tasks on CrowdFlower and MTurk using a common collection of Twitter statuses and asked workers to perform the same annotation task in order to fully understand the features that each provides, and to determine the total amount of work necessary to produce a result on each service. MTurk has the advantage of using standard HTML and Javascript instead of CrowdFlower's CML. However MTurk has inferior data verification, in that the service only provides a threshold on worker agreement as a form of quality control.

This is quite poor when tasks are more complicated than a single boolean judgment, as with the case at hand. CrowdFlower works across multiple services and does verification against gold standard data, and can get more judgements to improve quality in cases where it's necessary.

3 Annotation guidelines

The task asked workers to look at Twitter individual status messages (tweets) and use a toggle button to tag each word with person (PER), organization (ORG), location (LOC), or "none of the above" (NONE). Each word also had a check box (labeled ???) to indicate that uncertainty. We provided the workers with annotation guidelines adapted from the those developed by the Linguistic Data Consortium (Linguistic Data Consortium – LCTL Team, 2006) which were in turn based on guidelines used for MUC-7 (Chinchor and Robinson, 1997).

We deliberately kept our annotation goals simple: We only asked workers to identify three basic types of named entities.

Our guidelines read:

> An entity is a object in the world like a place or person and a *named entity* is a phrase that uniquely refers to an object by its proper name (Hillary Clinton), acronym (IBM), nickname (Opra) or abbreviation (Minn.).
>
> *Person* (PER) entities are limited to humans (living, deceased, fictional, deities, ...) identified by name, nickname or alias. Don't include titles or roles (Ms., President, coach). Include suffix that are part of a name (e.g., Jr., Sr. or III).
>
> *Organization* (ORG) entities are limited to corporations, institutions, government agencies and other groups of people defined by an established organizational structure. Some examples are businesses (Bridgestone Sports Co.), stock ticker symbols (NASDAQ), multinational organizations (European Union), political parties (GOP) non-generic government entities (the State Department), sports teams (the Yankees), and military groups (the Tamil Tigers). Do not tag 'generic' entities like "the government" since these are not unique proper names referring to a specific ORG.
>
> *Location* (LOC) entities include names of politically or geographically defined places (cities, provinces, countries, international regions, bodies of water, mountains, etc.). Locations also include man-made structures like airports, highways, streets, factories and monuments.

We instructed annotators to ignore other types of named entities, e.g., events (World War II), products (iPhone), animals (Cheetah), inanimate objects and monetary units (the Euro) and gave them four principles to follow when tagging:

- Tag words according to their *meaning* in the context of the tweet.
- Only tag *names*, i.e., words that directly and uniquely refer to entities.
- Only tag names of the types *PER*,*ORG*, and *LOC*.
- Use the *???* checkbox to indicate uncertainty in your tag.

3.1 Data selection

We created a "gold standard" data set of about 400 tweets to train and screen workers on MTurk, to salt the MTurk data with worker evaluation data, for use on CrowdFlower, and to evaluate the performance of the final NER system after training on the crowdsourced annotations. We preselected tweets to annotate using the NLTK named entity recognizer to select statuses that were thought to contain named entities of the desired types (PER, ORG, LOC).

Initial experiments suggested that a worker can annotate about 400 tweets an hour. Based on this, we loaded each MTurk Human Intelligence Tasks (HIT) with five tweets, and paid workers five cents per HIT. Thus, if we require that each tweet be annotated by two workers, we would be able to produce about 4,400 raw annotated tweets with the $100 grant from Amazon, accounting for their 10% overhead price.

3.2 CrowdFlower

We also experimented with CrowdFlower, a crowdsourcing service that uses various worker channels like MTurk and SamaSource[2] and provides an enhanced set of management and analytic tools. We were interested in understanding the advantages and disadvantages compared to using MTurk directly.

[2]http://www.samasource.org/

Figure 2: CrowdFlower is an enhanced service that feeds into MTurk and other crowdsourcing systems. It provides convenient management tools that show the performance of workers for a task.

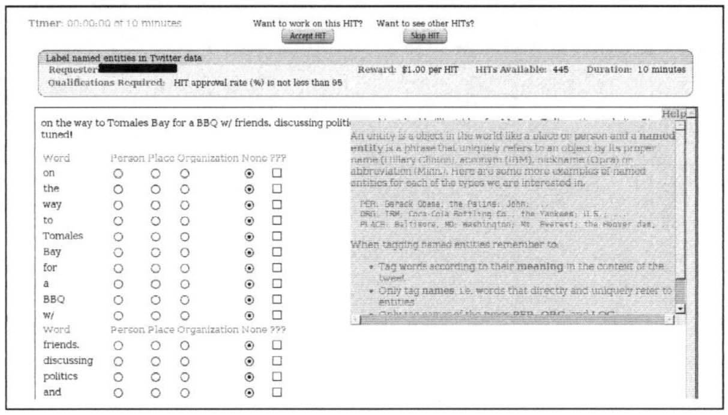

Figure 3: In the MTurk interface a tweet is shown in its entirety at the top, then a set of radio buttons and a checkbox is shown for each word of the tweet. These allow the user to pick the annotation for each word, and indicate uncertainty in labeling.

We prepared a basic front-end for our job using the CrowdFlower Markup Language (CML) and custom JavaScript. We used the CrowdFlower interface to calibrate our job and to decide the pay rate. It considers various parameters like amount of time required to complete a sample task and the desired accuracy level to come up with a pay rate.

One attractive feature lets one provide a set of "gold standard" tasks that pair data items with correct responses. These are automatically mixed into the stream of regular tasks that workers process. If a worker makes errors in one of these gold standard tasks, she gets immediate feedback about her error and the correct answer is shown. CrowdFlower claims that error rates are reduced by a factor of two when gold standards are used(crowdflower.com, 2010). The interface shown in Figure 2 shows the number of gold tasks the user has seen, and how many they have gotten correct.

CrowdFlower's management tools provides a detailed analysis of the workers for a job, including the trust level, accuracy and past accuracy history associated with each worker. In addition, the output records include the geographical region associated with each worker, information that may be useful for some tasks.

3.3 MTurk

The current iteration of our MTurk interface is shown in Figure 3. Each tweet is shown at the top of the HIT interface so that it can easily be read for context. Then a table is displayed with each word of the tweet down the side, and radio buttons to pick what kind of entity each word is. Every ten rows, the header is repeated, to allow the worker to scroll down the page and still see the column labels. The interface also provides a checkbox allows the worker to indicate uncertainty in labeling a word.

We expect that our data will include some tricky cases where an annotator, even an experienced one, may be unsure whether a word is part of a named entity and/or what type it is. For example, is 'Baltimore Visionary Art Museum' a LOC followed by a three word ORG, or a four-word ORG? We considered and rejected using hierarchical named entities in order to keep the annotation task simple. Another example that might give an annotator pause is a phrase like 'White House' can be used as a LOC or ORG, depending on the context.

This measure can act as a measure of a worker's quality: if they label many things as "uncertain", we might guess that they are not producing good results in general. Also, the uncertainty allows for a finer-grained measure of how closely the results from two workers for the same tweet match: if the workers disagree on the tagging of a particular word, but agree that it is not certain, we could decide that this word is a bad example and not use it as training data.

Finally, a help screen is available. When the user mouses over the word "Help" in the upper right, the guidelines discussed in Section 3 are displayed. The screenshot in Figure 3 shows the help dialog expanded.

The MTurk interface uses hand-written Javascript to produce the table of words, radio buttons, and

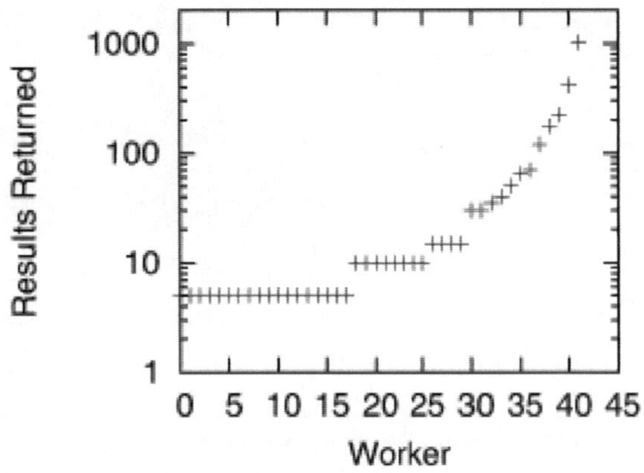

Figure 4: Only about one-third of the workers did more than three HITs and a a few prolific workers accounted for most of our data.

checkboxes. The form elements have automatically generated names, which MTurk handles neatly. Additional Javascript code collects location information from the workers, based on their IP address. A service provided by Geobytes[3] provides the location data.

4 Results from MTurk

Our dataset was broken into HITs of four previously unlabeled tweets, and one previously labeled tweet (analogous to the "gold" data used by CrowdFlower). We submitted 251 HITs, each of which was to be completed twice, and the job took about 15 hours. Total cost for this job was $27.61, for a total cost per tweet of about 2.75 cents each (although we also paid to have the gold tweets annotated again). 42 workers participated, mostly from the US and India, with Australia in a distant third place. Most workers did only a single HIT, but most HITs were done by a single worker. Figure 4 shows more detail.

After collecting results from MTurk, we had to come up with a strategy for determining which of the results (if any) were filled randomly. To do this, we implemented an algorithm much like Google's PageRank (Brin and Page, 1998) to judge the amount of inter-worker agreement. Pseudocode for our algorithm is presented in Figure 5.

This algorithm doesn't strictly measure worker quality, but rather worker agreement, so it's important to ensure that the workers it judges as having high agreement values are actually making high-quality judgements. Figure 6 shows the worker agreement values plotted against the number of results a particular worker completed. The slope of this plot (more results returned tends to give higher scores) is interpreted to be because practice makes perfect: the more HITs a worker completes, the more experience they have with the task, and the more accurate their results will be.

```
WORKER-AGREE : results → scores
1  worker_ids ← ENUMERATE(KEYS(results))
   ▷ Initialize A
2  for worker1 ∈ worker_ids
3      do for worker2 ∈ worker_ids
4             do A[worker1, worker2]
                   ← SIMILARITY(results[worker1],
                                results[worker2])
   ▷ Normalize columns of A so that they sum to 1 (elided)
   ▷ Initialize x to be normal: each worker
     is initially trusted equally.
5  x ← ⟨1/√n, ..., 1/√n⟩
   ▷ Find the largest eigenvector of A, which
     corresponds to the agreement-with-group
     value for each worker.
6  i ← 0
7  while i < max_iter
8      do xnew ← NORMALIZE(A × x)
9         diff ← xnew − x
10        x = xnew
11        if diff < tolerance
12          then break
13        i ← i + 1
14 for workerID, workerNum ∈ worker_ids
15     do scores[workerID] ← x[workerNum]
16 return scores
```

Figure 5: Intra-worker agreement algorithm. MTurk results are stored in an associative array, with worker IDs as keys and lists of HIT results as values, and worker scores are floating point values. Worker IDs are mapped to integers to allow standard matrix notation. The Similarity function in line four just returns the fraction of HITs done by two workers where their annotations agreed.

So, with this agreement metric established, we set out to find out how well it agreed with our expectation that it would also function as a quality metric. Consider those workers that completed only a single HIT (there are 18 of them): how well did they do their jobs, and where did they end up ranked as a result? Since each HIT is composed of five tweets,

[3] http://www.geobytes.com/

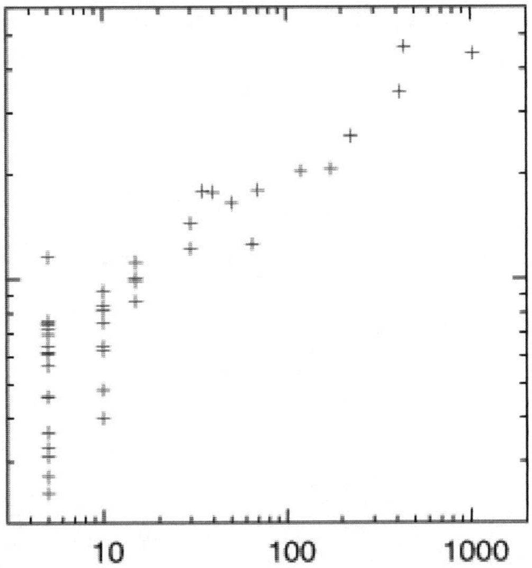

Figure 6: This log-log plot of worker agreement scores versus the number of results clearly shows that workers who have done more HITs have better inter-annotator agreement scores.

Score	0.0243	Score	0.0364	Score	0.0760
Trying	org	Newbie	person	Trying	none
to	org	here	none	out	none
decide	org	nice	none	TwittEarth	org
if	org	to	none	-	none
it's	org	meet	none	Good	none
worth	place	you	none	graphics.	none
hanging	org	all	none	Fun	none
around	org			but	none
until	org			useless.	none
the	none			(URL)	none
final	org				
implosion	org				

Figure 7: These sample annotations represent the range of worker quality for three workers who did only one HIT. The first is an apparently random annotation, the second a plausible but incorrect one, and the third a correct annotation. Our algorithm assigned these workers scores aligned with their product quality.

even such a small sample can contain a lot of data.

Figure 7 shows a sample annotation for three tweets, each from a worker who did only one HIT, and the ranking that the worker received for doing that annotation. The worst scoring one is apparently a random fill: there's no correlation at all between the answers and the correct ones. The middle tweet is improved: "Newbie" isn't a person in this context, but it's a mistake a non-native speaker might make, and everything else is right, and the score is higher. The last tweet is correctly labeled within our parameters, and scores the highest. This experiment shows that our agreement metric functions well as a correctness metric.

Also of interest is the raw effectiveness of MTurk workers; did they manage to tag tweets as well as our experts? After investigating the data, our verdict is that the answer is not quite—but by carefully combining the tags that two people give the same tweet it is possible to get good answers nevertheless, at much lower cost than employing a single expert.

5 Results from CrowdFlower

Our CrowdFlower task involved 30 tweets. Each tweet was further split into tokens resulting in 506 units as interpreted by CrowdFlower's system. We required a total 986 judgments. In addition, we were

Figure 8: CrowdFlower provides good interfaces to manage crowdsourcing tasks. This view lets us to monitor the number of judgements in each category.

required to generate thirteen "gold" data, which is the minimum required by the service. Every gold answer has an optional text with it to inform workers why we believe our answer is the correct one and theirs is incorrect. This facilitates gradually training workers up to the point where they can provide reliably correct results. Figure 8 shows the interface CrowdFlower provides to monitor the number of judgements in each category.

We used the calibration interface that CrowdFlower provides to fix the price for our task (Figure 9). It considers various parameters like the time required per unit and desired accuracy level, and also adds a flat 33% markup on the actual labor costs. We divided the task into a set of assignments where each assignment had three tweets and was paid five cents. We set the time per unit as 30 seconds, so, based on the desired accuracy level and markup overhead, our job's cost was \$2.19. This comes to \$2 hourly pay per worker, assuming they take the whole 30 sec-

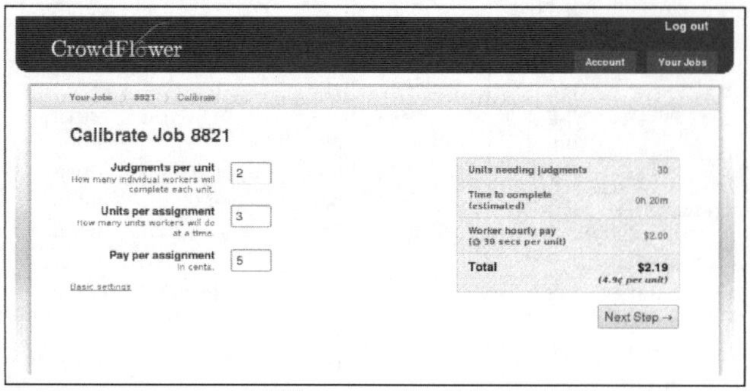

Figure 9: CrowdFlower has an interface that makes it easy to select an appropriate price for a task.

onds to complete the task.

6 Cloud Comparison

MTurk can also be used to efficiently evaluate results requiring human judgments. We implemented an additional HIT to evaluate a new technique we developed to generate "word clouds." In this task workers choose which of two word clouds generated from query results by two different algorithms provides a more useful high level description that can highlight important features and opinions about the query topic.

Evaluating how well a set of words describes and highlights the important features and opinions pertaining to the subject of the query is subjective, which necessitates human evaluations. MTurk workers were given two word clouds, one from our technique and the other from a baseline relevance feedback technique (Rocchio (Rocchio, 1971)), for each query. Queries were shown with a short descriptive blurb to disambiguate it from possible alternatives, reveal the intent of the user who created the query, and provide a short description of it for workers who were unfamiliar with the query subject. Wikipedia links were provided, when applicable, for anyone needing further information about the query subject. Workers were asked to use a slider to determine which cloud better represented the key concepts related to the query. The slider would snap into one of eleven positions, which were labeled with value judgments they represented. The center value indicates that the two clouds were equally good. Figure 10 shows the final query interface.

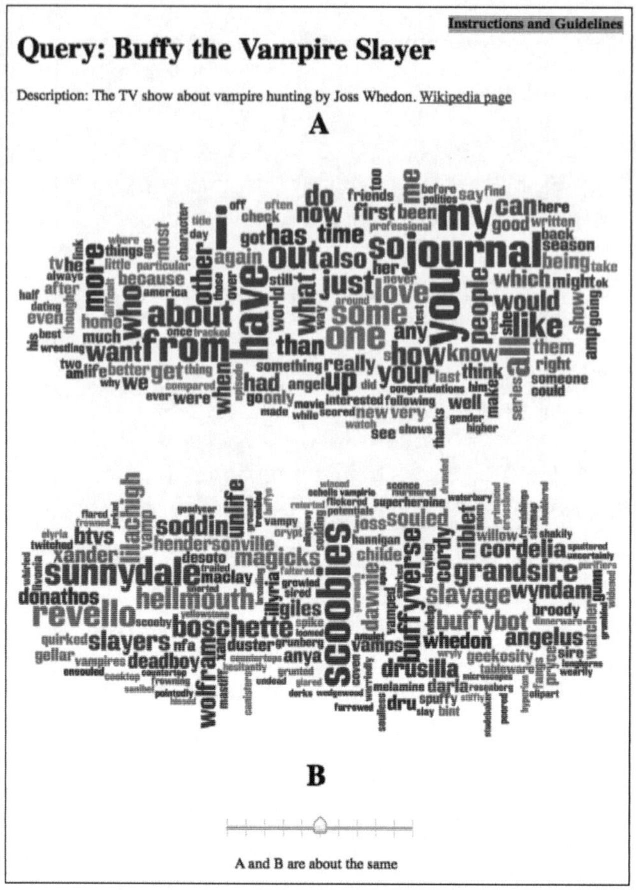

Figure 10: MTurk workers were asked which word cloud they thought best represented returned the results of a query, in this case "Buffy the Vampire Slayer".

6.1 Results

Since MTurk workers are paid per task they complete, there is an incentive to do low quality work and even to randomly guess to get tasks done as fast as possible. To ensure a high quality evaluation we included in every batch of five queries a quality control question. Quality control questions were designed to look exactly like the regular cloud comparisons, but only one of the two clouds displayed was actually from the query in the description. The other word cloud was generated from a different query with no relation to the real query, and hand checked to make sure that anyone who was doing a respectable job would agree that the off-topic word cloud was a poor result for the query. If a worker's response indicated that the off topic cloud was as good as or better than the real cloud then they failed that control question, otherwise they passed.

We asked that twelve workers label each set of questions. We only used results from workers that answered at least seven control questions with an average accuracy rating of at least 75%. This left us with a pool of eight reliable workers with an average accuracy on control questions of about 91%. Every question was labeled by at least five different workers with a mode of seven.

Workers were not told which technique produced which cloud. Techniques were randomly assigned to either cloud A or B to prevent people from entering into a "cloud A is always better" mentality. The position of the quality control questions were randomly assigned in each set of five cloud comparisons. The links to the cloud images were anonymized to random numbers followed by the letter A or B for their position to prevent workers from guessing anything about either the query or the technique that generated the cloud.

We applied a filter to remove the query words from all word clouds. First of all, it would be a dead giveaway on the control questions. Second, the query words are already known and thus provide no extra information about the query to the user while simultaneously taking up the space that could be used to represent other more interesting words. Third, their presence and relative size compared to the baseline could cause users to ignore other features especially when doing a quick scan.

The slider scores were converted into numerical scores ranging from -5 to +5, with zero representing that the two clouds were equal. We averaged the score for each cloud comparison, and determined that for 44 out of 55 clouds workers found our technique to be better than the baseline approach.

6.2 Issues

We faced some issues with the CrowdFlower system. These included incorrect calibration for jobs, errors downloading results from completed jobs, price displayed on MTurk being different that what was set through CrowdFlower and gold standard data not getting stored on CrowdFlower system. Another problem was with the system's 10-token limit on gold standards, which is not yet resolved at the time of this writing. On the whole, the CrowdFlower team has been very quick to respond to our problems and able to correct the problems we encountered.

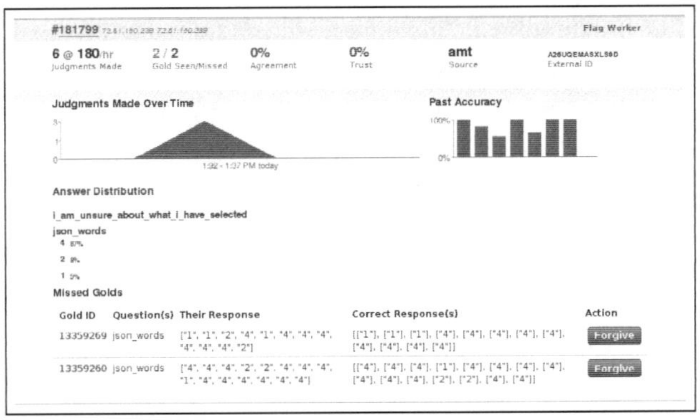

Figure 11: Statistics for worker #181799. The interface has an option to "forgive" the worker for missing gold and an option to "flag" the worker so that the answers are excluded while returning the final set of judgments. It also displays workers ID, past accuracy and source, e.g. MTurk.

6.3 Live Analytics

CrowdFlower'a analytics panel facilitates viewing the live responses. The trust associated with each worker can be seen under the workers panel. Workers who do a large amount of work with low trust are likely scammers or automated bots. Good gold data ensures that their work is rejected. The system automatically pauses a job when the ratio of untrusted to trusted judgments exceeds a certain mark. This was particularly helpful for us to rectify some of our gold data. Currently, the job is being completed with 61% accuracy for gold data. This could be due to the current issue we are facing as described above. It's also possible to view statistics for individual workers, as shown in Figure 11.

7 Conclusion

Crowdsourcing is an effective way to collect annotations for natural language and information retrieval research. We found both MTurk and CrowdFlower to be flexible, relatively easy to use, capable of producing usable data, and very cost effective.

Some of the extra features and interface options that CrowdFlower provided were very useful, but did their were problems with their "gold standard" agreement evaluation tools. Their support staff was very responsive and helpful, mitigating some of these problems. We were able to duplicate some of the "gold standard" functionality on MTurk directly by generating our own mix of regular and quality control queries. We did not attempt to provide immediate feedback to workers who enter a wrong answer for the "gold standard" queries, however.

With these labeled tweets, we plan to train an entity recognizer using the Stanford named entity recognizer[4], and run it on our dataset. After using this trained entity recognizer to find the entities in our data, we will compare its accuracy to the existing recognized entities, which were recognized by an ER trained on newswire articles. We will also attempt to do named entity linking and entity resolution on the entire corpus.

We look forward to making use of the data we collected in our research and expect that we will use these services in the future when we need human judgements.

Acknowledgments

This work was done with partial support from the Office of Naval Research and the Johns Hopkins University Human Language Technology Center of Excellence. We thank both Amazon and Dolores Labs for grants that allowed us to use their systems for the experiments.

References

S. Bird, E. Klein, and E. Loper. 2009. *Natural language processing with Python*. Oreilly & Associates Inc.

S. Brin and L. Page. 1998. The anatomy of a large-scale hypertextual web search engine. In *Seventh International World-Wide Web Conference (WWW 1998)*.

C. Callison-Burch. 2009. Fast, Cheap, and Creative: Evaluating Translation Quality Using Amazons Mechanical Turk. In *Proceedings of EMNLP 2009*.

N. Chinchor and P. Robinson. 1997. MUC-7 named entity task definition. In *Proceedings of the 7th Message Understanding Conference*. NIST.

crowdflower.com. 2010. The error rates without the gold standard is more than twice as high as when we do use a gold standard. http://crowdflower.com/general/examples. Accessed on April 11, 2010.

J.R. Finkel, T. Grenager, and C. Manning. 2005. Incorporating non-local information into information extraction systems by gibbs sampling. In *Proceedings of the 43nd Annual Meeting of the Association for Computational Linguistics (ACL 2005)*, volume 100, pages 363–370.

A. Java, X. Song, T. Finin, and B. Tseng. 2007. Why we twitter: understanding microblogging usage and communities. In *Proceedings of the 9th WebKDD and 1st SNA-KDD 2007 workshop on Web mining and social network analysis*, pages 56–65. ACM.

Linguistic Data Consortium – LCTL Team. 2006. Simple named entity guidelines for less commonly taught languages, March. Version 6.5.

pingdom.com. 2010. Twitter: Now more than 1 billion tweets per month. http://royal.pingdom.com/2010/02/10/twitter-now-more-than-1-billion-tweets-per-month/, February. Accessed on February 15, 2010.

T. Poibeau and L. Kosseim. 2001. Proper Name Extraction from Non-Journalistic Texts. In *Computational linguistics in the Netherlands 2000: selected papers from the eleventh CLIN Meeting*, page 144. Rodopi.

J. Rocchio. 1971. Relevance feedback in information retrieval. In G. Salton, editor, *The SMART Retrieval System: Experiments in Automatic Document Processing*. Prentice-Hall.

R. Snow, B. O'Connor, D. Jurafsky, and A.Y. Ng. 2008. Cheap and fast—but is it good?: evaluating non-expert annotations for natural language tasks. In *Proceedings of the Conference on Empirical Methods in Natural Language Processing*, pages 254–263. Association for Computational Linguistics.

Stephanie Strassel, Mark Przybocki, Kay Peterson, Zhiyi Song, and Kazuaki Maeda. 2008. Linguistic resources and evaluation techniques for evaluation of cross-document automatic content extraction. In *Proceedings of the 6th International Conference on Language Resources and Evaluation*.

[4]http://nlp.stanford.edu/software/CRF-NER.shtml

MTurk Crowdsourcing: A Viable Method for Rapid Discovery of Arabic Nicknames?

Chiara Higgins
George Mason University

Fairfax, VA. 22030, USA
chiara.higgins@gmail.com

Elizabeth McGrath
MITRE

McLean, VA. 20112, USA
emcgrath@mitre.org

Lailla Moretto
MITRE

McLean, VA. 20112, USA
lmoretto@mitre.org

Abstract

This paper presents findings on using crowdsourcing via Amazon Mechanical Turk (MTurk) to obtain Arabic nicknames as a contribution to exiting Named Entity (NE) lexicons. It demonstrates a strategy for increasing MTurk participation from Arab countries. The researchers validate the nicknames using experts, MTurk workers, and Google search and then compare them against the Database of Arabic Names (DAN). Additionally, the experiment looks at the effect of pay rate on speed of nickname collection and documents an advertising effect where MTurk workers respond to existing work batches, called Human Intelligence Tasks (HITs), more quickly once similar higher paying HITs are posted.

1 Introduction

The question this experiment investigates is: can MTurk crowdsourcing add undocumented nicknames to existing Named Entity (NE) lexicons?

This experiment seeks to produce nicknames to add to DAN Version 1.1, which contains 147,739 lines of names. While DAN does not list nicknames as a metadata type, it does include some commonly known nicknames.

1.1 Traditional collection methods are costly

According to DAN's website, administrators collect nicknames using a team of software engineers and native speakers. They also draw on a "large variety of sources including websites, corpora, books, phone directories, dictionaries, encyclopedias, and university rosters" (Halpern, 2009). Collecting names by searching various media sources or employing linguists and native speakers is a massive effort requiring significant expenditure of time and money.

1.2 Crowdsourcing might work better

The experiment uses crowdsourcing via MTurk since it offers a web-based problem-solving model and quickly engages a large number of international workers at low cost. Furthermore, previous research shows the effectiveness of crowdsourcing as a method of accomplishing labor intensive natural language processing tasks (Callison-Burch, 2009) and the effectiveness of using MTurk for a variety of natural language automation tasks (Snow, Jurafsy, & O'Connor, 2008).

The experiment answers the following questions:

- Can we discover valid nicknames not currently in DAN?
- What do we need to pay workers to gather nicknames rapidly?
- How do we convey the task to guide non-experts and increase participation from Arab countries?

Proceedings of the NAACL HLT 2010 Workshop on Creating Speech and Language Data with Amazon's Mechanical Turk, pages 89–92,
Los Angeles, California, June 2010.

2 Experiment Design

The experiment contains three main phases. First, nicknames are gathered from MTurk workers. Second, the collected names are validated via MTurk, internet searches, and expert opinion. Finally, the verified names are compared against the available list of names in the DAN.

2.1 Collecting nicknames on MTurk

In this phase, we open HITs on MTurk requesting workers to enter an Arabic nickname they have heard. In addition to writing a nickname, the workers input where they heard the name and their country of residence.

HIT instructions are kept simple and written in short sentences to guide non-experts and include a basic definition of a nickname. To encourage participation of native Arabic speakers, the instructions and search words are in Arabic as well as English. Workers are asked to input names in the Arabic alphabet, thus eliminating any worker who does not use Arabic often enough to warrant having an Arabic keyboard. Further clarifying the task, words highlighted in red, “Arabic alphabet”, emphasize what the worker needs to do.

While seeking to encourage participation from Arab countries, we choose not to block participation from other countries since there are Arabic speakers and immigrants in many countries where Arabic is not the main language.

To evaluate the effect of pay rate on nickname collection rate, HITs have a variety of pay rates. HITs paying $0.03 per HIT are kept up throughout the experiment, while HITs paying $0.05 and finally $0.25 are added later.

2.2 Nickname validation phase

Vetting the nicknames, involves a Google check and asking 3 experts and 5 MTurk workers to rate each name that is submitted in a valid format.

Each expert and MTurk worker has the opportunity to rate the likelihood the nickname would occur in the Arab world on a Likert scale (Strongly Agree, Agree, Neither Agree nor Disagree, Disagree, Strongly Disagree).

The entire validation process is completed twice, once paying the workers $.01 per validation and once paying $.05 per validation to allow us to further research the effect of pay on HIT collection rate.

The Google check vets the names to see if they occur on the web thus eliminating, any nicknames that are nowhere in print and therefore not currently necessary additions to NE lexicons.

2.3 Compare data to ground truth in DAN

The third phase is a search for exact matches for the validated nicknames in DAN to determine if they represent new additions to the lexicon.

3 Results

MTurk workers generated 332 nicknames during the course of this experiment. Because the initial collection rate was slower than expected, we validated and compared only the first 108 names to report results related to the usefulness of MTurk in nickname collection. Results involving pay and collection rate draw on the full data.

Based on self-reported data, approximately 35% of the respondents came from the Arabic speaking countries of Morocco, Egypt, Lebanon, Jordan, UAE, and Dubai. 46% were submitted from India, 13% from the U.S. and 5% elsewhere.

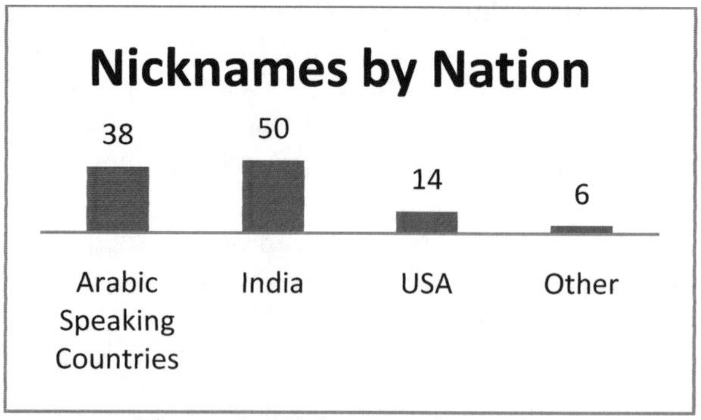

Figure 1. Nicknames by nation

3.1 Validation results

Each of the nicknames was verified by MTurk workers and three experts. On a five-point Likert scale with 1 representing strong disagreement and 5 showing strong agreement, we accepted 51 of the names as valid because the majority (3 of 5 MTurk workers and 2 of 3 experts) scored the name as 3 or higher.

One of the 51 names accepted by other means could not be found in a Google search leaving us with 50 valid nicknames.

Comparing the 50 remaining names to DAN we found that 11 of the valid names were already in the lexicon.

3.2 Effect of increased pay on responses

Holding everything else constant, we increased the worker's pay during nickname collection. On average, \$0.03 delivered 9.8 names a day, for \$0.05 we collected 25 names a day and for \$0.25 we collected 100 names in a day.

We also posted one of our MTurk verification files two times, once at \$0.01 per HIT and once at \$0.05 per HIT, holding everything constant except the pay. Figure 2 shows the speed with which the two batches of HITs were completed. The results show not only an increased collection speed for the higher paying HITs, but also an increased collection speed for the existing lower paying HIT once the higher paying HITs were posted.

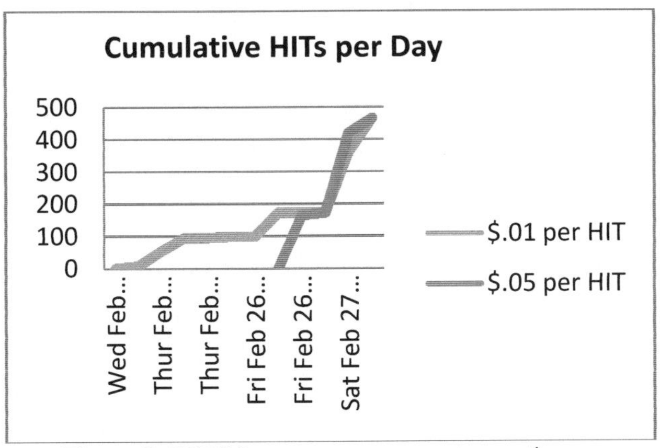

Figure 2. HITS by payment amount over time

4 Conclusions

As our most significant goal, we sought to investigate whether MTurk crowdsourcing could successfully collect undiscovered nicknames to add to an existing NE lexicon.

The results indicate that MTurk is a viable method for collecting nicknames; in the course of the experiment, we successfully produced 39 verified nicknames that we recommend adding to the DAN.

Another goal was to explore the effect of worker pay on HIT completion rate. Our initial collection rate, at \$0.03 per HIT, was only 9.8 names per day. By increasing pay, we were able to speed up the process. At \$0.05 per name, we increased the daily collection rate from 9.8 to 25, and by making the pay rate \$0.25 we collected 100 names in a day. So increasing pay significantly improved collection speed.

While working with pricing for the verification HITs, we were able to quantify an "advertising effect" we had noticed previously where the posting of a higher paying HIT causes existing similar lower paying HITs to be completed more quickly as well. Further research could be conducted to determine a mix of pay rates that maximizes collection rate while minimizing cost.

Furthermore, the experiment shows that by using bilingual directions and requiring typing in Arabic, we were able to increase the participation from Arabic speaking countries. Based on our previous experience where we posted Arabic language related HITs in English only, Arab country participation on MTurk is minimal. Other researchers have also found little MTurk participation from Arabic speaking countries (Ross, Zaldivar, Irani, & Tomlinson, 2009). In this experiment, however, we received more than 35% participation from workers in Arabic speaking countries.

Acknowledgments

Thanks to the MITRE Corporation for providing the ground truth DAN data under their research license agreement with the CJK Dictionary Institute. Also thanks to Trent Rockwood of MITRE for providing expert assistance in the Arabic language and on some technical issues.

References

Callison-Burch, C. (2009). Fast, Cheap, and Creative: Evaluating Translation Quality Using Amazon's Mechanical Turk. *Proceedings of the EMNLP*. Singapore.

Halpern, J. (2009). Lexicon-Driven Approach to the Recognition of Arabic Named Entities. *Second International Conference on Arabic Language Resources and Tools*. Cairo.

Ross, J., Zaldivar, A., Irani, L., & Tomlinson, B. (2009). *Who are the Turkers? Worker Demographics in Amazon*. Department of Informatics, University of California, Irvine.

Snow, R., Jurafsy, D., & O'Connor, B. (2008). Cheap and fast – but is it good?: Evaluating Non-Expert Annotations for Natural Language Tasks. *Proceedings of the 2008 Conference on Empirical Methods in Natural Language Processing*, (pp. 254-263). Honolulu.

An Enriched MT Grammar for Under $100

Omar F. Zaidan and **Juri Ganitkevitch**
Dept. of Computer Science, Johns Hopkins University
Baltimore, MD 21218, USA
{ozaidan, juri}@cs.jhu.edu

Abstract

We propose a framework for improving output quality of machine translation systems, by operating on the level of grammar rule features. Our framework aims to give a boost to grammar rules that appear in the derivations of translation candidates that are deemed to be of good quality, hence making those rules more preferable by the system. To that end, we ask human annotators on Amazon Mechanical Turk to compare translation candidates, and then interpret their preferences of one candidate over another as an implicit preference for one derivation over another, and therefore as an implicit preference for one or more grammar rules. Our framework also allows us to generalize these preferences to grammar rules corresponding to a previously unseen test set, namely rules for which no candidates have been judged.

1 Introduction

When translating between two languages, state-of-the-art statistical machine translation systems (Koehn et al., 2007; Li et al., 2009) generate candidate translations by relying on a set of relevant grammar (or phrase table) entries. Each of those entries, or *rules*, associates a string in the source language with a string in the target language, with these associations typically learned by examining a large parallel bitext. By the very nature of the translation process, a target side sentence $\mathbf{e}$ can be a candidate translation for a source sentence $\mathbf{f}$ only if $\mathbf{e}$ can be constructed using a small subset of the grammar, namely the subset of rules with source side sequences relevant to the word sequence of $\mathbf{f}$. However, even this limited set of candidates (call it $\mathcal{E}(\mathbf{f})$) is quite large, with $|\mathcal{E}(\mathbf{f})|$ growing exponentially in the length of $\mathbf{f}$. The system is able to rank the translations within $\mathcal{E}(\mathbf{f})$ by assigning a score $s(\mathbf{e})$ to each candidate translation. This score is the dot product:

$$s(\mathbf{e}) = \vec{\varphi}(\mathbf{e}) \cdot \vec{w} \tag{1}$$

where $\vec{\varphi}(\mathbf{e})$ is a feature vector characterizing $\mathbf{e}$, and $\vec{w}$ is a system-specific weight vector characterizing the system's belief of how much the different features reflect translation quality. The features of a candidate $\mathbf{e}$ are computed by examining the way $\mathbf{e}$ is constructed (or *derived*), and so if we let $\boldsymbol{d}(\mathbf{e})$ be the derivation of $\mathbf{e}$, the feature vector can be denoted:[1]

$$\vec{\varphi}(\boldsymbol{d}(\mathbf{e})) = \langle \varphi_1(\boldsymbol{d}(\mathbf{e})), \ldots, \varphi_m(\boldsymbol{d}(\mathbf{e})) \rangle \tag{2}$$

where $\varphi_i(\boldsymbol{d}(\mathbf{e}))$ is the value of ith feature function of $\boldsymbol{d}(\mathbf{e})$ (with a corresponding weight w_i in $\vec{w}$).

To compute the score for a candidate, we examine its derivation $\boldsymbol{d}(\mathbf{e})$, enumerating the grammar rules used to construct $\mathbf{e}$: $\boldsymbol{d}(\mathbf{e}) = (r_1, \ldots, r_k)$. Typically, each of the rules will itself have a vector of m features, and we calculate the value of a derivation feature $\varphi_i(\boldsymbol{d}(\mathbf{e}))$ as the sum of the ith feature over all rules in the derivation:

$$\varphi_i(\boldsymbol{d}(\mathbf{e})) = \sum_{r \in \boldsymbol{d}(\mathbf{e})} \varphi_i(r) \tag{3}$$

[1] There are other features computed directly, without examining the derivation (e.g. candidate length, language model score), but we omit these features from the motivation discussion for clarity.

Proceedings of the NAACL HLT 2010 Workshop on Creating Speech and Language Data with Amazon's Mechanical Turk, pages 93–98,
Los Angeles, California, June 2010.

These features are usually either relative frequencies estimated from the training corpus, relating the rule's source and target sides, or features that characterize the structure of the rule itself, independently from the corpus.

Either way, the weight w_i is chosen so as to reflect some belief regarding the correlation between the ith feature and translation quality. This is usually done by choosing weights that maximize performance on a tuning set separate from the training bitext. Unlike system weights, the grammar rule feature values are fixed once extracted, and are not modified during this tuning phase. In this paper, we propose a framework to augment the feature set to incorporate additional intuition about how likely a rule is to produce a translation preferred by a human annotator. This knowledge is acquired by directly asking human judges to compare candidate translations, therefore determining which subset of grammar rules annotators seem to prefer over others. We also seek to generalize this intuition to rules for which no candidates were judged, hence allowing us to impact a much larger set of rules than just those used in translating the tuning set.

The paper is organized as follows. We first give a general description of our framework. We then discuss our data collection efforts on Amazon Mechanical Turk for an Urdu-English translation task, and make explicit the type of judgments we collect and how they can be used to augment grammar rules. Before concluding, we propose a framework for generalizing judgments to unseen grammar rules, and analyze the data collection process.

2 The General Framework

As initially mentioned, when tuning a SMT system on a development set, we typically only perform high-level optimization of the system weights. In this section we outline an approach that could allow for lower-level optimization, on the level of individual grammar rules.

We kick off the process by soliciting judgments from human annotators regarding the quality of a subset of candidates (the following section outlines how candidates are chosen). The resulting judgments on sentences are interpreted to be judgments on individual grammar rules used in the derivations of these candidates. And so, if an annotator declares a candidate to be of high quality, this is considered a vote of confidence on the individual rules giving rise to this candidate, and if an annotator declares a candidate to be of lowl quality, this is considered a vote of no confidence on the individual rules.

To make use of the collected judgments, we extend the set of features used in the decoder by a new feature λ:

$$\vec{\varphi}' = \langle \varphi_1, \ldots, \varphi_m, \lambda \rangle \quad (4)$$

This feature is the cornerstone of our framework, as it will hold the quantified and cumulated judgments for each rule, and will be used by the system at decoding time, in addition to the existing m features, incorporating the annotators' judgments into the translation process.[2]

The range of possible values for this feature, and how the feature is computed, depends on how one chooses to ask annotators to score candidates, and what form those judgments assume (i.e. are those judgments scores on a scale? Are they "better" vs. "worse" judgments, and if so, compared to how many other possibilities?). At this point, we will only emphasize that the value of λ should reflect the annotators' preference for the rule, and that it should be computed from the collected judgments. We will propose one such method of computing λ in Section 4, after describing the type of judgments we collected.

3 Data Collection

We apply our approach to an Urdu-to-English translation task. We used a syntactically rich SAMT grammar (Venugopal and Zollmann, 2006), where each rule in the grammar is characterized by 12 features. The grammar was provided by Chris Callison-Burch (personal communication), and was extracted from a parallel corpus of 88k sentence pairs.[3] One system using this grammar produced significantly improved output over submissions to the NIST 2009 Urdu-English task (Baker et al., 2009).

We use the Joshua system (Li et al., 2009) as a decoder, with system weights tuned using

[2] In fact, the collected judgments can only cover a small portion of the grammar. We address this coverage problem in Section 4.

[3] LDC catalog number LDC2009E12.

Z-MERT (Zaidan, 2009) on a tuning set of 981 sentences, a subset of the 2008 NIST Urdu-English test set.[4] We choose candidates to be judged from the 300-best candidate lists.[5]

Asking a worker to make a quantitative judgment of the quality of a particular candidate translation (e.g. on a 1–7 scale) is a highly subjective and annotator-dependent process. Instead, we present workers with pairs of candidates, and ask them to judge which candidate is of better quality.

How are candidate pairs chosen? We would like a judgment to have the maximum potential for being informative about specific grammar rules. In essense, we prefer a pair of candidates if they have highly similar derivations, yet differ noticeably in terms of how the decoder ranks them. In other words, if a relatively minimal change in derivation causes a relatively large difference in the score assigned by the decoder, we are likely to attribute the difference to very few rule comparisons (or perhaps only one), hence focusing the comparison on individual rules, all the while shielding the annotators from having to compare grammar rules directly.

Specifically, each pair of candidates $(\mathbf{e}, \mathbf{e}')$ is assigned a potential score $\pi(\mathbf{e}, \mathbf{e}')$, defined as:

$$\pi(\mathbf{e}, \mathbf{e}') = \frac{s(\mathbf{e})s(\mathbf{e}')}{lev(\boldsymbol{d}(\mathbf{e}), \boldsymbol{d}(\mathbf{e}'))}, \quad (5)$$

where $s(\mathbf{e})$ is the score assigned by the decoder, and $lev(\boldsymbol{d}, \boldsymbol{d'})$ is a distance measure between two derivations which we will now descibe in more detail. In Joshua, the derivation of a candidate is captured fully and exactly by a derivation tree, and so we define $lev(\boldsymbol{d}, \boldsymbol{d'})$ as a tree distance metric as follows. We first represent the trees as strings, using the familiar nested string representation, then compute the word-based Levenshtein edit distance between the two strings. An edit has a cost of 1 in general, but we assign a cost of zero to edit operations on terminals, since we want to focus on the structure of the derivation trees, rather than on terminal-level lexical choices.[6] Furthermore, we ignore differences in "pure" pre-terminal rules, that only have terminals as their right-hand side. These decisions effectively allow us to focus our efforts on grammar rules with at least one nonterminal in their right-hand side.

We perform the above potential computation on all pairs formed by the cross product of the top 10 candidates and the top 300 candidates, and choose the top five pairs ranked by potential.

Our HIT template is rather simple. Each HIT screen corresponds to a single source sentence, which is shown to the worker along with the five chosen candidate pairs. To aid workers who are not fluent in Urdu[7] better judge translation quality, the HIT also displays one of the available references for that source sentence. To eliminate potential bias associated with the order in which candidates are presented (an annotator might be biased to choosing the first presented candidate, for example), we present the two candidates in random or- der. Furthermore, for quality assurance, we embed a sixth candidate pair to be judged, where we pair up a randomly chosen candidate with another reference for that sentence.[8] Presumably, a faithful worker would be unlikely to prefer a random candidate over the reference, and so this functions as an embedded self-verification test. The order of this test, relative to the five original pairs, is chosen randomly.

4 Incorporating the Judgements

4.1 Judgement Quantification

The judgments we obtain from the procedure described in the previous section relate pairs of candidate translations. However, we have defined the accumulation feature λ as a feature for each rule. Thus, in order to compute λ, we need to project the judgments onto the rules that tell the two candidates apart. A simple way to do this is the following: for a judged candidate pair $(\mathbf{e}, \mathbf{e}')$ let $U(\mathbf{e})$ be the set of

[4]LDC catalog number LDC2009E11.

[5]We exclude source sentences shorter than 4 words long or that have fewer than 4 candidate translations. This eliminates roughly 6% of the development set.

[6]This is not to say that lexical choices are not important, but lexical choice is heavily influenced by context, which is not captured well by grammar rules. Furthermore, lexical choice is a phenomenon already well captured by the score assigned to the candidate by the language model, a feature typically included when designing $\vec{\varphi}$.

[7]We exclude workers from India and restrict the task to workers with an existing approval rating of 90% or higher.

[8]The tuning set contains at least three different human references for each source sentence, and so the reference "candidate" shown to the worker is not the same as the sentence already identified as a reference.

rules that appear in $\boldsymbol{d}(\mathbf{e})$ but not in $\boldsymbol{d}(\mathbf{e}')$, and vice versa.[9] We will assume that the jugdment obtained for $(\mathbf{e}, \mathbf{e}')$ applies for every rule pair in the cartesian product of $U(\mathbf{e})$ and $U(\mathbf{e}')$. This expansion yields a set of judged grammar rule pairs $\mathcal{J} = \{(a, b)\}$ with associated vote counts $v_{a>b}$ and $v_{b>a}$, capturing how often the annotators preferred a candidate that was set apart by a over a candidate containing b, and vice versa.

So, following our prior definiton as an expression of the judges' preference, we can calculate the value of λ for a rule r as the relative frequency of favorable judgements:

$$\lambda(r) = \frac{\sum_{(r,b)\in\mathcal{J}} v_{r>b}}{\sum_{(r,b)\in\mathcal{J}} v_{b>r} + v_{r>b}} \quad (6)$$

4.2 Generalization to Unseen Rules

This approach has a substantial problem: λ, computed as given above, is undefined for a rule that was never judged (i.e. a rule that never set apart a pair of candidates presented to the annotators). Furthermore, as described, the coverage of the collected judgments will be limited to a small subset of the entire grammar, meaning that when the system is asked to translate a new source sentence, it is highly unlikely that the relevant grammar rules would have already been judged by an annotator. Therefore, it is necessary to generalize the collected judgments/votes and propagate them to previously unexamined rules.

In order to do this, we propose the following general approach: when observing a judgment for a pair of rules $(a, b) \in \mathcal{J}$, we view that judgement not as a vote on one of them specifically, but rather as a comparison of rules similar to a versus rules similar to b. When calculating $\lambda(r)$ for any rule r we use a distance measure over rules, Δ, to estimate how each judgment in $\mathcal{J}$ projects to r. This leads to the following modified computatio of $\lambda(r)$:

$$\lambda(r) = \sum_{(a,b)\in\mathcal{J}} \frac{\Delta(a,r)v'_{b>a} + \Delta(b,r)v'_{a>b}}{\Delta(a,r) + \Delta(b,r)} \quad (7)$$

[9]The way we select candidate pairs ensures that $U(\mathbf{e})$ and $U(\mathbf{e}')$ are both small and expressive in terms of impact on the decoder ranking. On our data $U(\mathbf{e})$ contained an average of 4 rules.

where $v'_{a>b}$ (and analogously $v'_{b>a}$) is defined as the relative frequency of a being preferred over b:

$$v'_{a>b} = \frac{v_{a>b}}{v_{a>b} + v_{b>a}}$$

4.3 A Vector Space Realization

Having presented a general framework for judgment generalization, we will now briefly sketch a concrete realization of this approach.

In order to be able to use the common distance metrics on rules, we define a *rule vector space*. The basis of this space will be a new set of rule features designed specifically for the purpose of describing the structure of a rule, $\vec{\psi} = \langle\psi_1, \ldots, \psi_k\rangle$. Provided the exact features chosen are expressive and well-distributed over the grammar, we expect any conventional distance metric to correlate with rule similarity.

We deem a particular ψ_i good if it quantifies a quality of the rule that describes the rule's nature rather than the particular lexical choices it makes, i.e. a statistic (such as the rule length, arity, number of lexical items in the target or source side or the average covered span in the training corpus), information relevant to the rule's effect on a derivation (such as nonterminals occuring in the rule and wheter they are re-ordered) or features that capture frequent lexical cues that carry syntactic information (such as the co-occurrence of function words in source and target language, possibly in conjunction with certain nonterminal types).

5 Results and Analysis

The judgments were collected over a period of about 12 days (Figure 1). A total of 16,374 labels were provided (2,729 embedded test labels + 13,645 'true' labels) by 658 distinct workers over 83.1 hours (i.e. each worker completed an average of 4.2 HITs over 7.6 minutes). The reward for each HIT was \$0.02, with an additional \$0.005 incurred for Amazon Fees. Since each HIT provides five labels, we obtain 200 (true) labels on the dollar. Each HIT took an average of 1.83 minutes to complete, for a labeling rate of 164 true labels/hour, and an effective wage of \$0.66/hour. The low reward does not seem to have deterred Turkers from completing our HITs faithfully, as the success rate on the embedded

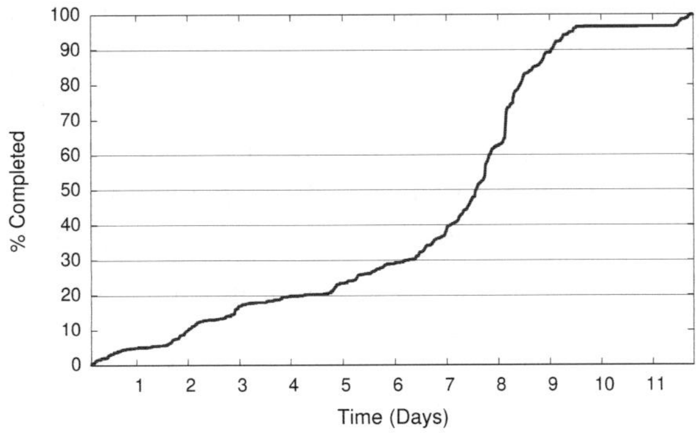

Figure 1: Progress of HIT submission over time. There was a hiatus of about a month during which we collected no data, which we are omitting for clairty.

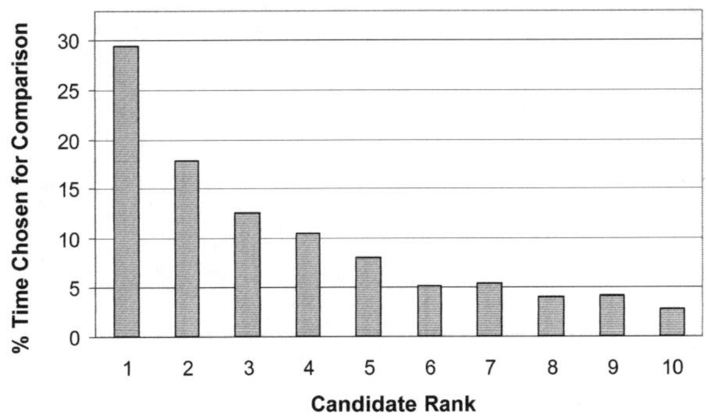

Figure 2: Histogram of the rank of the **higher**-ranked candidate chosen in pair comparisons. For instance, in about 29% of chosen pairs, the higher-ranked candidate was the top candidate (of 300) by decoder score.

True Questions	
Preferred	**%**
High-Ranked	40.0%
Low-Ranked	24.1%
No Difference	35.9%

Validation Questions	
Preferred	**%**
Reference	83.7%
Random Candidate	11.7%
No Difference	4.65%

Table 1: Distributions of the collected judgments over the true questions and over the embedded test questions. "High-Ranked" (resp. "Low-Ranked") refers to whether the decoder assigned a high (low) score to the candidate. And so, annotators agreed with the decoder 40.0% of the time, and disagreed 24.1% of the time.

(a) [NP] → ⟨ [NP] [NN+IN] کے | the [NN+IN] [NP] ⟩

(b) [NP] → ⟨ [NP] کے [NN] کے | [NN] of [NP] ⟩

Figure 3: A example pair of rules for which judgements were obtained. The first rule is preferred by the decoder, while human annotators favor the second rule.

questions was quite high (Table 1).[10] From our set of comparatively judged candidate translations we extracted competing rule pairs. To reduce the influence of lexical choices and improve comparability, we excluded pure preterminal rules and limited the extraction to rules covering the same span in the Urdu source. Figure 3 shows an interesting example of one such rule pair. While the decoder demonstrates a clear preference for rule (a) (including it into its higher-ranked translation 100% of the time), the Turkers tend to prefer translations generated using rule (b), disagreeing with the SMT system 60% of the time. This indicates that preferring the second rule in decoding may yield better results in terms of human judgment, in this case potentially due to the cleaner separation of noun phrases from the prepositional phrase.

We also examine the distribution of the chosen candidates. Recall that each pair consists of a **high**-ranked candidate from the top-ten list, and a **low**-ranked candidate from the top-300 list. The Histogram of the higher rank (Figure 2) shows that the high-ranked candidate is in fact a top-three candidate over 50% of the time. We also see (Figure 4) that the low-ranked candidate tends to be either close in rank to the top-ten list, or far away. This again makes sense given our definition of potential for a pair: potential is high if the derivations are very close (left mode) or if the decoder scores differ considerably (right mode).

Finally, we examine inter-annotator agreement, since we collect multiple judgments per query. We find that there is full agreement among the annotators in 20.6% of queries. That is, in 20.6% of queries, all three annotators answering that query gave the same answer (out of the three provided answers). This complete agreement rate is significantly higher than a rate caused by pure chance (11.5%). This is a positive result, especially given

[10]It should be mentioned that the human references themselves are of relatively low quality.

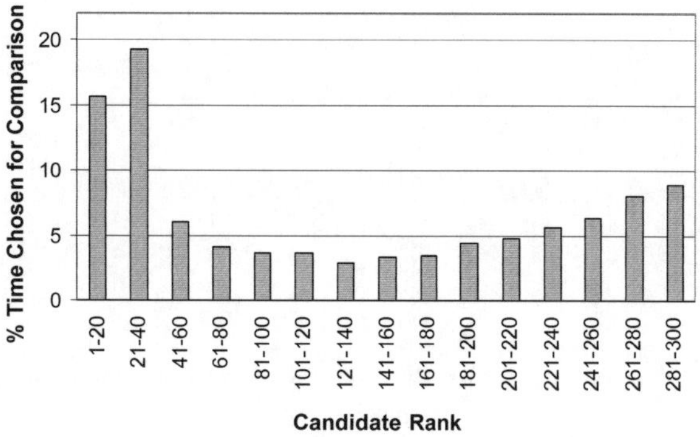

Figure 4: Histogram of the rank of the **lower**-ranked candidate chosen in pair comparisons. For instance, in about 16% of chosen candidate pairs, the lower-ranked candidate was ranked in the top 20.

how little diversity usually exists in n-best lists, a fact (purposely) exacerbated by our strategy of choosing highly similar pairs of candidates. On the other hand, we observe complete *dis*agreement in only 14.9% of queries, which is significantly lower than a rate caused by pure chance (which is 22.2%).

One thing to note is that these percentages are calculated after excluding the validation questions, where the complete agreement rate is an expectedly even higher 64.9%, and the complete disagreement rate is an expectedly even lower 3.60%.

6 Conclusions and Outlook

We presented a framework that allows us to "tune" MT systems on a finer level than system-level feature weights, going instead to the grammar rule level and augmenting the feature set to reflect collected human judgments. A system relying on this new feature during decoding is expected to have a slightly different ranking of translation candidates that takes human judgment into account. We presented one particular judgment collection procedure that relies on comparing candidate pairs (as opposed to evaluating a candidate in isolation) and complemented it with one possible method of propagating human judgments to cover grammar rules relevant to new sentences.

While the presented statistics over the collected data suggest that the proposed candidate selection procedure yields consistent and potentially informative data, the quantitative effects on a machine translation system remain to be seen.

Additionally, introducing λ as a new feature makes it necessary to find a viable weight for it. While this can be done trivially in running MERT on arbitrary development data, it may be of interest to extend the weight optimization procedure in order to preserve the partial ordering induced by the judgments as best as possible.

Acknowledgments

This research was supported by the EuroMatrix-Plus project funded by the European Commission, by the DARPA GALE program under Contract No. HR0011-06-2-0001, and the NSF under grant IIS-0713448.

References

Kathy Baker, Steven Bethard, Michael Bloodgood, Ralf Brown, Chris Callison-Burch, Glen Coppersmith, Bonnie Dorr, Wes Filardo, Kendall Giles, Anni Irvine, Mike Kayser, Lori Levin, Justin Martineau, Jim Mayfield, Scott Miller, Aaron Phillips, Andrew Philpot, Christine Piatko, Lane Schwartz, and David Zajic. 2009. Semantically informed machine translation (SIMT). In *SCALE 2009 Summer Workshop Final Report*, pages 135–139.

Philipp Koehn, Hieu Hoang, Alexandra Birch Mayne, Chris Callison-Burch, Marcello Federico, Nicola Bertoldi, Brooke Cowan, Wade Shen, Christine Moran, Richard Zens, Chris Dyer, Ondřej Bojar, Alexandra Constantin, and Evan Herbst. 2007. Moses: Open source toolkit for statistical machine translation. In *Proc. of ACL, Demonstration Session*, pages 177–180, June.

Zhifei Li, Chris Callison-Burch, Chris Dyer, Juri Ganitkevitch, Sanjeev Khudanpur, Lane Schwartz, Wren N. G. Thornton, Jonathan Weese, and Omar F. Zaidan. 2009. Joshua: An open source toolkit for parsing-based machine translation. In *Proc. of the Fourth Workshop on Statistical Machine Translation*, pages 135–139.

Ashish Venugopal and Andreas Zollmann. 2006. Syntax augmented machine translation via chart parsing. In *Proc. of the NAACL 2006 Workshop on Statistical Machine Translation*, pages 138–141. Association for Computational Linguistics.

Omar F. Zaidan. 2009. Z-MERT: A fully configurable open source tool for minimum error rate training of machine translation systems. *The Prague Bulletin of Mathematical Linguistics*, 91:79–88.

Using the Amazon Mechanical Turk to Transcribe and Annotate Meeting Speech for Extractive Summarization

Matthew Marge Satanjeev Banerjee Alexander I. Rudnicky
School of Computer Science, Carnegie Mellon University
Pittsburgh, PA 15213, USA
{mrmarge,banerjee,air}@cs.cmu.edu

Abstract

Due to its complexity, meeting speech provides a challenge for both transcription and annotation. While Amazon's Mechanical Turk (MTurk) has been shown to produce good results for some types of speech, its suitability for transcription and annotation of spontaneous speech has not been established. We find that MTurk can be used to produce high-quality transcription and describe two techniques for doing so (voting and corrective). We also show that using a similar approach, high quality annotations useful for summarization systems can also be produced. In both cases, accuracy is comparable to that obtained using trained personnel.

1 Introduction

Recently, Amazon's Mechanical Turk (MTurk) has been shown to produce useful transcriptions of speech data; Gruenstein et al. (2009) have successfully used MTurk to correct the transcription output from a speech recognizer, while Novotney and Callison-Burch (2010) used MTurk for transcribing a corpus of conversational speech. These studies suggest that transcription, formerly considered to be an exacting task requiring at least some training, could be carried out by casual workers. However, only fairly simple transcription tasks were studied.

We propose to assess the suitability of MTurk for processing more challenging material, specifically recordings of meeting speech. Spontaneous speech can be difficult to transcribe because it may contain false starts, disfluencies, mispronunciations and other defects. Similarly for annotation, meeting content may be difficult to follow and conventions difficult to apply consistently.

Our first goal is to ascertain whether MTurk transcribers can accurately transcribe spontaneous speech, containing speech errors and of variable utterance length.

Our second goal is to use MTurk for creating annotations suitable for extractive summarization research, specifically labeling each utterance as either "in-summary" or "not in-summary". Among other challenges, this task cannot be decomposed into small independent sub-tasks—for example, annotators cannot be asked to annotate a single utterance independent of other utterances. To our knowledge, MTurk has not been previously explored for the purpose of summarization annotation.

2 Meeting Speech Transcription Task

We recently explored the use of MTurk for transcription of short-duration clean speech (Marge et al., 2010) and found that combining independent transcripts using ROVER yields very close agreement with a gold standard (2.14%, comparable to expert agreement). But simply collecting independent transcriptions seemed inefficient: the "easy" parts of each utterance are all transcribed the same. In the current study our goal is determine whether a smaller number of initial transcriptions can be used to identify easy- and difficult-to-transcribe regions, so that the attention of subsequent transcribers can be focused on the more difficult regions.

2.1 Procedure

In this *corrective* strategy for transcription, we have two turkers to independently produce transcripts. A word-level minimum edit distance metric is then used to align the two transcripts and locate disagreements. These regions are replaced with underscores, and new turkers are asked to transcribe those regions.

Utterances were balanced for transcription difficulty (measured by the native English back-

Proceedings of the NAACL HLT 2010 Workshop on Creating Speech and Language Data with Amazon's Mechanical Turk, pages 99–107,
Los Angeles, California, June 2010.

ground of the speaker and utterance length). For the first pass transcription task, four sets of jobs were posted for turkers to perform, with each paying $0.01, $0.02, $0.04, or $0.07 per approved transcription. Payment was linearly scaled with the length of the utterance to be transcribed at a rate of $0.01 per 10 seconds of speech, with an additional payment of $0.01 for providing feedback. In each job set, there were 12 utterances to be transcribed (yielding a total of 24 jobs available given two transcribers per utterance). Turkers were free to transcribe as many utterances as they could across all payment amounts.

After acquiring two transcriptions, we aligned them, identified points of disagreement and reposted the transcripts and the audio as part of a next round of job sets. Payment amounts were kept the same based on utterance length. In this second pass of transcriptions, three turkers were recruited to correct and amend each transcription. Thus, a total of five workers worked on every transcription after both iterations of the corrective task. In our experiment 23 turkers performed the first phase of the task, and 28 turkers the corrective task (4 workers did both passes).

2.2 First and Second Pass Instructions

First-pass instructions asked turkers to listen to utterances with an embedded audio player provided with the HIT. Turkers were instructed to transcribe every word heard in the audio and to follow guidelines for marking speaker mispronunciations and false starts. Filled pauses ('uh', 'um', etc.) were not to be transcribed in the first pass. Turkers could replay the audio as many times as necessary.

In the second pass, turkers were instructed to focus on the portions of the transcript marked with underscores, but also to correct any other words they thought were incorrect. The instructions also asked turkers to identify three types of filler words: "uh", "um", and "lg" (laughter). We selected this set since they were the most frequent in the gold standard transcripts. Again, turkers could replay the audio.

2.3 Speech Corpus

The data were sampled from a previously-collected corpus of natural meetings (Banerjee and Rudnicky, 2007). The material used in this paper comes from four speakers, two native English speakers and two non-Native English speakers (all male). We selected 48 audio clips; 12 from each of the four speakers. Within each speaker's set of clips, we further divided the material into four length categories: ~5, ~10, ~30 and ~60 sec. The speech material is conversational in nature; the gold standard transcriptions of this data included approximately 15 mispronunciations and 125 false starts. Table 1 presents word count information related to the utterances in each length category.

Utterance Length	Word Count (mean)	Standard Deviation	Utterance Count
5 sec	14	5.58	12
10 sec	24.5	7.26	12
30 sec	84	22.09	12
60 sec	146.6	53.17	12

Table 1. Utterance characteristics.

3 Meeting Transcription Analysis

Evaluation of first and second pass corrections was done by calculating word error rate (WER) with a gold standard, obtained using the transcription process described in (Bennett and Rudnicky, 2002). Before doing so, we normalized the candidate MTurk transcriptions as follows: spell-checking (with included domain-specific technical terms), and removal of punctuation (periods, commas, etc.). Apostrophes were retained.

Utterance Length	First-Pass WER	Second-Pass WER	ROVER-3 WER
5 sec.	31.5%	19.8%	15.3%
10 sec.	26.7%	20.3%	13.8%
30 sec.	20.8%	16.9%	15.0%
60 sec.	24.3%	17.1%	15.4%
Aggregate	23.8%	17.5%	15.1%

Table 2. WER across transcription iterations.

3.1 First-Pass Transcription Results

Results from aligning our first-pass transcriptions with a gold standard are shown in the second column of Table 2. Overall error rate was 23.8%, which reveals the inadequacy of individual turker transcriptions, if no further processing is done. (Remember that first-pass transcribers were asked to leave out fillers even though the gold standard contained them, thus increasing WER).

In this first pass, speech from non-native speakers was transcribed more poorly (25.4% WER) than speech from native English speakers (21.7% WER). In their comments sections, 17% of turkers noted the difficulty in transcribing non-native speakers, while 13% found native English speech difficult. More than 80% of turkers thought the amount of work "about right" for the payment received.

3.2 Second-Pass Transcription Results

The corrective process greatly improved agreement with our expert transcriptions. Aggregate WER was reduced from 23.8% to 17.5% (27% relative reduction) when turkers corrected initial transcripts with highlighted disagreements (third column of Table 2). In fact, transcriptions after corrections were significantly more accurate than initial transcriptions ($F(1, 238) = 13.4$, $p < 0.05$). With respect to duration, the WER of the 5-second utterances had the greatest improvement, a relative reduction of WER by 37%. Transcription alignment with the gold standard experienced a 39% improvement to 13.3% for native English speech, and a 19% improvement to 20.6% for non-native English speech (columns 2 and 3 of Table 3).

We found that 30% of turkers indicated that the second-pass correction task was difficult, as compared with 15% for the first-pass transcription task. Work amount was perceived to be about right (85% of the votes) in this phase, similar to the first.

3.3 Combining Corrected Transcriptions

In order to improve the transcriptions further, we combined the three second-pass transcriptions of each utterance using ROVER's word-level voting scheme (Fiscus, 1997). The WER of the resulting transcripts are presented in the fourth column of Table 2. Aggregate WER was further reduced by 14% relative to 15.1%. This result is close to typical disagreement rates of 6-12% reported in the literature (Roy and Roy, 2009). The best improvements using ROVER were found with the transcriptions of the shorter utterances: WER from the second-pass of 5-second utterances transcriptions was reduced by 23% to 15.3%. The 10-second utterance transcriptions experienced the best improvement, 32%, to a WER of 13.8%.

Although segmenting audio into shorter segments may yield fast turnaround times, we found that utterance length is not a significant factor in determining alignment between combined, corrected transcriptions and gold-standard transcriptions ($F(3, 44) = 0.16$, $p = 0.92$). We speculate that longer utterances show good accuracy due to the increased context available to transcribers.

Speaker Background	First-Pass WER	Second-Pass WER	ROVER-3 WER
Native	21.7%	13.3%	10.8%
Non-native	25.4%	20.6%	18.4%

Table 3. WER across transcription iterations based on speaker background.

3.4 Error Analysis

Out of 3,281 words (48 merged transcriptions of 48 utterances), 496 were errors. Among the errors were 37 insertions, 315 deletions, and 144 substitutions. Thus the most common error was to miss a word.

Further analysis revealed that two common cases of errors occurred: the misplacement or exclusion of filler words (even though the second phase explicitly instructed turkers to insert filler words) and failure to transcribe words considered to be out of the range of the transcriber's vocabulary, such as technical terms and foreign names. Filler words accounted for 112 errors (23%). Removing fillers from both the combined transcripts and the gold standard improved WER by 14% relative to 13.0%. Further, WER for native English speech transcriptions was reduced to 8.9%. This difference was however not statistically significant ($F(1,94) = 1.64$, $p = 0.2$).

Turkers had difficulty transcribing uncommon words, technical terms, names, acronyms, etc. (e.g., "Speechalyzer", "CTM", "PQs"). Investigation showed that at least 41 errors (8%) could be attributed to this out-of-vocabulary problem. It is unclear if there is any way to completely eradicate such errors, short of asking the original speakers.

3.5 Comparison to One-Pass Approach

Although the corrective model provides significant gain from individual transcriptions, this approach is logistically more complex. We compared it to our one-pass approach, in which five turkers independently transcribe all utterances (Marge et al., 2010). Five new transcribers per utterance were recruited for this task (yielding 240 transcriptions).

Individual error rate was 24.0%, comparable to the overall error rate for the first step of the corrective approach (Table 2).

After combining all five transcriptions with ROVER, we found similar gains to the corrective approach: an overall improvement to 15.2% error rate. Thus both approaches can effectively produce high-quality transcriptions. We speculate that if higher accuracy is required, the corrective process could be extended to iteratively re-focus effort on the regions of greatest disagreement.

3.6 Latency

Although payment scaled with the duration of utterances, we observed a consistent disparity in turnaround time. All HITs were posted at the same time in both iterations (Thursday afternoon, EST). Turkers were able to transcribe 48 utterances twice in about a day in the first pass for the shorter utterances (5- and 10-second utterances), while it took nearly a week to transcribe the 30- and 60-second utterances. Turkers were likely discouraged by the long duration of the transcriptions compounded with the nature of the speech. To increase turnaround time on lengthy utterances, we speculate that it may be necessary to scale payment non-linearly with length (or another measure of perceived effort).

3.7 Conclusion

Spontaneous speech, even in long segments, can indeed be transcribed on MTurk with a level of accuracy that approaches expert agreement rates for spontaneous speech. However, we expect segmentation of audio materials into smaller segments would yield fast turnaround time, and may keep costs low. In addition, we find that ROVER works more effectively on shorter segments because lengths of candidate transcriptions are less likely to have large disparities. Thus, multiple transcriptions per utterance can be utilized best when their lengths are shorter.

4 Annotating for Summarization

4.1 Motivation

Transcribing audio data into text is the first step towards making information contained in audio easily accessible to humans. A next step is to condense the information in the raw transcription, and produce a short summary that includes the most important information. Good summaries can provide readers with a general sense of the meeting, or help them to drill down into the raw transcript (or the audio itself) for additional information.

4.2 Annotation Challenges

Unfortunately, summary creation is a difficult task because "importance" is inherently subjective and varies from consumer to consumer. For example, the manager of a project, browsing a summary of a meeting, might be interested in all agenda items, whereas a project participant may be interested in only those parts of the meeting that pertain to his portion of the project.

Despite this subjectivity, the usefulness of a summary is clear, and audio summarization is an active area of research. Within this field, two kinds of human annotations are generally created—annotators are either asked to write a short summary of the audio, or they are asked to label each transcribed utterance as either "in summary" or "out of summary". The latter annotation is particularly useful for training and evaluating *extractive* summarization systems—systems that create summaries by selecting a subset of the utterances.

Due to the subjectivity involved, we find very low inter-annotator agreement for this labeling task. Liu and Liu (2008) reported Kappa agreement scores of between 0.11 and 0.35 across 6 annotators, Penn and Zhu (2008) reported 0.38 on telephone conversation and 0.37 on lecture speech, using 3 annotators, and Galley (2006) reported 0.32 on meeting data. Such low levels of agreement imply that the resulting training data is likely to contain a great deal of "noise"—utterances labeled "in summary" or "out of summary", when in fact they are not good examples of those classes.

Disagreements arise due to the fact that utterance importance is a spectrum. While some utterances are clearly important or unimportant, there are many utterances that lie between these extremes. In order to label utterances as either "in-summary" or not, annotators must choose an arbitrary threshold at which to make this decision. Simply asking annotators to provide a continuous "importance value" between 0 and 1 is also likely to be infeasible as the exact value for a given utterance is difficult to ascertain.

4.3 3-Class Formulation

One way to alleviate this problem is to redefine the task as a 3-class labeling problem. Annotators can be asked to label utterances as either "important", "unimportant" or "in-between". Although this formulation creates two decision boundaries, instead of the single one in the 2-class formulation, the expectation is that a large number of utterances with middling importance will simply be assigned to the "in between" class, thus reducing the amount of noise in the data. Indeed we have shown (Banerjee and Rudnicky, 2009) that in-house annotators achieve high inter-annotator agreement when provided with the 3-class formulation.

Another way to alleviate the problem of low agreement is to obtain annotations from many annotators, and identify the utterances that a majority of the annotators appear to agree on; such utterances may be considered as good examples of their class. Using multiple annotators is typically not feasible due to cost. In this paper we investigate using MTurk to create 3-class-based summarization annotations from multiple annotators per meeting, and to combine and filter these annotations to create high quality labels.

5 Using Mechanical Turk for Annotations

5.1 Challenges of Using Mechanical Turk

Unlike some other tasks that require little or no context in order to perform the annotation, summarization annotation requires a great deal of context. It is unlikely that an annotator can determine the importance of an utterance without being aware of neighboring utterances. Moreover, the appropriate length of context for a given utterance is likely to vary. Presenting all contiguous utterances that discuss the same topic might be appropriate, but would require manual segmentation of the meeting into topics. In this paper we experiment with showing *all* utterances of a meeting. This is a challenge however, because MTurk is typically applied to quick low-cost tasks that need little context. It is unclear whether turkers would be willing to perform such a time-consuming task, even for higher payment.

Another challenge for turkers is being able to understand the discussion well enough to perform the annotation. We experiment here with meetings

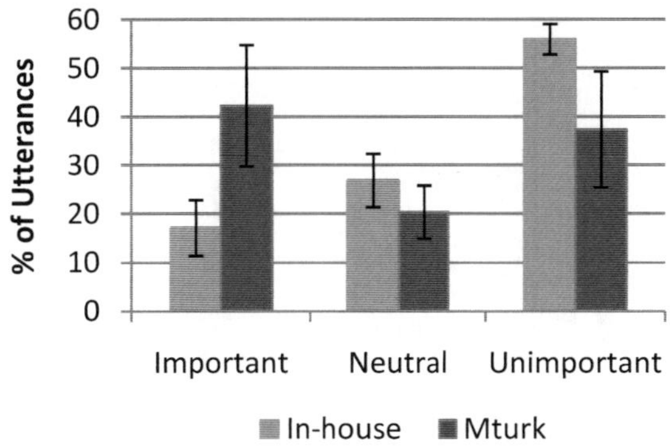

Figure 1. Label distribution of in-house and MTurk annotators.

that include significant technical content. While in-house annotators can be trained over time to understand the material well enough to perform the task, it is impractical to provide turkers with such training. We investigate the degree to which turkers can provide summarization annotation with minimal training.

5.2 Data Used

We selected 5 recorded meetings for our study. These meetings were not scripted—and would have taken place even if they weren't being recorded. They were project meetings containing discussions about software deliverables, problems, resolution plans, etc. The contents included technical jargon and concepts that non-experts are unlikely to grasp by reading the meeting transcript alone.

The 5 meetings had 2 to 4 participants each (mean: 3.5). For all meetings, the speech from each participant was recorded separately using head-mounted close-talking microphones. We manually split these audio streams into utterances—ensuring that utterances did not have more than a 0.5 second pause in them, and then transcribed them using an established process (Bennett and Rudnicky, 2002). The meetings varied widely in length from 15 minutes and 282 utterances to 40 minutes and 948 utterances (means: 30 minutes, 610 utterances). There were 3,052 utterances across the 5 meetings, each containing an mean of 7 words. The utterances in the meetings were annotated using the 3-class formulation by two in-house annotators. Their inter-annotator agreement is presented along with the rest of the evaluation results in Section 6.

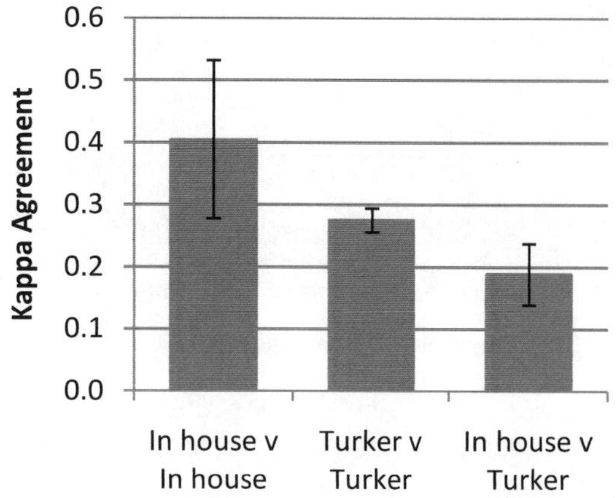

Figure 2. Average kappa agreement between in-house annotators, turkers, and in-house annotators and turkers.

5.3 HIT Design and Instructions

We instructed turkers to imagine that someone else (not them) was going to eventually write a report about the meeting, and it was their task to identify those utterances that should be included in the report. We asked annotators to label utterances as "important" if they should be included in the report and "unimportant" otherwise. In addition, utterances that they thought were of medium importance and that *may or may not* need to be included in the report were to be labeled as "neutral". We provided examples of utterances in each of these classes. For the "important" class, for instance, we included "talking about a problem" and "discussing future plan of action" as examples. For the "unimportant" class, we included "off topic joking", and for the "neutral" class "minute details of an algorithm" was an example.

In addition to these instructions and examples, we gave turkers a general guideline to the effect that in these meetings typically 1/4th of the utterances are "important", 1/4th "neutral" and the rest "unimportant". As we discuss in section 6, it is unclear whether most turkers followed this guideline.

Following these instructions, examples and tips, we provided the text of the utterances in the form of an HTML table. Each row contained a single utterance, prefixed with the name of the speaker. The row also contained three radio buttons for the three classes into which the annotator was asked to classify the utterance. Although we did not ensure that annotators annotated every utterance before submitting their work, we observed that for 95% of the utterances every annotator did provide a judgment; we ignore the remaining 5% of the utterances in our evaluation below.

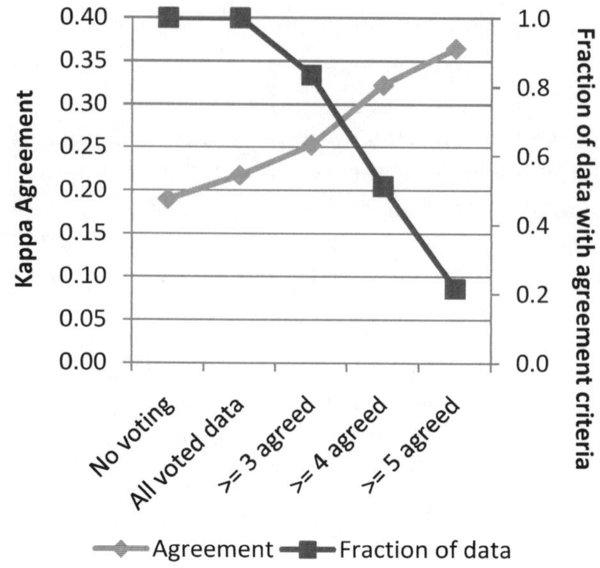

Figure 3. Agreement with in-house annotators when turker annotations are merged through voting.

5.4 Number of Turkers and Payment

For each meeting, we used 5 turkers and paid each one the same. That is, we did not vary the payment amount as an experimental variable. We calculated the amount to pay for a meeting based on in the length of that meeting. Specifically, we multiplied the number of utterances by 0.13 US cents to arrive at the payment. This resulted in payments ranging from 35 cents to $1.25 per meeting (mean 79 cents). The effective hourly rate (based on how much time turkers took to actually finish each job) was $0.87.

6 Annotation Results

6.1 Label Distribution

We first examine the average distribution of labels across the 3 classes. Figure 1 shows the distributions (expressed as percentages of the number of utterances) for in-house and MTurk annotators, averaged across the 5 meetings. Observe that the distribution for the in-house annotators is far more skewed away from a uniform 33% assignment, whereas the label distribution of turkers is less skewed. The likely reason for this difference is that turkers have a poorer understanding of the meetings, and are more likely than in-house annotators to make arbitrary judgments about utterances. This poor understanding perhaps also explains the large difference in the percentage of utterances labeled as important—for many utterances that are difficult to understand, turkers probably play it safe by marking it important.

The error bars represent the standard deviations of these averages, and capture the difference in label distribution from meeting to meeting. While different meetings are likely to inherently have different ratios of the 3 classes, observe that the standard deviations for the in-house annotators are much lower than those for the turkers. For example, the percentage of utterances labeled "important" by in-house annotators varies from 9% to 22% across the 5 meetings, whereas it varies from 30% to 57% for turkers, a much wider range. These differences in standard deviation persist for each meeting as well—that is, for any given meeting, the label distribution of the turkers varies much more between each other than the distribution of the in-house annotators.

6.2 Inter-Annotator Agreement

Figure 2 shows the kappa values for pairs of annotators, averaged across the 5 meetings, while the error bars represent the standard deviations. The kappa between the two in-house annotators. (0.4) is well within the range of values reported in the summarization literature (see section 4). The kappa values range from 0.24 to 0.50 across the 5 meetings. The inter-annotator agreement between pairs of turkers, averaged across the 10 possible pairs per meeting (5 choose 2), and across the 5 meetings show that turkers tend to agree less between each other than in-house annotators, although this kappa (0.28) is still within the range of typical agreement (this kappa has lower variance because the sample size is larger). The kappa between in-house annotators and turkers[1] (0.19) is on the lower end of the scale but remains within the range of agreement reported in the literature, suggesting that Mechanical Turk may be a useful tool for summarization.

[1] For each meeting, we measure agreement between every possible pair of annotators such that one of the annotators was an in-house annotator, and the other a turker. Here we present the average agreement across all such pairs, and across all the meetings.

6.3 Agreement after Voting

We consider merging the annotations from multiple turkers using a simple voting scheme as follows. For each utterance, if 3, 4 or 5 annotators labeled the utterance with the same class, we labeled the utterance with that class. For utterances in which 2 annotators voted for one class, 2 for another and 1 for the third, we randomly picked from one of the classes in which 2 annotators voted the same way. We then computed agreement between this "voted turker" and each of the two in-house annotators, and averaged across the 5 meetings. Figure 3 shows these agreement values. The left-most point on the "Kappa Agreement" curve shows the average agreement obtained using individual turkers (0.19) while the second point shows the agreement with the "voted turker" (0.22). This is only a marginal improvement, implying that simply voting and using all the data does not improve much over the average agreement of individual annotators.

The agreement does improve when we consider only those utterances that a clear majority of annotators agreed on. The 3rd, 4th and 5th points on the "Agreement" curve plot the average agreement when considering only those utterances that at least 3, 4 and 5 turkers agreed on. The "Fraction of data" curve plots the fraction of the meeting utterances that fit these agreement criteria. For utterances that at least 3 turkers agreed on, the kappa agreement value with in-house annotators is 0.25, and this represents 84% of the data. For about 50% of the data 4 of 5 turkers agreed, and these utterances had a kappa of 0.32. Finally utterances for which annotators were unanimous had a kappa of 0.37, but represented only 22% of the data. It is particularly encouraging to note that although the amount of data reduces as we focus on utterances that more and more turkers agree on, the utterances so labeled are not dominated by any one class. For example, among utterances that 4 or more turkers agree on, 48% belong to the important class, 48% to unimportant class, and the remaining 4% to the neutral class. These results show that with voting, it is possible to select a subset of utterances that have higher agreement rates, implying that they are annotated with higher confidence. For future work we will investigate whether a summarization system trained on only the highly agreed-upon data outperforms one trained on all the annotation data.

7 Conclusions

In this study, we found that MTurk can be used to create accurate transcriptions of spontaneous meeting speech when using a two-stage corrective process. Our best technique yielded a disagreement rate of 15.1%, which is competitive with reported disagreement in the literature of 6-12%. We found that both fillers and out-of-vocabulary words proved troublesome. We also observed that the length of the utterance being transcribed wasn't a significant factor in determining WER, but that the native language of the speaker was indeed a significant factor.

We also experimented with using MTurk for the purpose of labeling utterances for extractive summarization research. We showed that despite the lack of training, turkers produce labels with better than random agreement with in-house annotators. Further, when combined using voting, and with the low-agreement utterances filtered out, we can identify a set of utterances that agree significantly better with in-house annotations.

In summary, MTurk appears to be a viable resource for producing transcription and annotation of meeting speech. Producing high-quality outputs, however, may require the use of techniques such as ensemble voting and iterative correction or refinement that leverage performance of the same task by multiple workers.

References

S. Banerjee and A. I. Rudnicky. 2007. Segmenting meetings into agenda items by extracting implicit supervision from human note-taking. In *Proceedings of IUI.*

S. Banerjee and A. I. Rudnicky. 2009. Detecting the noteworthiness of utterances in human meetings. In *Proceedings of SIGDial.*

C. Bennett and A. I. Rudnicky. 2002. The Carnegie Mellon Communicator corpus. In *Proceedings of ICSLP.*

J. G. Fiscus. 1997. A post-processing system to yield word error rates: Recognizer Output Voting Error Reduction (ROVER). In *Proceedings of ASRU Workshop.*

M. Galley. (2006). A skip-chain conditional random field for ranking meeting utterances by im portance. In *Proceedings of EMNLP.*

A. Gruenstein, I. McGraw, and A. Sutherland. 2009. A self-transcribing speech corpus: collecting continuous speech with an online educational game. In *Proceedings of SLaTE Workshop.*

F. Liu and Y. Liu. 2008. Correlation between ROUGE and human evaluation of extractive meeting summaries. In *Proceedings of ACL-HLT.*

M. Marge, S. Banerjee, and A. I. Rudnicky. 2010. Using the Amazon Mechanical Turk for transcription of spoken language. In *Proceedings of ICASSP.*

S. Novotney and C. Callison-Burch. 2010. Cheap, fast and good enough: Automatic speech recognition with non-expert transcription. In *Proceedings of NAACL.*

G. Penn and X. Zhu. 2008. A critical reassessment of evaluation baselines for speech summarization. In *Proceedings of ACL-HLT.*

B. Roy and D. Roy. 2009. Fast transcription of unstructured audio recordings. In *Proceedings of In terspeech.*

Appendix

Transcription task HIT type 1:

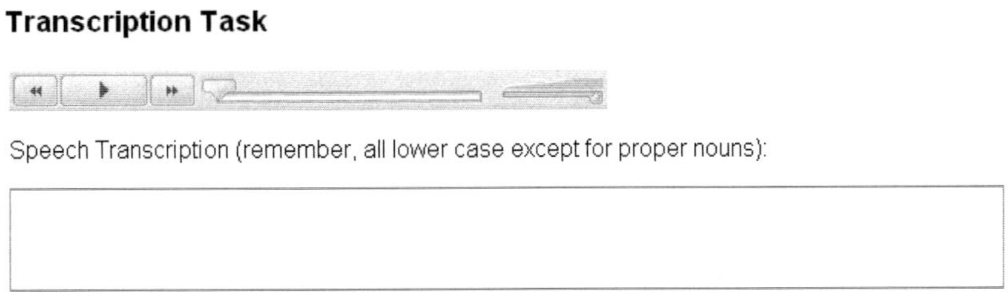

Transcription task HIT type 2:

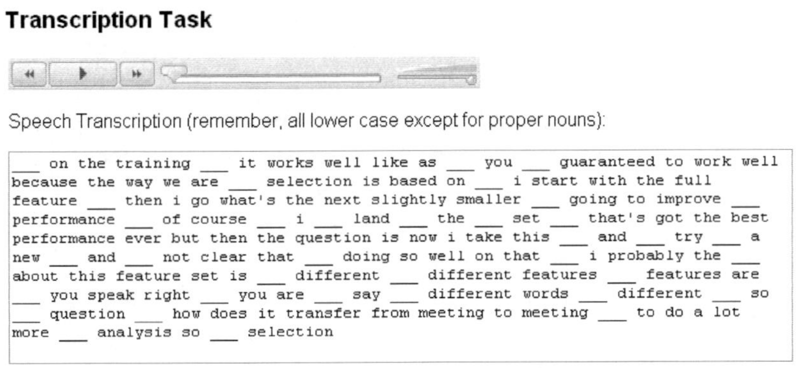

Annotation task HIT:

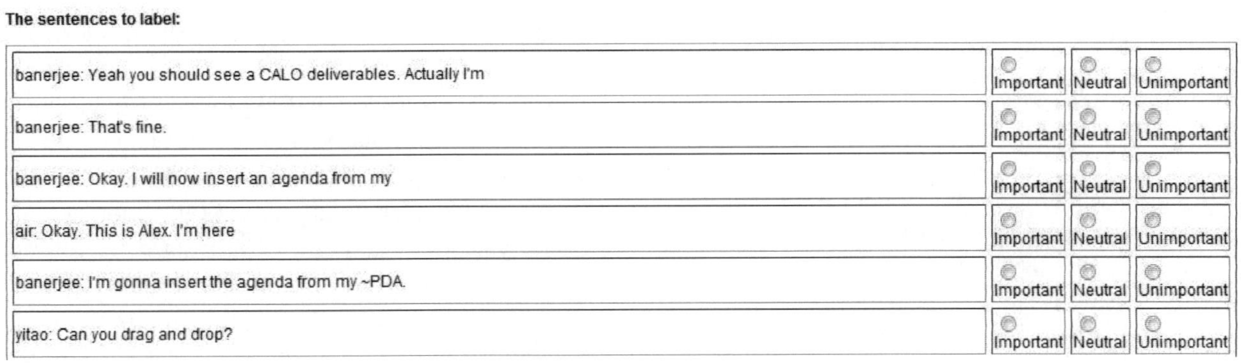

Using Mechanical Turk to Annotate Lexicons for Less Commonly Used Languages

Ann Irvine and Alexandre Klementiev
Computer Science Department
Johns Hopkins University
Baltimore, MD 21218
{anni,aklement}@jhu.edu

Abstract

In this work we present results from using Amazon's Mechanical Turk (MTurk) to annotate translation lexicons between English and a large set of less commonly used languages. We generate candidate translations for 100 English words in each of 42 foreign languages using Wikipedia and a lexicon induction framework. We evaluate the MTurk annotations by using positive and negative control candidate translations. Additionally, we evaluate the annotations by adding pairs to our seed dictionaries, providing a feedback loop into the induction system. MTurk workers are more successful in annotating some languages than others and are not evenly distributed around the world or among the world's languages. However, in general, we find that MTurk is a valuable resource for gathering cheap and simple annotations for most of the languages that we explored, and these annotations provide useful feedback in building a larger, more accurate lexicon.

1 Introduction

In this work, we make use of several free and cheap resources to create high quality lexicons for less commonly used languages. First, we take advantage of small existing dictionaries and freely available Wikipedia monolingual data to induce additional lexical translation pairs. Then, we pay Mechanical Turk workers a small amount to check and correct our system output. We can then use the updated lexicons to inform another iteration of lexicon induction, gather a second set of MTurk annotations, and so on.

Here, we provide results of one iteration of MTurk annotation. We discuss the feasibility of using MTurk for annotating translation lexicons between English and 42 less commonly used languages. Our primary goal is to enlarge and enrich the small, noisy bilingual dictionaries that we have for each language. Our secondary goal is to study the quality of annotations that we can expect to obtain for our set of low resource languages. We evaluate the annotations both alone and as feedback into our lexicon induction system.

2 Inducing Translation Candidates

Various linguistic and corpus cues are helpful for relating word translations across a pair of languages. A plethora of prior work has exploited orthographic, topic, and contextual similarity, to name a few (Rapp, 1999; Fung and Yee, 1998; Koehn and Knight, 2000; Mimno et al., 2009; Schafer and Yarowsky, 2002; Haghighi et al., 2008; Garera et al., 2008). In this work, our aim is to induce translation candidates for further MTurk annotation for a large number of language pairs with varying degrees of relatedness and resource availability. Therefore, we opt for a simple and language agnostic approach of using contextual information to score translations and discover a set of candidates for further annotation. Table 1 shows our 42 languages of interest and the number of Wikipedia articles with interlingual links to their English counterparts. The idea is that tokens which tend to appear in the context of a given type in one language should be similar to contextual tokens of its translation in the other language. Each word can thus be represented as a

Proceedings of the NAACL HLT 2010 Workshop on Creating Speech and Language Data with Amazon's Mechanical Turk, pages 108–113,
Los Angeles, California, June 2010.

Tigrinya	36	Punjabi	401
Kyrgyz	492	Somali	585
Nepali	1293	Tibetan	1358
Uighur	1814	Maltese	1896
Turkmen	3137	Kazakh	3470
Mongolian	4009	Tatar	4180
Kurdish	5059	Uzbek	5875
Kapampangan	6827	Urdu	7674
Irish	9859	Azeri	12568
Tamil	13470	Albanian	13714
Afrikaans	14315	Hindi	14824
Bangla	16026	Tagalog	17757
Latvian	22737	Bosnian	23144
Welsh	25292	Latin	31195
Basque	38594	Thai	40182
Farsi	58651	Bulgarian	68446
Serbian	71018	Indonesian	73962
Slovak	76421	Korean	84385
Turkish	86277	Ukrainan	91022
Romanian	97351	Russian	295944
Spanish	371130	Polish	438053

Table 1: Our 42 languages of interest and the number of Wikipedia pages for each that have interlanguage links with English.

vector of contextual word indices. Following Rapp (1999), we use a small seed dictionary to project[1] the contextual vector of a source word into the target language, and score its overlap with contextual vectors of candidate translations, see Figure 1. Top scoring target language words obtained in this manner are used as candidate translations for MTurk annotation. While longer lists will increase the chance of including correct translations and their morphological variants, they require more effort on the part of annotators. To strike a reasonable balance, we extracted relatively short candidate lists, but allowed MTurk users to type their own translations as well.

3 Mechanical Turk Task

Following previous work on posting NLP tasks on MTurk (Snow et al., 2008; Callison-Burch, 2009), we use the service to gather annotations for proposed bilingual lexicon entries. For 32 of our 42 languages of interest, we were able to induce lexical translation

[1]A simple string match is used for projection. While we expect that more sophisticated approaches (e.g. exploiting morphological analyses) are likely to help, we cannot assume that such linguistic resources are available for our languages.

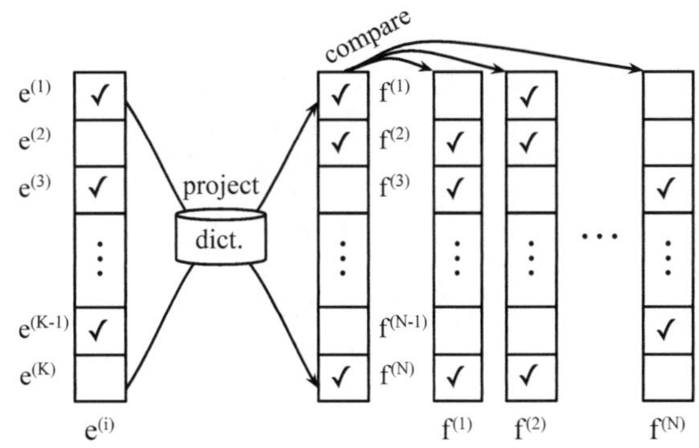

Figure 1: Lexicon induction using contextual information. First, contextual vectors are projected using small dictionaries and then they are compared with the target language candidates.

candidates and post them on MTurk for annotation. We do not have dictionaries for the remaining ten, so, for those languages, we simply posted a set of 100 English words and asked workers for manual translations. We had three distinct workers translate each word.

For the 32 languages for which we proposed translation candidates, we divided our set of 100 English words into sets of ten English words to be completed within a single HIT. MTurk defines HIT (Human Intelligence Task) as a self-contained unit of work that requesters can post and pay workers a small fee for completing. We requested that three MTurk workers complete each of the ten HITs for each language. For each English word within a HIT, we posted ten candidate translations in the foreign language and asked users to check the boxes beside any and all of the words that were translations of the English word. We paid workers $0.10 for completing each HIT. If our seed dictionary included an entry for a given English word, we included that in the candidate list as a positive control. Additionally, we included a random word in the foreign language as a negative control. The remaining eight or nine candidate translations were proposed by our induction system. We randomized the order in which the candidates appeared to workers and presented the words as images rather than text to discourage copying and pasting into online translation systems.

In addition to gathering annotations on candidate

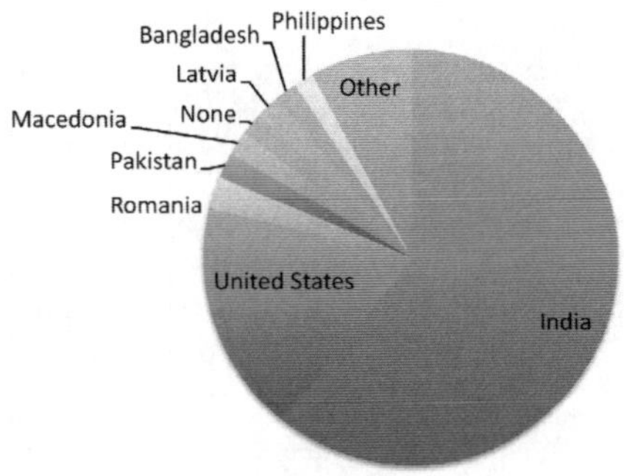

Figure 2: Distribution of MTurk workers around the world

translations, we gathered the following information in each HIT:

- Manual translations of each English word, especially for the cases where none of our proposed candidate translations were accurate
- Geographical locations via IP addresses
- How the HIT was completed: knowledge of the languages, paper dictionary, online dictionary
- Whether the workers were native speakers of each language (English and foreign), and for how many years they have spoken each

4 Results

Figure 2 shows the percent of HITs that were completed in different countries. More than 60% of HITs were completed by workers in India, more than half of which were completed in the single city of Chennai. Another 18% were completed in the United States, and roughly 2% were completed in Romania, Pakistan, Macedonia, Latvia, Bangladesh, and the Philippines. Of all annotations, 54% reported that the worker used knowledge of the two languages, while 28% and 18% reported using paper and online dictionaries, respectively, to complete the HITs.

Ninety-three MTurk workers completed at least one of our HITs, and 53 completed at least two. The average number of HITs completed per worker was 12. One worker completed HITs for 17 different languages, and nine workers completed HITs in more than three languages. Of the ten prolific workers, one was located in the United States, one in the United Kingdom, and eight in India. Because we posted each HIT three times, the minimum number of workers per language was three. Exactly three workers completed all ten HITs posted in the following languages: Kurdish, Maltese, Tatar, Kapampangan, Uzbek, and Latvian. We found that the average number of workers per language was 5.2. Ten distinct workers (identified with MTurk worker IDs) completed Tamil HITs, and nine worked on the Farsi HITs.

4.1 Completion Time

Figure 3 shows the time that it took for our HITs for 37 languages to be completed on MTurk. The HITs for the following languages were posted for a week and were never completed: Tigrinya, Uighur, Tibetan, Kyrgyz, and Kazakh. All five of the uncompleted HIT sets required typing annotations, a more time consuming task than checking translation candidates. Not surprisingly, languages with many speakers (Hindi, Spanish, and Russian) and languages spoken in and near India (Hindi, Tamil, Urdu) were completed very quickly. The languages for which we posted a manual translation only HIT are marked with a * in Figure 3. The HIT type does not seem to have affected the completion time.

4.2 Annotation Quality

Lexicon Check Agreement. Figure 4 shows the percent of positive control candidate translations that were checked by the majority of workers (at least two of three). The highest amounts of agreement with the controls were for Spanish and Polish, which indicates that those workers completed the HITs more accurately than the workers who completed, for example, the Tatar and Thai HITs. However, as already mentioned, the seed dictionaries are very noisy, so this finding may be confounded by discrepancies in the quality of our dictionaries. The noisy dictionaries also explain why agreement with the positive controls is, in general, relatively low.

We also looked at the degree to which workers agreed upon negative controls. The average percent agreement between the (majority of) workers and the negative controls over all 32 languages is only 0.21%. The highest amount of agreement with negative controls is for Kapampangan and Turkmen (1.28% and 1.26%, respectively). These are two of

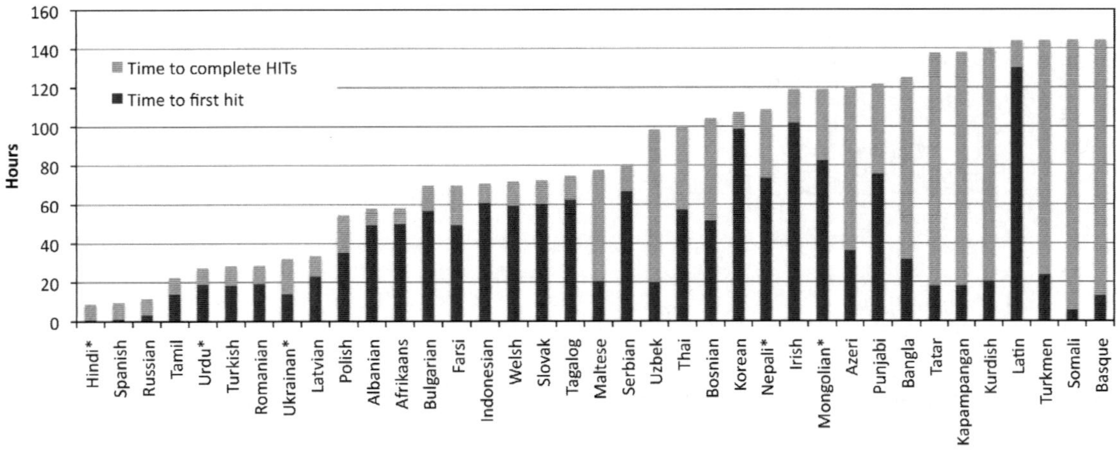

Figure 3: Number of hours HITs posted on MTurk before completion; division of the time between posting and the completion of one HIT and the time between the completion of the first and last HIT shown. HITs that required lexical translation only (not checking candidate translations) are marked with an *.

the languages for which there was little agreement with the positive controls, substantiating our claim that those HITs were completed less accurately than for other languages.

Manual Translation Agreement. For each English word, we encouraged workers to manually provide one or more translations into the foreign language. Figure 5 shows the percent of English words for which the MTurk workers provided and agreed upon at least one manual translation. We defined agreement as exact string match between at least two of three workers, which is a conservative measure, especially for morphologically rich languages. As shown, there was a large amount of agreement among the manual translations for Ukrainian, Farsi, Thai, and Korean. The MTurk workers did not provide any manual translations at all for the following languages: Somali, Kurdish, Turkmen, Uzbek, Kapampangan, and Tatar.

It's easy to speculate that, despite discouraging the use of online dictionaries and translation systems by presenting text as images, users reached this high level of agreement for manual translations by using the same online translation systems. However, we searched for 20 of the 57 English words for which the workers agreed upon a manually entered Russian translation in Google translate, and we found that the Russian translation was the top Google translation for only 11 of the 20 English words. Six of the Russian words did not appear at all in the list of translations for the given English word. Thus, we conclude that, at least for some of our languages of interest, MTurk workers did provide accurate, human-generated lexical translations.

4.3 Using MTurk Annotations in Induction

To further test the usefulness of MTurk generated bilingual lexicons, we supplemented our dictionaries for each of the 37 languages for which we gathered MTurk annotations with translation pairs that workers agreed were good (both chosen from the candidate set and manually translated). We compared seed dictionaries of size 200 with those supplemented with, on average, 69 translation pairs. We found an average relative increase in accuracy of our output candidate set (evaluated against complete available dictionaries) of 53%. This improvement is further evidence that we are able to gather high quality translations from MTurk, which can assist the lexicon induction process. Additionally, this shows that we could iteratively produce lexical translation candidates and have MTurk workers annotate them, supplementing the induction dictionaries over many iterations. This framework would allow us to gener-

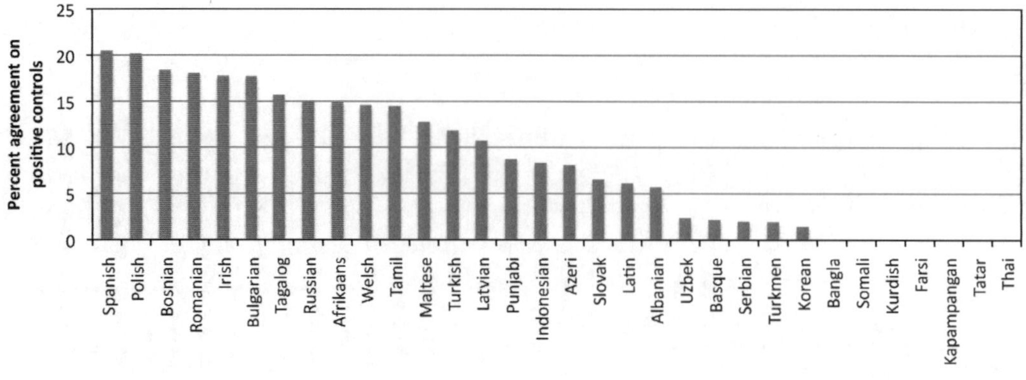

Figure 4: Percent of positive control candidate translations for which two or three workers checked as accurate.

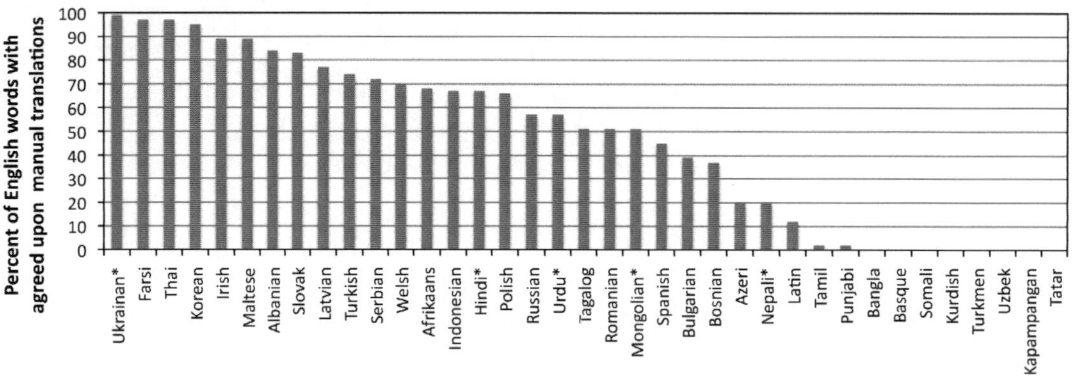

Figure 5: Percent of 100 English words for which at least two of three MTurk workers provided at least one matching manual translation; HITs that required lexical translation only (not checking candidate translations) are marked with an *.

ate very large and high quality dictionaries starting with a very small set of seed translation pairs.

5 Conclusion

The goal of this work was to use Amazon's Mechanical Turk to collect and evaluate the quality of translation lexicons for a large set of low resource languages. In order to make the annotation task easier and maximize the amount of annotation given our budget and time constraints, we used contextual similarity along with small bilingual dictionaries to extract a set of translation candidates for MTurk annotation. For ten of our languages without dictionaries, we asked workers to type translations directly. We were able to get complete annotations of both types quickly for 37 of our languages. The other five languages required annotations of the latter type, which may explain why they remained unfinished.

We used annotator agreement with positive and negative controls to assess the quality of generated lexicons and provide an indication of the relative difficulty of obtaining high quality annotations for each language. Not surprisingly, annotation agreement tends to be low for those languages which are especially low resource, as measured by the number of Wikipedia pages. Because there are relatively few native speakers of these languages in the online community, those HITs were likely completed by non-native speakers. Finally, we demonstrated that augmenting small seed dictionaries with the obtained lexicons substantially impacts contextual lexicon induction with an average relative gain of 53% in accuracy across languages.

In sum, we found that the iterative approach of automatically generating noisy annotation and asking MTurk users to correct it to be an effective means of obtaining supervision. Our manual annotation tasks are simple and annotation can be obtained quickly for a large number of low resource languages.

References

Chris Callison-Burch. 2009. Fast, cheap, and creative: Evaluating translation quality using amazons mechanical turk. In *Proceedings of EMNLP*.

Pascale Fung and Lo Yuen Yee. 1998. An IR approach for translating new words from nonparallel, comparable texts. In *Proceedings of ACL*, pages 414–420.

Nikesh Garera, Chris Callison-Burch, and David Yarowsky. 2008. Improving translation lexicon induction from monolingual corpora via dependency contexts and part-of-speech equivalences. In *Proceedings of CoNLL*.

Aria Haghighi, Percy Liang, Taylor Berg-Kirkpatrick, and Dan Klein. 2008. Learning bilingual lexicons from monolingual corpora. In *Proceedings of ACL*, pages 771–779.

Philipp Koehn and Kevin Knight. 2000. Estimating word translation probabilities from unrelated monolingual corpora using the EM algorithm. In *Proceedings of AAAI*.

David Mimno, Hanna Wallach, Jason Naradowsky, David Smith, and Andrew McCallum. 2009. Polylingual topic models. In *Proceedings of EMNLP*.

Reinhard Rapp. 1999. Automatic identification of word translations from unrelated English and German corpora. In *Proceedings of ACL*, pages 519–526.

Charles Schafer and David Yarowsky. 2002. Inducing translation lexicons via diverse similarity measures and bridge languages. In *Proceedings of CoNLL*, pages 146–152.

Rion Snow, Brendan OConnor, Daniel Jurafsky, and Andrew Y. Ng. 2008. Cheap and fast - but is it good? evaluating non-expert annotations for natural language tasks. In *Proceedings of EMNLP*.

Opinion Mining of Spanish Customer Comments with Non-Expert Annotations on Mechanical Turk

Bart Mellebeek, Francesc Benavent, Jens Grivolla,
Joan Codina, Marta R. Costa-jussà and Rafael Banchs
Barcelona Media Innovation Center
Av. Diagonal, 177, planta 9
08018 Barcelona, Spain
{bart.mellebeek|francesc.benavent|jens.grivolla|joan.codina|marta.ruiz|rafael.banchs}@barcelonamedia.org

Abstract

One of the major bottlenecks in the development of data-driven AI Systems is the cost of reliable human annotations. The recent advent of several crowdsourcing platforms such as Amazon's Mechanical Turk, allowing requesters the access to affordable and rapid results of a global workforce, greatly facilitates the creation of massive training data. Most of the available studies on the effectiveness of crowdsourcing report on English data. We use Mechanical Turk annotations to train an Opinion Mining System to classify Spanish consumer comments. We design three different Human Intelligence Task (HIT) strategies and report high inter-annotator agreement between non-experts and expert annotators. We evaluate the advantages/drawbacks of each HIT design and show that, in our case, the use of non-expert annotations is a viable and cost-effective alternative to expert annotations.

1 Introduction

Obtaining reliable human annotations to train data-driven AI systems is often an arduous and expensive process. For this reason, crowdsourcing platforms such as Amazon's Mechanical Turk[1], Crowdflower[2] and others have recently attracted a lot of attention from both companies and academia. Crowdsourcing enables requesters to tap from a global pool of non-experts to obtain rapid and affordable answers to simple Human Intelligence Tasks (HITs), which can be subsequently used to train data-driven applications.

A number of recent papers on this subject point out that non-expert annotations, if produced in a sufficient quantity, can rival and even surpass the quality of expert annotations, often at a much lower cost (Snow et al., 2008), (Su et al., 2007). However, this possible increase in quality depends on the task at hand and on an adequate HIT design (Kittur et al., 2008).

In this paper, we evaluate the usefulness of MTurk annotations to train an Opinion Mining System to detect opinionated contents (Polarity Detection) in Spanish customer comments on car brands. Currently, a large majority of MTurk tasks is designed for English speakers. One of our reasons for participating in this shared task was to find out how easy it is to obtain annotated data for Spanish. In addition, we want to find out how useful these data are by comparing them to expert annotations and using them as training data of an Opinion Mining System for polarity detection.

This paper is structured as follows. Section 2 contains an explanation of the task outline and our goals. Section 3 contains a description of three different HIT designs that we used in this task. In Section 4, we provide a detailed analysis of the retrieved HITs and focus on geographical information of the workers, the correlation between the different HIT designs, the quality of the retrieved answers and on the cost-effectiveness of the experiment. In Section 5, we evaluate the incidence of MTurk-generated annotations on a polarity classification task using two different experimental settings. Finally, we conclude

[1] https://www.mturk.com
[2] http://crowdflower.com/

Proceedings of the NAACL HLT 2010 Workshop on Creating Speech and Language Data with Amazon's Mechanical Turk, pages 114–121,
Los Angeles, California, June 2010.

in Section 6.

2 Task Outline and Goals

We compare different HIT design strategies by evaluating the usefulness of resulting Mechanical Turk (MTurk) annotations to train an Opinion Mining System on Spanish consumer data. More specifically, we address the following research questions:

(i) Annotation quality: how do the different MTurk annotations compare to expert annotations?

(ii) Annotation applicability: how does the performance of an Opinion Mining classifier vary after training on different (sub)sets of MTurk and expert annotations?

(iii) Return on Investment: how does the use of MTurk annotations compare economically against the use of expert annotations?

(iv) Language barriers: currently, most MTurk tasks are designed for English speakers. How easy is it to obtain reliable MTurk results for Spanish?

3 HIT Design

We selected a dataset of 1000 sentences containing user opinions on cars from the automotive section of `www.ciao.es` (Spanish). This website was chosen because it contains a large and varied pool of Spanish customer comments suitable to train an Opinion Mining System and because opinions include simultaneously global numeric and specific ratings over particular attributes of the subject matter. Section 5.1 contains more detailed information about the selection of the dataset. An example of a sentence from the data set can be found in (1):

(1) 'No te lo pienses más, cómpratelo!'
(= 'Don't think twice, buy it!')

The sentences in the dataset were presented to the MTurk workers in three different HIT designs. Each HIT design contains a single sentence to be evaluated. HIT1 is a simple categorization scheme in which workers are asked to classify the sentence as being either *positive*, *negative* or *neutral*, as is shown in Figure 1b. HIT2 is a graded categorization template in which workers had to assign a score between -5 (negative) and +5 (positive) to the example sentence, as is shown in Figure 1c. Finally, HIT3 is a continuous triangular scoring template that allows

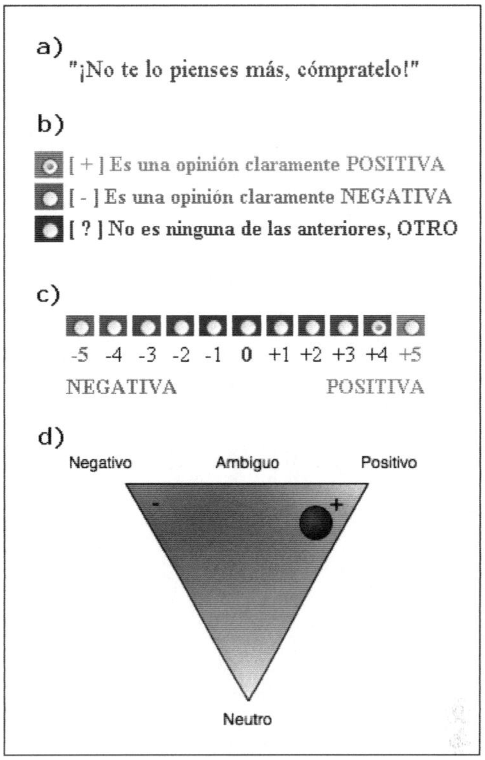

Figure 1: An example sentence (a) and the three HIT designs used in the experiments: (b) HIT1: a simple categorization scheme, (c) HIT2: a graded categorization scheme, and (d) HIT3: a continuous triangular scoring scheme containing both a horizontal positive-negative axis and a vertical subjective-objective axis.

workers to use both a horizontal positive-negative axis and a vertical subjective-objective axis by placing the example sentence anywhere inside the triangle. The subjective-objective axis expresses the degree to which the sentence contains opinionated content and was earlier used by (Esuli and Sebastiani, 2006). For example, the sentence *'I think this is a wonderful car'* clearly marks an opinion and should be positioned towards the subjective end, while the sentence *'The car has six cilinders'* should be located towards the objective end. Figure 1d contains an example of HIT3. In order not to burden the workers with overly complex instructions, we did not mention this subjective-objective axis but asked them instead to place ambiguous sentences towards the center of the horizontal positive-negative axis and more objective, non-opinionated sentences towards the lower *neutral* tip of the triangle.

For each of the three HIT designs, we specified the requirement of three different unique assignments per HIT, which led to a total amount of $3 \times 3 \times 1000 = 9000$ HIT assignments being uploaded on MTurk. Mind that setting the requirement of unique assigments ensures a number of unique workers *per individual HIT*, but does not ensure a consistency of workers over a single batch of 1000 HITs. This is in the line with the philosophy of crowdsourcing, which allows many different people to participate in the same task.

4 Annotation Task Results and Analysis

After designing the HITs, we uploaded 30 random samples for testing purposes. These HITs were completed in a matter of seconds, mostly by workers in India. After a brief inspection of the results, it was obvious that most answers corresponded to random clicks. Therefore, we decided to include a small competence test to ensure that future workers would possess the necessary linguistic skills to perform the task. The test consists of six simple categorisation questions of the type of HIT1 that a skilled worker would be able to perform in under a minute. In order to discourage the use of automatic translation tools, a time limit of two minutes was imposed and most test sentences contain idiomatic constructions that are known to pose problems to Machine Translation Systems.

4.1 HIT Statistics

Table 1 contains statistics on the workers who completed our HITs. A total of 19 workers passed the competence test and submitted at least one HIT. Of those, four workers completed HITs belonging to two different designs and six submitted HITs in all three designs. Twelve workers are located in the US (64%), three in Spain (16%), one in Mexico (5%), Equador (5%), The Netherlands (5%) and an unknown location (5%).

As to a comparison of completion times, it took a worker on average 11 seconds to complete an instance of HIT1, and 9 seconds to complete an instance of HIT2 and HIT3. At first sight, this result might seem surprising, since conceptually there is an increase in complexity when moving from HIT1 to HIT2 and from HIT2 to HIT3. These results might

Overall			HIT1		HIT2		HIT3	
ID	C	%	#	sec.	#	sec.	#	sec.
1	mx	29.9	794	11.0	967	8.6	930	11.6
2	us	27.6	980	8.3	507	7.8	994	7.4
3	nl	11.0	85	8.3	573	10.9	333	11.4
4	us	9.5	853	16.8	-	-	-	-
5	es	9.4	-	-	579	9.1	265	8.0
6	ec	4.1	151	9.4	14	16.7	200	13.0
7	us	3.6	3	15.7	139	8.5	133	11.6
8	us	2.2	77	8.2	106	7.3	11	10.5
9	us	0.6	-	-	-	-	50	11.2
10	us	0.5	43	5.3	1	5	-	-
11	us	0.4	-	-	38	25.2	-	-
12	us	0.4	-	-	10	9.5	27	10.8
13	es	0.4	-	-	-	-	35	15.1
14	es	0.3	-	-	30	13.5	-	-
15	us	0.3	8	24.7	18	21.5	-	-
16	us	0.2	-	-	-	-	22	8.9
17	us	0.2	-	-	17	16.5	-	-
18	?	0.1	6	20	-	-	-	-
19	us	0.1	-	-	1	33	-	-

Table 1: Statistics on MTurk workers for all three HIT designs: (fictional) worker ID, country code, % of total number of HITs completed, number of HITs completed per design and average completion time.

suggest that users find it easier to classify items on a graded or continuous scale such as HIT2 and HIT3, which allows for a certain degree of flexibility, than on a stricter categorical template such as HIT1, where there is no room for error.

4.2 Annotation Distributions

In order to get an overview of distribution of the results of each HIT, a histogram was plotted for each different task. Figure 2a shows a uniform distribution of the three categories used in the simple categorization scheme of HIT1, as could be expected from a balanced dataset.

Figure 2b shows the distribution of the graded categorization template of HIT2. Compared to the distribution in 2a, two observations can be made: (i) the proportion of the zero values is almost identical to the proportion of the neutral category in Figure 2a, and (ii) the proportion of the sum of the positive values [+1,+5] and the proportion of the sum of the negative values [-5,-1] are equally similar to the proportion of the positive and negative categories in 2a. This suggests that in order to map the graded annotations of HIT2 to the categories of HIT1, an intuitive partitioning of the graded scale into three equal parts should be avoided. Instead, a more adequate alternative would consist of mapping [-5,-1] to *negative*, 0

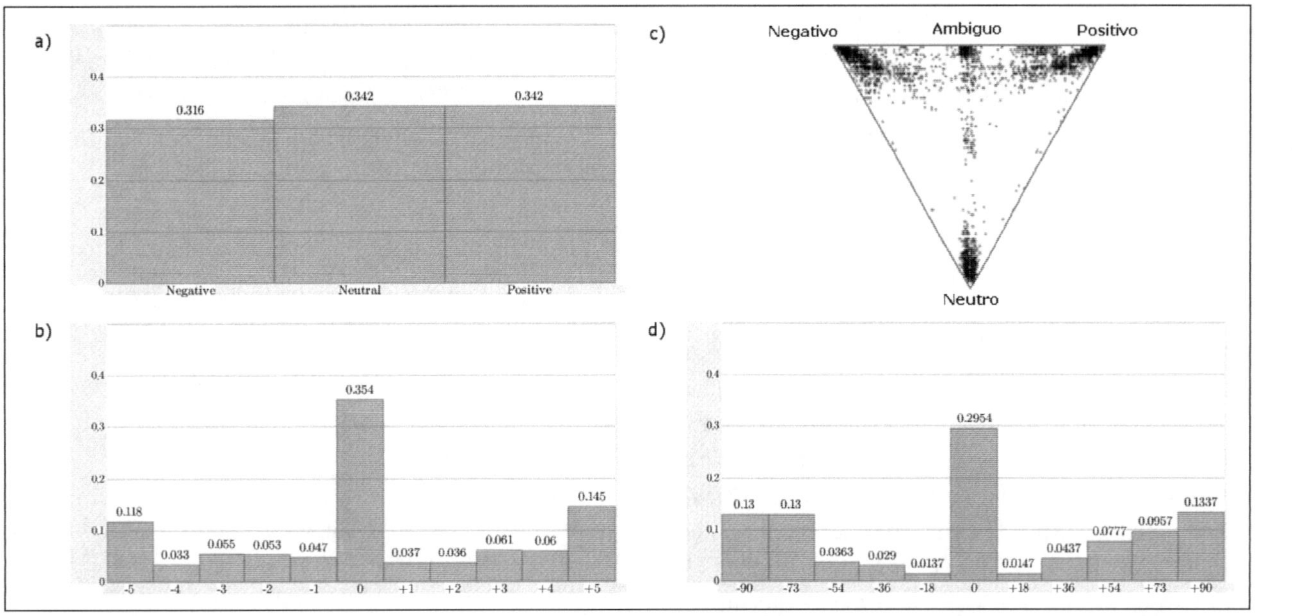

Figure 2: Overview of HIT results: a) distribution of the three categories used in HIT1, b) distribution of results in the scaled format of HIT2, c) heat map of the distribution of results in the HIT3 triangle, d) distribution of projection of triangle data points onto the X-axis (positive/negative).

to *neutral* and [+1,+5] to *positive*. This means that even slightly positive/negative grades correspond to positive/negative categories.

Figure 2c shows a heat map that plots the distribution of the annotations in the triangle of HIT3. It appears that worker annotations show a spontaneous tendency of clustering, despite the continuous nature of the design. This suggests that this HIT design, originally conceived as continuous, was transformed by the workers as a simpler categorization task using five labels: *negative*, *ambiguous* and *positive* at the top, *neutral* at the bottom, and *other* in the center.

Figure 2d shows the distribution of all datapoints in the triangle of Figure 2c, projected onto the X-axis (positive/negative). Although similar to the graded scale in HIT2, the distribution shows a slightly higher polarization.

These results suggest that, out of all three HIT designs, HIT2 is the one that contains the best balance between the amount of information that can be obtained and the simplicity of a one-dimensional annotation.

4.3 Annotation Quality

The annotation quality of MTurk workers can be measured by comparing them to expert annotations. This is usually done by calculating inter-annotator agreement (ITA) scores. Note that, since a single HIT can contain more than one assignment and each assignment is typically performed by more than one annotator, we can only calculate ITA scores between batches of assignments, rather than between individual workers. Therefore, we describe the ITA scores in terms of batches. In Table 4.4, we present a comparison of standard kappa[3] calculations (Eugenio and Glass, 2004) between batches of assignments in HIT1 and expert annotations.

We found an inter-batch ITA score of 0.598, which indicates a moderate agreement due to fairly consistent annotations between workers. When comparing individual batches with expert annotations, we found similar ITA scores, in the range between 0.628 and 0.649. This increase with respect to the inter-batch score suggests a higher variability among MTurk workers than between workers and experts. In order to filter out noise in worker annotations, we applied a simple majority voting procedure in which we selected, for each sentence in HIT1, the most voted category. This results in an additional

[3] In reality, we found that fixed and free margin Kappa values were almost identical, which reflects the balanced distribution of the dataset.

batch of annotations. This batch, refered in Table 4.4 as *Majority*, produced a considerably higher ITA score of 0.716, which confirms the validity of the majority voting scheme to obtain better annotations.

In addition, we calculated ITA scores between three expert annotators on a separate, 500-sentence dataset, randomly selected from the same corpus as described at the start of Section 3. This collection was later used as test set in the experiments described in Section 5. The inter-expert ITA scores on this separate dataset contains values of 0.725 for κ_1 and 0.729 for κ_2, only marginally higher than the *Majority* ITA scores. Although we are comparing results on different data sets, these results seem to indicate that multiple MTurk annotations are able to produce a similar quality to expert annotations. This might suggest that a further increase in the number of HIT assignments would outperform expert ITA scores, as was previously reported in (Snow et al., 2008).

4.4 Annotation Costs

As explained in Section 3, a total amount of 9000 assignments were uploaded on MTurk. At a reward of .02$ per assignment, a total sum of 225$ (180$ + 45$ Amazon fees) was spent on the task. Workers perceived an average hourly rate of 6.5$/hour for HIT1 and 8$/hour for HIT2 and HIT3. These figures suggest that, at least for assignments of type HIT2 and HIT3, a lower reward/assignment might have been considered. This would also be consistent with the recommendations of (Mason and Watts, 2009), who claim that lower rewards might have an effect on the speed at which the task will be completed - more workers will be competing for the task at any given moment - but not on the quality. Since we were not certain whether a large enough crowd existed with the necessary skills to perform our task, we explicitly decided not to try to offer the lowest possible price.

An in-house expert annotator (working at approximately 70$/hour, including overhead) finished a batch of 1000 HIT assignments in approximately three hours, which leads to a total expert annotator cost of 210$. By comparing this figure to the cost of uploading 3×1000 HIT assignments (75$), we saved $210 - 75 = 135$$, which constitutes almost 65% of the cost of an expert annotator. These figures do not take into account the costs of preparing the data and HIT templates, but it can be assumed that these costs will be marginal when large data sets are used. Moreover, most of this effort is equally needed for preparing data for in-house annotation.

	κ_1	κ_2
Inter-batch	0.598	0.598
Batch_1 vs. Expert	0.628	0.628
Batch_2 vs. Expert	0.649	0.649
Batch_3 vs. Expert	0.626	0.626
Majority vs. Expert	0.716	0.716
Experts[4]	0.725	0.729

Table 2: Interannotation Agreement as a measure of quality of the annotations in HIT1. κ_1 = Fixed Margin Kappa. κ_2 = Free Margin Kappa.

5 Incidence of annotations on supervised polarity classification

This section intends to evaluate the incidence of MTurk-generated annotations on a polarity classification task. We present two different evaluations. In section 5.2, we compare the results of training a polarity classification system with noisy available metadata and with MTurk generated annotations of HIT1. In section 5.3, we compare the results of training several polarity classifiers using different training sets, comparing expert annotations to those obtained with MTurk.

5.1 Description of datasets

As was mentioned in Section 3, all sentences were extracted from a corpus of user opinions on cars from the automotive section of `www.ciao.es` (Spanish). For conducting the experimental evaluation, the following datasets were used:

1. Baseline: constitutes the dataset used for training the baseline or reference classifiers in Experiment 1. Automatic annotation for this dataset was obtained by using the following naive approach: those sentences extracted from comments with ratings[5] equal to 5 were assigned to category 'positive', those extracted

[5]The corpus at `www.ciao.es` contains consumer opinions marked with a score between 1 (negative) and 5 (positive).

from comments with ratings equal to 3 were assigned to 'neutral', and those extracted from comments with ratings equal to 1 were assigned to 'negative'. This dataset contains a total of 5570 sentences, with a vocabulary coverage of 11797 words.

2. MTurk Annotated: constitutes the dataset that was manually annotated by MTurk workers in HIT1. This dataset is used for training the contrastive classifiers which are to be compared with the baseline system in Experiment 1. It is also used in various ways in Experiment 2. The three independent annotations generated by MTurk workers for each sentence within this dataset were consolidated into one unique annotation by majority voting: if the three provided annotations happened to be different[6], the sentence was assigned to category 'neutral'; otherwise, the sentence was assigned to the category with at least two annotation agreements. This dataset contains a total of 1000 sentences, with a vocabulary coverage of 3022 words.

3. Expert Annotated: this dataset contains the same sentences as the MTurk Annotated one, but with annotations produced internally by known reliable annotators[7]. Each sentence received one annotation, while the dataset was split between a total of five annotators.

4. Evaluation: constitutes the gold standard used for evaluating the performance of classifiers. This dataset was manually annotated by three experts in an independent manner. The gold standard annotation was consolidated by using the same criterion used in the case of the previous dataset[8]. This dataset contains a total of 500 sentences, with a vocabulary coverage of 2004 words.

[6]This kind of total disagreement among annotators occurred only in 13 sentences out of 1000.

[7]While annotations of this kind are necessarily somewhat subjective, these annotations are guaranteed to have been produced in good faith by competent annotators with an excellent understanding of the Spanish language (native or near-native speakers)

[8]In this case, annotator inter-agreement was above 80%, and total disagreement among annotators occurred only in 1 sentence out of 500

	Baseline	Annotated	Evaluation
Positive	1882	341	200
Negative	1876	323	137
Neutral	1812	336	161
Totals	5570	1000	500

Table 3: Sentence-per-category distributions for baseline, annotated and evaluation datasets.

These three datasets were constructed by randomly extracting sample sentences from an original corpus of over 25000 user comments containing more than 1000000 sentences in total. The sampling was conducted with the following constraints in mind: (i) the three resulting datasets should not overlap, (ii) only sentences containing more than 3 tokens are considered, and (iii) each resulting dataset must be balanced, as much as possible, in terms of the amount of sentences per category. Table 3 presents the distribution of sentences per category for each of the three considered datasets.

5.2 Experiment one: MTurk annotations vs. original Ciao annotations

A simple SVM-based supervised classification approach was considered for the polarity detection task under consideration. According to this, two different groups of classifiers were used: a baseline or reference group, and a contrastive group. Classifiers within these two groups were trained with data samples extracted from the baseline and annotated datasets, respectively. Within each group of classifiers, three different binary classification subtasks were considered: positive/not_positive, negative/not_negative and neutral/not_neutral. All trained binary classifiers were evaluated by computing precision and recall for each considered category, as well as overall classification accuracy, over the evaluation dataset.

A feature space model representation of the data was constructed by considering the standard bag-of-words approach. In this way, a sparse vector was obtained for each sentence in the datasets. Stop-word removal was not conducted before computing vector models, and standard normalization and TF-IDF weighting schemes were used.

Multiple-fold cross-validation was used in all conducted experiments to tackle with statistical vari-

classifier	baseline	annotated
positive/not_positive	59.63 (3.04)	69.53 (1.70)
negative/not_negative	60.09 (2.90)	63.73 (1.60)
neutral/not_neutral	51.27 (2.49)	62.57 (2.08)

Table 4: Mean accuracy over 20 independent simulations (with standard deviations provided in parenthesis) for each classification subtasks trained with either the baseline or the annotated dataset.

ability of the data. In this sense, twenty independent realizations were actually conducted for each experiment presented and, instead of individual output results, mean values and standard deviations of evaluation metrics are reported.

Each binary classifier realization was trained with a random subsample set of 600 sentences extracted from the training dataset corresponding to the classifier group, i.e. baseline dataset for reference systems, and annotated dataset for contrastive systems. Training subsample sets were always balanced with respect to the original three categories: 'positive', 'negative' and 'neutral'.

Table 4 presents the resulting mean values of accuracy for each considered subtask in classifiers trained with either the baseline or the annotated dataset. As observed in the table, all subtasks benefit from using the annotated dataset for training the classifiers; however, it is important to mention that while similar absolute gains are observed for the 'positive/not_positive' and 'neutral/not_neutral' subtasks, this is not the case for the subtask 'negative/not_negative', which actually gains much less than the other two subtasks.

After considering all evaluation metrics, the benefit provided by human-annotated data availability for categories 'neutral' and 'positive' is evident. However, in the case of category 'negative', although some gain is also observed, the benefit of human-annotated data does not seem to be as much as for the two other categories. This, along with the fact that the 'negative/not_negative' subtask is actually the best performing one (in terms of accuracy) when baseline training data is used, might suggest that low rating comments contains a better representation of sentences belonging to category 'negative' than medium and high rating comments do with respect to classes 'neutral' and 'positive'.

In any case, this experimental work only verifies the feasibility of constructing training datasets for opinionated content analysis, as well as it provides an approximated idea of costs involved in the generation of this type of resources, by using MTurk.

5.3 Experiment two: MTurk annotations vs. expert annotations

In this section, we compare the results of training several polarity classifiers on six different training sets, each of them generated from the MTurk annotations of HIT1. The different training sets are: (i) the original dataset of 1000 sentences annotated by experts (*Experts*), (ii) the first set of 1000 MTurk results (*Batch1*), (iii) the second set of 1000 MTurk results (*Batch2*), (iv) the third set of 1000 MTurk results (*Batch3*), (v) the batch obtained by majority voting between Batch1, Batch2 and Batch3 (*Majority*), and (vi) a batch of 3000 training instances obtained by aggregating Batch1, Batch2 and Batch3 (*All*). We used classifiers as implemented in Mallet (McCallum, 2002) and Weka (Hall et al., 2009), based on a simple bag-of-words representation of the sentences. As the objective was not to obtain optimum performance but only to evaluate the differences between different sets of annotations, all classifiers were used with their default settings.

Table 5 contains results of four different classifiers (Maxent, C45, Winnow and SVM), trained on these six different datasets and evaluated on the same 500-sentence test set as explained in Section 5.1. Classification using expert annotations usually outperforms classification using a single batch (one annotation per sentence) of annotations produced using MTurk. Using the tree annotations per sentence available from MTurk, all classifiers reach similar or better performance compared to the single set of expert annotations, at a much lower cost (as explained in section 4.4).

It is interesting to note that most classifiers benefit from using the full 3000 training examples (1000 sentences with 3 annotations each), which intuitively makes sense as the unanimously labeled examples will have more weight in defining the model of the corresponding class, whereas ambiguous or unclear cases will have their impact reduced as their characteristics are attributed to various classes.

On the contrary, Support Vector Machines show

System	Experts	Batch1	Batch2	Batch3	Majority	All
Winnow	44.2	43.6	40.4	47.6	46.2	**50.6**
SVM	**57.6**	53.0	55.4	54.0	57.2	52.8
C45	42.2	33.6	42.0	41.2	41.6	**45.0**
Maxent	**59.2**	55.8	57.6	54.0	57.6	58.6

Table 5: Accuracy figures of four different classifiers (Winnow, SVM, C45 and Maxent) trained on six different datasets (see text for details).

an important drop in performance when using multiple annotations, but perform well when using the majority vote. As a first intuition, this may be due to the fact that SVMs focus on detecting class boundaries (and optimizing the margin between classes) rather than developing a model of each class. As such, having the same data point appear several times with the same label will not aid in finding appropriate support vectors, whereas having the same data point with conflicting labels may have a negative impact on the margin maximization.

Having only evaluated each classifier (and training set) once on a static test set it is unfortunately not possible to reliably infer the significance of the performance differences (or determine confidence intervals, etc.). For a more in-depth analysis it might be interesting to use bootstrapping or similar techniques to evaluate the robustness of the results.

6 Conclusions

In this paper we have examined the usefulness of non-expert annotations on Amazon's Mechanical Turk to annotate the polarity of Spanish consumer comments. We discussed the advantages/drawbacks of three different HIT designs, ranging from a simple categorization scheme to a continous scoring template. We report high inter-annotator agreement scores between non-experts and expert annotators and show that training an Opinion Mining System with non-expert MTurk annotations outperforms original noisy annotations and obtains competitive results when compared to expert annotations using a variety of classifiers. In conclusion, we found that, in our case, the use of non-expert annotations through crowdsourcing is a viable and cost-effective alternative to the use of expert annotations.

In the classification experiments reported in this paper, we have relied exclusively on MTurk annotations from HIT1. Further work is needed to fully analyze the impact of each of the HIT designs for Opinion Mining tasks. We hope that the added richness of annotation of HIT2 and HIT3 will enable us to use more sophisticated classification methods.

References

A. Esuli and F. Sebastiani. 2006. SentiWordNet: a publicly available lexical resource for opinion mining. In *Proceedings of LREC*, volume 6.

B. D Eugenio and M. Glass. 2004. The kappa statistic: A second look. *Computational linguistics*, 30(1):95101.

Mark Hall, Eibe Frank, Geoffrey Holmes, Bernhard Pfahringer, Peter Reutemann, and Ian H. Witten. 2009. The weka data mining software: an update. *SIGKDD Explor. Newsl.*, 11(1):10–18.

A. Kittur, E. H Chi, and B. Suh. 2008. Crowdsourcing user studies with mechanical turk.

W. Mason and D. J Watts. 2009. Financial incentives and the performance of crowds. In *Proceedings of the ACM SIGKDD Workshop on Human Computation*, pages 77–85.

A. K. McCallum. 2002. Mallet: A machine learning for language toolkit. http://mallet.cs.umass.edu.

R. Snow, B. O'Connor, D. Jurafsky, and A. Y Ng. 2008. Cheap and fastbut is it good?: evaluating non-expert annotations for natural language tasks. In *Proceedings of the Conference on Empirical Methods in Natural Language Processing*, pages 254–263.

Q. Su, D. Pavlov, J. H Chow, and W. C Baker. 2007. Internet-scale collection of human-reviewed data. In *Proceedings of the 16th international conference on World Wide Web*, pages 231–240.

Crowdsourcing and language studies: the new generation of linguistic data

Robert Munro[a] **Steven Bethard**[b] **Victor Kuperman**[a] **Vicky Tzuyin Lai**[c]
Robin Melnick[a] **Christopher Potts**[a] **Tyler Schnoebelen**[a] **Harry Tily**[a]
[a]Department of Linguistics, Stanford University
[b]Department of Computer Science, Stanford University
[c]Department of Linguistics, University of Colorado
{rmunro,bethard,vickup,rmelnick,cgpotts,tylers,hjt}
@stanford.edu
vicky.lai@colorado.edu

Abstract

We present a compendium of recent and current projects that utilize crowdsourcing technologies for language studies, finding that the quality is comparable to controlled laboratory experiments, and in some cases superior. While crowdsourcing has primarily been used for annotation in recent language studies, the results here demonstrate that far richer data may be generated in a range of linguistic disciplines from semantics to psycholinguistics. For these, we report a number of successful methods for evaluating data quality in the absence of a 'correct' response for any given data point.

1 Introduction

Crowdsourcing's greatest contribution to language studies might be the ability to generate new *kinds* of data, especially within experimental paradigms. The speed and cost benefits for annotation are certainly impressive (Snow et al., 2008; Callison-Burch, 2009; Hsueh et al., 2009) but we hope to show that some of the greatest gains are in the very nature of the phenomena that we can now study.

For psycholinguistic experiments in particular, we are not so much utilizing 'artificial artificial' intelligence as the plain intelligence and linguistic intuitions of each crowdsourced worker – the 'voices in the crowd', so to speak. In many experiments we are studying gradient phenomena where there are no right answers. Even when there is binary response we are often interested in the distribution of responses over many speakers rather than specific data points. This differentiates experimentation from more common means of determining the quality of crowdsourced results as there is no gold standard against which to evaluate the quality or 'correctness' of each individual response.

The purpose of this paper is therefore two-fold. We summarize seven current projects that are utilizing crowdsourcing technologies, all of them somewhat novel to the NLP community but with potential for future research in computational linguistics. For each, we also discuss methods for evaluating quality, finding the crowdsourced results to often be indistinguishable from controlled laboratory experiments.

In Section 2 we present the results from semantic transparency experiments showing near-perfect interworker reliability and a strong correlation between crowdsourced data and lab results. Extending to audio data, we show in Section 3 that crowdsourced subjects were statistically indistinguishable from a lab control group in segmentation tasks. Section 4 shows that laboratory results from simple Cloze tasks can be reproduced with crowdsourcing. In Section 5 we offer strong evidence that crowdsourcing can also replicate limited-population, controlled-condition lab results for grammaticality judgments. In Section 6 we use crowdsourcing to support corpus studies with a precision not possible with even very large corpora. Moving to the brain itself, Section 7 demonstrates that ERP brainwave analysis can be enhanced by crowdsourced analysis of experimental stimuli. Finally, in Section 8 we outline simple heuristics for ensuring that microtasking workers are applying the linguistic attentiveness required to undertake more complex tasks.

Proceedings of the NAACL HLT 2010 Workshop on Creating Speech and Language Data with Amazon's Mechanical Turk, pages 122–130,
Los Angeles, California, June 2010.

2 Transparency of phrasal verbs

Phrasal verbs are those verbs that spread their meaning out across both a verb and a particle, as in 'lift up'. *Semantic transparency* is a measure of how strongly the phrasal verb entails the component verb. For example, to what extent does 'lifting up' entail 'lifting'? We can see the variation between phrasal verbs when we compare the transparency of 'lift up' to the opacity of 'give up'.

We conducted five experiments around semantic transparency, with results showing that crowdsourced results correlate well with each other and against lab data (ρ up to 0.9). Interrater reliability is also very high: $\kappa = 0.823$, which Landis and Koch (1977) would call 'almost perfect agreement.'

The crowdsourced results reported here represent judgments by 215 people. Two experiments were performed using Stanford University undergraduates. The first involved a questionnaire asking participants to rate the semantic transparency of 96 phrasal verbs. The second experiment consisted of a paper questionnaire with the phrasal verbs in context. That is, the first group of 'StudentLong' participants rated the similarity of 'cool' to 'cool down' on a scale 1-7:

cool   cool down   ______

The 'StudentContext' participants performed the same basic task but saw each verb/phrasal verb pair with an example of the phrasal verb in context.

With Mechanical Turk, we had three conditions:

TurkLong: A replication of the first questionnaire and its 96 questions.

TurkShort: The 96-questions were randomized into batches of 6. Thus, some participants ended up giving responses to all phrasal verbs, while others only gave 6, 12, 18, etc responses.

TurkContext: A variation of the 'StudentContext' task – participants were given examples of the phrasal verbs, though as with 'TurkShort', they were only asked to rate 6 phrasal verbs at a time.

What we find is a split into relatively high and low correlations, as Figure 1 shows. All Mechanical Turk tests correlate very well with one another (all $\rho > 0.7$), although the tasks and raters are different. The correlation between the student participants who were given sentence contexts and the workers

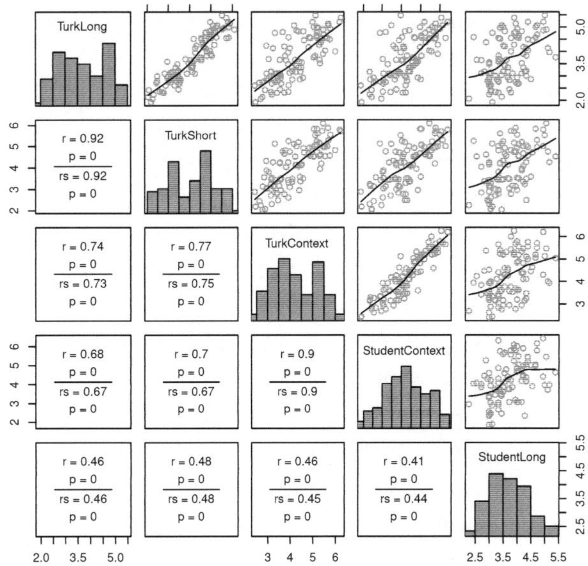

Figure 1: Panels at the diagonal report histograms of distributions of ratings across populations of participants; panels above the diagonal plot the locally weighted scatterplot smoothing Lowess functions for a pair of correlated variables; panels below the diagonal report correlation coefficients (the r value is Pearson's r, the rs value is Spearman's ρ) and respective ρ values.

who saw context is especially high (0.9). All correlations with StudentLong are relatively low, but this is actually true for StudentLong vs. StudentContext, too ($\rho = 0.44$), even though both groups are Stanford undergraduates.

Intra-class correlation coefficients (ICC) measure the agreement among participants, and these are high for all groups except StudentLong. Just among StudentLong participants, the ICC consistency is only 0.0934 and their ICC agreement is 0.0854. Once we drop StudentLong, we see that all of the remaining tests have high consistency (average of 0.78 for ICC consistency, 0.74 for ICC agreement). For example, if we combine TurkContext and StudentContext, ICC consistency is 0.899 and ICC agreement of 0.900. Cohen's kappa measurement also measures how well raters agree, weeding out chance agreements. Again, StudentLong is an outlier. Together, TurkContext / StudentContext gets a weighted kappa score of 0.823 – the overall average (excepting StudentLong) is $\kappa = 0.700$.

More details about the results in this section can be found in Schnoebelen and Kuperman (submitted).

3 Segmentation of an audio speech stream

The ability of browsers to present multimedia resources makes it feasible to use crowdsourcing techniques to generate data using spoken as well as written stimuli. In this section we report an MTurk replication of a classic psycholinguistic result that relies on audio presentation of speech. We developed a web-based interface that allows us to collect data in a statistical word segmentation paradigm. The core is a Flash applet developed using Adobe Flex which presents audio stimuli and collects participant responses (Frank et al., submitted).

Human children possess a remarkable ability to learn the words and structures of languages they are exposed to without explicit instruction. One particularly remarkable aspect is that unlike many written languages, spoken language lacks spaces between words: from spoken input, children learn not only the mapping between meanings and words but also what the words themselves are, with no direct information about where one ends and the next begins. Research in *statistical word segmentation* has shown that both infants and adults use statistical properties of speech in an unknown language to infer a probable vocabulary. In one classic study, Saffran, Newport & Aslin (1996) showed that after a few minutes of exposure to a language made by randomly concatenating copies of invented words, adult participants could discriminate those words from syllable sequences that also occurred in the input but crossed a word boundary. We replicated this study showing that cheap and readily accessible data from crowdsourced workers compares well to data from participants recorded in person in the lab.

Participants heard 75 sentences from one of 16 artificially constructed languages. Each language contained 2 two-syllable, 2 three-syllable, and 2 four syllable words, with syllables drawn from a possible set of 18. Each sentence consisted of four words sampled without replacement from this set and concatenated. Sentences were rendered as audio by the MBROLA synthesizer (Dutoit et al., 1996) at a constant pitch of 100Hz with 25ms consonants and 225ms vowels. Between each sentence, participants were required to click a "next" button to continue, preventing workers from leaving their computer during this training phase. To ensure workers could actually hear the stimuli, they were first asked to enter an English word presented auditorily.

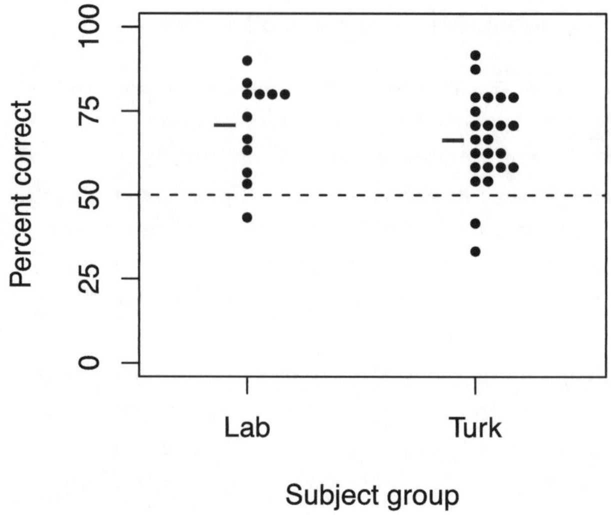

Figure 2: Per-subject correct responses for lab and MTurk participants. Bars show group means, and the dashed line indicates the chance baseline.

Workers then completed ten test trials in which they heard one word from the language and one nonword made by concatenating all but the first syllable of one word with the first syllable of another. If the words "bapu" and "gudi" had been presented adjacently, the string "pugu" would have been heard, despite not being a word of the language. Both were also displayed orthographically, and the worker was instructed to click on the one which had appeared in the previously heard language.

The language materials described above were taken from a Saffran et al. (1996) replication reported as Experiment 2 in Frank, Goldwater, Griffiths & Tenenbaum (under review). We compared the results from lab participants reported in that article to data from MTurk workers using the applet described above. Each response was marked "correct" if the participant chose the word rather than the nonword. 12 lab subjects achieved 71% correct responses, while 24 MTurk workers were only slightly lower at 66%. The MTurk results proved significantly different from a "random clicking" baseline of 50% ($t(23) = 5.92$, $p = 4.95 \times 10^{-06}$) but not significantly different from the lab subjects (Welch two-sample t-test for unequal sample sizes, $t(21.21) = -.92$, $p = .37$). Per-subject means for the lab and MTurk data are plotted in Figure 2.

4 Contextual predictability

As psycholinguists build models of sentence processing (e.g., from eye tracking studies), they need to understand the effect of the available sentence context. One way to gauge this is the Cloze task proposed in Taylor (1953): participants are presented with a sentence fragment and asked to provide the upcoming word. Researchers do this for every word in every stimulus and use the percentage of 'correct' guesses as input into their statistical and computational models.

Rather than running such norming studies on undergraduates in lab settings (as is typical), our results suggest that psycholinguists will be able to crowdsource these tasks, saving time and money without sacrificing reliability (Schnoebelen and Kuperman, submitted).

Our results are taken from 488 Americans, ranging from age 16-80 (mean: 34.49, median: 32, mode: 27) with about 25% each from the East and Midwest, 31% from the South, the rest from the West and Alaska. They represent a range of education levels, though the majority had been to college: about 33.8% had bachelor's degrees, another 28.1% had some college but without a degree.

By contrast, the lab data was gathered from 20 participants, all undergraduates at the University of Massachusetts at Amherst in the mid-1990's (Reichle et al., 1998). Both populations provided judgments on 488 words in 48 sentences. In general, crowdsourcing gave more diverse responses, as we would expect from a more diverse population.

The correlation between lab and crowdsourced data by Spearman's rank correlation is 0.823 ($\rho < 0.0001$), but we can be even more conservative by eliminating the 124 words that had predictability scores of 0 across both groups. By and large, the lab participants and the workers are consistent in which words they fail to predict. Even when we eliminate these shared zeros, the correlation is still high between the two data sets: weighted $\kappa = 0.759$ ($\rho < 0.0001$).

5 Judgment studies of fine-grained probabilistic grammatical knowledge

Moving to syntax, we demonstrate here that grammaticality judgments from lab studies can also be reproduced through crowdsourcing.

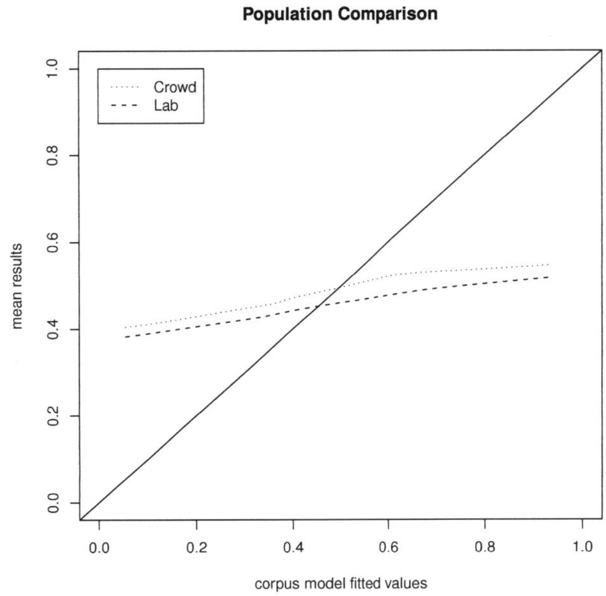

Figure 3: Mean 'that'-inclusion ratings plotted against corresponding corpus-model predictions. The solid line would represent perfect alignment between judgments and corpus model. Non-parametric Lowess smoothers illustrate the significant correlation between lab and crowd population results.

Corpus studies of spontaneous speech suggest that grammaticality is gradient (Wasow, 2008), and models of English complement clause (CC) and relative clause (RC) 'that'-optionality have as their most significant factor the predictability of embedding, given verb (CC) and head noun (RC) lemma (Jaeger, 2006; Jaeger, in press). Establishing that these highly gradient factors are similarly involved in judgments could provide evidence that such fine-grained probabilistic knowledge is part of linguistic competence.

We undertook six such judgment experiments: two baseline studies with lab populations then four additional crowdsourced trials via MTurk.

Experiment 1, a lab trial (26 participants, 30 items), began with the models of RC-reduction developed in Jaeger (2006). Corpus tokens were binned by relative model-predicted probability of 'that'-omission. Six tokens were extracted at random from each of five bins ($0 \leq \rho < 20\%$ likelihood of 'that'-inclusion; $20 \leq \rho < 40\%$; and so on). In a gradient scoring paradigm with 100 points distributed between available options (Bresnan, 2007) participants rated how likely each choice – with or without 'that' – was as the continuation of a segment of discourse. As hypothesized, mean participant ratings significantly correlate with corpus model predictions ($r = 0.614$, $\rho = 0.0003$).

Experiment 2 (29 participants) replicated Experiment 1 to address concerns that subjects might be 'over-thinking' the process. We used a timed forced-choice paradigm where participants had from 5 to 24 seconds (varied as a linear function of token length) to choose between the reduced/unreduced RC stimuli. These results correlate even more closely with predictions ($r = 0.838$, $\rho < 0.0001$).

Experiments 3 and 4 replicated 1 and 2 on MTurk (1200 tasks each). Results were filtered by volunteered demographics to select the same subject profile as the lab experiments. Response-time outliers were also excluded to avoid fast-click-through and distracted-worker data. Combined, these steps eliminated 384 (32.0%) and 378 (31.5%) tasks, respectively, with 89 and 66 unique participants remaining. While crowdsourced measures might be expected to yield lower correlations due to such unbalanced data sets, the results remain significant in both trials ($r = 0.562$, $\rho = 0.0009$; $r = 0.364$, $\rho = 0.0285$), offering strong evidence that crowdsourcing can replicate limited-population, controlled-condition lab results, and of the robustness of the alignment between production and judgment models. Figure 3 compares lab and crowd population results in the 100-point task (Experiments 1 and 3).

Experiments 5 and 6 (1600 hits each) employed the same paradigms via MTurk to investigate 'that'-mentioning in CCs, where predictability of embedding is an even stronger factor in the corpus model. Filtering reduced the data by 590 (36.9%) and 863 (53.9%) hits. As with the first four experiments, each of these trials produced significant correlations ($r = 0.433$, $\rho = 0.0107$; $r = 0.500$, $\rho = 0.0034$; respectively). Finally, mixed-effect binary logistic regression models – with verb lemma and test subject ID as random effects – were fitted to these judgment data. As in the corpus-derived models, predictability of embedding remains the most significant factor in all experimental models.

The results across both lab and crowdsourced studies suggest that speakers consider the same factors in judgment as in production, offering evidence that competence grammar includes access to probability distributions. Meanwhile, the strong correlations across populations offer encouraging evidence in support of using the latter in psycholinguistic judgment research.

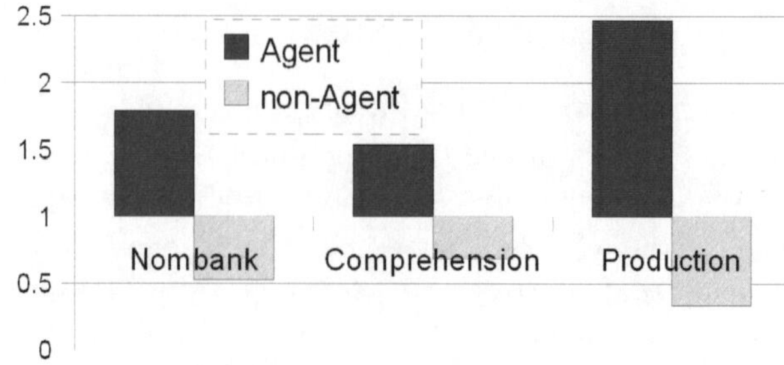

Figure 4: Odds ratio of a Nominal Agent being embedded within a Sentential Agent or non-Agent, relative to random chance. ($\rho < 0.001$ for all)

6 Confirming corpus trends

Crowdsourcing can also be used to establish the validity of corpus trends found in otherwise skewed data. The experiments in this section were motivated by the NomBank corpus of nominal predicate/arguments (Meyers et al., 2004) where we found that an Agent semantic role was much more likely to be embedded within a sentential Agent. For example, (1) is more likely than (2) to receive the Agent interpretation for the 'the police', but both have same potential range of meanings:

(1) "The investigation of the police took 3 weeks to complete"

(2) "It took 3 weeks to complete the investigation of the police"

While the trend is significant ($\rho < 0.001$), the corpus is not representative speech.

First, there are no minimal pairs of sentences in NomBank like (1) and (2) that have the same potential range of meanings. Second, the *s-genitive* ("the police's investigation") is inherently more Agentive than the *of-genitive* ("the investigation of the police") and it is also more compact. Sentential subjects tend to be lighter than objects, and more likely to realize Agents, so the resulting correlation could be indirect. Finally, if we sampled only the predicates/arguments in NomBank that are frequent in different sentential positions, we are limited to:

"earning, product, profit, trading, loss, share, rate, sale, price". This purely financial terminology is not representative of a typical acquisition environment – no child should be exposed to only such language – so it is difficult to draw broad conclusions about the cognitive viability of this correlation, even within English. It is because of factors like these that corpus linguistics has been somewhat of a 'poor cousin' to theoretical linguistics.

Therefore, two sets of experiments were undertaken to confirm that the trend is not epiphenomenal, one testing comprehension and one testing production.

The first tested thousands of workers' interpretations of sentences like those in (1) and (2), over a number of predicate/argument pairs ("shooting of the hunters", "destruction of the army" etc). Workers were asked their interpretation of the most likely meaning. For example, does (1) mean: "a: the police were doing the investigation" or "b: the police are being investigated". To control for errors or click-throughs, two plainly incorrect options were included. We estimate the erroneous response rate at about 0.4% – less than many lab studies.

For the second set of experiments, workers were asked to reword an *unambiguous* sentence using a given phrase. For example, rewording the following using "the investigation of the police":

(3) "Following the shooting of a commuter in Oakland last week, a reporter has uncovered new evidence while investigating the police involved."

We then (manually) recorded whether the required phrase was in a sentential Agent or non-Agent position.

Figure 4 gives the results from the corpus analysis and both experiments. The results clearly show a significant trend for all, and that the NomBank trend falls between the comprehension and production tasks, which would be expected for this highly edited register. It therefore supports the validity of the corpus results.

The phenomena likely exists to aid comprehension, as the cognitive realization of just one role needs to be activated at a given moment. Despite the near-ubiquity of 'Agent' in studies of semantic roles, we do not yet have a clear theory of this linguistic entity, or even firm evidence of its existence (Parikh, 2010). This study therefore goes some way towards illuminating this. More broadly, the experiments in this section support the wider use of crowdsourcing as a tool for language cognition research in conjunction with more traditional corpus studies.

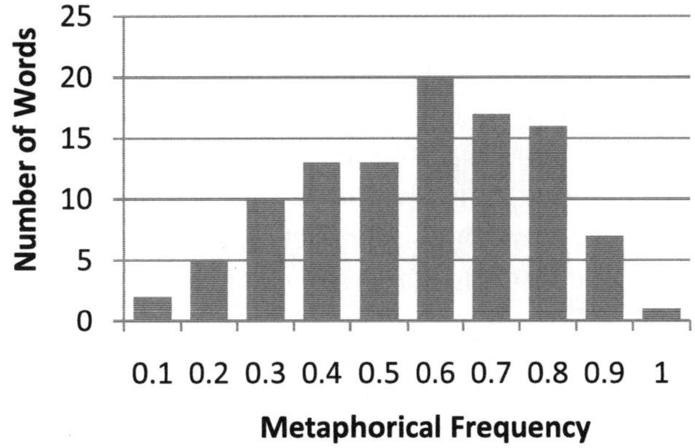

Figure 5: Distribution of metaphorical frequencies.

7 Post-hoc metaphorical frequency analysis of electrophysiological responses

Beyond reproducing laboratory and corpus studies, crowdsourcing also offers the opportunity to newly analyze data drawn from many other experimental stimuli. In this section, we demonstrate that crowdsourced workers can help us better understand ERP brainwave data by looking at how frequently words are used metaphorically.

Recent work in event related potentials (ERP) has suggested that even conventional metaphors, such as "All my ideas were attacked" require additional processing effort in the brain as compared to literal sentences like "All the soldiers were attacked" (Lai et al., 2009). This study in particular observed an N400 effect where negative waves 400 milliseconds after the presentation of the target words (e.g. *attacked*) were larger when the word was used metaphorically than when used literally.

The proposed explanation for this effect is that metaphors really do demand more from the brain than literal sentences. However, N400 effects are also observed when subjects encounter something that is semantically inappropriate or unexpected. While the Lai experiment controlled for overall word frequency, it might be possible to explain away these N400 effects if it turned out that in the real world the target words were almost always used literally, so that seeing them used metaphorically would be semantically incongruous.

To test this alternative hypothesis, we gathered sense frequency distributions for each of the target words – the hypothesis predicts that these should be skewed towards literal senses. For each of the 104 target words, we selected 50 random sentences from the American National Corpus (ANC), filling in with British National Corpus sentences when there were too few in the ANC. We gave the sentences to crowdsourced workers and asked them to label each target word as being used literally or metaphorically. Each task contained one sentence for each of the 104 target words, with the order of words and the literal/metaphorical buttons randomized. Each sentence was annotated 5 times.

To encourage native speakers of English, we had the MTurk service require that our workers be within the United States, and posted the text "Please accept this HIT only if you are a native speaker of English" in bold at the top of each HIT. We also used Javascript to force workers to spend at least 2 seconds on each sentence and we rejected results from workers that had chance level (50%) agreement with the other workers.

Though our tasks produced words annotated with literal and metaphorical tags, we were less interested in the individual annotations (though agreement was decent at 73%) and more interested in the overall pattern for each target word. Some words, like *fruit*, were almost always used literally (92%), while other words, like *hurdle* were almost always used metaphorically (91%) .

Overall, the target words had a mean metaphorical frequency of 53%, indicating that their literal and metaphorical senses were used in nearly equal proportions. Figure 5 shows that the metaphorical frequencies follow roughly a bell-curved distribution[1], which is especially interesting given that the target words were hand-selected for the Lai experiment and not drawn randomly from a corpus. We did not observe any skew towards literal senses as the alternative hypothesis would have predicted. This suggests that the findings of Lai, Curran, and Menn

[1]A Shapiro-Wilk test fails to reject the null hypothesis of a normal distribution (p=0.09).

Item type	correct	incorrect
'easy'	60	2
'promise'	59	3
stacked genitive	55	7

Table 1: Response data for three control items, with the goal of identifying workers who lack the requisite attentiveness. All show high attentiveness. The difference between the 'easy' and 'stacked genitive' is trending but not significant ($\rho = 0.0835$), indicating that any of these may be used.

(2009) cannot be dismissed based on a sense frequency argument.

We also took advantage of the collected sense frequency distributions to re-analyze data from the Lai experiment. We split the target words into a high bin (average 72% metaphorical) and a low bin (average 33% metaphorical), matching the number of items and average word log-frequency per bin. Looking at the average ERPs (brain waves) over time for each bin revealed that when subjects were reading novel metaphors, there was a significant difference ($p = .01$) at about 200ms (P200) between the ERPs for the highly literal words and the ERPs for the highly metaphorical words. Thus, not only does metaphorical frequency influence figurative language processing, but it does so much earlier than semantic effects are usually observed (e.g. N400 effects at 400ms)[2].

8 Screening for linguistic attentiveness

For annotation tasks, crowdsourcing is most successful when the tasks are designed to be as simple as possible, but in experimental work we don't always want to target the shallowest knowledge of the workers, so here we seek to discover just how attentive the workers really are.

When running psycholinguistics experiments in the lab, the experimenters generally have the chance to interact with participants. It is not uncommon for prospective subjects to be visibly exhausted, distracted, or inebriated, or not fluent in the given language to a requisite level of competence. When these participants turn up as outliers in the experimental data, it is easy enough to see why — they fell asleep, couldn't understand the instructions, etc.

[2]These results are consistent with recent findings that irony frequency may also produce P200 effects (Regel et al., 2010).

With crowdsourcing we lose the chance to have these brief but valuable encounters, and so anomalous response data are harder to interpret.

We present two simple experiments for measuring linguistic attentiveness, which can be used as one component of a language study or to broadly evaluate the linguistic competency of the workers. Taking well-known constructions from the literature, we selected constructions that: (a) exist in most (perhaps all) dialects of English; (b) involve high frequency lexical items; and (c) tend to be acquired relatively late by first-language learners.

We have found two constructions from Carol Chomsky's (1969) work on first-language acquisition to be particularly useful:

(4) John is easy to see.

(5) John is eager to see.

Example (4) is accurately paraphrased as 'It is easy to see John', where John is the object of 'see', whereas (5) is accurately paraphrased as 'John is eager for John to see', where John is the subject of 'see'. A similar shift happens with 'promise':

(6) Bozo told Donald to sing.

(7) Bozo promised Donald to sing.

We presented workers with a multiple-choice question that contained both subject and object paraphrases as options.

In similar experiments, we adapted examples from Roeper (2007), who looked at stacked prenominal possessive constructions:

(8) John's sister's friend's car.

These are cross-linguistically rare and challenging even for native speakers. As above, the workers were asked to choose between paraphrases.

Workers who provide accurate judgments are likely to have a level of English competence and devotion to the task that suffices for many language experiments. The results from one short audio study are given in Table 1. They indicate a high degree of attentiveness; as a group, our subjects performed at the near-perfect levels we expect for fluent adults.

We predict that adding tasks like these to experiments will not only screen for attentiveness, but also prompt for greater attention from an otherwise distracted worker, improving results at both ends.

9 Conclusions

While crowdsourcing was first used by linguists for annotation, we hope that the results here demonstrate the potential for far richer studies. In a range of linguistic disciplines from semantics to psycholinguistics it enables systematic, large-scale judgment studies that are more affordable and convenient than expensive, time-consuming lab-based studies. With crowdsourcing technologies, linguists have a reliable new tool for experimentally investigating language processing and linguistic theory.

Here, we have reproduced many 'classic' large-scale lab studies with a relative ease. We can envision many more ways that crowdsourcing might come to shape new methodologies for language studies. The affordability and agility brings experimental linguistics closer to corpus linguistics, allowing the quick generation of targeted corpora. Multiple iterations that were previously possible only over many years and several grants (and therefore never attempted) are now possible in a matter of days. This could launch whole new multi-tiered experimental designs, or at the very least allow 'rapid prototyping' of experiments for later lab-based verification.

Crowdsourcing also brings psycholinguistics much closer to computational linguistics. The two fields have always shared empirical data-driven methodologies and computer-aided methods. We now share a work-space too. Historically, NLP has necessarily drawn corpora from the parts of linguistic theory that have stayed still long enough to support time-consuming annotation projects. The results here have implications for such tasks, including parsing, word-sense disambiguation and semantic role labeling, but the most static parts of a field are rarely the most exciting. We therefore predict that crowdsourcing will also lead to an expanded, more dynamic NLP repertoire.

Finally, for the past half-century theoretical linguistics has relied heavily on 'introspective' corpus generation, as the rare edge cases often tell us the most about the boundaries of a given language. Now that we can quickly and confidently generate empirical results to evaluate hypotheses drawn from intuitions about the most infrequent linguistic phenomena, the need for this particular fallback has diminished – the stimuli are abundant.

Acknowledgements

We owe thanks to many people, especially within the Department of Linguistics at Stanford, which has quickly become a hive of activitiy for crowdsourced linguistic research. In particular, we thank Tom Wasow for his guidance in Section 5, Chris Manning for his guidance in Section 6, and Florian T. Jaeger for providing the corpus-derived base models in Section 5 (Jaeger, 2006). We also thank Michael C. Frank for providing the design, materials, and lab data used to evaluate the methods in Section 3. Several of the projects reported here were supported by Stanford Graduate Fellowships.

References

Joan Bresnan. 2007. Is syntactic knowledge probabilistic? Experiments with the English dative alternation. In Sam Featherston and Wolfgang Sternefeld, editors, *Roots: Linguistics in search of its evidential base*, pages 75–96. Mouton de Gruyter, Berlin.

Chris Callison-Burch. 2009. Fast, cheap, and creative: evaluating translation quality using Amazon's Mechanical Turk. In *EMNLP '09: Proceedings of the 2009 Conference on Empirical Methods in Natural Language Processing*, pages 286–295.

Carol Chomsky. 1969. *The Acquisition of Syntax in Children from 5 to 10.* MIT Press, Cambridge, MA.

Thierry Dutoit, Vincent Pagel, Nicolas Pierret, Franois Bataille, and Olivier van der Vrecken. 1996. The MBROLA project: Towards a set of high quality speech synthesizers free of use for non commercial purposes. In *Fourth International Conference on Spoken Language Processing*, pages 75–96.

Michael Frank, Harry Tily, Inbal Arnon, and Sharon Goldwater. submitted. Beyond transitional probabilities: Human learners impose a parsimony bias in statistical word segmentation.

Michael Frank, Sharon Goldwater, Thomas Griffiths, and Joshua Tenenbaum. under review. Modeling human performance in statistical word segmentation.

Pei-Yun Hsueh, Prem Melville, and Vikas Sindhwani. 2009. Data quality from crowdsourcing: a study of annotation selection criteria. In *Proceedings of the NAACL HLT 2009 Workshop on Active Learning for Natural Language Processing*, pages 27–35.

Florian Jaeger. 2006. *Redundancy and syntactic reduction in spontaneous speech.* Ph.D. thesis, Stanford University, Stanford, CA.

Florian Jaeger. in press. Redundancy and reduction: Speakers manage syntactic information density. *Cognitive Psychology*.

Vicky Tzuyin Lai, Tim Curran, and Lise Menn. 2009. Comprehending conventional and novel metaphors: An ERP study. *Brain Research*, 1284:145–155, August.

Richard Landis and Gary Koch. 1977. The measurement of observer agreement for categorical data. *Biometrics*, 33(1).

Adam Meyers, Ruth Reeves, Catherine Macleod, Rachel Szekely, Veronika Zielinska, Brian Young, , and Ralph Grishman. 2004. Annotating noun argument structure for NomBank. In *Proceedings of LREC-2004*.

Prashant Parikh. 2010. *Language and Equilibrium.* MIT Press, Cambridge, MA.

Stefanie Regel, Seana Coulson, and Thomas C. Gunter. 2010. The communicative style of a speaker can affect language comprehension? ERP evidence from the comprehension of irony. *Brain Research*, 1311:121–135.

Erik D. Reichle, Alexander Pollatsek, Donald L. Fisher, and Keith Rayner. 1998. Toward a model of eye movement control in reading. *Psychological Review*, 105:125–157.

Tom Roeper. 2007. *The Prism of Grammar: How Child Language Illuminates Humanism.* MIT Press, Cambridge, MA.

Jenny R. Saffran, Richard N. Aslin, and Elissa L. Newport. 1996. Word segmentation: The role of distributional cues. *Journal of memory and language*, 35:606–621.

Tyler Schnoebelen and Victor Kuperman. submitted. Using Amazon Mechanical Turk for linguistic research: Fast, cheap, easy, and reliable.

Rion Snow, Brendan O'Connor, Daniel Jurafsky, and Andrew T. Ng. 2008. Cheap and fast—but is it good?: evaluating non-expert annotations for natural language tasks. In *EMNLP '08: Proceedings of the Conference on Empirical Methods in Natural Language Processing*, pages 254–263.

Wilson Taylor. 1953. Cloze procedure: A new tool for measuring readability. *Journalism Quarterly*, 30:415–433.

Tom Wasow. 2008. Gradient data and gradient grammars. In *Proceedings of the 43rd Annual Meeting of the Chicago Linguistics Society*, pages 255–271.

Not-So-Latent Dirichlet Allocation: Collapsed Gibbs Sampling Using Human Judgments

Jonathan Chang
Facebook
1601 S. California Ave.
Palo Alto, CA 94304
jonchang@facebook.com

Abstract

Probabilistic topic models are a popular tool for the unsupervised analysis of text, providing both a predictive model of future text and a latent topic representation of the corpus. Recent studies have found that while there are suggestive connections between topic models and the way humans interpret data, these two often disagree. In this paper, we explore this disagreement from the perspective of the learning process rather than the output. We present a novel task, *tag-and-cluster*, which asks subjects to simultaneously annotate documents and cluster those annotations. We use these annotations as a novel approach for constructing a topic model, grounded in human interpretations of documents. We demonstrate that these topic models have features which distinguish them from traditional topic models.

1 Introduction

Probabilistic topic models have become popular tools for the unsupervised analysis of large document collections (Deerwester et al., 1990; Griffiths and Steyvers, 2002; Blei and Lafferty, 2009). These models posit a set of latent *topics*, multinomial distributions over words, and assume that each document can be described as a mixture of these topics. With algorithms for fast approximate posterior inference, we can use topic models to discover both the topics and an assignment of topics to documents from a collection of documents. (See Figure 1.)

These modeling assumptions are useful in the sense that, empirically, they lead to good models of documents (Wallach et al., 2009). However, recent work has explored how these assumptions correspond to humans' understanding of language (Chang et al., 2009; Griffiths and Steyvers, 2006; Mei et al., 2007). Focusing on the latent space, i.e., the inferred mappings between topics and words and between documents and topics, this work has discovered that although there are some suggestive correspondences between human semantics and topic models, they are often discordant.

In this paper we build on this work to further explore how humans relate to topic models. But whereas previous work has focused on the results of topic models, here we focus on the process by which these models are learned. Topic models lend themselves to sequential procedures through which the latent space is inferred; these procedures are in effect programmatic encodings of the modeling assumptions. By substituting key steps in this program with human judgments, we obtain insights into the semantic model conceived by humans.

Here we present a novel task, *tag-and-cluster*, which asks subjects to simultaneously annotate a document and cluster that annotation. This task simulates the sampling step of the collapsed Gibbs sampler (described in the next section), except that the posterior defined by the model has been replaced by human judgments. The task is quick to complete and is robust against noise. We report the results of a large-scale human study of this task, and show that humans are indeed able to construct a topic model in this fashion, and that the learned topic model has semantic properties distinct from existing topic models. We also demonstrate that the judgments can be used to guide computer-learned topic models towards models which are more concordant with human intuitions.

2 Topic models and inference

Topic models posit that each document is expressed as a mixture of topics. These topic proportions are drawn once per document, and the topics are shared across the corpus. In this paper we focus on Latent Dirichlet allocation (LDA) (Blei et al., 2003) a topic model which treats each document's topic assignment as a multinomial random variable drawn from a symmetric Dirichlet prior. LDA, when applied to a collection of documents, will build a latent space: a collection of topics for the corpus and a collection of topic proportions for each of its documents.

Proceedings of the NAACL HLT 2010 Workshop on Creating Speech and Language Data with Amazon's Mechanical Turk, pages 131–138,
Los Angeles, California, June 2010.

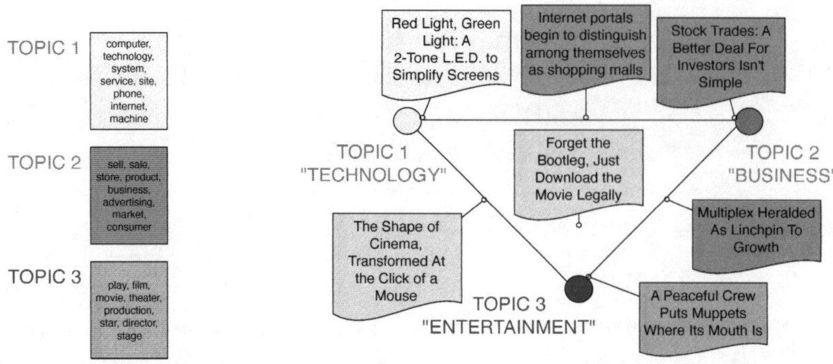

(a) Topics (b) Document Assignments to Topics

Figure 1: The latent space of a topic model consists of topics, which are distributions over words, and a distribution over these topics for each document. On the left are three topics from a fifty topic LDA model trained on articles from the New York Times. On the right is a simplex depicting the distribution over topics associated with seven documents. The line from each document's title shows the document's position in the topic space.

LDA can be described by the following generative process:

1. For each topic k,
   (a) Draw topic $\beta_k \sim \mathrm{Dir}(\eta)$
2. For each document d,
   (a) Draw topic proportions $\theta_d \sim \mathrm{Dir}(\alpha)$
   (b) For each word $w_{d,n}$,
      i. Draw topic assignment $z_{d,n} \sim \mathrm{Mult}(\theta_d)$
      ii. Draw word $w_{d,n} \sim \mathrm{Mult}(\beta_{z_{d,n}})$

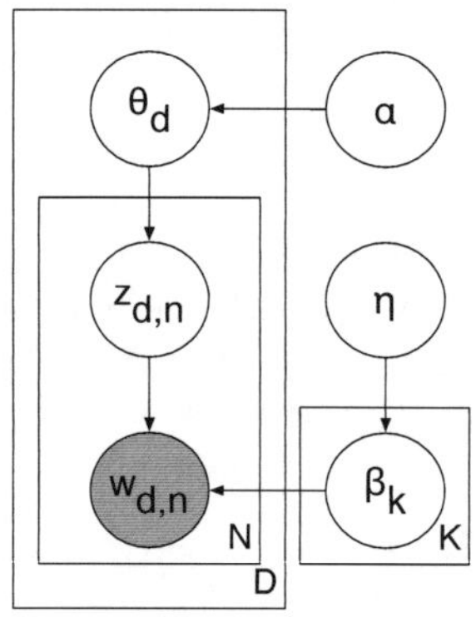

Figure 2: A graphical model depiction of latent Dirichlet allocation (LDA). Plates denote replication. The shaded circle denotes an observed variable and unshaded circles denote hidden variables.

This process is depicted graphically in Figure 2. The parameters of the model are the number of topics, K, as well as the Dirichlet priors on the topic-word distributions and document-topic distributions, α and η. The only observed variables of the model are the words, $w_{d,n}$. The remaining variables must be learned.

There are several techniques for performing posterior inference, i.e., inferring the distribution over hidden variables given a collection of documents, including variational inference (Blei et al., 2003) and Gibbs sampling (Griffiths and Steyvers, 2006). In the sequel, we focus on the latter approach.

Collapsed Gibbs sampling for LDA treats the topic-word and document-topic distributions, θ_d and β_k, as nuisance variables to be marginalized out. The posterior distribution over the remaining latent variables, the topic assignments $z_{d,n}$, can be expressed as

$$p(\boldsymbol{z}|\alpha,\eta,\boldsymbol{w}) \propto \prod_d \prod_k \left[\Gamma(n_{d,k}+\alpha_k) \frac{\Gamma(\eta_{w_{d,n}} + n_{w_{d,n},k})}{\Gamma(\sum_w n_{w,k} + \eta_w)} \right],$$

where $n_{d,k}$ denotes the number of words in document d assigned to topic k and $n_{w,k}$ the number of times word w is assigned to topic k. This leads to the sampling equations,

$$p(z_{d,i} = k|\alpha,\eta,\boldsymbol{w},\boldsymbol{z}y) \propto (n_{d,k}^{\neg d,i} + \alpha_k) \frac{\eta_{w_{d,i}} + n_{w_{d,i},k}^{\neg d,i}}{\sum_w n_{w,k}^{\neg d,i} + \eta_w}, \quad (1)$$

where the superscript $\neg d, i$ indicates that these statistics should exclude the current variable under consideration, $z_{d,i}$.

In essence, the model performs inference by looking at each word in succession, and probabilistically assigning it to a topic according to Equation 1. Equation 1 is derived through the modeling assumptions and choice of parameters. By replacing Equation 1 with a different equation or with empirical observations, we may construct new models which reflect different assumptions about the underlying data.

3 Constructing topics using human judgments

In this section we propose a task which creates a formal setting where humans can create a latent space representation of the corpus. Our task, *tag-and-cluster*, replaces the collapsed Gibbs sampling step of Equation 1 with a human judgment. In essence, we are constructing a gold-standard series of samples from the posterior.[1]

Figure 3 shows how *tag-and-cluster* is presented to users. The user is shown a document along with its title; the document is randomly selected from a pool of available documents. The user is asked to select a word from the document which is discriminative, i.e, a word which would help someone looking for the document find it. Once the word is selected, the user is then asked to assign the word to the topic which best suits the sense of the word used in the document. Users are specifically instructed to focus on the meanings of words, not their syntactic usage or orthography.

The user assigns a word to a topic by selecting an entry out of a menu of topics. Each topic is represented by the five words occuring most frequently in that topic. The order of the topics presented to the user is determined by the number of words in that document already assigned to each topic. Once an instance of a word in a document has been assigned, it cannot be reassigned and will be marked in red when subsequent users encounter this document. In practice, we also prohibit users from selecting infrequently occurring words and stop words.

[1]Additionally, since Gibbs sampling is by nature stochastic, we believe that the task is robust against small perturbations in the quality of the assignments, so long as in aggregate they tend toward the mode.

4 Experimental results

We conducted our experiments using Amazon Mechanical Turk, which allows workers (our pool of prospective subjects) to perform small jobs for a fee through a Web interface. No specialized training or knowledge is typically expected of the workers. Amazon Mechanical Turk has been successfully used in the past to develop gold-standard data for natural language processing (Snow et al., 2008).

We prepare two randomly-chosen, 100-document subsets of English Wikipedia. For convenience, we denote these two sets of documents as *set1* and *set2*. For each document, we keep only the first 150 words for our experiments. Because of the encyclopedic nature of the corpus, the first 150 words typically provides a broad overview of the themes in the article. We also removed from the corpus stop words and words which occur infrequently[2], leading to a lexicon of 8263 words. After this pruning *set1* contained 11614 words and *set2* contained 11318 words.

Workers were asked to perform twenty of the taggings described in Section 3 for each task; workers were paid \$0.25 for each such task. The number of latent topics, K, is a free parameter. Here we explore two values of this parameter, $K = 10$ and $K = 15$, leading to a total of four experiments — two for each set of documents and two for each value of K.

4.1 Tagging behavior

For each experiment we issued 100 HITs, leading to a total of 2000 tags per experiment. Figure 4 shows the number of HITs performed per person in each experiment. Between 12 and 30 distinct workers participated in each experiment. The number of HITs performed per person is heavily skewed, with the most active participants completing an order of magnitude more HITs than other particpants.

Figure 5 shows the amount of time taken per tag, in log seconds. Each color represents a different experiment. The bulk of the tags took less than a minute to perform and more than a few seconds.

4.2 Comparison with LDA

Learned topics As described in Section 3, the tag-and-cluster task is a way of allowing humans to con-

[2]Infrequently occurring words were identified as those appearing fewer than eight times on a larger collection of 7726 articles.

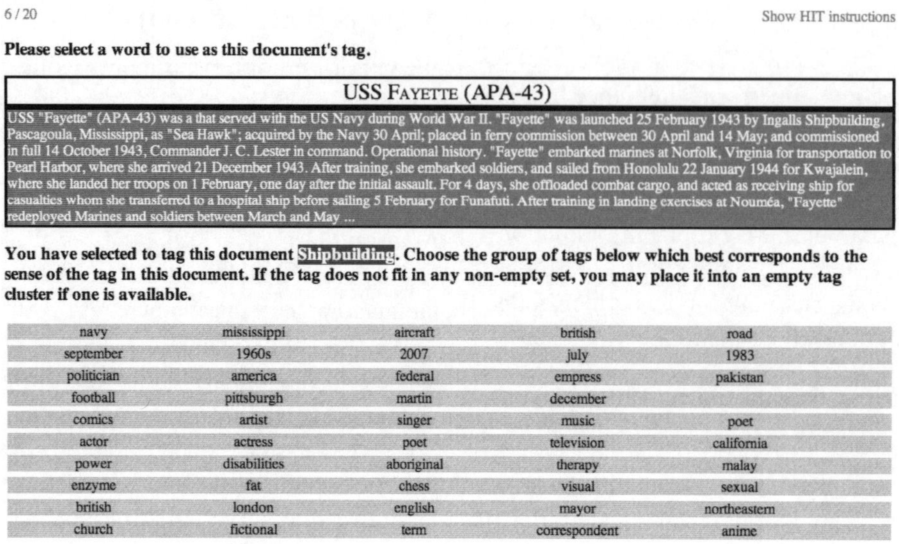

Figure 3: Screenshots of our task. In the center, the document along with its title is shown. Words which cannot be selected, e.g., distractors and words previously selected, are shown in red. Once a word is selected, the user is asked to find a topic in which to place the word. The user selects a topic by clicking on an entry in a menu of topics, where each topic is expressed by the five words which occur most frequently in that topic.

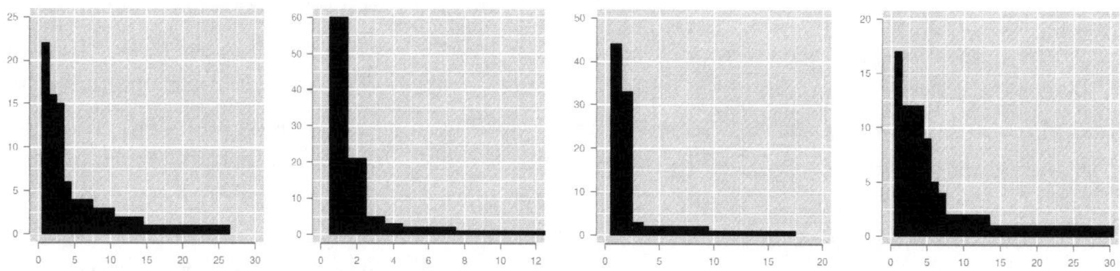

(a) *set1*, $K = 10$ (b) *set1*, $K = 15$ (c) *set2*, $K = 10$ (d) *set2*, $K = 15$

Figure 4: The number of HITs performed (y-axis) by each participant (x-axis). Between 12 and 30 people participated in each experiment.

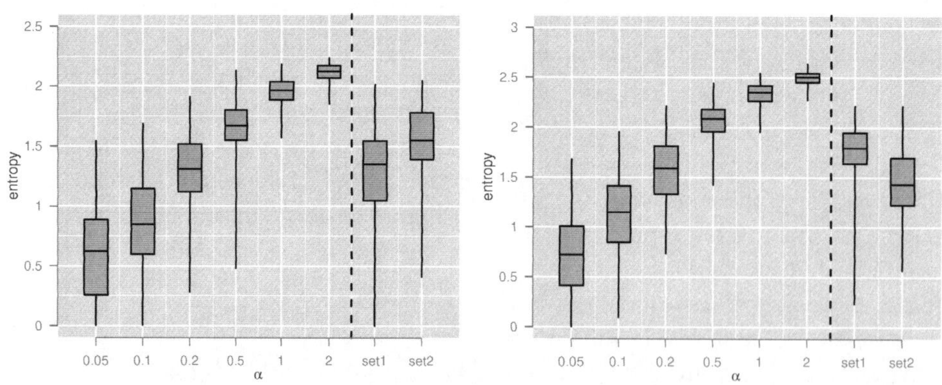

(a) $K = 10$ (b) $K = 15$

Figure 6: A comparison of the entropy of distributions drawn from a Dirichlet distribution versus the entropy of the topic proportions inferred by workers. Each column of the boxplot shows the distribution of entropies for 100 draws from a Dirichlet distribution with parameter α. The two rightmost columns show the distribution of the entropy of the topic proportions inferred by workers on *set1* and *set2*. The α of workers typically falls between 0.2 and 0.5.

Table 1: The five words with the highest probability mass in each topic inferred by humans using the task described in Section 3. Each subtable shows the results for a particular experimental setup. Each row is a topic; the most probable words are ordered from left to right.

(a) *set1*, $K = 10$

railway	lighthouse	rail	huddersfield	station
school	college	education	history	conference
catholic	church	film	music	actor
runners	team	championships	match	racing
engine	company	power	dwight	engines
university	london	british	college	county
food	novel	book	series	superman
november	february	april	august	december
paint	photographs	american	austin	black
war	history	army	american	battle

(b) *set2*, $K = 10$

president	emperor	politician	election	government
american	players	swedish	team	zealand
war	world	navy	road	torpedo
system	pop	microsoft	music	singer
september	2007	october	december	1999
television	dog	name	george	film
people	malay	town	tribes	cliff
diet	chest	enzyme	hair	therapy
british	city	london	english	county
school	university	college	church	center

(c) *set1*, $K = 15$

australia	knee	british	israel	set
catholic	roman	island	village	columbia
john	devon	michael	austin	charles
school	university	class	community	district
november	february	2007	2009	2005
lighthouse	period	architects	construction	design
railway	rail	huddersfield	ownership	services
cyprus	archdiocese	diocese	king	miss
carson	gordon	hugo	ward	whitney
significant	application	campaign	comic	considered
born	london	american	england	black
war	defense	history	military	artillery
actor	film	actress	band	designer
york	michigan	florida	north	photographs
church	catholic	county	2001	agricultural

(d) *set2*, $K = 15$

music	pop	records	singer	artist
film	paintings	movie	painting	art
school	university	english	students	british
drama	headquarters	chess	poet	stories
family	church	sea	christmas	emperor
dog	broadcast	television	bbc	breed
champagne	regular	character	characteristic	common
election	government	parliament	minister	politician
enzyme	diet	protein	hair	oxygen
war	navy	weapons	aircraft	military
september	october	december	2008	1967
district	town	marin	america	american
car	power	system	device	devices
hockey	players	football	therapy	champions
california	zealand	georgia	india	kolkata

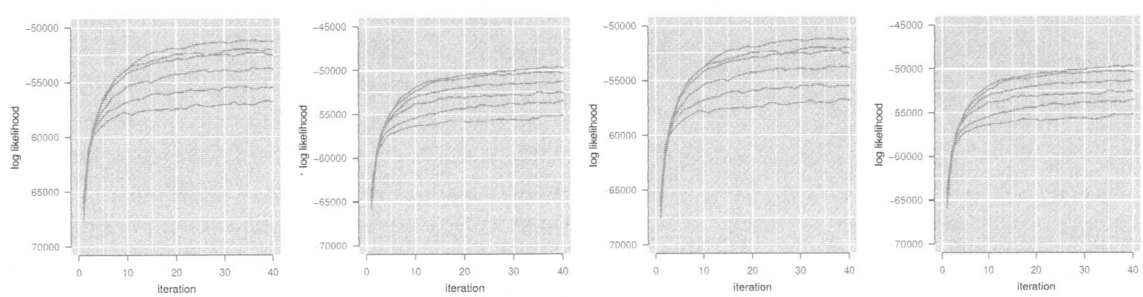

(a) *set1*, $K = 10$ (b) *set2*, $K = 10$ (c) *set1*, $K = 15$ (d) *set2*, $K = 15$

Figure 7: The log-likelihood achieved by LDA as a function of iteration. There is one series for each value of $\alpha \in \{0.05, 0.1, 0.2, 0.5, 1.0, 2.0\}$ from top to bottom.

Table 2: The five words with the highest probability mass in each topic inferred by LDA, with $\alpha = 0.2$. Each subtable shows the results for a particular experimental setup. Each row is a topic; the most probable words are ordered from left to right.

(a) *set1*, $K = 10$

born	2004	team	award	sydney
regiment	army	artillery	served	scouting
line	station	main	island	railway
region	street	located	site	knee
food	february	conference	day	2009
pride	greek	knowledge	portland	study
catholic	church	roman	black	time
class	series	film	actor	engine
travel	human	office	management	defense
school	born	war	world	university

(b) *set2*, $K = 10$

september	english	edit	nord	hockey
black	hole	current	england	model
training	program	war	election	navy
school	university	district	city	college
family	word	international	road	japan
publication	time	day	india	bridge
born	pop	world	released	march
won	video	microsoft	project	hungary
film	hair	bank	national	town
people	name	french	therapy	artist

(c) *set1*, $K = 15$

time	michael	written	experience	match
line	station	railway	branch	knowledge
film	land	pass	set	battle
william	florida	carson	virginia	newfoundland
war	regiment	british	army	south
reaction	terminal	copper	running	complex
born	school	world	college	black
food	conference	flight	medium	rail
township	scouting	census	square	county
travel	defense	training	management	edges
series	actor	engine	november	award
pride	portland	band	northwest	god
team	knee	2004	sydney	israel
catholic	located	site	region	church
class	february	time	public	king

(d) *set2*, $K = 15$

family	protein	enzyme	acting	oxygen
england	producer	popular	canadian	sea
system	death	artist	running	car
character	series	dark	main	village
english	word	publication	stream	day
training	program	hair	students	electrical
district	town	city	local	kolkata
september	edit	music	records	recorded
black	pop	bank	usually	hole
people	choir	road	diet	related
war	built	navy	british	service
center	million	cut	champagne	players
born	television	current	drama	won
school	university	college	election	born
film	nord	played	league	hockey

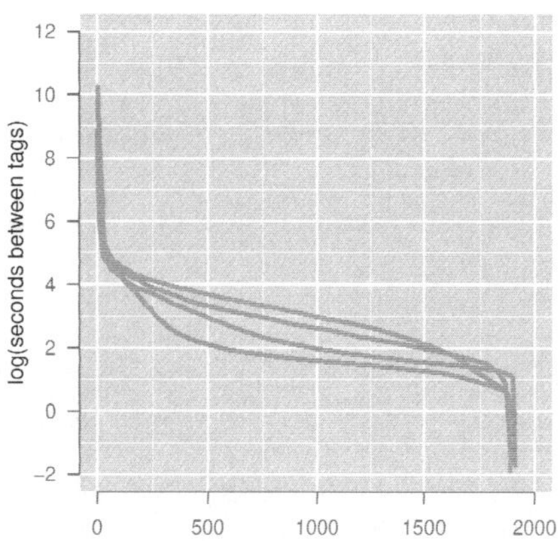

Figure 5: The distribution of times taken per HIT. Each series represents a different experiment. The bulk of the tags took less than one minute and more than a few seconds.

struct a topic model. One way of visualizing a learned topic model is by examining its topics. Table 1 shows the topics constructed by human judgments. Each subtable shows a different experimental setup and each row shows an individual topic. The five most frequently occurring words in each topic are shown, ordered from left to right.

Many of the topics inferred by humans have straightforward interpretations. For example, the {`november, february, april, august, december`} topic for the *set1* corpus with $K = 10$ is simply a collection of months. Similar topics (with years and months combined) can be found in the other experimental configurations. Other topics also cover specific semantic domains, such as {`president, emperor, politican, election, government`} or {`music, pop, records, singer, artist`}. Several of the topics are combinations of distinct concepts, such as {`catholic, church, film, music, actor`}, which is often indicative of the number of clusters, K, being too low.

Table 2 shows the topics learned by LDA under the same experimental conditions, with the Dirichlet hyperparameter $\alpha = 0.2$ (we justify this choice in the following section). These topics are more difficult to interpret than the ones created by humans. Some topics seem to largely make sense except for some anomalous words, such as {`district, town, city, local, kolkata`} or {`school, university, college, election, born`}. But the small amount of data means that it is difficult for a model which does not leverage prior knowledge to infer meaningful topic. In contrast, several humans, even working independently, can leverage prior knowledge to construct meaningful topics with little data.

There is another qualitative difference between the topics found by the tag-and-cluster task and LDA. Whereas LDA must rely on co-occurrence, humans can use ontological information. Thus, a topic which has ontological meaning, such as a list of months, may rarely be discovered by LDA since the co-occurrence patterns of months do not form a strong pattern. But users in every experimental configuration constructed this topic, suggesting that the users were consistently leveraging information that would not be available to LDA, even with a larger corpus.

Hyperparameter values A persistent question among practitioners of topic models is how to set or learn the value of the hyperparameter α. α is a Dirichlet parameter which acts as a control on sparsity — smaller values of α lead to sparser document-topic distributions. By comparing the sparsity patterns of human judgments to those of LDA for different settings of α, we can infer the value of α that would best match human judgments.

Figure 6 shows a boxplot comparison of the entropy of draws from a Dirichlet distribution (the generative process in LDA), versus the observed entropy of the models learned by humans. The first six columns show the distributions for the Dirichlet draws for various values of α; the last two columns show the observed entropy distributions on the two corpora, *set1* and *set2*.

The empirical entropy distributions across the corpora are comparable to those of a Dirichlet distribution with α between approximately 0.2 and 0.5.

Table 3: The five words with the highest probability mass in each topic inferred by LDA on *set1* with $\alpha = 0.2$, $K = 10$, and initialized using human judgments. Each row is a topic; the most probable words are ordered from left to right.

line	station	lighthouse	local	main
school	history	greek	knowledge	university
catholic	church	city	roman	york
team	club	2004	scouting	career
engine	knee	series	medium	reaction
located	south	site	land	region
food	film	conference	north	little
february	class	born	august	2009
pride	portland	time	northwest	june
war	regiment	army	civil	black

These settings of α are slightly higher than, but still in line with a common rule-of-thumb of $\alpha = 1/K$. Figure 7 shows the log-likelihood, a measure of model fit, achieved by LDA for each value of α. Higher log-likelihoods indicate better fits. Commensurate with the rule of thumb, using log-likelihoods to select α would encourage values smaller than human judgments.

However, while the entropy of the Dirichlet draws increases significantly when the number of clusters is increased from $K = 10$ to $K = 15$, the entropies assigned by humans does not vary as dramatically. This suggests that for any given document, humans are likely to pull words from only a small number of topics, regardless of how many topics are available, whereas a model will continue to spread probability mass across all topics even as the number of topics increases.

Improving LDA using human judgments The results of the previous sections suggests that human behavior differs from that of LDA, and that humans conceptualize documents in ways LDA does not. This motivates using the human judgments to augment the information available to LDA. To do so, we initialize the topic assignments used by LDA's Gibbs sampler to those made by humans. We then run the LDA sampler till convergence. This provides a method to weakly incorporate human knowledge into the model.

Table 3 shows the topics inferred by LDA when initialized with human judgments. These topics resemble those directly inferred by humans, although as we predicted in the previous sections, the topic consisting of months has largely disappeared. Other semantically coherent topics, such as {`located,`

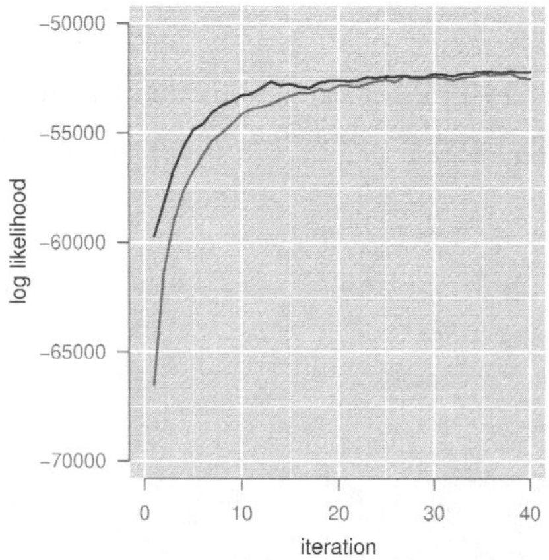

Figure 8: The log likelihood achieved by LDA on *set1* with $\alpha = 0.2$, $K = 10$, and initialized using human judgments (blue). The red line shows the log likelihood without incorporating human judgments. LDA with human judgments dominates LDA without human judgments and helps the model converge more quickly.

`south, site, land, region`}, have appeared in its place.

Figure 8 shows the log-likelihood course of LDA when initialized by human judgments (blue), versus LDA without human judgments (red). Adding human judgments strictly helps the model converge to a higher likelihood and converge more quickly. In short, incorporating human judgments shows promise at improving both the interpretability and convergence of LDA.

5 Discussion

We presented a new method for constructing topic models using human judgments. Our approach relies on a novel task, *tag-and-cluster*, which asks users to simultaneously annotate a document with one of its words and to cluster those annotations. We demonstrate using experiments on Amazon Mechanical Turk that our method constructs topic models quickly and robustly. We also show that while our topic models bear many similarities to traditionally constructed topic models, our human-learned topic models have unique features such as fixed sparsity and a tendency for topics to be constructed around concepts which models such as LDA typically fail to find.

We also underscore that the collapsed Gibbs sampling framework is expressive enough to use as the basis for human-guided topic model inference. This may motivate, as future work, the construction of different modeling assumptions which lead to sampling equations which more closely match the empirically observed sampling performed by humans. In effect, our method constructs a series of samples from the posterior, a gold standard which future topic models can aim to emulate.

Acknowledgments

The author would like to thank Eytan Bakshy and Professor Jordan Boyd-Graber-Ying for their helpful comments and discussions.

References

David Blei and John Lafferty, 2009. *Text Mining: Theory and Applications*, chapter Topic Models. Taylor and Francis.

David Blei, Andrew Ng, and Michael Jordan. 2003. Latent Dirichlet allocation. *JMLR*, 3:993–1022.

Jonathan Chang, Jordan Boyd-Graber, Sean Gerrish, Chong Wang, and David M. Blei. 2009. Reading tea leaves: How humans interpret topic models. In *NIPS*.

Scott Deerwester, Susan Dumais, Thomas Landauer, George Furnas, and Richard Harshman. 1990. Indexing by latent semantic analysis. *Journal of the American Society of Information Science*, 41(6):391–407.

Thomas L. Griffiths and Mark Steyvers. 2002. A probabilistic approach to semantic representation. In *Proceedings of the 24th Annual Conference of the Cognitive Science Society*.

T. Griffiths and M. Steyvers. 2006. Probabilistic topic models. In T. Landauer, D. McNamara, S. Dennis, and W. Kintsch, editors, *Latent Semantic Analysis: A Road to Meaning*. Laurence Erlbaum.

Qiaozhu Mei, Xuehua Shen, and ChengXiang Zhai. 2007. Automatic labeling of multinomial topic models. In *KDD*.

R. Snow, Brendan O'Connor, D. Jurafsky, and A. Ng. 2008. Cheap and fast—but is it good? Evaluating non-expert annotations for natural language tasks. In *EMNLP*.

Hanna M. Wallach, Iain Murray, Ruslan Salakhutdinov, and David Mimno. 2009. Evaluation methods for topic models. In *ICML*.

Collecting Image Annotations Using Amazon's Mechanical Turk

Cyrus Rashtchian Peter Young Micah Hodosh Julia Hockenmaier
Department of Computer Science
University of Illinois at Urbana-Champaign
201 North Goodwin Ave, Urbana, IL 61801-2302
{crashtc2, pyoung2, mhodosh2, juliahmr}@illinois.edu

Abstract

Crowd-sourcing approaches such as Amazon's Mechanical Turk (MTurk) make it possible to annotate or collect large amounts of linguistic data at a relatively low cost and high speed. However, MTurk offers only limited control over who is allowed to particpate in a particular task. This is particularly problematic for tasks requiring free-form text entry. Unlike multiple-choice tasks there is no correct answer, and therefore control items for which the correct answer is known cannot be used. Furthermore, MTurk has no effective built-in mechanism to guarantee workers are proficient English writers. We describe our experience in creating corpora of images annotated with multiple one-sentence descriptions on MTurk and explore the effectiveness of different quality control strategies for collecting linguistic data using Mechanical MTurk. We find that the use of a qualification test provides the highest improvement of quality, whereas refining the annotations through follow-up tasks works rather poorly. Using our best setup, we construct two image corpora, totaling more than 40,000 descriptive captions for 9000 images.

1 Introduction

Although many generic NLP applications can be developed by using existing corpora or text collections as test and training data, there are many areas where NLP could be useful if there was a suitable corpus available. For example, computer vision researchers are becoming interested in developing methods that can predict not just the presence and location of certain objects in an image, but also the relations between objects, their attributes, or the actions and events they participate in. Such information can neither be obtained from standard computer vision data sets such as the COREL collection nor from the user-provided keyword tag annotations or captions on photo-sharing sites such as Flickr. Similarly, although the text near an image on a website may provide cues about the entities depicted in the image, an explicit description of the image content itself is typically only provided if it is not immediately obvious to a human what is depicted (in which case we may not expect a computer vision system to be able to recognize the image content either). We therefore set out to collect a corpus of images annotated with simple full-sentence descriptions of their content. To obtain these descriptions, we used Amazon's Mechanical Turk (MTurk).[1] MTurk is an online framework that allows researchers to post annotation tasks, called HITs ("Human Intelligence Task"), then, for a small fee, be completed by thousands of anonymous non-expert users (Turkers). Although MTurk has been used for a variety of tasks in NLP, our use of MTurk differs from other research in NLP that uses MTurk mostly for annotation of existing text. Similar to crowdsourcing-based annotation, quality control is an essential component of crowdsourcing-based data collection efforts, and needs to be factored into the overall costs. For us, the quality of the text produced by the Turkers is particularly important since we are interested in us-

[1] All of our experiments on Mechanical Turk were administered and paid for through the services offered by Dolores Labs.

Proceedings of the NAACL HLT 2010 Workshop on Creating Speech and Language Data with Amazon's Mechanical Turk, pages 139–147,
Los Angeles, California, June 2010. ©2010 Association for Computational Linguistics

ing this corpus for future research at the intersection of computer vision and natural language processing. However, MTurk provides limited ways to implement such quality control directly. For example, our initial experiments yielded a data set that contained many sentences that were clearly not written by native speakers. We learned that several steps must be taken to ensure that Turkers both understand the task and produce quality data.

This paper describes our experiences with Turk (based on data collection efforts in spring and summer 2009), comparing two different approaches to quality control. Although we did not set out to run a scientific experiment comparing different strategies of how to collect linguistic data on Turk, our experience points towards certain recommendations for how to collect linguistic data on Turk.

2 The core task: image annotation

The PASCAL Data Set Every year, the Pattern Analysis, Statistical Modeling, and Computational Learning (PASCAL) organization hosts the Visual Object Classes Challenge (Everingham et al., 2008). This is a competition similar to the shared tasks familiar to the ACL community, where a common data set of images with classification and detection information is released, and computer vision researchers compete to create the best classification, detection, and segmentation systems. We chose to use this collection of images because it is a standard resource for computer vision, and will therefore faciliate further research.

The VOC2008 development and training set contains around 6000 images. It is categorized by objects that appear in the image, with some images appearing in multiple categories.[2]. The images contain a wide variety of actions and scenery. Our corpus consists of 1000 of these images, fifty randomly chosen from each of the twenty categories.

MTurk setup We asked Turkers to write one descriptive sentence for each of ten images. An example annotation screen is shown in Figure 1. We first showed the Turkers a list of instructive guidelines describing the task (Figure 6). The instructions told them to write ten complete but simple sentences, to include adjectives if possible, to describe the main characters, the setting, or the relation of the objects in the image, to pay attention to grammar and spelling, and to try to be concise. These instructions were meant to both explain the task and to prepare Turkers to write quality sentences. We then showed each Turker a set of ten images, chosen randomly from the 1000 total images, and displayed one at a time. The Turkers navigated using "Next" buttons through the ten annotation screens, each displaying one image and one text-box. We allowed Turkers ten minutes to complete one task.[3] We restricted the task to Turkers who have previously had at least 95% of their results approved. We paid \$0.10 to complete one task. The total cost for all 5000 descriptions was \$50 (plus Amazon's 10% fee).

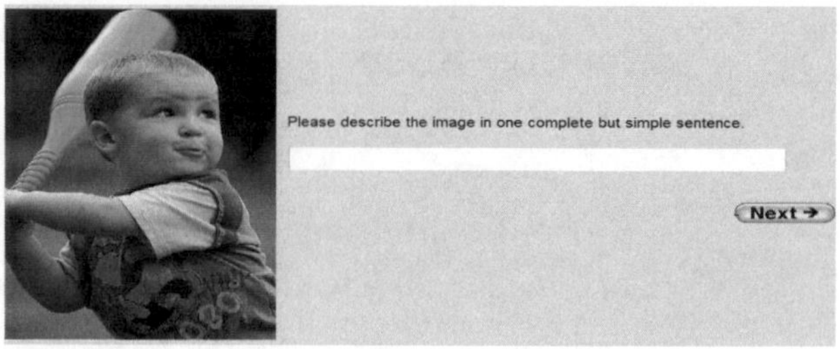

Figure 1: Screenshot of the image annotation task.

2.1 Results

On average, Turkers wrote the ten sentences in a total of four minutes. The average pay rate was \$1.30 per hour, and the whole experiment finished in under two days. Five different people described each image, and in the end, most of the Turkers completed the task successfully, although 2.5% of the 5000 sentences were empty strings. Turkers varied in the time they took to complete the experiment, in the length of their sentences, and in the level of detail they included about the image. An example captioned image is shown in Figure 2.

Problems with the data The quality of descriptions varied greatly. We were hoping to collect simple sentences, written in correct English, describing the entities and actions in the images. More-

[2]The twenty categories include people, various animals, vehicles and other objects: `person, bird, cat, cow, dog, horse, sheep, aeroplane, bicycle, boat, bus, car, motorbike, train, bottle, chair, dining table, potted plant, sofa, tv/monitor`

[3]This proved to be more than enough time for the task.

Two men playing cards at a table.
The two men are in an intense card game.
Two men playing cards on a kitchen counter are lit by a strong flash.
The men are playing cards
The scene shows two people playing cards.

Figure 2: An image along with the five captions that were written by Turkers.

over, these are explicitly the types of descriptions we asked for in the MTurk task instructions. Although we found the descriptions acceptable more than half of the time, a large number of the remaining descriptions had at least one of the following two problems:

1. Some descriptions did not mention the salient entities in the image, some were simply noun phrases (or less), and some were humorous or speculative.[4] We find all of these to be problems because future computer vision and natural language processing research will require accurate and consistent image captions.

2. A number of Turkers were not sufficiently proficient in English. Many descriptions contained grammar and spelling errors, and some included very awkward constructions. For example, the phrase "X giving pose" showed up several times in descriptions of images containing people (e.g. *"The lady and man giving pose."*). Such spelling and grammar errors will pose difficulties for any standard text-processing algorithms trained on native English.

Spell checking Due to the large number of misspellings in in the initial data set, we first ran the sentences first through our spell checker before putting them up on Turk to assess their quality. We tokenized the captions with OpenNLP, and first checked a manually created list of spelling corrections for each token. These included canonicalizations (correcting "surf board" as "surfboard"), words our automatic spell checker did not recognize ("mown"), and the most common misspellings in our data set ("shepard" to "shepherd"). If the token was not in our manual list, we passed the word to aspell. From aspell's candidate corrections, we selected the most frequent word that appeared either in other captions of the same image, of images of the same topic, or any caption in our data set.

[4]For example, some Turkers commented on the feelings of animals (e.g. *"the dog is not very happy next to the dumpster"*), and others made jokes about the content of the image (e.g. *"The goat is ready for hair cut"*)

3 Post-hoc quality control

Because our initial data collection efforts resulted in relatively noisy data, we created a new set of MTurk tasks designed to provide post-hoc quality control. Our aim was to filter out captions containing misspellings and incorrect grammar.

MTurk setup Each HIT consisted of fifty different image descriptions and asked Turkers to decide for each of them whether they contained correct grammar and spelling or not. At the beginning of each HIT, we included a brief training phase, where we showed the Turkers five example descriptions labeled as "correct" or "incorrect" (Figure 7). In the HIT itself, the fifty descriptions were displayed in blocks of five (albeit not for the same image) , and each description was followed by two radio buttons labeled "correct" and "incorrect". We did not show the corresponding images. A screenshot is shown in Figure 3. Each block of five captions contained one control item that we use for later assessment of the Turkers' spell-checking ability. We wrote these control captions ourselves, modeling them after actual image descriptions. We paid $0.08 for one task, and three people completed each task.

3.1 Results

On average, Turkers completed a HIT (judging fifty sentences) in four minutes, at an average hourly rate of $1.04. Each sentence in our data set was judged by three Turkers. The whole experiment finished

Figure 3: Screenshot from the grammar/spelling checking task. This is a block of five sentences that Turkers had to label as using correct or incorrect grammar and spelling. The first sentence is a control item that we included to monitor the Turkers' performance, and the other four are captions generated by other Turkers in a previous task.

Data set produced by...	Quality control performed by...	% Votes for "correct English" 0	1	2	3
Unqualified writers	three Turkers	18.9%	31.2%	26.4%	23.5%
Unqualified writers	three experts	11.8%	12.7%	15.3%	60.2%
Qualified writers	three experts	0.5%	2.5%	15.0%	82.0%

Table 1: Quality control by Turkers and Experts. The three experts judged 600 sentences from each data set. 565 sentences produced by unqualified workers were also judged by three Turkers.

in under two days, at a total cost of $28.80 (plus Amazon's 10% fee). We also selected randomly 600 spell-checked sentences for expert annotation. Three members of our team (all native speakers of English) judged each of these sentences in the same manner as the Turkers. Each sentence could therefore get between 0 and 3 Turker votes and between 0 and 3 expert votes for good English. The top two rows of Table 1 show the distribution of votes in each of the two groups. We also assess whether the judgments of the Turkers correlate with our own expert judgments. Table 2(a) shows the overall agreement between Turkers and expert annotators. The rest of Table 2 shows how performance of the Turkers on the control items affected agreement with expert judgments. We define the performance of a Turker in terms of the average the number of control items that they got right in each HIT they took. For each threshold in Tables 2(a)-(d), we considered only those images for which we have three quality judgments by workers whose performance is above the specified threshold.

Our results show that the effectiveness of using Turkers to filter for grammar and spelling issues is limited. Overall, the Turker judgments were overly harsh. The majority Turker vote agrees with the majority vote of the trained annotators on only 65.1% of the sentences. Manual inspection of the differences reveals that the Turkers marked many perfectly grammatical English sentences as incorrect (although they also marked a few which we had missed). Agreement with experts decreases among those Turkers that performed better on the control sentences, with only 56.7% agreement for Turkers that got all the controls right. In addition, the Turkers are significantly more likely to report false negatives over false positives and this also increases with performance on the control sentences. (Overall, the Turkers marked 29.9% of the sentences as false negatives, whereas the Turkers that scored perfectly on the controls marked 39.3% as false negatives.) Examination of the areas of high disagreement reveal that the Turkers were much more likely to vote down noun phrases than the experts were. The correct example captions provided in the instructions of the quality control test were complete sentences. Some of the control captions were noun phrases, but all of the noun phrase controls had some other error in them. Thus it was possible to either believe that noun phrases were correct or incorrect, and still be consistent with the provided examples, and provide correct judgments on the control sentences.

(a) ≥ 0 controls correct: 565 sentences

Turk votes	Expert votes 0	1	2	3
0	6.9%	4.4%	3.7%	3.9%
1	3.2%	5.7%	5.0%	17.3%
2	1.8%	2.8%	3.5%	18.2%
3	0.0%	0.4%	2.5%	20.7%

(b) ≥ 5 controls correct: 553 sentences

Turk votes	Expert votes 0	1	2	3
0	6.9%	4.5%	3.8%	4.0%
1	3.1%	5.4%	5.1%	17.5%
2	1.8%	2.7%	3.6%	18.4%
3	0.0%	0.4%	2.5%	20.3%

(c) ≥ 7 controls correct: 331 sentences

Turk votes	Expert votes 0	1	2	3
0	6.9%	6.3%	3.9%	5.1%
1	3.0%	4.5%	5.1%	24.5%
2	1.8%	1.8%	2.4%	15.1%
3	0.0%	0.0%	2.1%	17.2%

(d) ≥ 9 controls correct: 127 sentences

Turk votes	Expert votes 0	1	2	3
0	7.9%	6.3%	3.1%	6.3%
1	1.6%	4.7%	6.3%	23.6%
2	0.8%	3.1%	1.6%	15.7%
3	0.0%	0.0%	1.6%	17.3%

Table 2: Quality control: Agreement between Turker and Expert votes, depending on the average number of control items the Turker voters got right.

4 Quality control through pre-screening

Quality control can also be imposed through a pre-screening of the Turkers allowed to take the HIT. We collected another set of five descriptions per image, but restricted participation to Turkers residing in the US[5], and created a brief qualification test to check their English. We would like to be able to restrict our tasks to Turkers who are native speakers and competent spellers and writers of English, regardless of their country of residence. However, this seems to be difficult to verify within the current MTurk setup.

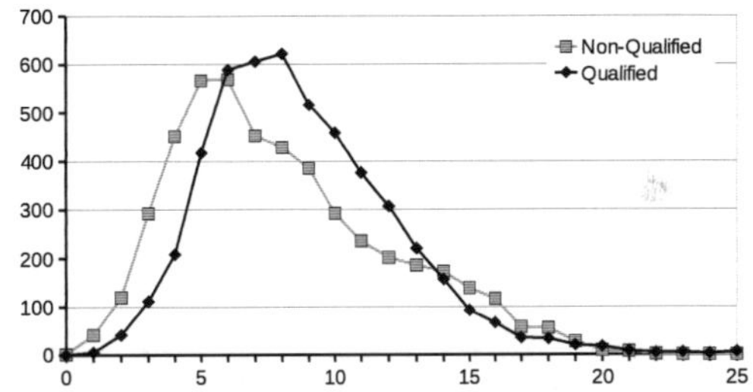

Figure 4: Average caption length (5000 images)

Qualification Test Design The qualification test consists of forty binary questions: fifteen testing spelling, fifteen testing grammar, and ten testing the ability to identify good image descriptions.

In all three cases, we started the section with a set of instructions displaying examples of positive and negative answers to the tasks. Each spelling question consisted of a single sentence, and Turkers were asked to determine if all of the words in the sentence were spelled correctly and if the correct word was being used ("lose" versus "loose"). Each grammar question consisted of a single sentence that was either correct or included a grammatical error. Both spelling and grammar checking questions were based on common mistakes made by foreign English speakers and on grammatical or spelling errors that occurred in our initial set of image captions. The grammar and spelling questions are listed in Table 3. The image description questions consisted of one image shown with two actual captions, and the Turkers were asked which caption better described the image. In order to pass the qualification test, we required each annotator to correctly answer at least twenty-four spelling and grammar questions and at least eight image description questions. To prevent Turkers from using the number of question they got correct to do a brute force search for the correct answers, we simply told them if they passed ("1") or failed ("0"). Currently, 1504 people have taken the qualification test, with a 67.2% passing rate. Since this qualification test was only required for our HITs that were restricted to US residents, we assume (but are not able to verify) that most, if not all, of the people who took this test are actually US residents.

[5]As of March 2010, 46.80% of Turkers reside in the U.S (`http://behind-the-enemy-lines.blogspot.com/` 03/09/2010)

MTurk Set-up We use the same MTurk set-up as before, but to encourage Turkers to complete the task even though they first have to pass a qualification test, we pay them $0.10 to annotate five images.

4.1 Results

We found that the Turkers who passed the qualification provided much better captions for the images. The average time spent on each image was longer (four minutes per ten images for the non-qualified workers versus five minutes per ten images for the qualified workers). On average, qualified Turkers produced slightly longer sentences (avg. 10.7 words) than non-qualified workers (avg. 10.0 words) (Figure 4), and the awkward constructions produced by the unqualified workers were mostly absent. The entire corpus was annotated in 253 hours at a cost of $100.00 (plus Amazon's 10% fee).

We also looked at the rate of misspellings (approximated by how often our spell-checker indicated a misspelling). Without the qualification test, Out of the 600 sentences produced without the qualification test, 78 contained misspellings, whereas only 25 sentences out of the 600 produced by the qualified workers contained misspellings. Furthermore, misspellings in the no-qualification group include many genuine errors (*"the boys are playing in tabel"*, *"bycycles"*, *"eatting"*), whereas misspellings in the qualification group are largely typos (e.g. *Ywo* for *Two*, *tableclothe*, *chari* for *chair*). Furthermore, the spell checker corrected all 25 misspellings in the qualified data set to the intended word, but 27 out of the 78 misspellings in the data produced by the unqualified workers got changed to some other word.

The same three members of our team rated again the English of 600 randomly selected sentences written by Turkers residing in the US who passed our test. We found a significant improvement in quality (Table 1, bottom row), with the majority expert vote accepting over 97% of the sentences. This is also corroborated by qualitative analysis of the data (see Figure 5 for examples). Inspection reveals that sentences that are deemed ungrammatical by the experts typically contain some undetected typo, and would be correct if these typos could be fixed. Without a qualification test, there is a significantly greater percentage of nonsensical responses such as: "Is this a bird squirrel?" and "thecentury". In addition, grammatically correct but useless fragments such as "very dark" and "peace" only appear without a test. After requiring the qualification test, the major reasons for rejection by Turkers are typos such as in "The two dogs blend in with the stuff animals" or missing determiners such as in "a train on tracks in town".

Overall cost effectiveness Using the no qualification test approach, we first paid $50.00 to get 5000 sentences written by unqualified Turkers (which resulted in 4851 non-empty sentences). This resulted in low-quality data which required further verification. Since this is too time-consuming for expert annotators, we then paid another $28.80 to get each of these sentences subsequently checked by three Turkers for grammaticality, resulting in 2222 sentences which received at least two positive votes for grammaticality. With the qualification test approach, we paid $100.00 to get 5000 sentences written. Based on our experiments on the set of 600 sentences, experts would judge over 97% of these sentences as correct, thus obviating the immediate need for further control. That is, it effectively costs more for non-qualified Turkers to produce sentences that are judged to be good than for qualified Turkers. Furthermore, their sentences will probably be of lower quality even after they have been judged acceptable.

5 A corpus of captions for Flickr photos

Encouraged by the success of the qualification test approach, we extended our corpus to contain 8000 images collected from Flickr. We again paid the Turkers $0.10 to annotate five images. Our data set consists of 8108 hand-selected images from Flickr, depicting actions and events (rather than images depicting scenery and mood). These images are more likely to require full sentence descriptions than the PASCAL images. We chose six large Flickr groups[6] and downloaded a few thousand images from each, giving us a total of 15,000 candidate images. We removed all black and white or sepia images as well as images containing photographer signatures or seals. Next, we manually identified pictures that depicted the actions of people or animals. For example, we kept images of people walking in parks, but not of

[6] The groups: strangers!, Wild-Child (Kids in Action), Dogs in Action (Read the Rules), Outdoor Activities, Action Photography and Flickr-Social (two or more people in the photo)

Without qualification test
(1) lady with birds
(2) Some parrots are have speaking skill.
(3) A lady in their dining table with birds on her shoulder and head.
(4) Asian woman with two cockatiels, on shoulder
head, room with oak cabinets.,
(5) The lady loves the parrot
With qualification test
(1) A woman has a bird on her shoulder, and another bird on her head
(2) A woman with a bird on her head and a bird on her shoulder.
(3) A women sitting at a dining table with two small birds sitting on her.
(4) A young Asian woman sitting at a kitchen
table with a bird on her head and another on her shoulder.
(5) Two birds are perched on a woman sitting in a kitchen.

Figure 5: Comparison of captions written by Turkers with and without qualification test

empty parks; we kept several people posing, but not a close-up of a single person.[7] Each HIT asked Turkers to describe five images. We required the qualification test and US residency. Average completion time was a little above 3 minutes for 5 sentences. The corpus was annotated in 284 hours[8], at a total cost of $812.00 (plus Amazon's 10% fee).

6 Related work and conclusions

Related work MTurk has been used for many different NLP and vision tasks (Tietze et al., 2009; Zaidan and Callison-Burch, 2009; Snow et al., 2008; Sorokin and Forsyth, 2008). Due to the noise inherent in non-expert annotations, many other attempts at quality control have been made. Kittur et al. (2008) solicit ratings about different aspects of Wikipedia articles. At first they receive very noisy results, due to Turkers' not paying attention when completing the task or specifically trying to cheat the requester. They remade the task, this time starting by asking the Turkers verifiable questions, speculating that the users would produce better quality responses when they suspect their answers will be checked. They also added a question that required the Turkers to comprehend the content of the Wikipedia article. With this new setup, they find that the quality greatly increases and carelessness is reduced. Kaisser and Lowe (2008) collected question and answer pairs by presenting Turkers with a question and telling them to copy and paste from a document of text they know to contain the answer. They achieve a good but far from perfect interannotator agreement based on the extracted answers. We speculate that the quality would be much worse if the Turkers wrote the sentences themselves. Callison-Burch (2009) asks Turkers to produce translations when given reference sentences in other languages. Overall, he finds find that Turkers produce better translations than machine translation systems. To eliminate translations from Turkers who simply put the reference sentence into an online translation website, he performs a follow-up task, where he asks other Turkers to vote on if they believe that sentences were generated using an online translation system. Mihalcea and Strapparava (2009) ask Turkers to produce 4-5 sentence opinion paragraphs about the death penalty, about abortion and describing a friend. They report that aside from a small number of invalid responses, all of the paragraphs were of good quality and followed their instructions. Their success is surprising to us because they do not report using a qualification test, and when we did this our responses contained a large amount of incorrect English spelling and grammar.

The TurKit toolkit (Little et al., 2009) provides another approach to improving the quality of MTurk annotations. Their iterative framework allows the requester to set up a series of tasks that first solicits text annotations from Turkers and then asks other Turkers to improve the annotations. They report successful results using this methodology, but we chose

[7]Our final data set consists of 1482 pictures from action photography, 1904 from dogs, 776 from flickr-social, 916 from outdoor, 1257 from strangers and 1773 from wild-child.

[8]Note that the annotation process scaled pretty well, considering that annotating more than eight times the number of images took only 31 hours longer.

to stick with simply using the qualification test because it achieves the desired results already. Furthermore, although using TurKit would have probably done away with our few remaining grammar and spelling mistakes, it may have caused the captions for an image to be a little too similar, and we value a diversity in the use of words and points of view.

Our experiences We have described our experiences in using Amazon's Mechanical Turk in the first half of 2009 to create a corpus of images annotated with descriptive sentences. We implemented two different approaches to quality control: first, we did not impose any restrictions on who could write image descriptions. This was then followed by a second set of MTurk tasks where Turkers had to judge the quality of the sentences generated in our initial Turk experiments. This approach to quality control would be cost-effective if the initial data were not too noisy and the subsequent judgments were accurate and cheap. However, this was not the case, and quality control on the judgments in the form of control items turned out to result in even lower accuracy. We then repeated our data collection effort, but required that Turkers live in the US and take a brief qualification test that we created to test their English. This is cost-effective if English proficiency can be accurately assessed in such a brief qualification test. We found that the latter approach was indeed far cheaper, and produced significantly better data. We did not set out to run a scientific experiment comparing different strategies of how to collect linguistic data on Turk, and therefore there may be multiple explanations for the effects we observe. Nevertheless, our experience indicates strongly that even very simple prescreening measures can provide very effective quality control.

We also extended our corpus to include 8000 images collected from Flickr. We hope to release this data to the public for future natural language processing and computer vision research.

Recommended practices for using MTurk in NLP Our experience indicates that with simple prescreening, linguistic data can be elicited fairly cheaply and rapidly from crowd-sourcing services such as Mechanical Turk. However, many applications may require more control over where the data comes from. Even though NLP data collection differs fundamentally from psycholinguistic experiments that may elicit production data, our community will typically also need to know whether data was produced by native speakers or not. Until MTurk provides a better mechanism to check the native language of its workers, linguistic data collection on MTurk will have to rely on potentially very noisy input.

Acknowledgements

This research was funded by NSF grant IIS 08-03603 *INT2-Medium: Understanding the Meaning of Images*. We are grateful for David Forsyth's advice and for Alex Sorokin's support with MTurk.

References

Chris Callison-Burch. 2009. Fast, cheap, and creative: Evaluating translation quality using Amazon's Mechanical Turk. In *Proceedings of EMNLP 2009*.

M. Everingham, L. Van Gool, C. K. I. Williams, J. Winn, and A. Zisserman. 2008. The PASCAL Visual Object Classes Challenge 2008 (VOC2008) Results. http://www.pascal-network.org/challenges/VOC/voc2008/workshop/.

Michael Kaisser and John Lowe. 2008. Creating a research collection of question answer sentence pairs with amazons mechanical turk. In *LREC 2008*.

Aniket Kittur, Ed H. Chi, and Bongwon Suh. 2008. Crowdsourcing user studies with mechanical turk. In *Proceedings of SIGCHI 2008*.

Greg Little, Lydia B. Chilton, Max Goldman, and Robert C. Miller. 2009. Turkit: tools for iterative tasks on mechanical turk. In *HCOMP '09: Proceedings of the ACM SIGKDD Workshop on Human Computation*.

Rada Mihalcea and Carlo Strapparava. 2009. The lie detector: Explorations in the automatic recognition of deceptive language. In *Proceedings of the ACL-IJCNLP 2009 Conference Short Papers*.

Rion Snow, Brendan O'Connor, Daniel Jurafsky, and Andrew Ng. 2008. Cheap and fast – but is it good? evaluating non-expert annotations for natural language tasks. In *Proceedings of EMNLP 2008*.

Alexander Sorokin and David Forsyth. 2008. Utility data annotation with amazon mechanical turk. In *Computer Vision and Pattern Recognition Workshop*.

Martin I. Tietze, Andi Winterboer, and Johanna D. Moore. 2009. The effect of linguistic devices in information presentation messages on comprehension and recall. In *Proceedings of ENLG 2009*.

Omar F. Zaidan and Chris Callison-Burch. 2009. Feasibility of human-in-the-loop minimum error rate training. In *Proceedings of EMNLP 2009*.

Are all of the words correctly spelled and correctly used?	Is the sentence grammatically correct?
A group of children playing with thier toys (N)	A man giving pose to camera. (N)
He accepts the crowd's praise graciously. (Y)	The white sheep walks on the grass. (Y)
The coffee is kept at a very hot temperture. (N)	She is good woman. (N)
A green car is parked in front of a resturant. (N)	He should have talk to him. (N)
An orange cat sleeping with a dog that is much larger then it. (N)	He has many wonderful toy. (N)
I ate a tasty desert after lunch. (N)	He sended the children home to their parents. (N)
A group of people getting ready for a surprise party. (Y)	The passage through the hills was narrow. (Y)
A small refrigerator filled with colorful fruits and vegetables. (Y)	A sleeping dog. (Y)
Two men fly by in a red plain. (N)	The questions on the test was difficult. (N)
A causal picture of a man and a woman. (N)	In Finland, we are used to live in a cold climate. (N)
Three men are going out for a special occasion. (Y)	Three white sheeps graze on the grassy field. (N)
Woman eatting lots of food. (N)	Between you and me, this is wrong. (Y)
Dyning room with chairs. (N)	They are living there during six months. (N)
A woman recieving a package. (N)	I was given lots of advices about buying new furnitures. (N)
This is a relatively uncommon occurance. (Y)	A horse being led back to it's stall. (N)

Table 3: The spelling and grammar portions of the qualification test. The test may be found on MTurk by searching for the qualification entitled "Image Annotation Qualification".

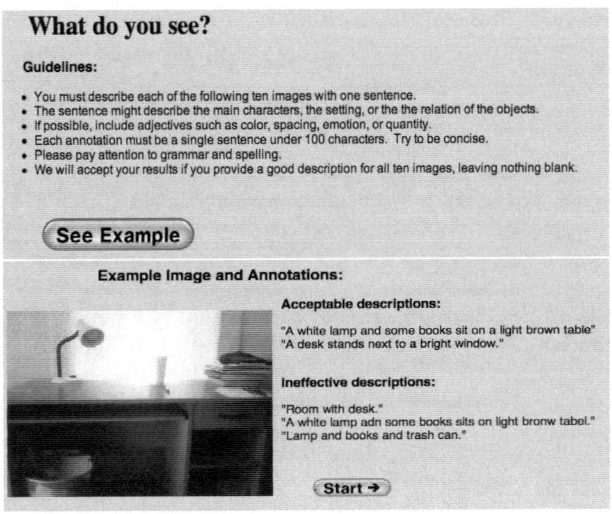

Figure 6: Screenshot of the image annotation instructions: guidelines (top) and examples (bottom).

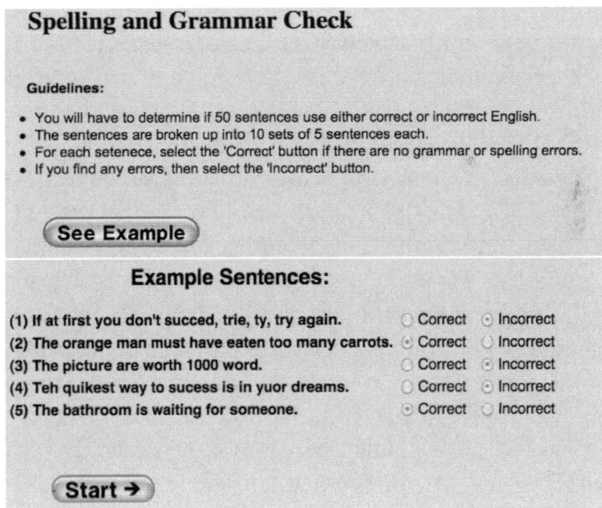

Figure 7: Screenshot of the quality control test instructions: guidelines (top) and examples (bottom).

Non-Expert Evaluation of Summarization Systems is Risky

Dan Gillick
University of California, Berkeley
Computer Science Division
dgillick@cs.berkeley.edu

Yang Liu
University of Texas, Dallas
Department of Computer Science
yangl@hlt.utdallas.edu

Abstract

We provide evidence that intrinsic evaluation of summaries using Amazon's Mechanical Turk is quite difficult. Experiments mirroring evaluation at the Text Analysis Conference's summarization track show that non-expert judges are not able to recover system rankings derived from experts.

1 Introduction

Automatic summarization is a particularly difficult task to evaluate. What makes a good summary? What information is relevant? Is it possible to separate information content from linguistic quality?

Besides subjectivity issues, evaluation is time-consuming. Ideally, a judge would read the original set of documents before deciding how well the important aspects are conveyed by a summary. A typical 10-document problem could reasonably involve 25 minutes of reading or skimming and 5 more minutes for assessing a 100-word summary. Since summary output can be quite variable, at least 30 topics should be evaluated to get a robust estimate of performance. Assuming a single judge evaluates all summaries for a topic (more redundancy would be better), we get a rough time estimate: 17.5 hours to evaluate two systems.

Thus it is of great interest to find ways of speeding up evaluation while minimizing subjectivity. Amazon's Mechanical Turk (MTurk) system has been used for a variety of labeling and annotation tasks (Snow et al., 2008), but such crowd-sourcing has not been tested for summarization.

We describe an experiment to test whether MTurk is able to reproduce system-level rankings that match expert opinion. Unlike the results of other crowd-sourcing annotations for natural language tasks, we find that non-expert judges are unable to provide expert-like scores and tend to disagree significantly with each other.

This paper is organized as follows: Section 2 introduces the particular summarization task and data we use in our experiments; Section 3 describes the design of our Human Intelligence Task (HIT). Section 4 shows experimental results and gives some analysis. Section 5 reviews our main findings and provides suggestions for researchers wishing to conduct their own crowd-sourcing evaluations.

2 TAC Summarization Task

Topic: Peter Jennings **Description:** Describe Peter Jennings' lung cancer and its effects.
Reference: Peter Jennings's announcement April 5, 2005, that he had lung cancer left his colleagues at ABC News saddened and dismayed. He had been "World News Tonight" anchorman since 1983. By the end of the week, ABC had received 3,400 e-mails offering him prayers and good wishes. A former heavy smoker, Jennings had not been well for some time and was unable to travel abroad to cover foreign events. However, his diagnosis came as a surprise to him. ABC announced that Jennings would continue to anchor the news during chemotherapy treatment, but he was unable to do so.

Table 1: An example topic and reference summary from the TAC 2009 summarization task.

Our data comes from the submissions to the Text Analysis Conference (TAC) summarization track in 2009 (Dang, 2009). The main task involved 44 query-focused topics, each requiring a system to produce a 100-word summary of 10 related news documents. Experts provided four reference summaries for each topic. Table 1 shows an example.

Proceedings of the NAACL HLT 2010 Workshop on Creating Speech and Language Data with Amazon's Mechanical Turk, pages 148–151,

Score Difference					
	0	1	2	3	mean
OQ	119	92	15	0	0.54
LQ	117	82	20	7	0.63

Table 2: Identical summaries often were given different scores by the same expert human judge at TAC 2009. Counts of absolute score differences are shown for Overall Quality (OQ) and Linguistic Quality (LQ).

2.1 Agreement and consistency

In the official TAC evaluation, each summary was judged by one of eight experts for "Overall Quality" and "Linguistic Quality" on a 1 ("very poor") to 10 ("very good") scale. Unfortunately, the lack of redundant judgments means we cannot estimate inter-annotator agreement. However, we note that out of all 4576 submitted summaries, there are 226 pairs that are identical, which allows us to estimate annotator consistency. Table 2 shows that an expert annotator will give the same summary the same score just over half the time.

2.2 Evaluation without source documents

One way to dramatically speed up evaluation is to use the experts' reference summaries as a gold standard, leaving the source documents out entirely. This is the idea behind automatic evaluation with ROUGE (Lin, 2004), which measures ngram overlap with the references, and assisted evaluation with Pyramid (Nenkova and Passonneau, 2004), which measures overlap of facts or "Semantic Content Units" with the references. The same idea has also been employed in various manual evaluations, for example by Haghighi and Vanderwende (2009), to directly compare the summaries of two different systems. The potential bias introduced by such abbreviated evaluation has not been explored.

3 HIT design

The overall structure of the HIT we designed for summary evaluation is as follows: The worker is asked to read the topic and description, and then two reference summaries (there is no mention of the source documents). The candidate summary appears next, followed by instructions to provide scores between 1 (very poor) and 10 (very good) in each category[1]. Mouse-over on the category names provides extra details, copied with slight modifications from Dang (2007).

Our initial HIT design asked workers to perform a head-to-head comparison of two candidate summaries, but we found this unsatisfactory for a number of reasons. First, many of the resulting scores did not obey the transitive property: given summaries x, y, and z, a single worker showed a preference for $y > x$ and $z > y$, but also $x > z$. Second, while this kind of head-to-head evaluation may be useful for system development, we are specifically interested here in comparing non-expert MTurk evaluation with expert TAC evaluation.

We went through a few rounds of revisions to the language in the HIT after observing worker feedback. Specifically, we found it was important to emphasize that a good summary not only responds to the topic and description, but also conveys the information in the references.

3.1 Quality control

Only workers with at least a 96% HIT approval rating[2] were allowed access to this task. We monitored results manually and blocked workers (rejecting their work) if they completed a HIT in under 25 seconds. Such suspect work typically showed uniform scores (usually all 10s). Nearly 30% of HITs were rejected for this reason.

To encourage careful work, we included this note in our HITs: "High annotator consistency is important. If the scores you provide deviate from the average scores of other annotators on the same HIT, your work will be rejected. We will award bonuses for particularly good work." We gave a few small bonuses ($0.50) to workers who left thoughtful comments.

3.2 Compensation

We experimented with a few different compensation levels and observed a somewhat counter-intuitive result. Higher compensation ($.10 per HIT) yielded lower quality work than lower compensation ($.07 per HIT), judging by the number of HITs we rejected. It seems that lower compensation attracts workers who are less interested in making money, and thus willing to spend more time and effort. There is a trade-off, though, as there are fewer workers willing to do the task for less money.

[1]Besides Overall Quality and Linguistic Quality, we include Information Content, to encourage judges to distinguish between content and readability.

[2]MTurk approval ratings calculated as the fraction of HITs approved by requesters.

Sys	TAC		MTurk		
	OQ	LQ	OQ	LQ	C
A	5.16	5.64	7.03	7.27	7.27
B	4.84	5.27	6.78	6.97	6.78
C	4.50	4.93	6.51	6.85	6.49
D	4.20	4.09	6.15	6.59	6.50
E	3.91	4.70	6.19	6.54	6.58
F	3.64	6.70	7.06	7.78	6.56
G	3.57	3.43	5.82	6.33	6.28
H	3.20	5.23	5.75	6.06	5.62

Table 3: Comparison of Overall Quality (OQ) and Linguistic Quality (LQ) scores between the TAC and MTurk evaluations. Content (C) is evaluated by MTurk workers as well. Note that system F is the lead baseline.

4 Experiments and Analysis

To assess how well MTurk workers are able to emulate the work of expert judges employed by TAC, we chose a subset of systems and analyze the results of the two evaluations. The systems were chosen to represent the entire range of average Overall Quality scores. System F is a simple lead baseline, which generates a summary by selecting the first sentences up to 100 words of the most recent document. The rest of the systems were submitted by various track participants. The MTurk evaluation included two-times redundancy. That is, each summary was evaluated by two different people. The cost for the full evaluation, including 44 topics, 8 systems, and $2x$ redundancy, at $.07 per HIT, plus 10% commission for Amazon, was $55.

Table 3 shows average scores for the two evaluations. The data suggest that the MTurk judges are better at evaluating Linguistic Quality than Content or Overall Quality. In particular, the MTurk judges appear to have difficulty distinguishing Linguistic Quality from Content. We will defend these claims with more analysis, below.

4.1 Worker variability

The first important question to address involves the consistency of the workers. We cannot compare agreement between TAC and MTurk evaluations, but the MTurk agreement statistics suggest considerable variability. In Overall Quality, the mean score difference between two workers for the same HIT is 2.4 (the standard deviation is 2.0). The mean is 2.2 for Linguistic Quality (the standard deviation is 1.5).

In addition, the TAC judges show more similarity with each other—as if they are roughly in agreement about what makes a good summary. We compute each judge's average score and look at the standard deviation of these averages for the two groups. The TAC standard deviation is 1.0 (ranging from 3.0 to 6.1), whereas the MTurk standard deviation is 2.3 (ranging from 1.0 to 9.5). Note that the average number of HITs performed by each MTurk worker was just over 5.

Finally, we can use regression analysis to show what fraction of the total score variance is captured by judges, topics, and systems. We fit linear models in **R** using binary indicators for each judge, topic, and system. Redundant evaluations in the MTurk set are removed for unbiased comparison with the TAC set. Table 4 shows that the differences between the TAC and MTurk evaluations are quite striking: Taking the TAC data alone, the topics are the major source of variance, whereas the judges are the major source of variance in the MTurk data. The systems account for only a small fraction of the variance in the MTurk evaluation, which makes system ranking more difficult.

Eval	Judges	Topics	Systems
TAC	0.28	0.40	0.13
MTurk	0.44	0.13	0.05

Table 4: Linear regression is used to model Overall Quality scores as a function of judges, topics, and systems, respectively, for each data set. The R^2 values, which give the fraction of variance explained by each of the six models, are shown.

4.2 Ranking comparisons

The TAC evaluation, while lacking redundant judgments, was a balanced experiment. That is, each judge scored every system for a single topic. The same is not true for the MTurk evaluation, and as a result, the average per-system scores shown in Table 3 may be biased. As a result, and because we need to test multiple system-level differences simultaneously, a simple t-test is not quite sufficient. We use Tukey's Honestly Significant Differences (HSD), explained in detail by Yandell (1997), to assess statistical significance.

Tukey's HSD test computes significance intervals based on the range of the sample means rather than individual differences, and includes an adjustment to correct for imbalanced experimental designs. The **R** implementation takes as input a linear model, so we

Eval	Ranking							
TAC (OQ)	A	B	C	D^A	E^B	F^C	G^C	H^D
MTurk (OQ)	F	A	B	C	E^F	G^F	D^B	H^B
TAC (LQ)	F	A^F	B^F	H^F	C^F	E^A	D^B	G^E
MTurk (LQ)	F	A	B^F	C^F	D^F	E^F	H^C	G^C
MTurk (C)	A	B	E	F	D	C	G^A	H^D

Table 5: Systems are shown in rank order from highest (left) to lowest (right) for each scoring metric: Overall Quality (OQ), Linguistic Quality (LQ), and Content (C). The superscripts indicate the rightmost system that is significantly different (at 95% confidence) according to Tukey's HSD test.

model scores using binary indicators for (J)udges, (T)opics, and (S)ystems (see equation 1), and measure significance in the differences between system coefficients (δ_k).

$$score = \alpha + \sum_i \beta_i J_i + \sum_j \gamma_j T_j + \sum_k \delta_k S_k \quad (1)$$

Table 5 shows system rankings for the two evaluations. The most obvious discrepancy between the TAC and MTurk rankings is system F, the baseline. Both TAC and MTurk judges gave F the highest scores for Linguistic Quality, a reasonable result given its construction, whereas the other summaries tend to pull sentences out of context. But the MTurk judges also gave F the highest scores in Overall Quality, suggesting that readability is more important to amateur judges than experts, or at least easier to identify. Content appears the most difficult category for the MTurk judges, as few significant score differences emerge. Even with more redundancy, it seems unlikely that MTurk judges could produce a ranking resembling the TAC Overall Quality ranking using this evaluation framework.

5 Discussion

Through parallel evaluations by experts at TAC and non-experts on MTurk, we have shown two main results. First, as expected, MTurk workers produce considerably noisier work than experts. That is, more redundancy is required to achieve statistical significance on par with expert judgments. This finding matches prior work with MTurk. Second, MTurk workers are unlikely to produce a score ranking that matches expert rankings for Overall Quality. This seems to be the result of some confusion in separating content from readability.

What does this mean for future evaluations? If we want to assess overall summary quality—that is, balancing content and linguistic quality like expert judges do—we will need to redesign the task for non-experts. Perhaps MTurk workers will be better able to understand Nenkova's Pyramid evaluation (2004), which is designed to isolate content. Extrinsic evaluation, where judges use the summary to answer questions derived from the source documents or the references, as done by Callison-Burch for evaluation of Machine Translation systems (2009), is another possibility.

Finally, our results suggest that anyone conducting an evaluation of summarization systems using non-experts should calibrate their results by asking their judges to score summaries that have already been evaluated by experts.

Acknowledgments

Thanks to Benoit Favre for discussing the evaluation format and to the anonymous reviewers for helpful, detailed feedback.

References

C. Callison-Burch. 2009. Fast, cheap, and creative: Evaluating translation quality using Amazons Mechanical Turk. *Proceedings of EMNLP*.

H.T. Dang. 2007. Overview of DUC 2007. In *Proceedings of the Document Understanding Conference*.

H.T. Dang. 2009. Overview of the TAC 2009 opinion question answering and summarization tasks. In *Proceedings of Text Analysis Conference (TAC 2009)*.

A. Haghighi and L. Vanderwende. 2009. Exploring content models for multi-document summarization. In *Proceedings of HLT-NAACL*.

C.Y. Lin. 2004. Rouge: A package for automatic evaluation of summaries. In *Proceedings of the Workshop: Text Summarization Branches Out*.

A. Nenkova and R. Passonneau. 2004. Evaluating content selection in summarization: The pyramid method. In *Proceedings of HLT-NAACL*.

R. Snow, B. O'Connor, D. Jurafsky, and A.Y. Ng. 2008. Cheap and fast—but is it good?: Evaluating non-expert annotations for natural language tasks. In *Proceedings of EMNLP*.

B.S. Yandell. 1997. *Practical data analysis for designed experiments*. Chapman & Hall/CRC.

Shedding (a Thousand Points of) Light on Biased Language

Tae Yano
School of Computer Science
Carnegie Mellon University
Pittsburgh, PA 15213, USA
taey@cs.cmu.edu

Philip Resnik
Department of Linguistics and UMIACS
University of Maryland
College Park, MD 20742, USA
resnik@umiacs.umd.edu

Noah A. Smith
School of Computer Science
Carnegie Mellon University
Pittsburgh, PA 15213, USA
nasmith@cs.cmu.edu

Abstract

This paper considers the linguistic indicators of bias in political text. We used Amazon Mechanical Turk judgments about sentences from American political blogs, asking annotators to indicate whether a sentence showed bias, and if so, in which political direction and through which word tokens. We also asked annotators questions about their own political views. We conducted a preliminary analysis of the data, exploring how different groups perceive bias in different blogs, and showing some lexical indicators strongly associated with perceived bias.

1 Introduction

Bias and framing are central topics in the study of communications, media, and political discourse (Scheufele, 1999; Entman, 2007), but they have received relatively little attention in computational linguistics. What are the linguistic indicators of bias? Are there lexical, syntactic, topical, or other clues that can be computationally modeled and automatically detected?

Here we use Amazon Mechanical Turk (MTurk) to engage in a systematic, empirical study of linguistic indicators of bias in the political domain, using text drawn from political blogs. Using the MTurk framework, we collected judgments connected with the two dominant schools of thought in American politics, as exhibited in single sentences. Since no one person can claim to be an unbiased judge of political bias in language, MTurk is an attractive framework that lets us measure perception of bias across a population.

2 Annotation Task

We drew sentences from a corpus of American political blog posts from 2008. (Details in Section 2.1.) Sentences were presented to participants one at a time, without context. Participants were asked to judge the following (see Figure 1 for interface design):

- To what extent a sentence or clause is biased (none, somewhat, very);
- The nature of the bias (very liberal, moderately liberal, moderately conservative, very conservative, biased but not sure which direction); and
- Which words in the sentence give away the author's bias, similar to "rationale" annotations in Zaidan et al. (2007).

For example, a participant might identify a moderate liberal bias in this sentence,

> Without Sestak's challenge, we would have Specter, comfortably ensconced as a Democrat in name only.

adding checkmarks on the underlined words. A more neutral paraphrase is:

> Without Sestak's challenge, Specter would have no incentive to side more frequently with Democrats.

It is worth noting that "bias," in the sense we are using it here, is distinct from "subjectivity" as that topic has been studied in computational linguistics. Wiebe et al. (1999) characterize subjective sentences as those that "are used to communicate the speaker's evaluations, opinions, and speculations," as distinguished from sentences whose primary intention is "to objectively communicate material that is factual to the reporter." In contrast, a biased sentence reflects a "tendency or preference towards a particular perspective, ideology or result."[1] A subjective sentence can be unbiased (*I think that movie was terrible*), and a biased sentence can purport to communicate factually (*Nationalizing our health care system*

[1] http://en.wikipedia.org/wiki/Bias as of 13 April, 2010.

Proceedings of the NAACL HLT 2010 Workshop on Creating Speech and Language Data with Amazon's Mechanical Turk, pages 152–158,
Los Angeles, California, June 2010.

is a point of no return for government interference in the lives of its citizens[2]).

In addition to annotating sentences, each participant was asked to complete a brief questionnaire about his or her own political views. The survey asked:

1. Whether the participant is a resident of the United States;

2. Who the participant voted for in the 2008 U.S. presidential election (Barack Obama, John McCain, other, decline to answer);

3. Which side of political spectrum he/she identified with for social issues (liberal, conservative, decline to answer); and

4. Which side of political spectrum he/she identified with for fiscal/economic issues (liberal, conservative, decline to answer).

This information was gathered to allow us to measure variation in bias perception as it relates to the stance of the annotator, e.g., whether people who view themselves as liberal perceive more bias in conservative sources, and vice versa.

2.1 Dataset

We extracted our sentences from the collection of blog posts in Eisenstein and Xing (2010). The corpus consists of 2008 blog posts gathered from six sites focused on American politics:

- American Thinker (conservative),[3]
- Digby (liberal),[4]
- Hot Air (conservative),[5]
- Michelle Malkin (conservative),[6]
- Think Progress (liberal),[7] and
- Talking Points Memo (liberal).[8]

13,246 posts were gathered in total, and 261,073 sentences were extracted using WebHarvest[9] and OpenNLP 1.3.0.[10] Conservative and liberal sites are evenly represented (130,980 sentences from conservative sites, 130,093 from liberal sites). OpenNLP was also used for tokenization.

[2]Sarah Palin, `http://www.facebook.com/note.php?note_id=113851103434`, August 7, 2009.

[3]`http://www.americanthinker.com`

[4]`http://digbysblog.blogspot.com`

[5]`http://hotair.com`

[6]`http://michellemalkin.com`

[7]`http://thinkprogress.org`

[8]`http://www.talkingpointsmemo.com`

[9]`http://web-harvest.sourceforge.net`

[10]`http://opennlp.sourceforge.net`

Liberal	Conservative
thinkprogress org	exit question
video thinkprogress	hat tip
et rally	ed lasky
org 2008	hot air
gi bill	tony rezko
wonk room	ed morrissey
dana perino	track record
phil gramm	confirmed dead
senator mccain	american thinker
abu ghraib	illegal alien

Table 1: Top ten "sticky" partisan bigrams for each side.

2.2 Sentence Selection

To support exploratory data analysis, we sought a diverse sample of sentences for annotation, but we were also guided by some factors known or likely to correlate with bias. We extracted sentences from our corpus that matched at least one of the categories below, filtering to keep those of length between 8 and 40 tokens. Then, for each category, we first sampled 100 sentences without replacement. We then randomly extracted sentences up to 1,100 from the remaining pool. We selected the sentences this way so that the collection has variety, while including enough examples for individual categories. Our goal was to gather at least 1,000 annotated sentences; ultimately we collected 1,041. The categories are as follows.

"Sticky" partisan bigrams. One likely indicator of bias is the use of terms that are particular to one side or the other in a debate (Monroe et al., 2008). In order to identify such terms, we independently created two lists of "sticky" (i.e., strongly associated) bigrams in liberal and conservative subcorpora, measuring association using the log-likelihood ratio (Dunning, 1993) and omitting bigrams containing stopwords.[11] We identified a bigram as "liberal" if it was among the top 1,000 bigrams from the liberal blogs, as measured by strength of association, and was also not among the top 1,000 bigrams on the conservative side. The reverse definition yielded the "conservative" bigrams. The resulting liberal list contained 495 bigrams, and the conservative list contained 539. We then manually filtered cases that were clearly remnant HTML tags and other markup, arriving at lists of 433 and 535, respectively. Table 1 shows the strongest weighted bigrams.

As an example, consider this sentence (with a preceding sentence of context), which contains *gi bill*. There is no reason to think the bigram itself is inherently biased (in contrast to, for example, *death tax*, which we would

[11]We made use of Pedersen's N-gram Statistics Package (Banerjee and Pedersen, 2003).

perceive as biased in virtually any unquoted context), but we do perceive bias in the full sentence.

> Their hard fiscal line softens in the face of American imperialist adventures. According to CongressDaily the Bush dogs are also whining because one of their members, Stephanie Herseth Sandlin, didn't get HER GI Bill to the floor in favor of Jim Webb's .

Emotional lexical categories. Emotional words might be another indicator of bias. We extracted four categories of words from Pennebaker's LIWC dictionary: Negative Emotion, Positive Emotion, Causation, and Anger.[12] The following is one example of a biased sentence in our dataset that matched these lexicons, in this case the Anger category; the match is in bold.

> A bunch of **ugly** facts are nailing the biggest scare story in history.

The five most frequent matches in the corpus for each category are as follows.[13]

Negative Emotion: war attack* problem* numb* argu*

Positive Emotion: like well good party* secur*

Causation: how because lead* make why

Anger: war attack* argu* fight* threat*

***Kill* verbs.** Greene and Resnik (2009) discuss the relevance of syntactic structure to the perception of sentiment. For example, their psycholinguistic experiments would predict that when comparing *Millions of people starved under Stalin* (inchoative) with *Stalin starved millions of people* (transitive), the latter will be perceived as more negative toward Stalin, because the transitive syntactic frame tends to be connected with semantic properties such as intended action by the subject and change of state in the object. "Kill verbs" provide particularly strong examples of such phenomena, because they exhibit a large set of semantic properties canonically associated with the transitive frame (Dowty, 1991). The study by Greene and Resnik used 11 verbs of killing and similar action to study the effect of syntactic "packaging" on perceptions of sentiment.[14] We included membership on this list (in any morphological form) as a selection criterion, both because these verbs may be likely to appear in sentences containing bias (they overlap significantly with Pennebaker's Negative Emotion list), and because annotation of bias will provide further data relevant to Greene and Resnik's hypothesis about the connections among semantic propeties, syntactic structures, and positive or negative perceptions (which are strongly connected with bias).

In our final 1,041-sentence sample, "sticky bigrams" occur 235 times (liberal 113, conservative 122), the lexical category features occur 1,619 times (Positive Emotion 577, Negative Emotion 466, Causation 332, and Anger 244), and "kill" verbs appear as a feature in 94 sentences. Note that one sentence often matches multiple selection criteria. Of the 1,041-sentence sample, 232 (22.3%) are from American Thinker, 169 (16.2%) from Digby, 246 (23.6%) from Hot Air, 73 (7.0%) from Michelle Malkin, 166 (15.9%) from Think Progress, and 155 (14.9%) from Talking Points Memo.

3 Mechanical Turk Experiment

We prepared 1,100 Human Intelligence Tasks (HITs), each containing one sentence annotation task. 1,041 sentences were annotated five times each (5,205 judgements total). One annotation task consists of three bias judgement questions plus four survey questions. We priced each HIT between $0.02 and $0.04 (moving from less to more to encourage faster completion). The total cost was $212.[15] We restricted access to our tasks to those who resided in United States and who had above 90% approval history, to ensure quality and awareness of American political issues. We also discarded HITs annotated by workers with particularly low agreement scores. The time allowance for each HIT was set at 5 minutes.

3.1 Annotation Results

3.1.1 Distribution of Judgments

Overall, more than half the judgments are "not biased," and the "very biased" label is used sparingly (Table 2). There is a slight tendency among the annotators to assign the "very conservative" label, although moderate bias is distributed evenly on both side (Table 3). Interestingly, there are many "biased, but not sure" labels, indicating that the annotators are capable of perceiving bias (or manipulative language), without fully decoding the intent of the author, given sentences out of context.

Bias	1	1.5	2	2.5	3
% judged	36.0	26.6	25.5	9.4	2.4

Table 2: Strength of perceived bias per sentence, averaged over the annotators (rounded to nearest half point). Annotators rate bias on a scale of 1 (no bias), 2 (some bias), and 3 (very biased).

[12] `http://www.liwc.net`. See Pennebaker et al. (2007) for detailed description of background theory, and how these lexicons were constructed. Our gratitude to Jamie Pennebaker for the use of this dictionary.

[13] Note that some LIWC lexical entries are specified as prefixes/stems, e.g. `ugl*`, which matches *ugly uglier*, etc.

[14] The verbs are: *kill, slaughter, assassinate, shoot, poison, strangle, smother, choke, drown, suffocate*, and *starve*.

[15] This includes the cost for the discarded annotations.

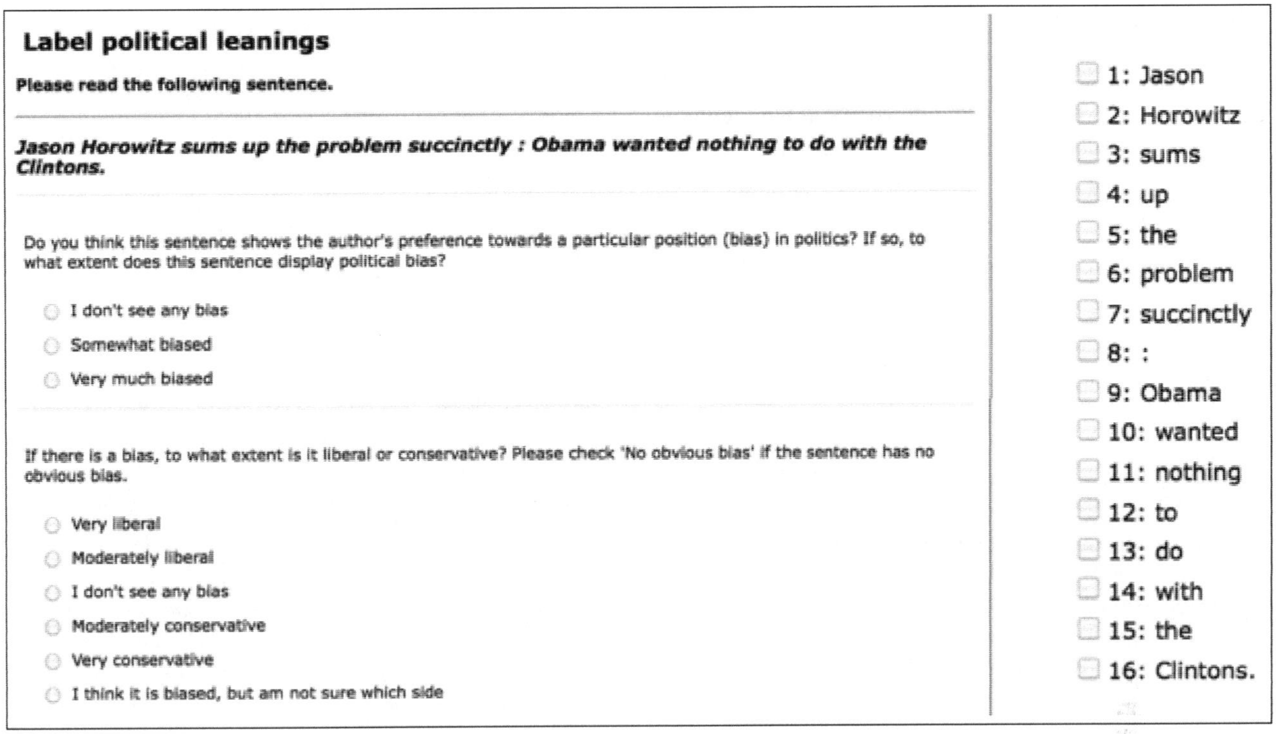

Figure 1: HIT: Three judgment questions. We first ask for the strength of bisa, then the direction. For the word-level annotation question (right), workers are asked to check the box to indicate the region which "give away" the bias.

Bias type	VL	ML	NB	MC	VC	B
% judged	4.0	8.5	54.8	8.2	6.7	17.9

Table 3: Direction of perceived bias, per judgment (very liberal, moderately liberal, no bias, moderately conservative, very conservative, biased but not sure which).

		Economic			
		L	M	C	NA
Social	L	20.1	10.1	4.9	0.7
	M	0.0	21.9	4.7	0.0
	C	0.1	0.4	11.7	0.0
	NA	0.1	0.0	11.2	14.1

Table 4: Distribution of judgements by annotators' self-identification on social issues (row) and fiscal issue (column); {L, C, M, NA} denote liberal, conservative, moderate, and decline to answer, respectively.

3.1.2 Annotation Quality

In this study, we are interested in where the wisdom of the crowd will take us, or where the majority consensus on bias may emerge. For this reason we did not contrive a gold standard for "correct" annotation. We are, however, mindful of its overall quality—whether annotations have reasonable agreement, and whether there are fraudulent responses tainting the results.

To validate our data, we measured the pair-wise Kappa statistic (Cohen, 1960) among the 50 most frequent workers[16] and took the average over all the scores.[17]. The average of the agreement score for the first question is 0.55, and the second 0.50. Those are within the range of reasonable agreement for moderately difficult task. We also inspected per worker average scores for frequent workers[18] and found one with consistently low agreement scores. We discarded all the HITs by this worker from our results. We also manually inspected the first 200 HITs for apparent frauds. The annotations appeared to be consistent. Often annotators agreed (many "no bias" cases were unanimous), or differed in only the degree of strength ("very biased" vs. "biased") or specificity ("biased but I am not sure" vs. "moderately liberal"). The direction of bias, if specified, was very rarely inconsistent.

Along with the annotation tasks, we asked workers how we could improve our HITs. Some comments were

[16]258 workers participated; only 50 of them completed more than 10 annotations.

[17]Unlike traditional subjects for a user-annotation study, our annotators have not judged all the sentences considered in the study. Therefore, to compute the agreement, we considered only the case where two annotators share 20 or more sentences.

[18]We consider only those with 10 or more annotations.

insightful for our study (as well as for the interface design). A few pointed out that an impolite statement or a statement of negative fact is not the same as bias, and therefore should be marked separately from bias. Others mentioned that some sentences are difficult to judge out of context. These comments will be taken into account in future research.

4 Analysis and Significance

In the following section we report some of the interesting trends we found in our annotation results. We consider a few questions and report the answers the data provide for each.

4.1 Is a sentence from a liberal blog more likely be seen as liberal?

In our sample sentence pool, conservatives and liberals are equally represented, though each blog site has a different representation.[19] We grouped sentences by source site, then computed the percentage representation of each site within each bias label; see Table 5. In the top row, we show the percentage representation of each group in overall judgements.

In general, a site yields more sentences that match its known political leanings. Note that in our annotation task, we did not disclose the sentence's source to the workers. The annotators formed their judgements solely based on the content of the sentence. This result can be taken as confirming people's ability to perceive bias within a sentence, or, conversely, as confirming our *a priori* categorizations of the blogs.

	at	ha	mm	db	tp	tpm
Overall	22.3	23.6	7.0	16.2	15.9	14.9
NB	23.7	22.3	6.1	15.7	17.0	15.3
VC	**24.8**	**32.3**	**19.3**	6.9	7.5	9.2
MC	**24.4**	**33.6**	**8.0**	8.2	13.6	12.2
ML	16.6	15.2	3.4	**21.1**	**22.9**	**20.9**
VL	16.7	9.0	4.3	**31.0**	**22.4**	**16.7**
B	20.1	25.4	7.2	19.5	12.3	13.7

Table 5: Percentage representation of each site within bias label pools from question 2 (direction of perceived bias): very liberal, moderately liberal, no bias, moderately conservative, very conservative, biased but not sure which. Rows sum to 100. Boldface indicates rates higher than the site's overall representation in the pool.

4.2 Does a liberal leaning annotator see more conservative bias?

In Table 5, we see that blogs are very different from each other in terms of the bias annotators perceive in their language. In general, conservative sites seemingly produced much more identifiable partisan bias than liberal sites.[20]

[19]Posts appear on different sites at different rates.

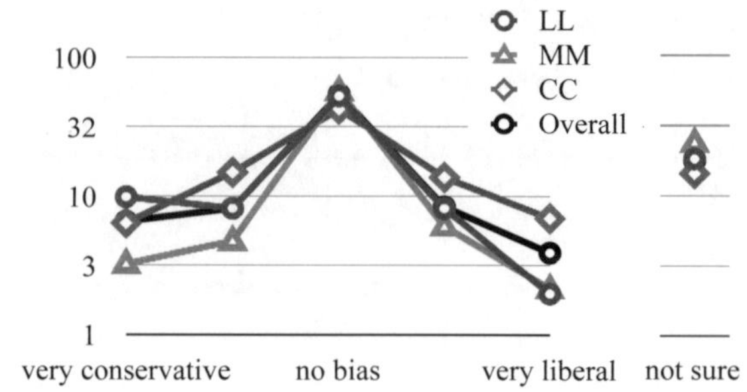

Figure 2: Distribution of bias labels (by judgment) for social and economic liberals (LL), social and economic moderates (MM), and social and economic conservatives (CC), and overall. Note that this plot uses a logarithmic scale, to tease apart the differences among groups.

This impression, however, might be an artifact of the distribution of the annotators' own bias. As seen in Table 4, a large portion of our annotators identified themselves as liberal in some way. People might call a statement biased if they disagree with it, while showing leniency toward hyperbole more consistent with their opinions.

To answer this question, we break down the judgement labels by the annotators' self-identification, and check the percentage of each bias type within key groups (see Figure 2). In general, moderates perceive less bias than partisans (another useful reality check, in the sense that this is to be expected), but conservatives show a much stronger tendency to label sentences as biased, in *both* directions. (We caution that the underrepresentation of self-identifying conservatives in our worker pool means that only 608 judgments from 48 distinct workers were used to estimate these statistics.) Liberals in this sample are less balanced, perceiving conservative bias at double the rate of liberal bias.

4.3 What are the lexical indicators of perceived bias?

For a given word type w, we calculate the frequency that it was marked as indicating bias, normalized by its total number of occurrences. To combine the judgments of different annotators, we increment w's count by k/n whenever k judgments out of n marked the word as showing bias. We perform similar calculations with a restriction to liberal and conservative judgments on the sentence as a

[20]Liberal sites cumulatively produced 64.9% of the *moderately liberal* bias label and 70.1 % of *very liberal*, while conservative sites produced 66.0% of *moderately conservative* and 76.4% of *very conservative*, respectively.

Overall		Liberal		Conservative		Not Sure Which	
bad	0.60	Administration	0.28	illegal	0.40	pass	0.32
personally	0.56	Americans	0.24	Obama's	0.38	bad	0.32
illegal	0.53	woman	0.24	corruption	0.32	sure	0.28
woman	0.52	single	0.24	rich	0.28	blame	0.28
single	0.52	personally	0.24	stop	0.26	they're	0.24
rich	0.52	lobbyists	0.23	tax	0.25	happen	0.24
corruption	0.52	Republican	0.22	claimed	0.25	doubt	0.24
Administration	0.52	union	0.20	human	0.24	doing	0.24
Americans	0.51	torture	0.20	doesn't	0.24	death	0.24
conservative	0.50	rich	0.20	difficult	0.24	actually	0.24
doubt	0.48	interests	0.20	Democrats	0.24	exactly	0.22
torture	0.47	doing	0.20	less	0.23	wrong	0.22

Table 6: Most strongly biased words, ranked by relative frequency of receiving a bias mark, normalized by total frequency. Only words appearing five times or more in our annotation set are ranked.

whole. Top-ranked words for each calculation are shown in Table 6.

Some of the patterns we see are consistent with what we found in our automatic method for proposing biased bigrams. For example, the bigrams tended to include terms that refer to members or groups on the opposing side. Here we find that *Republican* and *Administration* (referring in 2008 to the Bush administration) tends to show liberal bias, while *Obama's* and *Democrats* show conservative bias.

5 Discussion and Future Work

The study we have conducted here represents an initial pass at empirical, corpus-driven analysis of bias using the methods of computational linguistics. The results thus far suggest that it is possible to automatically extract a sample that is rich in examples that annotators would consider biased; that naïve annotators can achieve reasonable agreement with minimal instructions and no training; and that basic exploratory analysis of results yields interpretable patterns that comport with prior expectations, as well as interesting observations that merit further investigation.

In future work, enabled by annotations of biased and non-biased material, we plan to delve more deeply into the linguistic characteristics associated with biased expression. These will include, for example, an analysis of the extent to which explicit "lexical framing" (use of partisan terms, e.g., Monroe et al., 2008) is used to convey bias, versus use of more subtle cues such as syntactic framing (Greene and Resnik, 2009). We will also explore the extent to which idiomatic usages are connected with bias, with the prediction that partisan "memes" tend to be more idiomatic than compositional in nature.

In our current analysis, the issue of subjectivity was not directly addressed. Previous work has shown that opinions are closely related to subjective language (Pang and Lee, 2008). It is possible that asking annotators about sentiment while asking about bias would provide a deeper understanding of the latter. Interestingly, annotator feedback included remarks that mere negative "facts" do not convey an author's opinion or bias. The nature of subjectivity as a factor in bias perception is an important issue for future investigation.

6 Conclusion

This paper considered the linguistic indicators of bias in political text. We used Amazon Mechanical Turk judgments about sentences from American political blogs, asking annotators to indicate whether a sentence showed bias, and if so, in which political direction and through which word tokens; these data were augmented by a political questionnaire for each annotator. Our preliminary analysis suggests that bias can be annotated reasonably consistently, that bias perception varies based on personal views, and that there are some consistent lexical cues for bias in political blog data.

Acknowledgments

The authors acknowledge research support from HP Labs, help with data from Jacob Eisenstein, and helpful comments from the reviewers, Olivia Buzek, Michael Heilman, and Brendan O'Connor.

References

Satanjeev Banerjee and Ted Pedersen. 2003. The design, implementation and use of the ngram statistics package. In *the Fourth International Conference on Intelligent Text Processing and Computational Linguistics*.

Jacob Cohen. 1960. A coefficient of agreement for nominal scales. *Educational and Psychological Measurement*, 20(1):37–46.

David Dowty. 1991. Thematic Proto-Roles and Argument Selection. *Language*, 67:547–619.

Ted Dunning. 1993. Accurate methods for the statistics of surprise and coincidence. *Computational Linguistics*, 19(1):61–74.

Jacob Eisenstein and Eric Xing. 2010. The CMU 2008 political blog corpus. Technical report CMU-ML-10-101.

Robert M. Entman. 2007. Framing bias: Media in the distribution of power. *Journal of Communication*, 57(1):163–173.

Stephan Greene and Philip Resnik. 2009. More than words: Syntactic packaging and implicit sentiment. In *NAACL*, pages 503–511, June.

Burt L. Monroe, Michael P. Colaresi, and Kevin M. Quinn. 2008. Fightin' words: Lexical feature selection and evaluation for identifying the content of political conflict. *Political Analysis*, 16(4):372–403, October.

Bo Pang and Lillian Lee. 2008. Opinion mining and sentiment analysis. *Foundations and Trends in Information Retrieval*, 2(1-2):1–135.

J.W. Pennebaker, C.K Chung, M. Ireland, A Gonzales, and R J. Booth, 2007. *The development and psychometric properties of LIWC2007*.

Dietram A. Scheufele. 1999. Framing as a theory of media effects. *Journal of Communication*, 49(1):103–122.

Janyce M. Wiebe, Rebecca F. Bruce, and Thomas P. O'Hara. 1999. Development and use of a gold standard data set for subjectivity classifications. In *Proceedings of the Association for Computational Linguistics (ACL)*, pages 246–253.

Omar Zaidan, Jason Eisner, and Christine Piatko. 2007. Using "annotator rationales" to improve machine learning for text categorization. In *NAACL*, pages 260–267, April.

Evaluation of Commonsense Knowledge with Mechanical Turk

Jonathan Gordon
Dept. of Computer Science
University of Rochester
Rochester, NY, USA
jgordon@cs.rochester.edu

Benjamin Van Durme
HLTCOE
Johns Hopkins University
Baltimore, MD, USA
vandurme@cs.jhu.edu

Lenhart K. Schubert
Dept. of Computer Science
University of Rochester
Rochester, NY, USA
schubert@cs.rochester.edu

Abstract

Efforts to automatically acquire world knowledge from text suffer from the lack of an easy means of evaluating the resulting knowledge. We describe initial experiments using Mechanical Turk to crowdsource evaluation to non-experts for little cost, resulting in a collection of factoids with associated quality judgements. We describe the method of acquiring usable judgements from the public and the impact of such large-scale evaluation on the task of knowledge acquisition.

1 Introduction

The creation of intelligent artifacts that can achieve human-level performance at problems like question-answering ultimately depends on the availability of considerable knowledge. Specifically, what is needed is commonsense knowledge about the world in a form suitable for reasoning. *Open knowledge extraction* (Van Durme and Schubert, 2008) is the task of mining text corpora to create useful, high-quality collections of such knowledge.

Efforts to encode knowledge by hand, such as Cyc (Lenat, 1995), require expensive man-hours of labor by experts. Indeed, results from Project Halo (Friedland *et al.*, 2004) suggest that properly encoding the (domain-specific) knowledge from just one page of a textbook can cost $10,000. OKE, on the other hand, creates logical formulas automatically from existing stores of human knowledge, such as books, newspapers, and the Web. And while crowdsourced efforts to gather knowledge, such as Open Mind (Singh, 2002), learn factoids people come up with off the tops of their heads to contribute, OKE learns from what people normally write about and thus consider important. Open *knowledge* extraction differs from open *information* extraction (Banko *et al.*, 2007) in the focus on everyday, commonsense knowledge rather than specific facts, and on the logical interpretability of the outputs. While an OIE system might learn that Tolstoy wrote using a dip pen, an OKE system would prefer to learn that an author may write using a pen.

An example of an OKE effort is the KNEXT system[1] (Schubert, 2002), which uses compositional semantic interpretation rules to produce logical formulas from the knowledge implicit in parsed text. These formulas are then automatically expressed as English-like "factoids", such as 'A PHILOSOPHER MAY HAVE A CONVICTION' or 'NEGOTIATIONS CAN BE LIKELY TO GO ON FOR SOME HOURS'.

While it is expected that eventually sufficiently clean knowledge bases will be produced for inferences to be made about everyday things and events, currently the average quality of automatically acquired knowledge is not good enough to be used in traditional reasoning systems. An obstacle for knowledge extraction is the lack of an easy method for evaluating – and thus improving – the quality of results. Evaluation in acquisition systems is typically done by human judging of random samples of output, usually by the reporting authors themselves (*e.g.*, Lin and Pantel, 2002; Schubert and Tong, 2003; Banko *et al.*, 2007). This is time-consuming, and it has the potential for bias: it would be preferable to have people other than AI researchers label whether an output is commonsense knowledge or not. We explore the use of Amazon's Mechanical Turk service, an online labor market, as a means of acquiring many non-expert judgements for little cost.

2 Related Work

While Open Mind Commons (Speer, 2007) asks users to vote for or against commonsense statements contributed by others users in order to come to a consensus, we seek to evaluate an automatic system. Snow *et al.* (2008) compared the quality of labels produced by non-expert Turkers against those made by experts for a variety of NLP tasks and found that they required only four responses per item to emulate expert annotations. Kittur *et al.* (2008) describe the use and

[1] Public release of the basic KNEXT engine is forthcoming.

Proceedings of the NAACL HLT 2010 Workshop on Creating Speech and Language Data with Amazon's Mechanical Turk, pages 159–162,
Los Angeles, California, June 2010.

The statement above is a reasonably clear, entirely plausible, generic claim and seems neither too specific nor too general or vague to be useful:

- I agree.
- I lean towards agreement.
- I'm not sure.
- I lean towards disagreement.
- I disagree.

Figure 1: Rating instructions and answers.

Examples of *good* statements:

- A SONG CAN BE POPULAR
- A PERSON MAY HAVE A HEAD
- MANEUVERS MAY BE HOLD -ED IN SECRET
  It's fine if verb conjugations are not attached or are a bit unnatural, *e.g.* "hold -ed" instead of "held".

Examples of *bad* statements:

- A THING MAY SEEK A WAY
  This is *too vague*. What sort of thing? A way for/to what?
- A COCKTAIL PARTY CAN BE AT SCOTCH_PLAINS_COUNTRY_CLUB
  This is *too specific*. We want to know that a cocktail party can be at a country club, not at this particular one. The underscores are not a problem.
- A PIG MAY FLY
  This is *not literally true* even though it happens to be an expression.
- A WORD MAY MEAN
  This is *missing information*. What might a word mean?

Figure 2: The provided examples of good and bad factoids.

necessity of verifiable questions in acquiring accurate ratings of Wikipedia articles from Mechanical Turk users. These results contribute to our methods below.

3 Experiments

Previous evaluations of KNEXT output have tried to judge the relative quality of knowledge learned from different sources and by different techniques. Here the goal is simply to see whether the means of evaluation can be made to work reasonably, including at what scale it can be done for limited cost. For these experiments, we relied on $100 in credit provided by Amazon as part of the workshop shared task. This amount was used for several small experiments in order to empirically estimate what $100 could achieve, given a tuned method of presentation and evaluation.

We took a random selection of factoids generated from the British National Corpus (BNC Consortium, 2001), split into sets of 20, and removed those most easily filtered out as probably being of low quality or malformed. We skipped the more stringent filters (originally created for dealing with noisy Web text), leaving more variety in the quality of the factoids Turkers were asked to rate.

The first evaluation followed the format of previous, offline ratings. For each factoid, Turkers were given the instructions and choices in Fig. 1, where the options correspond in our analysis to the numbers 1–5, with 1 being agreement. To help Turkers make such judgements, they were given a brief background statement: "*We're gathering the sort of everyday, commonsense knowledge an intelligent computer system should know. You're asked to rate several possible statements based on how well you think they meet this goal.*" Mason and Watts (2009) suggest that while money may increase the number and speed of responses, other motivations such as wanting to help with something worthwhile or interesting are more likely to lead to high-quality responses.

Participants were then shown the examples and explanations in Fig. 2. Note that while they are told some categories that bad factoids can fall into, the Turkers are not asked to make such classifications themselves, as this is a task where even experts have low agreement (Van Durme and Schubert, 2008).

An initial experiment (Round 1) only required Turkers to have a high (90%) approval rate. Under these conditions, out of 100 HITs[2], 60 were completed by participants whose IP addresses indicated they were in India, 38 from the United States, and 2 from Australia. The average Pearson correlation between the ratings of different Indian Turkers answering the same questions was a very weak 0.065, and between the Indian responders and those from the US and Australia was 0.132. On the other hand, the average correlation among non-Indian Turkers was 0.508, which is close to the 0.6–0.8 range seen between the authors in the past, and which can be taken as an upper bound on agreement for the task.

Given the sometimes subtle judgements of meaning required, being a native English speaker has previously been assumed to be a prerequisite. This difference in raters' agreements may thus be due to levels of language understanding, or perhaps to different levels of attentiveness to the task. However, it does not seem to be the case that the Indian respondents rushed: They took a median time of 201.5 seconds (249.18 avg. with a high standard deviation of 256.3 s – some took more than a minute per factoid). The non-Indian responders took a median time of just 115.5 s (124.5 avg., 49.2 std dev.).

Regardless of the cause, given these results, we restricted the availability of all following experiments to Turkers in the US.Ideally we would include other English-speaking countries, but there is no straight-

[2]Human Intelligence Tasks – Mechanical Turk assignments. In this case, each HIT was a set of twenty factoids to be rated.

	All		High Corr. (> 0.3)	
Round	*Avg.*	*Std. Dev.*	*Avg.*	*Std. Dev.*
1 (BNC)	2.59	1.55	2.71	1.64
3 (BNC)	2.80	1.66	2.83	1.68
4 (BNC)	2.61	1.64	2.62	1.64
5 (BNC)	2.76	1.61	2.89	1.68
6 (Weblogs)	2.83	1.67	2.85	1.67
7 (Wikipedia)	2.75	1.64	2.75	1.64

Table 1: Average ratings for all responses and for highly correlated responses. to other responses. Lower numbers are more positive. Round 2 was withdrawn without being completed.

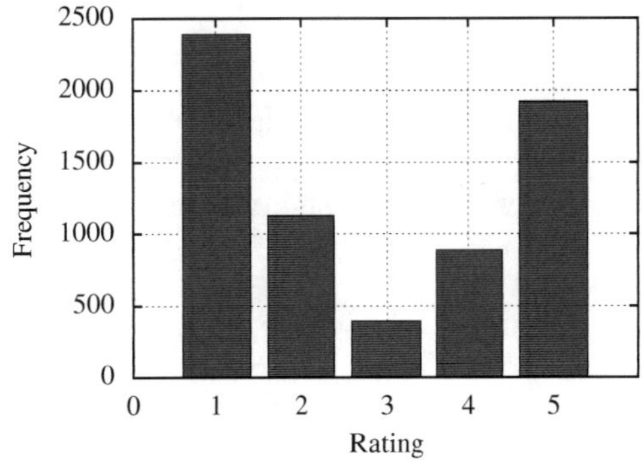

Figure 3: Frequency of ratings in the high-corr. results of Round 3.

forward way to set multiple allowable countries on Mechanical Turk.When Round 2 was posted with a larger set of factoids to be rated and the location requirement, responses fell off sharply, leading us to abort and repost with a higher payrate (7¢ for 20 factoids *vs* 5¢ originally) in Round 3.

To avoid inaccurate ratings, we rejected submissions that were improbably quick or were strongly uncorrelated with other Turkers' responses. We collected five Turkers' ratings for each set of factoids, and for each persons' response to a HIT computed the average of their three highest correlations with others' responses. We then rejected if the correlations were so low as to indicate random responses. The scores serve a second purpose of identifying a more trustworthy subset of the responses. (A cut-off score of 0.3 was chosen based on hand-examination.) In Table 1, we can see that these more strongly correlated responses rate factoids as slightly worse overall, possibly because those who either casual or uncertain are more likely to judge favorably on the assumption that this is what the task authors would prefer, or they are simply more likely to select the top-most option, which was "I agree".

An example of a factoid that was labeled incorrectly by one of the filtered out users is 'A PERSON MAY LOOK AT SOME THING-REFERRED-TO OF PRESS RELEASES', for which a Turker from Madras in Round 1 selected "I agree". Factoids containing the vague 'THING-REFERRED-TO' are often filtered out of our results automatically, but leaving them in gave us some obviously bad inputs for checking Turkers' responses. Another (US) Turker chose "I agree" when told 'TES MAY HAVE 1991ES' but "I disagree" when shown 'A TRIP CAN BE TO A SUPERMARKET'.

We are interested not only in whether there is a general consensus to be found among the Turkers but also how that consensus correlates with the judgements of AI researchers. To this end, one of the authors rated five sets (100 factoids) presented in Round 3, which yielded an average correlation between all the Turkers and the author of 0.507, which rises slightly to 0.532 if we only count those Turkers considered "highly correlated" as described above.

As another test of agreement, for ten of the sets in Round 3, two factoids were designated as fixpoints – the single best and worst factoid in the set, assigned ratings 1 and 5 respectively. From the Turkers who rated these factoids, 65 of the 100 ratings matched the researchers' designations and 77 were within one point of the chosen rating.[3]

A few of the Turkers who participated had fairly strong negative correlations to the other Turkers, suggesting that they may have misunderstood the task and were rating backwards.[4] Furthermore, one Turker commented that she was unsure whether the statement she was being asked to agree with (Fig. 1) "was a positive or negative". To see how it would affect the results, we ran (as Round 4) twenty sets of factoids, asking simplified question "Do you agree this is a good statement of general knowledge?" The choices were also reversed in order, running from "I disagree" to "I agree" and color-coded, with agree being green and disagree red. This corresponded to the coloring of the good and bad examples at the top of the page, which the Turkers were told to reread when they were halfway through the HIT. The average correlation for responses in Round 4 was 0.47, which is an improvement over the 0.34 avg. correlation of Round 3.

Using the same format as Round 4, we ran factoids from two other corpora. Round 6 consisted of 300 random factoids taken from running KNEXT on weblog data (Gordon *et al.*, 2009) and Round 7 300 random factoids taken from running KNEXT on Wikipedia.

[3] If we only look at the highly correlated responses, this increases slightly to 68% exact match, 82% within one point.

[4] This was true for one Turker who completed many HITs, a problem that might be prevented by accepting/rejecting HITs as soon as all scores for that set of factoids were available rather than waiting for the entire experiment to finish.

The average ratings for factoids from these sources are lower than for the BNC, reflecting the noisy nature of much writing on weblogs and the many overly specific or esoteric factoids learned from Wikipedia.

The results achieved can be quite sensitive to the display of the task. For instance, the frequency of ratings in Fig. 3 shows that Turkers tended toward the extremes: "I agree" and "I disagree" but rarely "I'm not sure". This option might have a negative connotation ("Waffling is undesirable") that another phrasing would not. As an alternative presentation of the task (Round 5), for 300 factoids, we asked Turkers to first decide whether a factoid was "incoherent (not understandable)" and, otherwise, whether it was "bad", "not very good", "so-so", "not so bad", or "good" commonsense knowledge. Turkers indicated factoids were incoherent 14% of the time, with a corresponding reduction in the number rated as "bad", but no real increase in middle ratings. The average ratings for the "coherent" factoids are in Table 1.

4 Uses of Results

Beyond exploring the potential of Mechanical Turk as a mechanism for evaluating the output of KNEXT and other open knowledge extraction systems, these experiments have two useful outcomes:

First, they give us a large collection of almost 3000 factoids that have associated average ratings and allow for the release of the subset of those factoids that are believed to probably be good (rated 1–2). This data set is being publicly released at `http://www.cs.rochester.edu/research/knext`, and it includes a wide range of factoids, such as 'A REPRESENTATION MAY SHOW REALITY' and 'DEMONSTRATIONS MAY MARK AN ANNIVERSARY OF AN UPRISING'.

Second, the factoids rated from Round 2 onward were associated with the KNEXT extraction rules used to generate them: The factoids generated by different rules have average ratings from 1.6 to 4.8. We hope in future to use this data to improve KNEXT's extraction methods, improving or eliminating rules that often produce factoids judged to be bad. Inexpensive, fast evaluation of output on Mechanical Turk could be a way to measure incremental improvements in output quality coming from the same source.

5 Conclusions

These initial experiments have shown that untrained Turkers evaluating the natural-language verbalizations of an open knowledge extraction system will generally give ratings that correlate strongly with those of AI researchers. Some simple methods were described to find those responses that are likely to be accurate. This work shows promise for cheap and quick means of measuring the quality of automatically constructed knowledge bases and thus improving the tools that create them.

Acknowledgements

This work was supported by NSF grants IIS-0535105 and IIS-0916599.

References

Michele Banko, Michael J. Cafarella, Stephen Soderland, Matt Broadhead, and Oren Etzioni. 2007. Open information extraction from the Web. In *Proc. of IJCAI-07*.

BNC Consortium. 2001. The British National Corpus, v.2. Dist. by Oxford University Computing Services.

Noah S. Friedland *et al.*. 2004. Project Halo: Towards a digital Aristotle. *AI Magazine*, 25(4).

Jonathan Gordon, Benjamin Van Durme, and Lenhart K. Schubert. 2009. Weblogs as a source for extracting general world knowledge. In *Proc. of K-CAP-09*.

Aniket Kittur, Ed H. Chi, and Bongwon Suh. 2008. Crowdsourcing user studies with Mechanical Turk. In *Proc. of CHI '08*.

Douglas B. Lenat. 1995. Cyc: A Large-scale Investment in Knowledge Infrastructure. *Communications of the ACM*, 38(11):33–48.

Dekang Lin and Patrick Pantel. 2002. Concept discovery from text. In *Proc. of COLING-02*.

Winter Mason and Duncan J. Watts. 2009. Financial incentives and the "performance of crowds". In *Proc. of HCOMP '09*.

Lenhart K. Schubert and Matthew H. Tong. 2003. Extracting and evaluating general world knowledge from the Brown corpus. In *Proc. of the HLT-NAACL Workshop on Text Meaning*.

Lenhart K. Schubert. 2002. Can we derive general world knowledge from texts? In *Proc. of HLT-02*.

Push Singh. 2002. The public acquisition of commonsense knowledge. In *Proc. of AAAI Spring Symposium on Acquiring (and Using) Linguistic (and World) Knowledge for Information Access*.

Rion Snow, Brendan O'Connor, Daniel Jurafsky, and Andrew Y. Ng. 2008. Cheap and fast – but is it good? In *Proc. of EMNLP-08*.

Robert Speer. 2007. Open mind commons: An inquisitive approach to learning common sense. In *Workshop on Common Sense and Intelligent User Interfaces*.

Benjamin Van Durme and Lenhart K. Schubert. 2008. Open knowledge extraction through compositional language processing. In *Proc. of STEP 2008*.

Cheap Facts and Counter-Facts

Rui Wang
Computational Linguistics Department
Saarland University
Room 2.04, Building C 7.4
Saarbruecken, 66123 Germany
rwang@coli.uni-sb.de

Chris Callison-Burch
Computer Science Department
Johns Hopkins University
3400 N. Charles Street (CSEB 226-B)
Baltimore, MD 21218, USA
ccb@cs.jhu.com.edu

Abstract

This paper describes our experiments of using Amazon's Mechanical Turk to generate (counter-)facts from texts for certain named-entities. We give the human annotators a paragraph of text and a highlighted named-entity. They will write down several (counter-)facts about this named-entity in that context. The analysis of the results is performed by comparing the acquired data with the recognizing textual entailment (RTE) challenge dataset.

1 Motivation

The task of RTE (Dagan et al., 2005) is to say whether a person would reasonably infer some short passage of text, the *Hypothesis* (H), given a longer passage, the *Text* (T). However, collections of such T-H pairs are rare to find and these resources are the key to solving the problem.

The datasets used in the RTE task were collected by extracting paragraphs of news text and manually constructing hypotheses. For the data collected from information extraction task, the H is usually a statement about a relation between two named-entities (NEs), which is written by expertise. Similarly, the H in question answering data is constructed using both the question and the (in)correct answers. Therefore, the research questions we could ask are,

1. Are these hypotheses really those ones people interested in?
2. Are hypotheses different if we construct them in other ways?
3. What would be a good negative hypotheses compared with the positive ones?

In this paper, we address these issues by using Amazon's Mechanical Turk (MTurk), online non-expert annotators (Snow et al., 2008). Instead of constructing the hypotheses targeted to IE or QA, we just ask the human annotators to come up with some facts they consider as relevant to the given text. For negative hypotheses, we change the instruction and ask them to write counter-factual but still relevant statements. In order to narrow down the content of the generated hypotheses, we give a focused named-entity (NE) for each text to guide the annotators.

2 Related Work

The early related research was done by Cooper et al. (1996), where they manually construct a textbook-style corpus aiming at different semantic phenomena involved in inference. However, the dataset is not large enough to train a robust machine-learning-based RTE system. The recent research from the RTE community focused on acquiring large quantities of textual entailment pairs from news headlines (Burger and Ferro, 2005) and negative examples from sequential sentences with transitional discourse connectives (Hickl et al., 2006). Although the quality of the data collected were quite good, most of the positive examples are similar to summarization and the negative examples are more like a comparison/contrast between two sentences instead of a contradiction. Those data are the real sentences used in news articles, but the way of obtaining them is not necessarily the (only) best way to

Proceedings of the NAACL HLT 2010 Workshop on Creating Speech and Language Data with Amazon's Mechanical Turk, pages 163–167,
Los Angeles, California, June 2010. ©2010 Association for Computational Linguistics

find entailment pairs. In this paper, we investigate an alternative inexpensive way of collecting entailment/contradiction text pairs by crowdsourcing.

In addition to the information given by the text, common knowledge is also allowed to be involved in the inference procedure. The Boeing-Princeton-ISI (BPI) textual entailment test suite[1] is specifically designed to look at entailment problems requiring world knowledge. We will also allow this in the design of our task.

3 Design of the Task

The basic idea of the task is to give the human annotators a paragraph of text with one highlighted named-entity and ask them to write some (counter-)facts about it. In particular, we first preprocess an existing RTE corpus using a named-entity recognizer to mark all the named-entities appearing in both T and H. When we show the texts to Turkers, we highlight one named-entity and give them one of these two sets of instructions:

Facts: Please write several facts about the highlighted words according to the paragraph. You may add additional common knowledge (e.g. Paris is in France), but please mainly use the information contained in the text. But please **do not copy and paste**!

Counter-Facts: Please write several statements that are contradictory to the text. Make your statements about the highlighted words. Please use the information mainly in the text. Avoid using words like **not** or **never**.

Then there are three blank lines given for the annotators to fill in facts or counter-factual statements. For each HIT, we gather facts or counter-facts for five texts, and for each text, we ask three annotators to perform the task. We give Turkers one example as a guide along with the instructions.

4 Experiments and Results

The texts we use in our experiments are the development set of the RTE-5 challenge (Bentivogli et al., 2009), and we preprocess the data using the Stanford named-entity recognizer (Finkel et al., 2005). In all, it contains 600 T-H pairs, and we use the texts to generate facts and counter-facts and hypotheses as references. We put our task online through CrowdFlower[2], and on average, we pay one cent for each (counter-)fact to the Turkers. CrowdFlower can help with finding trustful Turkers and the data were collected within a few hours.

	Total	Average (per Text)
Extracted NEs		
Facts	244	1.19
Counter-Facts	121	1.11
Generated Hypotheses		
Facts	790	3.85
Counter-Facts	203	1.86

Table 1: The statistics of the (valid) data we collect. The *Total* column presents the number of extracted NEs and generated hypotheses and the *Average* column shows the average numbers per text respectively.

To get a sense of the quality of the data we collect, we mainly focus on analyzing the following three aspects: 1) the statistics of the datasets themselves; 2) the comparison between the data we collect and the original RTE dataset; and 3) the comparison between the facts and the counter-facts.

Table 1 show some basic statistics of the data we collect. After excluding invalid and trivial ones[3], we acquire 790 facts and 203 counter-facts. In general, the counter-facts seem to be more difficult to obtain than the facts, since both the total number and the average number of the counter-facts are less than those of the facts. Notice that the NEs are not many since they have to appear in both T and H.

The comparison between our data and the original RTE data is shown in Table 2. The average length of the generated hypotheses is longer than the original hypotheses, for both the facts and the counter-facts. Counter-facts seem to be more verbose, since additional (contradictory) information is added. For instance, example ID 425 in Table 4, Counter_Fact_1 can be viewed as the more informative but contradictory version of Fact_1 (and the original hypoth-

[1] http://www.cs.utexas.edu/~pclark/bpi-test-suite/

[2] http://crowdflower.com/

[3] Invalid data include empty string or single words; and the trivial ones are those sentences directly copied from the texts.

esis). The average bag-of-words similarity scores are calculated by dividing the number of overlapping words of T and H by the total number of words in H. In the original RTE dataset, the entailed hypotheses have a higher BoW score than the contradictory ones; while in our data, facts have a lower score than the counter-facts. This might be caused by the greater variety of the facts than the counter-facts. Fact_1 of example ID 425 in Table 4 is almost the same as the original hypothesis, and Fact_2 of example ID 374 as well, though the latter has some slight differences which make the answer different from the original one. The NE position in the sentence is another aspect to look at. We find that people tend to put the NEs at the beginning of the sentences more than other positions, while in the RTE datasets, NEs appear in the middle more frequently.

In order to get a feeling of the quality of the data, we randomly sampled 50 generated facts and counter-facts and manually compared them with the original hypotheses. Table 3 shows that generated facts are easier for the systems to recognize, and the counter-facts have the same difficulty on average.

Although it is subjective to evaluate the *difficulty* of the data by human reading, in general, we follow the criteria that

1. Abstraction is more difficult than extraction;
2. Inference is more difficult than the direct entailment;
3. The more sentences in T are involved, the more difficult that T-H pair is.

Therefore, we view the Counter_Fact_1 in example ID 16 in Table 4 is more difficult than the original hypothesis, since it requires more inference than the direct fact validation. However, in example ID 374, Fact_1 is easier to be verified than the original hypothesis, and same as those facts in example ID 506. Similar hypotheses (e.g. Fact_1 in example ID 425 and the original hypothesis) are treated as being at the same level of difficulty.

After the quantitive analysis, let's take a closer look at the examples in Table 4. The facts are usually constructed by rephrasing some parts of the text (e.g. in ID 425, "after a brief inspection" is paraphrased by "investigated by" in Fact_2) or making a short summary (e.g. Fact_1 in ID 374, "George Stranahan spoke of Thompson's death."). For counter-facts, removing the negation words or changing into another adjective is one common choice, e.g. in ID 374, Counter_Fact_1 removed "n't" and Counter_Fact_3 changed "never" into "fully". The antonyms can also make the contradiction, as "rotten" to "great" in Counter_Fact_2 in ID 374.

Example ID 506 in Table 4 is another interesting case. There are many facts about Yemen, but no valid counter-facts are generated. Furthermore, if we compare the generated facts with the original hypothesis, we find that people tend to give straightforward facts instead of abstracts[4].

At last, we show some preliminary results on testing a baseline RTE system on this dataset. For the sake of comparison, we extract a subset of the dataset, which is balanced on entailment and contradiction text pairs, and compare the results with the same system on the original RTE-5 dataset. The baseline system uses a simple BoW-based similarity measurement between T and H (Bentivogli et al., 2009) and the results are shown in Table 5.

The results indicate that our data are slightly "easier" than the original RTE-5 dataset, which is consistent with our human evaluation on the sampled data

	Valid	Harder	Easier	Same
Facts	76%	16%	24%	36%
Counter-Facts	84%	36%	36%	12%

Table 3: The comparison of the generated (counter-)facts with the original hypotheses. The *Valid* column shows the percentage of the valid (counter-)facts; and other columns present the distribution of harder, easier cases than the original hypotheses or with the same difficulty.

	RTE-5	Our Data
Counter-/Facts	300/300	178/178
All "YES"	50%	50%
BoW Baseline	57.5%	58.4%

Table 5: The results of baseline RTE systems on the data we collected, compared with the original RTE-5 dataset. The *Counter-/Facts* row shows the number of the T-H pairs contained in the dataset; and the other scores in percentage are accuracy of the systems.

[4]But this might also be caused by the design of our task.

	Ave. Length	Ave. BoW	NE Position		
			Head	Middle	Tail
Original Entailment Hypotheses	7.6	0.76	46%	53%	1%
Facts	9.8	0.68	68%	29%	3%
Original Contradiction Hypotheses	7.5	0.72	44%	56%	0%
Counter-Facts	12.3	0.75	59%	38%	3%

Table 2: The comparison between the generated (counter-)facts and the original hypotheses from the RTE dataset. The *Ave. Length* column represents the average number of words in each hypothesis; The *Ave. BoW* shows the average bag-of-words similarity compared with the text. The three columns on the right are all about the position of the NE appearing in the sentence, how likely it is at the head, middle, or tail of the sentence.

(Table 3). However, it is still too early to draw conclusions based on the simple baseline results.

5 Conclusion and Future Work

In this paper, we report our experience of using MTurk to collect facts and counter-facts about the given NEs and texts. We find that the generated hypotheses are not entirely the same as the original hypotheses in the RTE data. One direct extension would be to use more than one NE at one time, but it may also cause problems, if those NEs do not have any relations in-between. Another line of research would be to test this generated resources using some real existing RTE systems and compare the results with the original RTE datasets, and also further explore the potential application of this resource.

Acknowledgments

The first author is supported by the PIRE scholarship program. The second author is supported by the EuroMatrixPlusProject (funded by the European Commission), by the DARPA GALE program under Contract No. HR0011-06-2-0001, and by the NSF under grant IIS-0713448. The views and findings are the authors' alone.

References

L. Bentivogli, B. Magnini, I. Dagan, H.T. Dang, and D. Giampiccolo. 2009. The fifth pascal recognizing textual entailment challenge. In *Proceedings of the Text Analysis Conference (TAC 2009) Workshop*, Gaithersburg, Maryland, USA, November. National Institute of Standards and Technology.

John Burger and Lisa Ferro. 2005. Generating an entailment corpus from news headlines. In *Proceedings of the ACL Workshop on Empirical Modeling of Semantic Equivalence and Entailment*, pages 49–54, Ann Arbor, Michigan, USA. Association for Computational Linguistics.

Robin Cooper, Dick Crouch, Jan Van Eijck, Chris Fox, Johan Van Genabith, Jan Jaspars, Hans Kamp, David Milward, Manfred Pinkal, Massimo Poesio, and Steve Pulman. 1996. Using the framework. Technical Report LRE 62-051 D-16, The FraCaS Consortium.

I. Dagan, O. Glickman, and B. Magnini. 2005. The pascal recognising textual entailment challenge. In *Proceedings of the PASCAL Challenges Workshop on Recognising Textual Entailment*.

Jenny Rose Finkel, Trond Grenager, and Christopher Manning. 2005. Incorporating non-local information into information extraction systems by gibbs sampling. In *Proceedings of the 43nd Annual Meeting of the Association for Computational Linguistics (ACL 2005)*, pages 363–370. Association for Computational Linguistics.

Andrew Hickl, John Williams, Jeremy Bensley, Kirk Roberts, Bryan Rink, and Ying Shi. 2006. Recognizing textual entailment with lcc's groundhog system. In *Proceedings of the Second PASCAL Challenges Workshop*.

Rion Snow, Brendan O'Connor, Daniel Jurafsky, and Andrew Y. Ng. 2008. Cheap and fast - but is it good? Evaluating non- expert annotations for natural language tasks. In *Proceedings of EMNLP*.

ID: 16	Answer: **Contradiction**
Original Text	*The father of an Oxnard teenager accused of gunning down a gay classmate who was romantically attracted to him has been found dead, Ventura County authorities said today. Bill McInerney, 45, was found shortly before 8 a.m. in the living room of his Silver Strand home by a friend, said James Baroni, Ventura County's chief deputy medical examiner. The friend was supposed to drive him to a court hearing in his son's murder trial, Baroni said. McInerney's 15-year-old son, Brandon, is accused of murder and a hate crime in the Feb. 12, 2008, shooting death of classmate Lawrence "Larry" King, 15. The two boys had been sparring in the days before the killing, allegedly because Larry had expressed a romantic interest in Brandon.*
Original Hypothesis	*Bill McInerney is accused of killing a gay teenager.*
NE_1: Bill McInerney	
Counter_Fact_1	*Bill McInerney is still alive.*
ID: 374	Answer: **Contradiction**
Original Text	*Other friends were not surprised at his death. "I wasn't surprised," said **George Stranahan**, a former owner of the **Woody Creek Tavern**, a favourite haunt of Thompson. "I never expected Hunter to die in a hospital bed with tubes coming out of him." Neighbours have said how his broken leg had prevented him from leaving his house as often as he had liked to. One neighbour and long-standing friend, Mike Cleverly, said Thompson was clearly hobbled by the broken leg. "Medically speaking, he's had a rotten year."*
Original Hypothesis	*The **Woody Creek Tavern** is owned by **George Stranahan**.*
NE_1: George Stranahan	
Fact_1	*George Stranahan spoke of Thompson's death.*
Fact_2	*George Stranahan once owned the Woody Creek Tavern.*
Counter_Fact_1	*George Stranahan was surprised by his friend's death.*
Counter_Fact_2	*Medically, George Stranahan's friend, Humter Thompson, had a great year.*
Counter_Fact_3	*George Stranahan fully expected Thompson to die in a hospital with tubes coming out of him.*
NE_2: Woody Creek Tavern	
Fact_1	*Woody Creek Tavern was previously owned by George Stranahan.*
ID: 425	Answer: **Entailment**
Original Text	*Merseyside Police concluded after a brief inspection that the controversial blog **Liverpool Evil Cabal** does not break criminal law. However the council officers continue to search for the editor. The blog has been blocked on computers controlled by Liverpool Direct Ltd, a company jointly owned by Liverpool City Council and British Telecom. The council's elected officials have denied ordering the block and are currently investigating its origin.*
Original Hypothesis	***Liverpool Evil Cabal** is the name of an online blog.*
NE_1: Liverpool Evil Cabal	
Fact_1	*Liverpool Evil Cabal is a web blog.*
Fact_2	*Liverpool Evil Cabal was a blog investigated by the Merseyside Police.*
Counter_Fact_1	*Liverpool Evil Cabal is a blog of Liverpool Direct Ltd.*
Counter_Fact_2	*Liverpool Evil Cabal is freed from the charges of law breaking.*
ID: 506	Answer: **Entailment**
Original Text	*At least 58 people are now dead as a result of the recent flooding in **Yemen**, and at least 20,000 in the country have no access to shelter. Five people are also reported missing. The Yemeni government has pledged to send tents to help the homeless. The flooding is caused by the recent heavy rain in Yemen, which came as a shock due to the fact that the country only receives several centimeters of rain per year.*
Original Hypothesis	*Heavy rain caused flooding in **Yemen**.*
NE_1: Yemen	
Fact_1	*58 people are dead in Yemen because of flooding.*
Fact_2	*5 people in Yemen are missing.*
Fact_3	*At least 58 people are dead in Yemen because of flooding.*

Table 4: Examples of facts and counter-facts, compared with the original texts and hypotheses. We ask the Turkers to write several (counter-)facts about the highlighted NEs, and only part of the results are shown here.

The Wisdom of the Crowd's Ear: Speech Accent Rating and Annotation with Amazon Mechanical Turk

Stephen A. Kunath
Linguistics Department
Georgetown University
Washington, D.C. 20057
sak68@georgetown.edu

Steven H. Weinberger
Program in Linguistics
3e4 George Mason University
Fairfax, VA 22030
weinberg@gmu.edu

Abstract

Human listeners can almost instantaneously judge whether or not another speaker is part of their speech community. The basis of this judgment is the speaker's accent. Even though humans judge speech accents with ease, it has been tremendously difficult to automatically evaluate and rate accents in any consistent manner. This paper describes an experiment using the Amazon Mechanical Turk to develop an automatic speech accent rating dataset.

1 Introduction

In linguistics literature and especially in second language acquisition research, the evaluation of human speech accents relies on human judges. Whenever humans listen to the speech of others they are almost instantly able to determine whether the speaker is from the same language community. Indeed, much of the research in accent evaluation relies on native speakers to listen to samples of accented speech and rate the accent severity (Anderson-Hsieh,et. al., 1992; Cunningham-Anderson and Engstrand 1989; Gut, 2007; Koster and Koet 1993; Magen, 1998, Flege, 1995; Munro, 1995, 2001). Two problems arise from the use of this methodology. One is that the purely linguistic judgments may be infiltrated by certain biases. So for example, all other things being equal, some native English judges may interpret certain Vietnamese accents as being more severe than say, Italian accents when listening to the English uttered by speakers from these language backgrounds. The second, and more theoretically interesting problem, is that human judges make these ratings based upon some hidden, abstract knowledge of phonology. The mystery of what this knowledge is and contains is real, for as Gut (2007) remarks, "…no exact, comprehensive and universally accepted definition of foreign accent exists" (p75). The task of this linguistic and computational study is to aid in defining and uncovering this knowledge.

This study aims to develop a method for integrating accent ratings and judgments from a large number of human listeners, provided through Amazon Mechanical Turk(MTurk), to construct a set of training data for an automated speaker accent evaluation system. This data and methodology will be a resource that accent researchers can utilize. It reflects the wisdom of the crowd's ear to help determine the components of speech that different listeners use to rate the accentedness of non-native speakers.

2 Source Data

This task required HIT workers to listen to and rate a selection of non-native English speech samples. The source of all the speech samples for this effort was George Mason University's Speech Accent Archive (http://accent.gmu.edu). The Speech Accent Archive was chosen because of the high quality of samples as well as the fact that each speech

Proceedings of the NAACL HLT 2010 Workshop on Creating Speech and Language Data with Amazon's Mechanical Turk, pages 168–171,
Los Angeles, California, June 2010.

sample had readings of the same elicitation paragraph. This elicitation paragraph was designed to include all of the phonological features considered part of native English speech. Additionally, narrow phonetic transcriptions and phonological generalizations are available for each sample. Each speaker's information record contains demographic information and language background information. Three native language groups were selected for this study: Arabic, Mandarin, and Russian. The motivation for this particular selection comes from the fact that each of these languages represents a different language family. These languages contain different phonetic inventories as well as phonological patterns.

3 HIT Description

Our HIT consisted of three sections. The first section asked the worker to describe their own native language background and any foreign language knowledge or experience. Asking about native and foreign language experience allowed us to estimate possible rating bias arising from experience with second language phonology. The second section of the HIT included two rating tasks for use as a baseline and to help the workers get acclimated to the task. Each worker was asked to listen to two audio samples of speakers reading the same elicitation paragraph, one of a native English speaker and one of a native Spanish speaker who started learning English late in life. The rating scale used was a five point Likert scale. After completing the baseline question, workers began the third section and were then asked to listen to fifteen samples of non-native English speakers read the same elicitation paragraph. After listening to each sample the workers were asked to rate the accentedness of the speech on the five point Likert scale. The five-point scale rates native accent as a 1 and heavy accent as a 5. Workers were additionally asked to group each speech sample into different native language categories. For this question they were presented with 3 language family groups: A, B, and C. Based on their perception of each speech sample they would attempt to categorize the fifteen speakers into distinct groups native language groups.

4 Worker Requirements and Cost

Due to the type of questions contained in our HIT we came up with several worker requirements for the HIT. The first and most important requirement was that HIT workers be located inside of the USA so as to limit the number of non-native English speakers. This requirement also helped to increase the likelihood that the listener would be familiar with varieties of English speech accents common in America. Additionally, due to the size of the

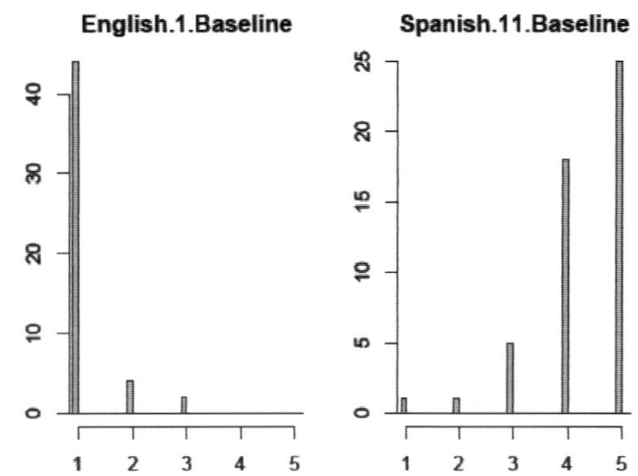

Figure 1. Mechanical Turk workers ratings of 2 baseline samples: English 1 and Spanish 11. The numbers on the horizontal axis represent the how native-like the speaker was rated. A (1) indicates that the speaker sounds like a native English speaker. A (5) indicates the presence of a heavy accent.

task we had a requirement that any worker must have at least a 65% approval record for previous HITs on other MTurk tasks. After looking at other-comparably difficult tasks we decided to offer our first HIT at $0.75. Subsequent HITs decreased the offered price to $0.50 for the task.

5 HIT Results

Two HITs were issued for this task. Each HIT had 25 workers. Average time for each worker on this task was approximately 12.5 minutes. Initial data analysis showed that users correctly carried out the tasks. Baseline question results, shown in figure 1, indicated that virtually every worker agreed that the native English speaker sample was a native speaker of English. The ratings of the baseline Spanish showed that workers generally agreed that it was heavily accented speech. In addition to the high quality of baseline evaluations, workers consistently provided their own native and foreign language information.

Ratings of the speech samples in each question, as seen in Figure 2, showed relatively consistent evaluations across workers. A more detailed statistical analysis of inter-worker ratings and groupings is currently underway, but the initial statistical tests show that there was a consistent correlation between certain phonological speech patterns and ratings of accentedness.

6 Future Work

This experiment has already provided a wealth of information on how human's rate accents and how consistent those ratings are across a large number of listeners. Currently, we are integrating the accent ratings with the phonetic transcriptions and the list of identified phonological speech processes to construct a set of features that are correlated with accent ratings. We have begun to capitalize on the Mechanical Turk paradigm and are constructing a qualification test to help us better understand inter-worker agreement on accent rating.

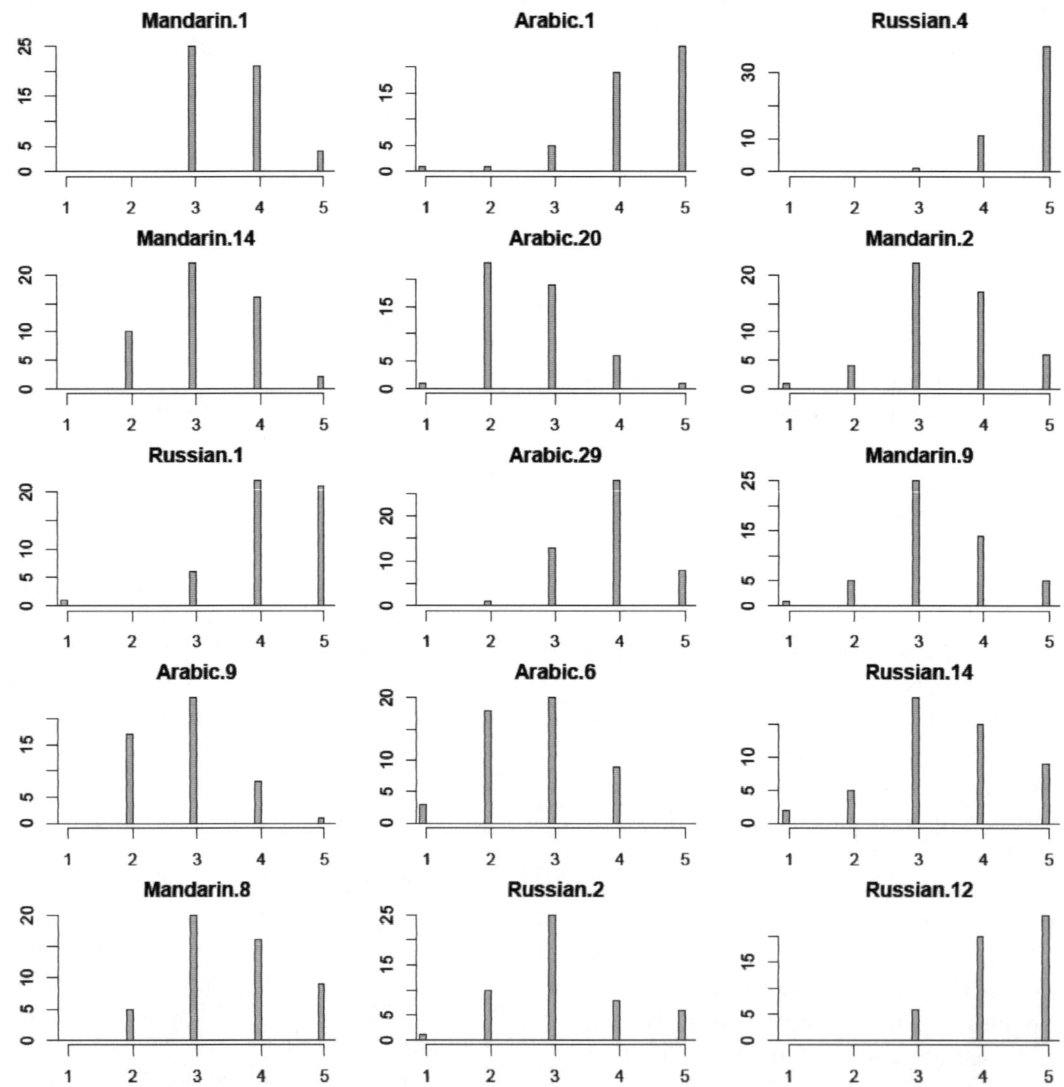

Figure 2. Workers accent ratings for all speech samples. The horizontal axis indicates the accentedness rating: (1) is a native English accent and (5) is heavily accented. The vertical axis indicates the number of HIT workers that provided the same rating for the sample. The numbers at the end of each language name represent the Speech Accent Archive sample id for the language, e.g. Mandarin.1 indicates that the sample was the Mandarin 1 speaker on the Archive.

This qualification test will include a larger sample of Native English speech data as well as a broader selection of foreign accents. In this new qualification test workers will be presented with a scale to rate the speakers accent from native-like to heavily accented. Additionally, the user will be asked to group the samples into native language families. Once the user passes this qualification test they will then be able to work on HITs that are considerably shorter than the original long-form HIT described in this paper. In the new HITs workers will listen to one or more speech samples at a time and both rate and, if required, attempt to group the sample relative to other speech samples. The selection criteria for these new samples will be based on the presence of phonological speech processes that have the highest correlation with accent ratings.

Acknowledgments

The authors would like to thank Amazon.com and the workshop organizers for providing MTurk credits to perform this research.

References

Anderson-Hsieh, J., Johnson, R., & Kohler, K. 1992. The relationship between native speaker judgments of non-native pronunciation and deviance in segmentals, prosody, and syllable structure. *Language Learning,* 42, 529-555.

Cunningham-Anderson, U., and Engstrand, E., 1989. Perceived strength and identity of foreign accent in Swedish. *Phonetica*, 46, 138-154.

Flege, James E., Murray J. Munro, and Ian R.A. MacKay (1995). Factors Affecting Strength of Perceived Foreign Accent in a Second Language. *Journal of the Acoustical Society of America*, 97, 5, pp 3125-3134.

Gut, U. 2007. Foreign Accent. In C. Muller, (ed.), *Speaker Classification I.* Berlin: Springer.

Koster, C., and Koet, T. 1993. The evaluation of accent in the English of Dutchmen. *Language Learning*, 43, 1, 69-92.

Lippi-Green, R. 1997. *English with an Accent.* New York: Routledge.

Magen, H. 1998. The perception of foreign-accented speech. *Journal of Phonetics*, 26, 381-400.

Munro, Murray J. (1995). Nonsegmental Factors in Foreign Accent: Ratings of Filtered Speech. *Studies in Second Language Acquisition,* 17, pp 17-34.

Munro, Murray J. and Tracey M. Derwing (2001). Modeling Perceptions of the Accentedness and Comprehensibility of L2 Speech: The Role of Speaking Rate. *Studies in Second Language Acquisition,* 23, pp 451-468.

Scovel, T. 1995. Differentiation, recognition, and identification in the discrimination of foreign accents. In J.Archibald (ed), *Phonological Acquisition and Phonological Theory.* Hillsdale, NJ: Lawrence Erlbaum.

Crowdsourcing Document Relevance Assessment with Mechanical Turk

Catherine Grady and Matthew Lease
School of Information
University of Texas at Austin
{cgrady,ml}@ischool.utexas.edu

Abstract

We investigate human factors involved in designing effective Human Intelligence Tasks (HITs) for Amazon's Mechanical Turk[1]. In particular, we assess document relevance to search queries via MTurk in order to evaluate search engine accuracy. Our study varies four human factors and measures resulting experimental outcomes of cost, time, and accuracy of the assessments. While results are largely inconclusive, we identify important obstacles encountered, lessons learned, related work, and interesting ideas for future investigation. Experimental data is also made publicly available for further study by the community[2].

1 Introduction

Evaluating accuracy of new search algorithms on ever-growing information repositories has become increasingly challenging in terms of the time and expense required by traditional evaluation techniques. In particular, while the Cranfield evaluation paradigm has proven remarkably effective for decades (Voorhees, 2002), enormous manual effort is involved in assessing topic relevance of many different documents to many different queries. Consequently, there has been significant recent interest in developing more scalable evaluation methodology. This has included developing robust accuracy metrics using few assessments (Buckley and Voorhees, 2004), inferring implicit relevance assessments from user behavior (Joachims, 2002), more carefully selecting documents for assessment (Aslam and Pavlu, 2008; Carterette et al., 2006), and leveraging crowdsourcing (Alonso et al., 2008).

We build on this line of work to investigating crowdsourcing-based relevance assessment via MTurk. While MTurk has quickly become popular as a means of obtaining data annotations quickly and inexpensively (Snow et al., 2008), relatively little attention has been given to addressing human-factors involved in crowdsourcing and their impact on resultant cost, time, and accuracy of the annotations obtained (Mason and Watts, 2009). The advent of crowdsourcing has led to many researchers, whose work might otherwise fall outside the realm of human-computer interaction (HCI), suddenly finding themselves creating HITs for MTurk and thereby directly confronting important issues of interface design and usability which could significantly impact the quality or quantity of annotations they obtain. A similar observation has been made recently regarding the importance of effective HCI for obtaining quality answers from users in a social search setting (Horowitz and Kamvar, 2010).

Our overarching hypothesis is that better addressing human factors in HIT design can yield significantly reduce cost, reduce time, and/or increase accuracy of the annotations obtained via crowdsourcing. Such improvement could come through a variety of complimentary effects, such as attracting more or better workers, incentivizing them to do better work, better explaining the task to be performed and reducing confusion, etc. While the results of this study are largely inconclusive with regard to our

[1]http://aws.amazon.com/mturk
[2]http://www.ischool.utexas.edu/~ml/data

Proceedings of the NAACL HLT 2010 Workshop on Creating Speech and Language Data with Amazon's Mechanical Turk, pages 172–179,
Los Angeles, California, June 2010.

experimental hypothesis, other contributions of the work are identified in the abstract above.

2 Background

To evaluate search accuracy in the Cranfield paradigm (Voorhees, 2002), a predefined set of documents (e.g., web pages) are typically manually assessed for relevance with respect to some fixed set of *topics*. Each topic corresponds to some static *information need* of a hypothetical user. Because language allows meaning to be conveyed in various ways and degrees of brevity, each topic can be expressed via a myriad of different *queries*. Table 1 shows the four topics used in our study which were generated by NIST for TREC[3]. We do use the paragraph-length "narrative" queries under an (untested) assumption that they are overly complex and technical for a layman assessor. Instead, we use (1) the short keyword "title" queries and (2) more verbose and informative "description" queries, which are typically expressed as a one-sentence question or statement.

NIST has typically invested significant time training annotators, something far less feasible in a crowdsourced setting. NIST has also typically employed a single human assessor per topic to ensure consistent topic interpretation and relevance assessment. One downside of this practice is limited scalability of annotation, particularly in a crowdsourced setting. When multiple annotators have been used, previous studies have also found relatively low inner-annotator agreement for relevance assessment due to the highly subjective nature of relevance (Voorhees, 2002). Thus in addition to reducing time and cost of assessment, crowdsourcing may also enable us to improve assessment accuracy by integrating assessment decisions by a committee of annotators. This is particularly important for generating reusable test collections for benchmarking. Practical costs involved in relevance assessment based on standard pooling methods is significant and becoming increasingly prohibitive as collection sizes grow (Carterette et al., 2009).

MTurk allows "requesters" to crowdsource large numbers of HITs online which workers can search, browse, preview, accept, and complete or abandon.

[3]http://trec.nist.gov

3. Joint Ventures. Document will announce a new joint venture involving a Japanese company.

13. Mitsubishi Heavy Industries Ltd. Document refers to Mitusbishi Heavy Industries Ltd.

68. Health Hazards from Fine-Diameter Fibers. Document will report actual studies, or even unsubstantiated concerns about the safety to manufacturing employees and installation workers of fine-diameter fibers used in insulation and other products.

78. Greenpeace. Document will report activity by Greenpeace to carry out their environmental protection goals.

Table 1: The four TREC topics used in our study. Topic number and <title> field are shown in bold. Remaining text constitutes the description (<desc>) field.

With regard to measuring the impact of different design alternatives on resulting HIT effectiveness, MTurk provides requesters with many useful statistics regarding completion of their HITs. Some effects cannot be measured, however, such as when HITs are skipped, when HITs are viewed in search results but not selected, and other outcomes which could usefully inform effective HIT design.

3 Methodology

Our study investigated how varying certain aspects of HIT design affected annotation accuracy and time, as well as the relationship between expense and these outcomes. In particular, workers were asked to make binary assessments regarding the relevance of various documents to different queries.

3.1 Experimental Variables

We varied four simple aspects of HIT design:

- **Query**: <title> vs. <desc>
- **Terminology**: HIT title of "binary relevance judgment" (technical) vs. "yes/no decision" (layman)
- **Pay**: $0.01 vs. $0.02
- **Bonus**: no bonus offered vs. $0.02

The **Query** is clearly central to relevance assessment since it provides the annotator's primary basis for judging relevance. Since altering a query can have enormous impact on the assessment, and because we were testing the ability of Mechanical Turk workers to replicate assessments made previously by TREC assessors, we preserved wording of the queries as they appeared in the original TREC topics (see §2). We hypothesized that the greater detail found in the topic description vs. the title would improve accuracy with some corresponding increase in HIT completion time (longer query to read, at times with more stilted language, and more specific relevance criteria requiring more careful reading of documents). An alternative hypothesis would be that a very conscientious worker might take longer wrestling with a vague title query.

Terminology: the HIT title is arguably one of a HIT's more prominent features since it is one of the first (and often the only) description of a HIT a potential worker sees. An attractive title could conceivably draw workers to a task while an unattractive one could repel them. Besides the simple variation studied here, future experiments could test other aspects of title formulation. For example, greater specificity as to the content of documents or topics within the HIT could attract workers that are knowledgeable or interested in a particular subject. Additionally, a title that indicates a task is for research purposes might attract workers motivated to contribute to society.

Pay: the base pay rate has obvious implications for attracting workers and incentivizing them to do quality work. While anecdotal knowledge suggested the "going rate" for simple HITs was about $0.02, we started at the lowest possible rate and increased from there. Although higher pay rates are certainly more attractive to legitimate workers, they also tend to attract more spammers, so determining appropriate pay is something of a careful balancing act.

Bonus: Two important questions are 1) How does knowing that one could receive a bonus affect performance on the current HIT?, and 2) How does actually receiving a bonus affect performance on future HITs? We focused on the first question. When bonuses were offered, we both advertised this fact in the HIT title (see Title 4 above) and appended the following statement to the instructions: "[b]onuses will be given for good work with good explanations of the reasoning behind your relevance assessment." If a worker's explanation made clear why she made the relevance judgment she did, bonuses were awarded regardless of the assessment's correctness with regard to ground truth. Decisions to award bonus pay were made manually (see §5).

3.2 Experimental Constants

Various factors kept constant in our study could also be interesting to investigate in future work:

- **Description**: the worker may optionally view a brief description of the task before accepting the HIT. For all HITs, our description was simply: "(1) Decide whether a document is relevant to a topic, 2) Click 'relevant' or 'not relevant', and 3) Submit".
- **Keywords**: HITs were advertised for search via keywords "judgment, document, relevance, search"
- **Duration**: once accepted, all HITs had to be completed within one hour
- **Approval Rate**: workers had to have a 95% approval rate to accept our HITs
- **HIT approval**: all HITs were accepted, but approval was not immediate to suggest that HITs were being carefully reviewed before pay was awarded
- **Feedback to workers**: none given

More careful selection of high-interest Keywords (e.g., "easy" or "fun") may be a surprisingly effective way to attract more workers. It would be very interesting to analyze the query logs for keywords used by Workers in searching for HITs of interest.

Omar Alonso suggests workers should always be paid (personal communication). Given the low cost involved, keeping Workers individually happy avoids the effort of having to justify rejections to angry Workers, maintains one's reputation for attracting Workers, and still allows problematic workers to be filtered out in future batches.

3.3 Experimental Outcomes

With regard to outcomes, we were principally interested in measuring accuracy, time, and expense. Base statistics, such as the completion time of a particular HIT, allowed us to compute derived statistics like averages per topic, per Worker, per Batch, per experimental variable, etc. We could then also look for correlations between outcomes as well as between experimental variables and outcomes.

Accuracy was measured by simply computing the annotator mean accuracy with regard to "ground truth" binary relevance labels from NIST. A variety of other possibilities exist, such as deciding binary annotations by majority vote and comparing these to ground truth. Recent work has explored ensemble methods for weighting and combining anno-

Topic	Relevant	Non-Relevant
3	48, 55, 84, 120	85
13	28, 30	*193*, 84, 117
68		157, 163, 170, 182, 186
78	*9978*	134, 166, 167,*0062*

Table 2: Documents assessed per topic, along with "true" binary relevance judgments according to official TREC NIST annotation. Document prefixes used in table: (3 and 13) WSJ920324-, except *WSJ920323-0193*, (68 and 78) AP901231- except *FBIS4-9978* and *WSJ920324-0062*. Only one document, 84, was shared across queries (3 and 13).

#	Name	Query	Term.	Pay	Bonus
1	Baseline	title	BRJ	\$0.01	-
2	P=0.02	title	BRJ	\$0.02	-
3	T=yes/no	title	yes/no	\$0.01	-
4	Q=desc.	desc.	yes/no	\$0.01	-
5	B=0.02	title	yes/no	\$0.01	\$0.02

Table 3: Experimental matrix. Batches 2 and 3 changed one variable with respect to Batch 1. Batches 4 and 5 changed one variable with respect to Batch 3. *Terminology* varied as specified in §3. For batch 5, 23 bonuses were awarded at total cost of \$0.46.

tations (Snow et al., 2008; Whitehill et al., 2009) which also could have been used like majority vote.

As for time, we measured HIT completion time (from acceptance to completion) and Batch completion time (from publishing the Batch to all its HITs being completed). We only anecdotally measured our own time required to generate HIT designs, shepherd the Batches, assess outcomes, etc.

Cost was measured solely with respect to what was paid to Workers and does not include overhead costs charged by Amazon (§2). We also did not account for the cost of our own salaries, equipment, or other indirect expenses associated with the work.

3.4 Additional Details

Assessment was performed on XML documents taken from the TREC TIPSTER collection of news articles. Documents were simply presented as text after simple pre-processing; a better alternative for the future would be to associate an attractive style sheet with the XML to enhance readability and attractiveness of HITs. Relatively little pre-processing

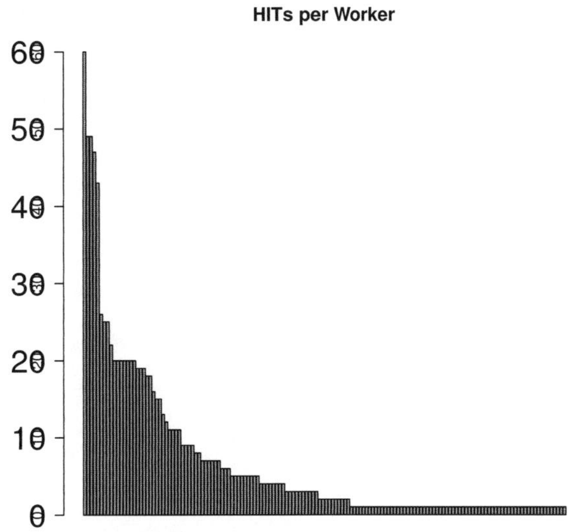

Figure 1: Number of HITs completed by each worker

was performed: (1) XML tags were replaced with HTML, (2) document ID, number, and TREC-related info was commented out, and (3) paragraph tags were added to break up text.

Our basic HIT layout was based on a pre-existing template for assessing binary relevance provided by Omar Alonso (personal communication). This template reflected several useful design decisions like having HITs be self-contained rather than referring to content at an external URL, a design previously found to be effective (Alonso et al., 2008).

4 Evaluation

We performed five batch evaluations, shown in Table 3. For each of the four topics shown in Table 1, five documents were assessed (Table 2), and ten assessments (one per HIT) were collected for each document. Each batch therefore consisted of $4 * 5 * 10 = 200$ HITs, for an overall total of 1000 HITs. Document length varied from 162 words to 2129 words per document (including HTML tags and single-character tokens). Each HIT required the worker to make a single binary relevance judgment (i.e. relevant or non-relevant) for a given query-document pair. In all cases, "ground truth" was available to us in the form of prior relevance assessments created by NIST. 149 unique Workers com-

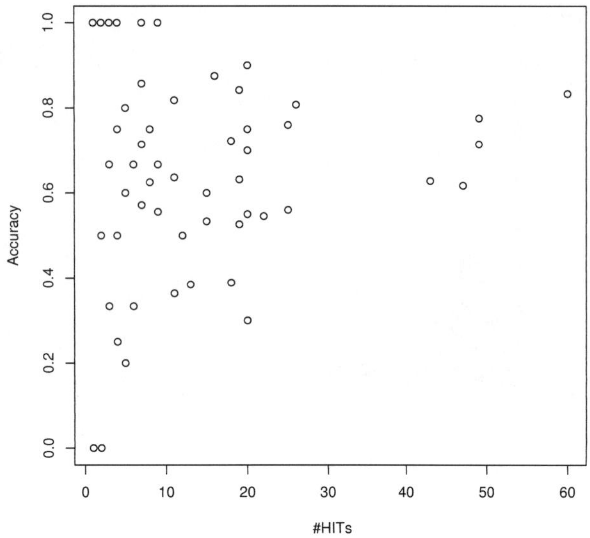

Figure 2: HITs completed vs. accuracy achieved shows negligible direct correlation: Pearson $|\rho| < 0.01$.

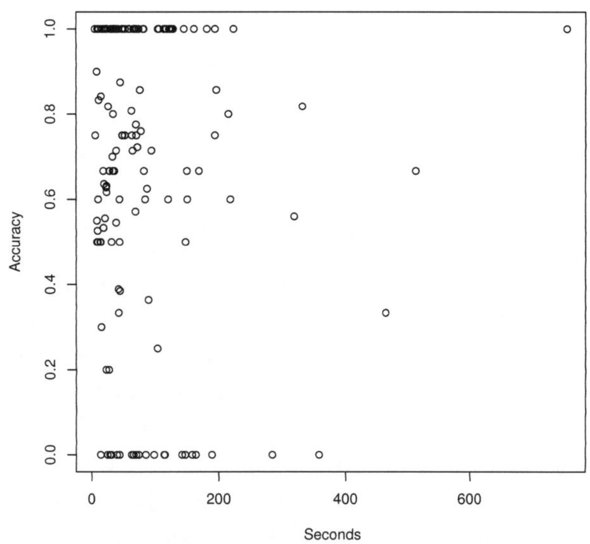

Figure 3: HIT completion time vs. accuracy achieved shows negligible direct correlation: Pearson $|\rho| \approx 0.06$.

pleted the 1000 HITs, with some Workers completing far more HITs than others (Figure 1).

We did not restrict Workers from accepting HITs from different batches, and some Workers even participated in all 5 Batches. Since in some cases a single Worker assessed the same query-document pair multiple times, our results likely reflect unanticipated effects of training or fatigue (see §5).

Statistical significance was measured via a two-tailed unpaired t-test. The only significant outcomes observed were increase in comment length and number of comments for higher-paying or bonus batches. We note p-values < 0.05 where they occur.

Maximum accuracy of 70.5% was achieved with Batch 3, which featured use of Title query and yes/no response. Similar accuracy of 69.5% was also achieved in both Batch 1 and 2. Accuracy fell in Batch 4 (using the Description query) to 66.5%, and fell further to 64% in Batch 5, which featured bonuses. With regard to varying use of Title vs. Description query (Batches 1-3,5 vs. 4), accuracy for the Title query HITs was 68.4% vs. the 66.5% reported above for Batch 4. Thus use of Description queries was not observed to lead to more accurate assessments. HIT completion time was also highest for Batch 4, with workers taking an average of 72s to complete a HIT, vs. mean HIT completion time of 63s over the four Title query batches.

The number of unique workers (UW) per Batch gives some sense of how attractive a Batch was, where a high number could alternatively suggest many workers were attracted (positive) or incentives were too weak to encourage a few Workers to do many HITs (negative). UW in batches 1-4 ranged from 64-72. This fell to 38 UW in Batch 5 (bonus batch), perhaps indicating that workers were incentivized to do more HITs to earn bonuses. At the same time that the number of workers went down, the accuracy per worker went up, with the average worker judging 3.37 documents correctly, compared to a range of 2.10 - 2.20 correct answers per average worker for Batches 1-3 and 1.85 correct answers per average worker for Batch 4 (which, interestingly, had slightly more UWs than the other batches).

Subset	#B	HITs	Cost noB	Cost withB	Batch Completion Time Total	MeanH	MeanB	sdB	HIT Completion Time Total	MeanH	MeanB	sdH
Query 3	5	250	$3.00	$3.14	N/A	N/A	N/A	N/A	16127	64.50	3225.4	92.48
Query 13	5	250	$3.00	$3.14	N/A	N/A	N/A	N/A	17148	68.59	3429.6	139.08
Query 68	5	250	$3.00	$3.06	N/A	N/A	N/A	N/A	14880	59.52	2976	111.23
Query 78	5	250	$3.00	$3.12	N/A	N/A	N/A	N/A	17117	68.46	3423.4	122.89
Pay=$0.01	4	800	$8.00	$8.46	1078821	1348.52	269705.25	47486.7	54379	67.97	13594.75	123.57
Pay=$0.02	1	200	$4.00	$4.00	386324	1931.62	386324	N/A	10893	54.465	10893	88.87
Title	4	800	$10.00	$10.46	1227585	1534.48	306896.25	67820.58	50968	63.71	12742	117.14
Desc.	1	200	$4.00	$4.00	237560	1187.8	237560	N/A	14304	71.52	14304	119.20
No Bonus	4	800	$10.00	$10.00	1124799	1405.99	281199.75	70347.43	51966	64.95	12991.5	111.32
Bonus	1	200	$2.00	$2.46	340346	1701.73	340346	N/A	13306	66.53	13306	139.97
Batch 1	1	200	$2.00	$2.00	249921	1249.60	249921	N/A	13935	69.67	13935	130.66
Batch 2	1	200	$4.00	$4.00	386324	1931.62	386324	N/A	10893	54.46	10893	88.87
Batch 3	1	200	$2.00	$2.00	250994	1254.97	250994	N/A	12834	64.17	12834	102.01
Batch 4	1	200	$2.00	$2.00	237560	1187.8	237560	N/A	14304	71.52	14304	119.20
Batch 5	1	200	$2.00	$2.46	340346	1701.73	340346	N/A	13306	66.53	13306	139.97
All	5	1000	$12.00	$12.46	1465145	1465.14	293029	66417.07	65272	65.272	13054.4	117.54

Table 4: Preliminary analysis 1. Column labels: #B: Number of Batches, # HITs, noB: Cost without bonuses, withB: Cost with bonuses, Total, MeanH/B: Mean per-HIT/Batch, sdB/H: std-deviation across Batches/HITs.

Recall that bonuses were awarded whenever Workers provided clear justification of their judgments (whether or not those judgments matched ground truth). In 74% of these cases (17 of the 23 HITs awarded bonuses), relevance assessments were correct. Thus there may be a useful correlation to exploit provided practical heuristics exist for automatically distinguishing quality feedback from spam.

Feedback length might serve as a more practical alternative to measuring quality while still correlating with accuracy. Mean comment length for Batches 2 and 5 was 38.6 and 28.1 characters per comment, whereas Batches 1, 3, and 4 had mean comment lengths of 13.9, 12.7, and 19.3 characters per comment. The mean difference in comment length between Batch 2 and Batch 1 was 24.7 characters ($p<0.01$), 25.9 characters between Batches 2 and 3 ($p<0.01$), and 19.3 characters between Batches 2 and 4 ($p<0.01$). Batch 5 and Batch 1 had a mean comment-length difference of 14.2 characters ($p<0.01$), and Batches 5 and 3 differed by 15.4 characters ($p<0.01$). Thus higher-paying HITs or HITs with bonus opportunities may correlate with greater Worker effort. Batches 2 (pay=$0.02) and 5 (bonus batch) garnered the highest number of comments, with each averaging 0.37 comments per HIT. In contrast, Batches 1, 3, and 4 averaged only 0.21, 0.18, and 0.23 comments per HIT, or a difference of 0.16 ($p<0.01$), 0.19 ($p<0.01$), and 0.14 ($p<0.01$) comments, respectively.

5 Discussion

How to control for the same worker participating in multiple experiments. We found many of the same workers completed HITs in multiple batches, compromising our experimental control and likely introducing effects of training or fatigue. It does not appear that MTurk provides an easy way to preventing this; one can block a worker from doing jobs, but blocking is more of a tool to prevent poor performance. It is also construed as a punishment: workers' ratings can be negatively affected by blocking. Because of this, blocking is not a substitute for a mechanism that simply allows requesters to hide HITs or otherwise disallow repeat workers from completing HITs. It would be nice to develop a simple mechanism for automatically ensuring each experiment involves a different set of workers.

Automatic HIT validation. MTurk does not appear to automatically ensure a submitted HIT was actually completed, i.e. a worker can submit a HIT without having actually done anything. While the submitted HIT can be rejected and re-requested, building some trivial validation of HITs to catch such cases automatically appears worthwhile.

Automatic bonus pay. For Batch 5 (which included bonus pay), one of the authors spent an hour manually processing/evaluating worker annotations and feedback, distributing bonus pay for 23 of the 200 HITs. While some time is certainly well spent in manually analyzing annotations and feedback, the

Subset	Accuracy				Unique Workers				HPW	Feedback Given		Feedback Length	
	#Correct	MeanH	MeanB	sdH	Total	MeanH	MeanB	Acc	Mean	Total	MeanH	MeanH	sd
Query 3	144	0.58	28.8	0.50	84	0.34	16.8	1.71	2.98	60	0.24	17.91	42.44
Query 13	191	0.76	38.2	0.43	88	0.35	17.6	2.17	2.84	71	0.28	25.04	55.82
Query 68	183	0.73	36.6	0.44	83	0.33	16.6	2.20	3.01	69	0.28	21.08	44.69
Query 78	162	0.65	32.4	0.48	83	0.33	16.6	1.95	3.01	76	0.30	26.02	56.52
Pay=$0.01	541	0.68	135.25	0.47	137	0.17	34.25	3.95	5.84	201	0.25	18.49	42.52
Pay=$0.02	139	0.70	139	0.46	64	0.32	64	2.17	3.13	75	0.38	38.60	71.53
Title	547	0.68	136.75	0.47	132	0.17	33	4.14	6.06	229	0.29	23.32	51.23
Desc.	133	0.67	133	0.47	72	0.36	72	1.85	2.78	47	0.24	19.29	46.40
No Bonus	552	0.69	138	0.46	121	0.15	30.25	4.56	6.61	201	0.25	21.12	50.26
Bonus	128	0.64	128	0.48	38	0.19	38	3.37	5.26	75	0.38	28.09	50.21
Batch 1	139	0.70	139	0.46	66	0.33	66	2.11	3.03	42	0.21	13.90	37.62
Batch 2	139	0.70	139	0.46	64	0.32	64	2.17	3.13	75	0.38	38.60	71.53
Batch 3	141	0.71	141	0.46	64	0.32	64	2.20	3.13	37	0.19	12.67	31.96
Batch 4	133	0.67	133	0.47	72	0.36	72	1.85	2.78	47	0.24	19.29	46.40
Batch 5	128	0.64	128	0.48	38	0.19	38	3.37	5.26	75	0.38	28.09	50.21
All	680	0.68	136	0.47	149	0.15	29.8	4.56	6.71	276	0.28	22.51	50.30

Table 5: Preliminary analysis 2. Column labels: HPW: HITs per worker, MeanH/B: Mean per-HIT/Batch, sd(H): std-deviation (across HITs), Acc: mean worker accuracy. Feedback length is in characters.

disparity in cost of our own salaries vs. bonus expenses suggests decisions on bonus pay should be automated if possible (and it likely pays to err on the side of being generous). Of course, automated bonus distribution may negatively affect quality of work if, for example, any string of characters in the feedback box yields bonus pay and workers catch on to this. Similarly, automation may fail to reward truly valuable qualitative feedback from workers which is harder to automatically assess than simply evaluating worker accuracy on known examples.

6 Future Work

Assessing relevance of Web pages. In the near-term, we will be using MTurk to evaluate search accuracy of systems participating in the TREC 2010 Relevance Feedback Track. This will involve addressing several significant challenges: (1) achieving scalable evaluation, (2) protecting workers from malicious attack pages while maintaining assessment accuracy, (3) addressing issues of Web spam, and (4) handling issues of unknown mature content workers may encounter during assessment.

With regard to (1), we will be scaling up Cranfield-based relevance assessment to support search evaluation on the massive ClueWeb09 Web crawl[4]. As for (2), many Web pages containing attack code designed to compromise the viewer's computer, and in a crowdsourced environment we cannot ensure all workers have installed the latest security patches for their Web browsers. Various tradeoffs may be involved between security and usability in pre-rendering Web pages to assess as static images, creating a "safe-viewer" applet, etc. Web spam (3) can be annoying to workers and thereby impact the quality of their work, wastes time and money since spam is never relevant to any query by definition, and spam detection is conceptually a distinct task and ought to be handled as such. In the short term, we may simply ask workers to not only decide relevance vs. non-relevance, but to simultaneously differentiate non-relevant content from non-relevant spam, but a better solution would be preferable. Mature content (4) is similar to spam but can be far worse than annoying to workers, touches on legal issues, and inability to filter it could significantly reduce the number of workers willing to accept HITs which may contain it. Our short-term solution will likely be to perform some simple pre-filtering and simply warn workers they may encounter such content, but this solution is not ideal.

Varying number of annotations in proportion to annotator agreement. While we collected a fixed number of relevance assessments for each query-document pair, it may be both more efficient and more effective to collect few assessments when inner-annotator agreement is high and proportionally more assessments when greater disagreement exists between annotators (Von Ahn et al., 2008).

[4]http://boston.lti.cs.cmu.edu/Data/clueweb09

Graded vs. binary relevance. We want assessors to be both maximally informative and maximally consistent, and there is an inherent tradeoff here. Allowing assessors to make graded relevance judgments corresponds to the intuitive notion that relevance is typically not a binary proposition. Evaluation of commercial search engines today often reports use of a five-point graded scale, and such graded feedback allows us to better distinguish relative effectiveness of different search algorithms at a finer scale. However, the right number of relevance levels to assess is unclear, and too many would likely involve making overly nuanced judgments that could overwhelm assessors and lead to low inner-annotator agreement. We may similarly ask assessors to further differentiate relevance judgment from cases of "I don't know" and "this HIT seems broken". There is also the possibility of inducing graded relevance levels from binary judgments, such as by averaging and rescaling. The utility could be measured by comparing benchmark algorithms using the explicit or induced assessments.

Evaluating annotation accuracy with regard to ground-truth labels vs. task accuracy. While much research with MTurk has measured accuracy in terms of reproducing a ground-truth label, ultimately we are not interested in the labels themselves but rather in what we can do with them. Relevance assessment in particular suffers from notoriously low inner-annotator agreement. Consequently, one alternative to comparing against "ground-truth" labels would be to evaluate the ability of crowdsourced labels for effectively distinguish between different benchmark algorithms.

Crowd demographics. While it is typically suggested that experts produce superior annotations, there are important questions of effects from who is judging the annotations. For example, if you want to know if the general public will think a particular web page is relevant to a particular query, more useful assessments might be obtained from a layman than from someone who builds search engines for a living. This also suggests another reason why it may even be preferable in some circumstances for crowdsource annotations to disagree with "ground-truth" expert labels. It also raises questions about generality of system comparisons based on expert labels when systems are to be used by the general public.

References

Omar Alonso, Daniel E. Rose, and Benjamin Stewart. 2008. Crowdsourcing for relevance evaluation. *SIGIR Forum*, 42(2):9–15.

J. Aslam and V. Pavlu. 2008. A practical sampling strategy for efficient retrieval evaluation. Technical report, Northeastern University.

C. Buckley and E.M. Voorhees. 2004. Retrieval evaluation with incomplete information. In *Proceedings of the 27th annual international ACM SIGIR conference on Research and development in information retrieval*, pages 25–32. ACM New York, NY, USA.

B. Carterette, J. Allan, and R. Sitaraman. 2006. Minimal test collections for retrieval evaluation. In *Proceedings of the 29th annual international ACM SIGIR conference on Research and development in information retrieval*, pages 268–275.

B. Carterette, V. Pavlu, E. Kanoulas, J.A. Aslam, and J. Allan. 2009. If I Had a Million Queries. In *Proceedings of the 31st European Conference on Information Retrieval*, pages 288–300.

D. Horowitz and S.D. Kamvar. 2010. The Anatomy of a Large-Scale Social Search Engine. In *Proc. of the 19th international conference on World wide web (WWW)*.

Thorsten Joachims. 2002. Optimizing search engines using clickthrough data. In *KDD '02: Proceedings of the 8th SIGKDD international conference on Knowledge discovery and data mining*, pages 133–142.

W. Mason and D.J. Watts. 2009. Financial incentives and the performance of crowds. In *Proceedings of the ACM SIGKDD Workshop on Human Computation*, pages 77–85. ACM.

R. Snow, B. O'Connor, D. Jurafsky, and A.Y. Ng. 2008. Cheap and fast—but is it good?: evaluating non-expert annotations for natural language tasks. In *Proceedings of the Conference on Empirical Methods in Natural Language Processing*, pages 254–263. Association for Computational Linguistics.

L. Von Ahn, B. Maurer, C. McMillen, D. Abraham, and M. Blum. 2008. recaptcha: Human-based character recognition via web security measures. *Science*, 321(5895):1465.

E.M. Voorhees. 2002. The philosophy of information retrieval evaluation. *Lecture Notes in Computer Science*, pages 355–370.

J. Whitehill, P. Ruvolo, T. Wu, J. Bergsma, and J. Movellan. 2009. Whose Vote Should Count More: Optimal Integration of Labels from Labelers of Unknown Expertise. *Proceedings of the 2009 Neural Information Processing Systems (NIPS) Conference*.

Preliminary Experience with Amazon's Mechanical Turk for Annotating Medical Named Entities

Meliha Yetisgen-Yildiz, Imre Solti
Biomedical & Health Informatics
University of Washington
Seattle, WA 98195, USA
{melihay,solti}@uw.edu

Fei Xia, Scott Russell Halgrim
Department of Linguistics
University of Washington
Seattle, WA 98195, USA
{fxia,captnpi}@uw.edu

Abstract

Amazon's Mechanical Turk (MTurk) service is becoming increasingly popular in Natural Language Processing (NLP) research. In this paper, we report our findings in using MTurk to annotate medical text extracted from clinical trial descriptions with three entity types: medical condition, medication, and laboratory test. We compared MTurk annotations with a gold standard manually created by a domain expert. Based on the good performance results, we conclude that MTurk is a very promising tool for annotating large-scale corpora for biomedical NLP tasks.

1 Introduction

The manual construction of annotated corpora is extremely expensive both in terms of time and money. Snow et al. (2008) demonstrated the potential power of Amazon's Mechanical Turk (MTurk) service in annotating large corpora for natural language tasks cheaply and quickly. We are working on a Natural Language Processing (NLP) project to automate the clinical trial eligibility screening of patients. This project involves building statistical models for medical named entity recognition which requires a large-scale annotated corpus for training. As part of corpus development, we tested the feasibility of using MTurk for the annotation of medical named entities in biomedical text and we report our findings in this paper.

In the following sections we describe how we used MTurk to annotate the biomedical corpus created from publicly available clinical trial announcements. The main goal of our study was to understand how well non-experts perform compared to medical expert in annotating the biomedical text.

2 Related Work

MTurk[1] is an online micro-task market that allows requesters to distribute work to a large number of workers from all over the world. The inspiration of the system was to have human workers complete simple tasks that would otherwise be extremely difficult for computers to perform (Kittur et al., 2008). A complex task is broken down into simple, one-time tasks called Human Intelligence Tasks (HITs). Requesters post their HITs on the MTurk marketplace by specifying the amount paid for the completion of each task, and the workers select from the available HITs the ones that they would like to work on. In 2007, Amazon claimed that the user base of MTurk consisted of over 100,000 users from 100 countries[2].

MTurk has been adopted for a variety of uses both in industry and academia, ranging from user studies (Kittur et al., 2008) to image labeling (Sorokin and Forsyth, 2008). Snow et al. (2008) examined the quality of labels created by MTurk workers for various NLP tasks including word sense disambiguation, word similarity, text entailment, and temporal ordering. Since the publication of Snow et al.'s paper, MTurk has become increasingly popular as an annotation tool for NLP research. Nakov (2008) used MTurk to create a manually annotated resource for noun-noun compound interpretation based on paraphrasing verbs. In a different NLP task, Callison-Burch (2009) used MTurk to evaluate machine translation quality. With a budget of only $10, Callison-Burch demonstrated the feasibility of performing manual evaluations of machine translation quality by recreating judgments from a WMT08 translation task.

In our pilot study we used MTurk to annotate entities in the biomedical text. To our knowledge, this is the first study that investigates the feasibility of MTurk for biomedical named entity annotation.

3 Annotation Task Description

In this section we will describe the types of entities in our annotation task and the details of our corpus creation process.

[1] https://www.MTurk.com/MTurk/welcome

[2] Source: New York Times article "Artificial Intelligence, With Help from the Humans", Available at: http://www.nytimes.com/2007/03/25/business/yourmoney/25Stream.html

Proceedings of the NAACL HLT 2010 Workshop on Creating Speech and Language Data with Amazon's Mechanical Turk, pages 180–183,
Los Angeles, California, June 2010. ©2010 Association for Computational Linguistics

3.1 Entity Types

We used MTurk to annotate the biomedical text for the following three entity types:

- Medical Conditions
  Example: First-degree relative who developed *<Medical_Condition>**breast cancer***
  </Medical_Condition> at ≤ 50 years of age.
- Medications
  Example: Previous treatment with an *<Medication>**anthracycline**</Medication>* in the metastatic breast cancer setting.
- Laboratory Test
  Example: *<Laboratory_Test>**Platelet count >=100,000 cells/mL**</Laboratory_Test>*.

3.2 Corpus

Our corpus came from the publicly available clinical trial announcements available at the ClinicalTrials.gov website. This website is a registry of federally and privately supported clinical trials conducted in the United States and around the world. The objectives and procedures of each clinical trial are explained in detail along with participant selection criteria and logistical information such as locations and contact information.

For this task we selected 50,109 announcements from the roughly 85,000 announcements posted on the ClinicalTrials.gov site. For selection criteria we relied on the following keywords: "heart | cancer | tumor | influenza | alzheimer | parkinson | malignant | stroke | respiratory | diabetes | pneumonia | nephritis | nephrotic | nephrosis | septicemia | liver | cirrhosis | hypertension | renal | neoplasm". We chose these keywords because they were part of the phrases of diagnoses for the top 12 leading causes of death excluding suicide, homicide and accidents (Heron et al., 2009). We limited the selection to trials for "Adult" or "Senior" patients.

After downloading the corpus of XML files we converted them to ANSI text using ABC Amber XML Converter[3]. 49,794 files successfully converted to ANSI text format. Using a simple regular expression search we selected documents that had both the "Inclusion Criteria" and "Exclusion Criteria" phrases. The final selection process resulted in 35,385 files. From this latest set we randomly selected 100 files to build the corpus for our pilot study. One of the authors, who has medical training, then manually annotated the three entity types in those selected files. We used this annotated set as the gold standard to measure the quality of the MTurk workers' annotations.

4 HIT Design

Biomedical text is full of jargon, and finding the three entity types in such text can be difficult for non-expert annotators. To make the annotation task more convenient for the MTurk workers, we used a customized user interface and provided detailed annotation guidelines. We also tested the bonus system available in the MTurk environment and evaluated the performance of the workers.

4.1 User Interface

In order to adapt the task of entity annotation to the MTurk format, we used an in-house web-based graphical user interface that allows the worker to select a span of text with the mouse cursor. The interface also uses simple tokenization heuristics to divide the text into highlightable spans and resolve partial token highlights or double-clicks into the next largest span. For instance, highlighting the word "cancer" from the second "c" to "e" will result in the entire span "cancer" being highlighted.

4.2 Annotation Guidelines

We created three separate annotation tasks, one for each entity type. For each task, we wrote annotation guidelines that explained the task and showed examples of entities that should be tagged and the ones that should not.

4.3 Bonus System

MTurk provides two methods for paying workers – fixed rates on each document and bonuses to workers for especially good work. In this study, we experimented with the bonus system to see its effect on performance and annotation time. Annotating a document would receive a base rate of \$0.01-\$0.05, but each tagged entity span could elicit a bonus of \$0.01. The base rate would cover the case where the document truly contained no entities, but the bonus amount could potentially be much larger than the base rate if the document was entity-rich. Bonuses for each tagged entity span were awarded based on an agreement threshold with peer workers. In this study, each document was annotated by four workers and we granted bonuses for entity spans that were agreed upon by at least three workers.

4.4 Performance Monitoring

We monitored a worker's performance by comparing the worker's annotations with his/her peer workers' annotations. After we posted the HITs, we continuously monitored the workers' performance and rejected the annotations from the ones who tried to cheat the system by either not doing any annotations (e.g., immediately submitting the document after accepting it) or con-

[3] ABC Amber XML Converter. Available at: http://www.processtext.com/abcxml.html.

Table 1. Cost analysis of annotation experiments ("File" in this table means the annotation of a document. There are 100 documents, and each document is annotated by four workers.)

Experiment Label	File Count		Total Worker Count	MONETARY COST				TIME COST	
				Pay Rate ($)		Total Cost ($)		Completion Time	
	Total	Completed		File	Bonus	File	Bonus	Per file (seconds)	Total (hours)
MedicalCondition-I	400	272	45	0.01	0	2.72	0	156.09	71.16
MedicalCondition-II	400	400	30	0.05	0.01	20	22.61	162.66	7.28
Medication-I	400	400	45	0.01	0.01	4	4.43	87.96	31.65
Medication-II	400	400	17	0.05	0.01	20	6.11	89.06	4.36
Laboratory Test	400	400	26	0.05	0.01	20	1.49	75.61	24.41

stantly doing wrong annotations (e.g., always annotating the first word of the text). Those rejected documents were automatically re-posted on the MTurk so other workers could work on them. In this pilot study, performance monitoring was done mainly manually. As future work, we plan to automate the process in order to scale it for larger annotation tasks.

4.5 Communication with Workers

The workers could send us their questions and comments about the individual documents or the general annotation task through a text box in the interface. During this study we received more than 100 messages from the workers. The majority of the messages were positive messages ("*thank you*", "*easy hit!*"). However, some of the comments included questions such as: "*Is pregnancy a medical condition?*" or "*Text doesn't mention the type of insulin but I highlighted it because insulin is a medication!*". We responded to the questions in a timely manner to increase the quality of annotations.

5 Annotation Experiments

In our annotation experiments, each of 100 documents in our corpus was annotated by four workers, resulting in 100×4=400 files per experiment. We experimented with different pay scales to understand how they affect the quality and speed of the annotations.

5.1 Cost of Annotations

We investigated the cost of annotations both in terms of money and time. The summary of the results is in Table 1. We ran five different MTurk annotation experiments for our corpus of 100 documents. A total of 139 workers were involved in our experiments, and we identified eight of those workers as cheaters and rejected their annotation. The remaining workers spent 138.86 hours to complete 1872 files. The slowest experiment was MedicalCondition-I, in which we paid a base document rate of $0.01 without any bonuses. With this pay scale, it took 71.16 hours for workers to annotate 272 out of 400 files. We suspected we could not attract enough workers to finish the annotation task on time so we stopped the experiment before all 400 files were completed. When we compiled the results, we noticed that there was a general tendency for the workers to tag the first one or two entities and then ignore the rest of the document. Based on this observation, we decided to add bonuses to motivate the workers to read through the whole document. We ran the same annotation task, MedicalCondition-II, with a higher base document rate of $0.05 and a bonus rate of $0.01. With this new payment scale the annotation task was fully completed in 7.28 hours.

We also compared the effect of base rates when the bonus amounts were kept the same. For medication annotations, increasing the base document rate from $0.01 to $0.05 decreased the total amount of annotation time from 31.65 hours to 4.36 hours and also decreased the number of workers from 45 to 17. We ordered the workers based on the number files they annotated. The top ranked 5 workers in Medication-I annotated 187 files (46%) and the top ranked 5 workers in Medication-II annotated 313 files (78%). The difference between those two values was interesting since it indicated that by increasing the base rate, we managed to attract workers who worked on more documents.

The average amount of time workers spent per document varied based on entity type. They spent the longest amount of time for medical condition and shortest amount of time for laboratory test. This can be explained by the richness of documents in terms of entities. In the manually created gold standard there were 1159 mentions of medical condition, 518 mentions of medication, and 249 mentions of laboratory tests. Another observation was that the change in pay scales did not affect the average annotation time per document.

5.2 Quality of Annotations

We measured the quality of the MTurk annotations at different inter-annotator agreement levels by comparing the agreed entity spans with the spans in the gold standard.

Table 2. Quality measurement of MTurk annotations (k: Agreement level, P: Precision, R: Recall, F: F-measure; the highest value for each column is in boldface)

k	Medical Condition-II						Medication-II						Laboratory Test					
	Exact			Overlap			Exact			Overlap			Exact			Overlap		
	P	R	F	P	R	F	P	R	F	P	R	F	P	R	F	P	R	F
1	0.51	**0.66**	0.58	0.70	**0.99**	0.79	0.43	**0.73**	0.54	0.50	**0.84**	0.62	0.30	**0.52**	0.38	0.42	**0.73**	0.53
2	**0.64**	**0.66**	**0.65**	0.84	0.87	**0.86**	0.71	0.66	**0.68**	0.79	0.73	**0.76**	**0.47**	0.43	**0.45**	0.72	0.65	**0.68**
3	0.63	0.52	0.57	0.89	0.73	0.80	**0.78**	0.38	0.51	**0.93**	0.45	0.61	0.29	0.13	0.18	0.86	0.40	0.54
4	0.60	0.31	0.41	**0.93**	0.48	0.63	0.76	0.10	0.18	0.89	0.12	0.21	0.05	0.00	0.01	**1.00**	0.08	0.14

Given a document annotated by multiple workers and an agreement level *k*, there are different ways of creating a new span file that includes only the spans that are agreed by at least k workers. One method is to go over each span in each annotation and output only the spans that are marked by at least k workers. This method does not work well when the spans are long and the workers could disagree on the boundary. We used an alternative method which first goes over each word position in the document and marks the positions that are part of spans in at least k annotations, and then outputs the spans that cover those marked positions. We call the new span file *agreement-k* file.

Once we have created agreement-k file, we compare it with the gold standard to calculate precision, recall, and F-measure. A span in agreement-k file and a span in the gold standard are called an *exact match* if they are identical and are called an *overlap match* if they overlap (exact match is a special case of overlap match). Table 2 shows the performance for the MedicalCondition-II, Medication-II, and LaboratoryTest experiments at different agreement levels (k). As can be seen from the table, as the value of k increased, the precision values increased and the recall values decreased. For all of the experiments, the best F-Score was achieved at agreement-level 2.

Of the three entity types, laboratory test was the hardest partly because laboratory test entities tend to be longer (the average length for entities in gold standard was 5.25 words, compared to 1.84 words for medication and 3.18 words for medical condition), making the exact boundary harder to define. The results for MedicalCondition-II and Medication-II were higher than LaboratoryTest. In addition, accuracy for Medication-I (not shown here due to space limit) and Medication-II were similar, indicating that pay rate did not affect accuracy much in our experiments. In the future, we plan to increase the number of annotations for each document, which we believe could further improve the performance.

6 Conclusion

Human annotation is crucial for many NLP tasks. In this paper, we demonstrated the potential of using MTurk for annotating medical text. By continuously monitoring the workers' performance and using the bonus system, we acquired high quality annotations from non-expert MTurk workers with limited time and budget.

As future work, we plan to analyze the MTurk annotations in detail in order to understand the problematic areas. Based on our observations, we will redesign our annotation tasks and continue our experiments with MTurk to create large-scale annotated corpora to be used in biomedical NLP projects.

Acknowledgement

This project was supported in part by NIH Grants 1K99LM010227-0110 and 5 U54 LM008748.

References

[1] Chris Callison-Burch. 2009. Fast, Cheap, and Creative: Evaluating Translation Quality Using Amazon's Mechanical Turk. In Proceedings of EMNLP'09.

[2] Melonie Heron, Donna L. Hoyert, Sherry L. Murphy, Jiaquan Xu, Kenneth D. Kochanek, and Betzaida Tejada-Vera. 2009. Deaths: Final data for 2006. National Vital Statistics Reports, 57:14.

[3] Aniket Kittur, Ed H. Chi, and Bongwon Suh. 2008. Crowdsourcing User Studies with Mechanical Turk. In Proceedings of CHI'08.

[4] Preslav Nakov. 2008. Noun compound interpretation using paraphrasing verbs: Feasibility study. In Proceedings of the 13th international conference on Artificial Intelligence: Methodology, Systems and Applications (AIMSA 2008), 103–117.

[5] Philip V. Ogren. 2006. Knowtator: a protégé plug-in for annotated corpus construction. In Proceedings NAACL HLT'06, 273-275.

[6] Rion Snow, Brendan O'Connor, Daniel Jurafsky and Andrew Y. Ng. 2008. Cheap and Fast - But is it Good? Evaluating Non-Expert Annotations for Natural Language Tasks. In Proceedings of EMNLP'08, 254-263.

[7] Alexander Sorokin and David Forsyth. Utility data annotation with Amazon Mechanical Turk. In Proceedings of Computer Vision and Pattern Recognition Workshop at CVPR'08.

Tools for Collecting Speech Corpora via Mechanical-Turk

Ian Lane[1,2], Alex Waibel[1,2]
[1]Language Technologies Institute
Carnegie Mellon University
Pittsburgh, PA 15213, USA
{ianlane,ahw}@cs.cmu.edu

Matthias Eck[2], Kay Rottmann[2]
[2]Mobile Technologies LLC
Pittsburgh, PA, USA
matthias.eck@jibbigo.com
kay.rottmann@jibbigo.com

Abstract

To rapidly port speech applications to new languages one of the most difficult tasks is the initial collection of sufficient speech corpora. State-of-the-art automatic speech recognition systems are typical trained on hundreds of hours of speech data. While pre-existing corpora do exist for major languages, a sufficient amount of quality speech data is not available for most world languages. While previous works have focused on the collection of translations and the transcription of audio via Mechanical-Turk mechanisms, in this paper we introduce two tools which enable the collection of speech data remotely. We then compare the quality of audio collected from paid part-time staff and unsupervised volunteers, and determine that basic user training is critical to obtain usable data.

1 Introduction

In order to port a spoken language application to a new language, first an automatic speech recognition (ASR) system must be developed. For many languages pre-existing corpora do not exist and thus speech data must be collected before development can begin. The collection of speech corpora is an expensive undertaking and obtaining this data rapidly, for example in response to a disaster, cannot be done using the typical methodology in which corpora are collected in controlled environments.

To build an ASR system for a new language, two sets of data are required; first, a text corpus consisting of written transcriptions of utterances users are likely to speak to the system, this is used to train the language model (LM) applied during ASR; and second, a corpora of recordings of speech, which are used to train an acoustic model (AM). Text corpora for a new language can be created by manually translating a pre-existing corpus (or a sub-set of that corpus) into the new language and crowd-sourcing methodologies can be used to rapidly perform this task. Rapidly creating corpora of speech data, however, is not trivial. Generally speech corpora are collected in controlled environments where speakers are supervised by experts to ensure the equipment is setup correctly and recordings are performed adequately. However, for most languages performing this task on-site, where developers are located, is impractical as there may not be a local community of speakers of the required language. An alternative is to perform the data collection remotely, allowing speakers to record speech on their own PCs or mobile devices in their home country or wherever they are located. While previous works have focused on the generation of translations (Razavian, 2009) and transcribing of audio (Marge, 2010) via Mechanical-Turk, in this paper we focus on the collection of speech corpora using a Mechanical-Turk type framework.

Previous works (Voxforge), (Gruenstein, 2009), (Schultz, 2007) have developed solutions for collecting speech data remotely via web-based interfaces. A web-based system for the collection of open-source speech corpora has been developed by the group at www.voxforge.org. Speech recordings are collected for ten major European languages and speakers can either record audio directly on the website or they can call in on a dedicated phone line. In (Gruenstein, 2009) spontaneous speech (US English) was collected via a web-based memory game. In this system speech prompts were not provided, but rather a voice-based memory game was used to gather and partially annotate

Proceedings of the NAACL HLT 2010 Workshop on Creating Speech and Language Data with Amazon's Mechanical Turk, pages 184–187,
Los Angeles, California, June 2010.

Figure 1: Screenshots from Speech Collection iPhone App

spontaneous speech. In comparison to the above works which focus on the collection of data for major languages, the SPICE project (Schultz, 2007) provides a set of web-based tools to enable developers to create voice-based applications for less-common languages. In addition to tools for defining the phonetic units of a language and creating pronunciation dictionaries, this system also includes tools to create prompts and collect speech data from volunteers over the web.

In this paper, we describe two tools we have developed to collect speech corpora remotely. The first, a Mobile smart-phone based system which allows speakers to record prompted speech directly on their phones and second, a web-based system which allows recordings to be collected remotely on PCs. We compare the quality of audio collected from paid part-time staff and unsupervised volunteers and determine that basic user training and automatic feedback mechanisms are required to obtain usable data.

2 Collection of Speech on Mobile Devices

Today's smart-phones are able to record quality audio onboard and generally have the ability to connect to the internet via a fast wifi-connection. This makes them an ideal platform for collecting speech data in the field. Speech data can be collected by a user at any time in any location, and the data can be uploaded at a later time when a wireless connection is available. At Mobile Technologies we have developed an iPhone application to perform this task.

The collection procedure consists of three steps. First, on start-up a small amount of personal information, namely, gender and age, are requested from the user. They then select the language for which they intend to provide speech data. The mobile-device ID, personal information and language selected is used as an identifier for individual speakers. Next, collection of speech data is performed. Collection is performed offline, enabling data to be collected in the field where there may not be a persistent internet connection. A prompt is randomly selected from an onboard database of sentences and is presented to the user, who reads the sentence aloud holding down a push-to-talk button while speaking. During the speech collection stage, the system automatically proceeds to the following prompt when the current recording is complete. The user however has the ability to go back to previous recordings, listen to it and re-speak the sentence if any issues are found. Finally, the speech data is uploaded using a wireless collection. Data is uploaded one utterance at a time to an FTP server. Uploading each utterance individually allows the user to halt the upload and continue it at a later time if required.

Figure 2: Java applet for Web-based recording

3 Collection via Web-based Recording

One of the most popular websites for crowd-sourcing is Amazon Mechanical Turk (AMT). "Requesters" post Human Intelligence Tasks (HITs) to this website and "Workers" browse the HITs, perform tasks and get paid a predefined amount after submitting their work. It has been reported that over 100,000 workers from 100 countries are using AMT (Pontin, 2007).

AMT allows two general types of HITs. A Question Form HIT is based on a provided XML template and only allows certain elements in the HIT. However, it is possible to integrate an external JAVA applet within a Question Form HIT which allows for some flexibility. Questions can also be hosted on an external website which increases flexibility for the HIT developer while remaining tightly integrated in the AMT environment.

For collection of audio data Amazon does not offer any integrated tools. We thus designed and implemented a Java applet for web based speech collection. The Java applet can easily be incorporated in the AMT Question-Form mechanism and could also be used as part of an External-Question HIT. Currently the Java applet provides the same basic functionality as outlined for the iPhone application. The applet sequentially shows a number of prompts to record. The user can skip a sentence, playback a recording to check the quality and also redo the recording for the current sentence (see screenshot in Figure 2).

After the user is finished, the recorded sentences are uploaded to a web-server using an HTTP Post request. An important difference is the necessity to be online during the speech recordings.

4 Evaluation of Recorded Audio

One issue when collecting speech data remotely is the quality of the resulting audio. When collection is performed in a controlled environment, the developer can ensure that the recording equipment is setup correctly, background noise is kept to a minimum and the speaker is adequately trained to use the recording equipment. However, the same is not guaranteed when collecting speech remotely via mechanical-turk frameworks.

Paid Employees	
Language	English
Number of Speakers	10
Utterances Evaluated	445
Volunteers	
Language	Haitian Creole
Number of Speakers	3
Utterances Evaluated	167

Table 1: Details of Evaluated Corpora

1	Recorded utterance is empty
2	Utterance is not segmented correctly
3	Recording is clipped
4	Recording contains audible echo
5	Recording contains audible noise

Table 2: Annotations used to label poor quality recordings

When recording prompted speech there are three types of issues that result in unsuitable data:

- **Garbage Audio:** recordings that are empty, clipped, have insufficient power, or are incorrectly segmented.
- **Low quality recordings:** low Signal-to-Noise recordings due to poor equipment or large background noise
- **Speaker errors:** Misspeaking of prompts, both accidental and malicious

To verify the quality of audio recorded in unsupervised environments we compared two sets of speech data. First, in an earlier data collection task we collected 445 prompted utterances from 10 US-English speakers. This data collection was performed in a quiet office environment with technical supervision. Speakers were paid a fee for their time. As a comparison a similar collection of Haitian Creole was performed. In this case data was collected on a volunteer basis and supervision was limited. Details of the collected data are shown in Table 1.

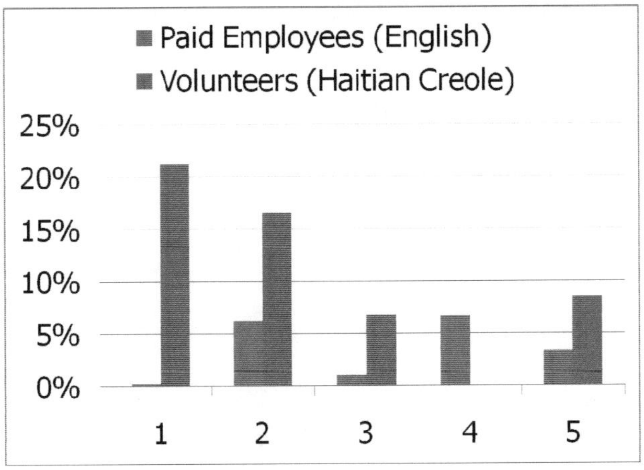

Figure 3: Percentage of recorded utterances determined to be inadequate for acoustic model training. Annotations limited to five issues listed in Table 1.

To determine the frequency of the quality issues listed above, we manually verified the two sets of collected speech. The recording of each utterance was listened to and if the audio file was determined to be of low quality it was annotated with one of the tags listed in Table 2. The percentage of utterances labeled with each annotation is shown for the English and volunteer Haitian Creole cases in Figure 3.

Around 10% of the English recordings were found to have issues. Clipping occurred in approximately 5% and a distinct echo was present in the recordings for one speaker. For the Haitian Creole case the yield of useable audio was significantly lower than that obtained for English. For all three speakers clipping was more prevalent and the level of background noise was higher. We discovered that due to lack of training, one of the volunteers had significant issues with the push-to-talk interface in our system. This led to many empty or incorrectly segmented recordings. In both cases, prompts were generally spoken accurately and technical problems caused poor quality recordings.

We believe the large difference in the yield of high quality recordings, 90% for English compared to 65% for Haitian Creole case, is directly due to the lack of training speakers received and the volunteer nature of the Haitian Creole task. By incorporating a basic tutorial when users first start our tools and an explicit feedback mechanism which automatically detects quality issues and prompts users to correct them we expect the yield of high quality recordings to increase significantly. In the near future we plan to use the tools to collect data from large communities of remote users.

5 Conclusions and Future Work

In this work, we have described two applications that allow speech corpora to be collected remotely, either directly on Mobile smart-phones or on a PC via a web-based interface. We also investigated the quality of recordings made by unsupervised volunteers and found that although prompts were generally read accurately, lack of training led to a significantly lower yield of high quality recordings.

In the near future we plan to use the tools to collect data from large communities of remote users. We will also investigate the user of tutorials and feedback to improve the yield of high quality data.

Acknowledgements

We would like to thank the Haitian volunteers who gave their time to help with this data collection.

References

N. S. Razavian, S Vogel, "The Web as a Platform to Build Machine Translation Resources", IWIC2009

M. Marge, S. Banerjee and A. Rudnicky, "Using the Amazon Mechanical Turk for Transcription of Spoken Language", IEEE-ICASSP, 2010

Voxforge, www.voxforge.org

A. Gruenstein, I. McGraw, and A. Sutherland, "A self-transcribing speech corpus: collecting continuous speech with an online educational game," Submitted to the Speech and Language Technology in Education (SLaTE) Workshop, 2009.

T. Schultz, et. al, "SPICE: Web-based Tools for Rapid Language Adaptation in Speech Processing Systems", In the Proceedings of INTERSPEECH, Antwerp, Belgium, 2007.

J. Pontin, "Artificial Intelligence, With Help From the Humans", The New York Times, 25 March 2007

Measuring Transitivity Using Untrained Annotators

Nitin Madnani[a,b] **Jordan Boyd-Graber**[a] **Philip Resnik**[a,c]
[a]Institute for Advanced Computer Studies
[b]Department of Computer Science
[c]Department of Linguistics
University of Maryland, College Park
{nmadnani, jbg, resnik}@umiacs.umd.edu

Abstract

Hopper and Thompson (1980) defined a multi-axis theory of transitivity that goes beyond simple syntactic transitivity and captures how much "action" takes place in a sentence. Detecting these features requires a deep understanding of lexical semantics and real-world pragmatics. We propose two general approaches for creating a corpus of sentences labeled with respect to the Hopper-Thompson transitivity schema using Amazon Mechanical Turk. Both approaches assume no existing resources and incorporate all necessary annotation into a single system; this is done to allow for future generalization to other languages. The first task attempts to use language-neutral videos to elicit human-composed sentences with specified transitivity attributes. The second task uses an iterative process to first label the actors and objects in sentences and then annotate the sentences' transitivity. We examine the success of these techniques and perform a preliminary classification of the transitivity of held-out data.

Hopper and Thompson (1980) created a multi-axis theory of Transitivity[1] that describes the volition of the subject, the affectedness of the object, and the duration of the action. In short, this theory goes beyond the simple grammatical notion of transitivity (whether verbs take objects — transitive — or not — intransitive) and captures how much "action" takes place in a sentence. Such notions of Transitivity are not apparent from surface features alone; identical syntactic constructions can have vastly different Transitivity. This well-established linguistic theory, however, is not useful for real-world applications without a Transitivity-annotated corpus.

Given such a substantive corpus, conventional machine learning techniques could help determine the Transitivity of verbs within sentences. Transitivity has been found to play a role in what is called "syntactic framing," which expresses implicit sentiment (Greene and Resnik, 2009). In these contexts, the perspective or sentiment of the writer is reflected in the constructions used to express ideas. For example, a less Transitive construction might be used to deflect responsibility (e.g. "John was killed" vs. "Benjamin killed John").

In the rest of this paper, we review the Hopper-Thompson transitivity schema and propose two relatively language-neutral methods to collect Transitivity ratings. The first asks humans to generate sentences with desired Transitivity characteristics. The second asks humans to rate sentences on dimensions from the Hopper-Thompson schema. We then discuss the difficulties of collecting such linguistically deep data and analyze the available results. We then pilot an initial classifier on the Hopper-Thompson dimensions.

1 Transitivity

Table 1 shows the subset of the Hopper-Thompson dimensions of Transitivity used in this study. We excluded noun-specific aspects as we felt that these were well covered by existing natural language processing (NLP) approaches (e.g. whether the object / subject is person, abstract entity, or abstract concept is handled well by existing named entity recognition systems) and also excluded aspects which we felt had significant overlap with the dimensions we were investigating (e.g. affirmation and mode).

We also distinguished the original Hopper-Thompson "Affectedness" aspect into separate "Benefit" and "Harm" components, as we suspect that these data will be useful to other applications such as sentiment analysis.

We believe that these dimensions of transitivity are simple and intuitive enough that they can be understood and labeled by the people on Amazon Mechanical Turk, a web service. Amazon Mechanical Turk (MTurk) allows individuals to post jobs on MTurk with a set fee that are then performed by workers on the Internet. MTurk connects workers to people with tasks and handles the coordination problems of payment and transferring data.

[1]We use capital "T" to differentiate from conventional syntactic transitivity throughout the paper.

Proceedings of the NAACL HLT 2010 Workshop on Creating Speech and Language Data with Amazon's Mechanical Turk, pages 188–194,
Los Angeles, California, June 2010.

Kinesis	Sentences where movement happens are perceived to be more Transitive. “Sue jumped out of an airplane” vs. “The corporation jumped to a silly conclusion.”
Punctuality	Sentences where the action happens quickly are perceived to be more Transitive. “She touched her ID to the scanner to enter” vs. “I was touched by how much she helped me.”
Mode	Sentences with no doubt about whether the action happened are perceived to be more Transitive. “Bob was too busy to fix the drain” vs. “Bob fixed the drain.”
Affectedness	Sentences where the object is more affected by the action are perceived to be more Transitive. “The St. Bernard saved the climber” vs. “Melanie looked at the model.”
Volition	Sentences where the actor chose to perform the action are perceived to be more Transitive. “Paul jumped out of the bushes and startled his poor sister” vs. “The picture startled George.”
Aspect	Sentences where the action is done to completion are perceived to be more Transitive. “Walter is eating the hamburger” vs. “Walter ate the pudding up.”

Table 1: The Hopper-Thompson dimensions of transitivity addressed in this paper. In experiments, “Affectedness” was divided into “Harm” and “Benefit.”

2 Experiments

Our goal is to create experiments for MTurk that will produce a large set of sentences with known values of Transitivity. With both experiments, we design the tasks to be as language independent as possible, thus not depending on language-specific preprocessing tools. This allows the data collection approach to be replicated in other languages.

2.1 Elicitation

The first task is not corpus specific, and requires no language-specific resources. We represent verbs using videos (Ma and Cook, 2009). This also provides a form of language independent sense disambiguation. We display videos illustrating verbs (Figure 1) and ask users on MTurk to identify the action and give nouns that can do the action and — in a separate task — the nouns that the action can be done to. For quality control, Turkers must match a previous Turker's response for one of their answers (a la the game show “Family Feud”).

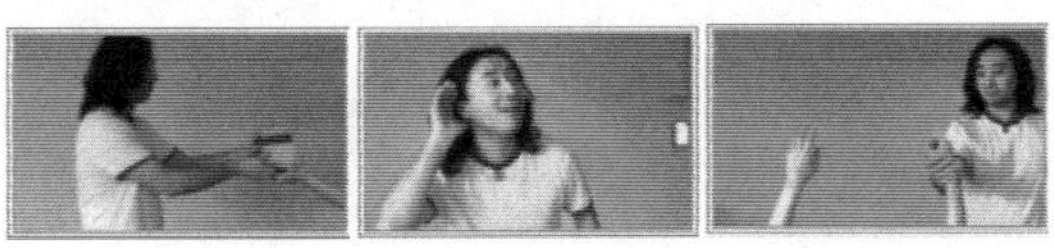

Figure 1: Stills from three videos depicting the verbs “receive,” “hear,” and “help.”

We initially found that subjects had difficulty distinguishing what things could do the action (subjects) vs. what things the action could be done to (objects). In order to suggest the appropriate syntactic frame, we use javascript to form their inputs into protosentences as they typed. For example, if they identified an action as “picking” and suggested “fruit” as a possible object, the protosentence “it is picking fruit” is displayed below their input (Figure 2). This helped ensure consistent answers. The subject and object tasks were done separately, and for the object task, users were allowed to say that there is nothing the action can be done to (for example, for an intransitive verb).

Figure 2: A screenshot of a user completing a task to find objects of a particular verb, where the verb is represented by a film. After the user has written a verb and a noun, a protosentence is formed and shown to ensure that the user is using the words in the appropriate roles.

These subjects and objects we collected were then used as inputs for a second task. We showed workers videos with potential subjects and objects and asked them to create pairs of sentences with opposite Transitivity attributes. For example, *Write a sentence where the thing to which the action is done benefits* and *Write a sentence where the thing to which the action is done is not affected by the action.* For both sides of the Transitivity dimension, we allowed users to say that writing such a sentence is impossible. We discuss the initial results of this task in Section 3.

2.2 Annotation

Our second task—one of annotation—depends on having a corpus available in the language of interest. For concreteness and availability, we use Wikipedia, a free multilingual encyclopedia. We extract a large pool of sentences from Wikipedia containing verbs of interest. We apply light preprocessing to remove long, unclear (e.g. starting with a pronoun), or uniquely Wikipedian sentences (e.g. very short sentences of the form "See *List of Star Trek Characters*"). We construct tasks, each for a single verb, that ask users to identify the subject and object for the verb in randomly selected sentences.[2] Users were prompted by an interactive javascript guide (Figure 3) that instructed them to click on the first word of the subject (or object) and then to click on the last word that made up the subject (or object). After they clicked, a text box was automatically populated with their answer; this decreased errors and made the tasks easier to finish. For quality control, each HIT has a simple sentence where subject and object were already determined by the authors; the user must match the annotation on that sentence for credit. We ended up rejecting less than one percent of submitted hits.

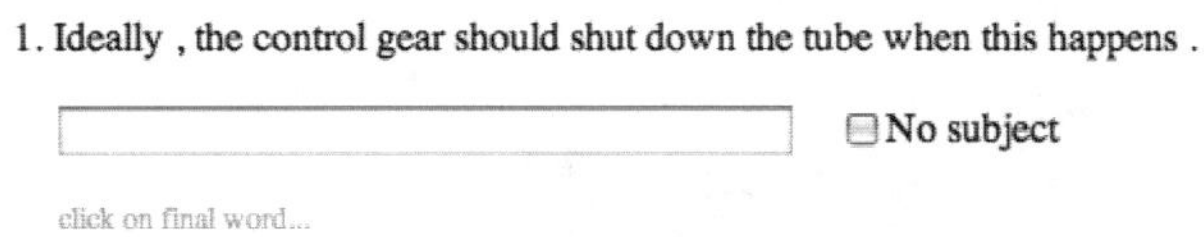

Figure 3: A screenshot of the subject identification task. The user has to click on the phrase that they believe is the subject.

Once objects and subjects have been identified, other users rate the sentence's Transitivity by answering the following questions like, where $VERB represents the verb of interest, $SUBJ is its subject and $OBJ is its object[3]:

- **Aspect**. After reading this sentence, do you know that $SUBJ is done $VERBing?
- **Affirmation**. From reading the sentence, how certain are you that $VERBing happened?
- **Benefit**. How much did $OBJ benefit?
- **Harm**. How much was $OBJ harmed?
- **Kinesis**. Did $SUBJ move?
- **Punctuality**. If you were to film $SUBJ's act of $VERBing in its entirety, how long would the movie be?
- **Volition**. Did the $SUBJ make a conscious choice to $VERB?

The answers were on a scale of 0 to 4 (higher numbers meant the sentence evinced more of the property in question), and each point in the scale had a description to anchor raters and to ensure consistent results.

2.3 Rewards

Table 2 summarizes the rewards for the tasks used in these experiments. Rewards were set at the minimal rate that could attract sufficient interest from users. For the "Video Elicitation" task, where users wrote sentences with specified Transitivity properties, we also offered bonuses for clever, clear sentences. However, this was our least popular task, and we struggled to attract users.

3 Results and Discussion

3.1 Creative but Unusable Elicitation Results

We initially thought that we would have difficulty coaxing users to provide full sentences. This turned out not to be the case. We had no difficulty getting (very imaginative) sentences, but the sentences were often inconsistent with the Transitivity aspects we are interested in. This shows both the difficulty of writing concise instructions for non-experts and the differences between everyday meanings of words and their meaning in linguistic contexts.

For example, the "volitional" elicitation task asked people to create sentences where the subject made a conscious decision to perform the action. In the cases where we asked users to create sentences where the subject did not make a conscious decision to perform an action, almost all of the sentences created by users focused on sentences where a person (rather than employ other tactics such as using a less individuated subject, e.g. replacing "Bob" with "freedom") was performing the action and was coerced into doing the action. For example:

- Sellers often give gifts to their clients when they are trying to make up for a wrongdoing.
- A man is forced to search for his money.
- The man, after protesting profusely, picked an exercise class to attend
- The vegetarian Sherpa had to eat the pepperoni pizza or he would surely have died.

While these data are likely still interesting for other purposes, their biased distribution is unlikely to be useful for helping identify whether an arbitrary sentence in a text expresses the volitional Transitivity attribute. The users prefer to have an animate agent that is compelled to take the action rather than create sentences where the action happens accidentally or is undertaken by an abstract or inanimate actor.

Similarly, for the aspect dimension, many users simply chose to represent actions that had not been completed

[2] Our goal of language independence and the unreliable correspondence between syntax and semantic roles precludes automatic labeling of the subjects and objects.

[3] These questions were developed using Greene and Resnik's (2009) surveys as a foundation.

Task	Questions / Hit	Pay	Repetition	Tasks	Total
Video Object	5	0.04	5	10	$2.00
Video Subject	5	0.04	5	10	$2.00
Corpus Object	10	0.03	5	50	$7.50
Corpus Subject	10	0.03	5	50	$7.50
Video Elicitation	5	0.10	2	70	$14.00
Corpus Annotation	7	0.03	3	400	$36.00
Total					$69.00

Table 2: The reward structure for the tasks presented in this paper (not including bonuses or MTurk overhead). "Video Subject" and "Video Object" are where users were presented with a video and supplied the subjects and objects of the depicted actions. "Corpus Subject" and "Corpus Object" are the tasks where users identified the subject and objects of sentences from Wikipedia. "Video Elicitation" refers to the task where users were asked to write sentences with specified Transitivity properties. "Corpus Annotation" is where users are presented with sentences with previously identified subjects and objects and must rate various dimensions of Transitivity.

using the future tense. For the kinesis task, users displayed amazing creativity in inventing situations where movement was correlated with the action. Unfortunately, as before, these data are not useful in generating predictive features for capturing the properties of Transitivity.

We hope to improve experiments and instructions to better align everyday intuitions with the linguistic properties of interest. While we have found that extensive directions tend to discourage users, perhaps there are ways incrementally building or modifying sentences that would allow us to elicit sentences with the desired Transitivity properties. This is discussed further in the conclusion, Section 4.

3.2 Annotation Task

For the annotation task, we observed that users often had a hard time keeping their focus on the words in question and not incorporating additional knowledge. For example, for each of the following sentences:

- Bonosus dealt with the eastern cities so harshly that his **severity** was remembered centuries later .
- On the way there, however, Joe and Jake pick another **fight** .
- The Black Sea was a significant naval theatre of World War I and saw both **naval and land battles** during World War II .
- Bush claimed that Zubaydah gave **information** that lead to al Shibh 's capture .

some users said that the objects in **bold** were greatly harmed, suggesting that users felt even abstract concepts could be harmed in these sentences. A rigorous interpretation of the affectedness dimension would argue that these abstract concepts were incapable of being harmed. We suspect that the negative associations (severity, fight, battles, capture) present in this sentence are causing users to make connections to harm, thus creating these ratings.

Similarly, world knowledge flavored other questions, such as kinesis, where users were able to understand from context that the person doing the action probably moved at some point near the time of the event, even if movement wasn't a part of the act of, for example, "calling" or "loving."

3.3 Quantitative Results

For the annotation task, we were able to get consistent ratings of transitivity. Table 3 shows the proportion of sentences where two or more annotators agreed on the a Transitivity label of the sentences for that dimension. All of the dimensions were significantly better than random chance agreement (0.52); the best was harm, which has an accessible, clear, and intuitive definition, and the worst was kinesis, which was more ambiguous and prone to disagreement among raters.

Dimension	Sentences with Agreement
HARM	0.87
AFFIRMATION	0.86
VOLITION	0.86
PUNCTUALITY	0.81
BENEFIT	0.81
ASPECT	0.80
KINESIS	0.70

Table 3: For each of the dimensions of transitivity, the proportion of sentences where at least two of three raters agreed on the label. Random chance agreement is 0.52.

Figure 4 shows a distribution for each of the Transitivity data on the Wikipedia corpus. These data are consistent with what one would expect from random sentences from an encyclopedic dataset; most of the sentences en-

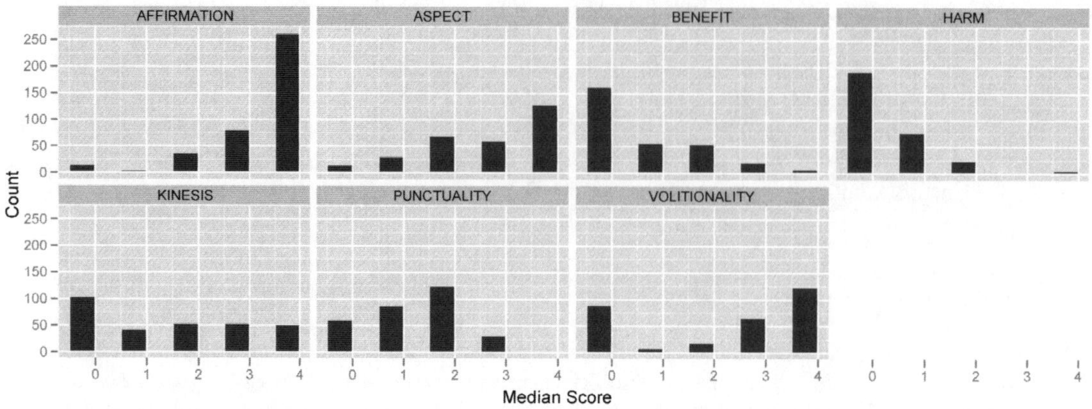

Figure 4: Histograms of median scores from raters by Transitivity dimension. Higher values represent greater levels of Transitivity.

code truthful statements, most actions have been completed, most objects are not affected, most events are over a long time span, and there is a bimodal distribution over volition. One surprising result is that for kinesis there is a fairly flat distribution. One would expect a larger skew toward non-kinetic words. Qualitative analysis of the data suggest that raters used real-world knowledge to associate motion with the context of actions (even if motion is not a part of the action), and that raters were less confident about their answers, prompting more hedging and a flat distribution.

3.4 Predicting Transitivity

We also performed an set of initial experiments to investigate our ability to predict Transitivity values for held out data. We extracted three sets of features from the sentences: lexical features, syntactic features, and features derived from WordNet (Miller, 1990).

Lexical Features A feature was created for each word in a sentence after being stemmed using the Porter stemmer (Porter, 1980).

Syntactic Features We parsed each sentence using the Stanford Parser (Klein and Manning, 2003) and used heuristics to identify cases where the main verb is transitive, where the subject is a nominalization (e.g. "running"), or whether the sentence is passive. If any of these constructions appear in the sentence, we generate a corresponding feature. These represent features identified by Greene and Resnik (2009).

WordNet Features For each word in the sentence, we extracted all the possible senses for each word. If any possible sense was a hyponym (i.e. an instance of) one of: *artifact*, *living thing*, *abstract entity*, *location*, or *food*, we added a feature corresponding to that top level synset. For example, the string "Lincoln" could be an instance of both a *location* (Lincoln, Nebraska) and a *living thing* (Abe Lincoln), so a feature was added for both the *location* and *living thing* senses. In addition to these noun-based features, features were added for each of the possible verb frames allowed by each of a word's possible senses (Fellbaum, 1998).

At first, we performed simple 5-way classification and found that we could not beat the most frequent class baseline for any dimension. We then decided to simplify the classification task to make binary predictions of low-vs-high instead of fine gradations along the particular dimension. To do this, we took all the rated sentences for each of the seven dimensions and divided the ratings into low (ratings of 0-1) and high (ratings of 2-4) values for that dimension. Table 4 shows the results for these binary classification experiments using different classifiers. All of the classification experiments were conducted using the Weka machine learning toolkit (Hall et al., 2009) and used 10-fold stratified cross validation.

Successfully rating Transitivity requires knowledge beyond individual tokens. For example, consider kinesis. Judging kinesis requires lexical semantics to realize whether a certain actor is capable of movement, pragmatics to determine if the described situation permits movement, and differentiating literal and figurative movement.

One source of real-world knowledge is WordNet; adding some initial features from WordNet appears to help aid some of these classifications. For example, classifiers trained on the volitionality data were not able to do better than the most frequent class baseline before the addition of WordNet-based features. This is a reasonable result, as WordNet features help the algorithm generalize which actors are capable of making decisions.

Dimension	Makeup	Classifier Accuracy						
		Baseline	NB		VP		SVM	
			-WN	+WN	-WN	+WN	-WN	+WN
HARM	269/35	**88.5**	83.9	84.9	87.2	87.8	88.5	88.5
AFFIRMATION	380/20	**95.0**	92.5	92.0	94.3	95.0	95.0	95.0
VOLITION	209/98	68.1	66.4	69.4	67.1	**73.3**	68.1	68.1
PUNCTUALITY	158/149	51.5	59.6	**61.2**	57.0	59.6	51.5	51.5
BENEFIT	220/84	72.4	69.1	65.1	**73.4**	71.4	72.4	72.4
ASPECT	261/46	**85.0**	76.5	74.3	81.1	84.7	85.0	85.0
KINESIS	160/147	52.1	**61.2**	**61.2**	56.4	60.9	52.1	52.1

Table 4: The results of preliminary binary classification experiments for predicting various transitivity dimensions using different classifiers such as Naive Bayes (NB), Voted Perceptron (VP) and Support Vector Machines (SVM). Classifier accuracies for two sets of experiments are shown: without WordNet features (-WN) and with WordNet features (+WN). The baseline simply predicts the most frequent class. For each dimension, the split between low Transitivity (rated 0-1) and high Transitivity (rated 2-4) is shown under the "Makeup" column. All reported accuracies are using 10-fold stratified cross validation.

4 Conclusion

We began with the goal of capturing a subtle linguistic property for which annotated datasets were not available. We created a annotated dataset of 400 sentences taken from the real-word dataset Wikipedia annotated for seven different Transitivity properties. Users were able to give consistent answers, and we collected results in a manner that is relatively language independent. Once we expand and improve this data collection scheme for English, we hope to perform similar data collection in other languages. We have available the translated versions of the questions used in this study for Arabic and German.

Our elicitation task was not as successful as we had hoped. We learned that while we could form tasks using everyday language that we thought captured these subtle linguistic properties, we also had many unspoken assumptions that the creative workers on MTurk did not necessarily share. As we articulated these assumptions in increasingly long instruction sets to workers, the sheer size of the instructions began to intimidate and scare off workers.

While it seems unlikely we can strike a balance that will give us the answers we want with the elegant instructions that workers need to feel comfortable for the tasks as we currently defined them, we hope to modify the task to embed further linguistic assumptions. For example, we hope to pilot another version of the elicitation task where workers modify an existing sentence to change one Transitivity dimension. Instead of reading and understanding a plodding discussion of potentially irrelevant details, the user can simply see a list of sentence versions that are not allowed.

Our initial classification results suggest that we do not yet have enough data to always detect these Transitivity dimensions from unlabeled text or that our algorithms are using features that do not impart enough information. It is also possible that using another corpus might yield greater variation in Transitivity that would aid classification; Wikipedia by design attempts to keep a neutral tone and eschews the highly charged prose that would contain a great deal of Transitivity.

Another possibility is that, instead of just the Transitivity ratings alone, tweaks to the data collection process could also help guide classification algorithms (Zaidan et al., 2008). Thus, instead of clicking on a single annotation label in our current data collection process, Turkers would click on a data label *and* the word that most helped them make a decision.

Our attempts to predict Transitivity are not exhaustive, and there are a number of reasonable algorithms and resources which could also be applied to the problem; for example, one might expect semantic role labeling or sense disambiguation to possibly aid the prediction of Transitivity. Determining which techniques are effective and the reasons why they are effective would aid not just in predicting Transitivity, which we believe to be an interesting problem, but also in *understanding* Transitivity.

Using services like MTurk allows us to tighten the loop between data collection, data annotation, and machine learning and better understand difficult problems. We hope to refine the data collection process to provide more consistent results on useful sentences, build classifiers, and extract features that are able to discover the Transitivity of unlabeled text. We believe that our efforts will help cast an interesting aspect of theoretical linguistics into a more pragmatic setting and make it accessible for use in more practical problems like sentiment analysis.

References

C. Fellbaum, 1998. *WordNet : An Electronic Lexical Database*, chapter A semantic network of English verbs. MIT Press, Cambridge, MA.

Stephan Greene and Philip Resnik. 2009. More than words: Syntactic packaging and implicit sentiment. In *Conference of the North American Chapter of the Association for Computational Linguistics*, pages 503–511.

Mark Hall, Eibe Frank, Geoffrey Holmes, Bernhard Pfahringer, Peter Reutemann, and Ian H. Witten. 2009. The WEKA Data Mining Software: An Update. *SIGKDD Explorations*, 11(1).

Paul J. Hopper and Sandra A. Thompson. 1980. Transitivity in grammar and discourse. *Language*, (56):251–299.

Dan Klein and Christopher D. Manning. 2003. Accurate unlexicalized parsing. In *Proceedings of the Association for Computational Linguistics*, pages 423–430.

Xiaojuan Ma and Perry R. Cook. 2009. How well do visual verbs work in daily communication for young and old adults? In *international conference on Human factors in computing systems*, pages 361–364.

George A. Miller. 1990. Nouns in WordNet: A lexical inheritance system. *International Journal of Lexicography*, 3(4):245–264.

M. F. Porter. 1980. An algorithm for suffix stripping. *Program*, 14(3):130–137.

Omar F. Zaidan, Jason Eisner, and Christine Piatko. 2008. Machine learning with annotator rationales to reduce annotation cost. In *Proceedings of the NIPS*2008 Workshop on Cost Sensitive Learning*, Whistler, BC, December. 10 pages.

Amazon Mechanical Turk for Subjectivity Word Sense Disambiguation

Cem Akkaya
University of Pittsburgh
cem@cs.pitt.edu

Alexander Conrad
University of Pittsburgh
conrada@cs.pitt.edu

Janyce Wiebe
University of Pittsburgh
wiebe@cs.pitt.edu

Rada Mihalcea
University of North Texas
rada@cs.unt.edu

Abstract

Amazon Mechanical Turk (MTurk) is a marketplace for so-called "human intelligence tasks" (HITs), or tasks that are easy for humans but currently difficult for automated processes. Providers upload tasks to MTurk which workers then complete. Natural language annotation is one such human intelligence task. In this paper, we investigate using MTurk to collect annotations for Subjectivity Word Sense Disambiguation (SWSD), a coarse-grained word sense disambiguation task. We investigate whether we can use MTurk to acquire good annotations with respect to gold-standard data, whether we can filter out low-quality workers (spammers), and whether there is a learning effect associated with repeatedly completing the same kind of task. While our results with respect to spammers are inconclusive, we are able to obtain high-quality annotations for the SWSD task. These results suggest a greater role for MTurk with respect to constructing a large scale SWSD system in the future, promising substantial improvement in subjectivity and sentiment analysis.

1 Introduction

Many Natural Language Processing (NLP) systems rely on large amounts of manually annotated data that is collected from domain experts. The annotation process to obtain this data is very laborious and expensive. This makes supervised NLP systems subject to a so-called knowledge acquisition bottleneck. For example, (Ng, 1997) estimates an effort of 16 person years to construct training data for a high-accuracy domain independent Word Sense Disambiguation (WSD) system.

Recently researchers have been investigating Amazon Mechanical Turk (MTurk) as a source of non-expert natural language annotation, which is a cheap and quick alternative to expert annotations (Kaisser and Lowe, 2008; Mrozinski et al., 2008). In this paper, we utilize MTurk to obtain training data for Subjectivity Word Sense Disambiguation (SWSD) as described in (Akkaya et al., 2009). The goal of SWSD is to automatically determine which word instances in a corpus are being used with subjective senses, and which are being used with objective senses. SWSD is a new task which suffers from the absence of a substantial amount of annotated data and thus can only be applied on a small scale. SWSD has strong connections to WSD. Like supervised WSD, it requires training data where target word instances – words which need to be disambiguated by the system – are labeled as having an objective sense or a subjective sense. (Akkaya et al., 2009) show that SWSD may bring substantial improvement in subjectivity and sentiment analysis, if it could be applied on a larger scale. The good news is that training data for 80 selected keywords is enough to make a substantial difference (Akkaya et al., 2009). Thus, large scale SWSD is feasible. We hypothesize that annotations for SWSD can be provided by non-experts reliably if the annotation task is presented in a simple way.

The annotations obtained from MTurk workers are noisy by nature, because MTurk workers are not trained for the underlying annotation task. That is why previous work explored methods to assess annotation quality and to aggregate multiple noisy annotations for high reliability (Snow et al., 2008; Callison-Burch, 2009). It is understandable that not every worker will provide high-quality annotations,

Proceedings of the NAACL HLT 2010 Workshop on Creating Speech and Language Data with Amazon's Mechanical Turk, pages 195–203,
Los Angeles, California, June 2010.

depending on their background and interest. Unfortunately, some MTurk workers do not follow the annotation guidelines and carelessly submit annotations in order to gain economic benefits with only minimal effort. We define this group of workers as spammers. We believe it is essential to distinguish between workers as well-meaning annotators and workers as spammers who should be filtered out as a first step when utilizing MTurk. In this work, we investigate how well the built-in qualifications in MTurk function as such a filter.

Another important question about MTurk workers is whether they learn to provide better annotations over time in the absence of any interaction and feedback. The presence of a learning effect may support working with the same workers over a long time and creating private groups of workers. In this work, we also examine if there is a learning effect associated with MTurk workers.

To summarize, in this work we investigate the following questions:

- Can MTurk be utilized to collect reliable training data for SWSD ?
- Are the built-in methods provided by MTurk enough to avoid spammers ?
- Is there a learning effect associated with MTurk workers ?

The remainder of the paper is organized as follows. In Section 2, we give general background information on the Amazon Mechanical Turk service. In Section 3, we discuss sense subjectivity. In Section 4, we describe the subjectivity word sense disambiguation task. In Section 5, we discuss the design of our experiment and our filtering mechanisms for workers. In Section 6, we evaluate MTurk annotations and relate results to our questions. In Section 7, we review related work. In Section 8, we draw conclusions and discuss future work.

2 Amazon Mechanical Turk

Amazon Mechanical Turk (MTurk)[1] is a marketplace for so-called "human intelligence tasks," or HITs. MTurk has two kinds of users: providers and workers. Providers create HITs using the Mechanical Turk API and, for a small fee, upload them to the HIT database. Workers search through the HIT database, choosing which to complete in exchange for monetary compensation. Anyone can sign up as a provider and/or worker. Each HIT has an associated monetary value, and after reviewing a worker's submission, a provider may choose whether to accept the submission and pay the worker the promised sum or to reject it and pay the worker nothing. HITs typically consist of tasks that are easy for humans but difficult or impossible for computers to complete quickly or effectively, such as annotating images, transcribing speech audio, or writing a summary of a video.

One challenge for requesters using MTurk is that of filtering out spammers and other workers who consistently produce low-quality annotations. In order to allow requesters to restrict the range of workers who can complete their tasks, MTurk provides several types of built-in statistics, known as qualifications. One such qualification is approval rating, a statistic that records a worker's ratio of accepted HITs compared to the total number of HITs submitted by that worker. Providers can require that a worker's approval rating be above a certain threshold before allowing that worker to submit one of his/her HITs. Country of residence and lifetime approved number of HITs completed also serve as built-in qualifications that providers may check before allowing workers to access their HITs.[2] Amazon also allows providers to define their own qualifications. Typically, provider-defined qualifications are used to ensure that HITs which require particular skills are only completed by qualified workers. In most cases, workers acquire provider-defined qualifications by completing an online test.

Amazon also provides a mechanism by which multiple unique workers can complete the same HIT. The number of times a HIT is to be completed is known as the number of assignments for the HIT. By having multiple workers complete the same HIT,

[1] `http://mturk.amazon.com`

[2] According to the terms of use, workers are prohibited from having more than one account, but to the writer's knowledge there is no method in place to enforce this restriction. Thus, a worker with a poor approval rating could simply create a new account, since all accounts start with an approval rating of 100%.

Subjective senses:

His **alarm** grew.
alarm, dismay, consternation – (fear resulting from the awareness of danger)

=> fear, fearfulness, fright – (an emotion experienced in anticipation of some specific pain or danger (usually accompanied by a desire to flee or fight))

What's the **catch**?
catch – (a hidden drawback; "it sounds good but what's the catch?")

=> drawback – (the quality of being a hindrance; "he pointed out all the drawbacks to my plan")

Objective senses:

The **alarm** went off.
alarm, warning device, alarm system – (a device that signals the occurrence of some undesirable event)

=> device – (an instrumentality invented for a particular purpose; "the device is small enough to wear on your wrist"; "a device intended to conserve water")

He sold his **catch** at the market.
catch, haul – (the quantity that was caught; "the catch was only 10 fish")

=> indefinite quantity – (an estimated quantity)

Figure 1: Subjective and objective word sense examples.

techniques such as majority voting among the submissions can be used to aggregate the results for some types of HITs, resulting in a higher-quality final answer. Previous work (Snow et al., 2008) demonstrates that aggregating worker submissions often leads to an increase in quality.

3 Word Sense Subjectivity

(Wiebe and Mihalcea, 2006) define subjective expressions as words and phrases being used to express mental and emotional states, such as speculations, evaluations, sentiments, and beliefs. Many approaches to sentiment and subjectivity analysis rely on lexicons of such words (subjectivity clues). However, such clues often have both subjective and objective senses, as illustrated by (Wiebe and Mihalcea, 2006). Figure 1 provides subjective and objective examples of senses.

(Akkaya et al., 2009) points out that most subjectivity lexicons are compiled as lists of keywords, rather than word meanings (senses). Thus, subjectivity clues used with objective senses – false hits – are a significant source of error in subjectivity and sentiment analysis. SWSD specifically deals with this source of errors. (Akkaya et al., 2009) shows that SWSD helps with various subjectivity and sentiment analysis systems by ignoring false hits.

4 Annotation Task

4.1 Subjectivity Word Sense Disambiguation

Our target task is Subjectivity Word Sense Disambiguation (SWSD). SWSD aims to determine which word instances in a corpus are being used with subjective senses and which are being used with objective senses. It can be considered to be a coarse-grained application-specific WSD that distinguishes between only two senses: (1) the subjective sense and (2) the objective sense.

Subjectivity word sense annotation is done in the following way. We try to keep the annotation task for the worker as simple as possible. Thus, we do not directly ask them if the instance of a target word has a subjective or an objective sense (without any sense inventory), because the concept of subjectivity is fairly difficult to explain to someone who does not have any linguistics background. Instead we show MTurk workers two sets of senses – one subjective set and one objective set – for a specific target word and a text passage in which the target word appears. Their job is to select the set that best reflects the meaning of the target word in the text passage. The specific sense set automatically gives us the subjectivity label of the instance. This makes the annotation task easier for them as (Snow et al., 2008) shows that WSD can be done reliably by MTurk workers. This approach presupposes a set of word senses that have been annotated as subjective or objective. The annotation of senses in a dictionary for subjectivity is not difficult for an expert annotator. Moreover, it needs to be done only once per target word, allowing us to collect hundreds of subjectivity labeled instances for each target word through MTurk.

In this annotation task, we do not inform the MTurk workers about the nature of the sets. This means the MTurk workers have no idea that they are annotating subjectivity of senses; they are just selecting the set which contains a sense matching the usage in the sentence or being as similar to it as possible. This ensures that MTurk workers are not biased by the contextual subjectivity of the sentence while tagging the target word instance.

Sense_Set1 (Subjective)

{ look, **appear**, seem } – give a certain impression or have a certain outward aspect; "She seems to be sleeping"; "This appears to be a very difficult problem"; "This project looks fishy"; "They appeared like people who had not eaten or slept for a long time"

{ **appear**, seem } – seem to be true, probable, or apparent; "It seems that he is very gifted"; "It appears that the weather in California is very bad"

Sense_Set2 (Objective)

{ **appear** } – come into sight or view; "He suddenly appeared at the wedding"; "A new star appeared on the horizon"

{ **appear**, come_out } – be issued or published, as of news in a paper, a book, or a movie; "Did your latest book appear yet?"; "The new Woody Allen film hasn't come out yet"

{ **appear**, come_along } – come into being or existence, or appear on the scene; "Then the computer came along and changed our lives"; "Homo sapiens appeared millions of years ago"

{ **appear** } – appear as a character on stage or appear in a play, etc.; "Gielgud appears briefly in this movie"; "She appeared in 'Hamlet' on the London

{ **appear** } – present oneself formally, as before a (judicial) authority; "He had to appear in court last month"; "She appeared on several charges of theft"

Figure 2: Sense sets for target word "appear".

Below, we describe a sample annotation problem. An MTurk worker has access to the following two sense sets of the target word "appear", as seen in Figure 2. The information that the first sense set is subjective and second sense set is objective is not available to the worker. The worker is presented with the following text passage holding the target word "appear".

> It's got so bad that I don't even know what to say. Charles |target| appeared |target| somewhat embarrassed by his own behavior. The hidden speech was coming, I could tell.

In this passage, the MTurk worker should be able to understand that "appeared" refers to the outward impression given by "Charles". This use of appear is most similar to the first entry in sense set one; thus, the correct answer for this problem is Sense_Set-1.

4.2 Gold Standard

The gold standard dataset, on which we evaluate MTurk worker annotations, is provided by (Akkaya et al., 2009). This dataset (called subjSENSEVAL) consists of target word instances in a corpus labeled as S or O, indicating whether they are used with a subjective or objective sense. It is based on the lexical sample corpora from SENSEVAL1 (Kilgarriff and Palmer, 2000), SENSEVAL2 (Preiss and Yarowsky, 2001), and SENSEVAL3 (Mihalcea and Edmonds, 2004). SubjSENSEVAL consists of instances for 39 ambiguous (having both subjective and objective meanings) target words.

(Akkaya et al., 2009) also provided us with subjectivity labels for word senses which are used in the creation of subjSENSEVAL. Sense labels of the target word senses are defined on the sense inventory of the underlying corpus (Hector for SENSEVAL1; WordNet1.7 for SENSEVAL2; and WordNet1.7.1 for SENSEVAL3). This means the target words from SENSEVAL1 have their senses annotated in the Hector dictionary, while the target words from SENSEVAL2 and SENSEVAL3 have their senses annotated in WordNet1.7. We make use of these labeled sense inventories to build our subjective and objective sets of senses, which we present to the MTurk worker as Sense_Set1 and Sense_Set2 respectively. We want to have a uniform sense representation for the words we ask subjectivity sense labels for. Thus, we consider only SENSEVAL2 and SENSEVAL3 subsets of subjSENSEVAL, because SENSEVAL1 relies on a sense inventory other than WordNet.

5 Experimental Design

We chose randomly 8 target words that have a distribution of subjective and objective instances in subjSENSEVAL with less skew than 75%. That is, no more than 75% of a word's senses are subjective or objective. Our concern is that using skewed data might bias the workers to choose from the more frequent label without thinking much about the problem. Another important fact is that these words with low skew are more ambiguous and responsible for more false hits. Thus, these target words are the ones for which we really need subjectivity word sense disambiguation. For each of these 8 target words, we select 40 passages from subjSENSEVAL in which the target word appears, to include in our experiments. Table 1 summarizes the selected target words

Word	FLP	Word	FLP
appear	55%	fine	72.5%
judgment	65%	solid	55%
strike	62.5%	difference	67.5%
restraint	70%	miss	50%
Average	62.2%		

Table 1: Frequent label percentages for target words.

Group1	Location: USA
Group2	Location: USA HIT Approval Rate $>$ 96%
Group3	Location: USA HIT Approval Rate $>$ 96% Approved HITs $>$ 500

Table 2: Constraints for each HIT group.

and their label distribution. In this table, frequent label percentage (FLP) represents the skew for each word. A word's FLP is equal to the percent of the senses that are of the most frequently occurring type of sense (subjective or objective) for that word.

We believe this annotation task is a good candidate for attracting spammers. This task requires only binary annotations, where the worker just chooses from one of the two given sets, which is not a difficult task. Since it is easy to provide labels, we believe that there will be a distinct line, with respect to quality of annotations, between spammers and mediocre annotators.

For our experiments, we created three different HIT groups each having different qualification requirements but sharing the same data. To be concrete, each HIT group consists of the same 320 instances: 40 instances for each target word listed in Table 1. Each HIT presents an MTurk worker with four instances of the same word in a text passage – this makes 80 HITs for each HIT group – and asks him to choose the set to which the activated sense belongs. We know for each HIT the mapping between sense set numbers and subjectivity. Thus, we can evaluate each HIT response on our gold-standard data, as discussed in Section 4.2. We pay seven cents per HIT. We consider this to be generous compensation for such a simple task.

There are many builtin qualifications in MTurk. We concentrated only on three of them: location, HIT approval rate, and approved HITs, as discussed in Section 2. In our experience, these qualifications are widely used for quality assurance. As mentioned before, we created three different HIT groups in order to see how well different built-in qualification combinations do with respect to filtering spammers. These groups – starting from the least constrained to the most constrained – are listed in Table 2.

Group1 required only that the MTurk workers are located in the US. This group is the least constrained one. Group2 additionally required an approval rate greater than 96%. Group3 is the most constrained one, requiring a lifetime approved HIT number to be greater than 500, in addition to the qualifications in Group1 and Group2.

We believe that neither location nor approval rate and location together is enough to avoid spammers. While being a US resident does to some extent guarantee English proficiency, it does not guarantee well-thought answers. Since there is no mechanism in place preventing users from creating new MTurk worker accounts at will and since all worker accounts are initialized with a 100% approval rate, we do not think that approval rate is sufficient to avoid serial spammers and other poor annotators. We hypothesize that the workers with high approval rate and a large number of approved HITs have a reputation to maintain, and thus will probably be careful in their answers. We think it is unlikely that spammers will have both a high approval rate and a large number of completed HITs. Thus, we anticipated that Group3's annotations will be of higher quality than those of the other groups.

Note that an MTurk worker who has access to the HITs in one of the HIT groups also has access to HITs in less constrained groups. For example, an MTurk worker who has access to HITs in Group3 also has access to HITs in Group2 and Group1. We did not prevent MTurk workers from working in multiple HIT groups because we did not want to influence worker behavior, but instead simulate the most realistic annotation scenario.

In addition to the qualifications described above, we also required each worker to take a qualification test in order to prove their competence in the annotation task. The qualification test consists of 10 sim-

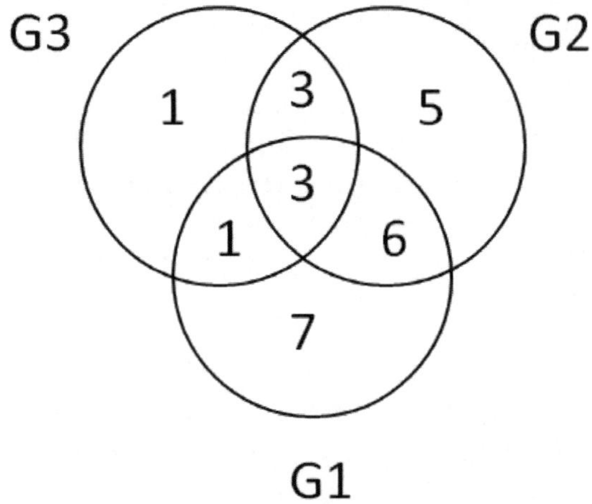

Figure 3: Venn diagram illustrating worker distribution.

ple annotation questions identical in form to those present in the HITs. These questions are split evenly between two target words, "appear" and "restraint". There are a total of five subjective and five objective usages in the test. We required an accuracy of 90% in the qualification test, corresponding to a Kappa score of .80, before a worker was allowed to submit any of our HITs. If a worker failed to achieve a score of 90% on an attempt, that worker could try the test again after a delay of 4 hours.

We collected three sets of assignments within each HIT group. In other words, each HIT was completed three times by three different workers in each group. This gives us a total of 960 assignments in each HIT group. A total of 26 unique workers participated in the experiment: 17 in Group1, 17 in Group2 and 8 in Group3. As mentioned before, a worker is able to participate in all the groups for which he is qualified. Thus the unique worker numbers in each group does not sum up to the total number of workers in the experiment, since some workers participated in the HITs for more than one group. Figure 3 summarizes how workers are distributed between groups.

6 Evaluation

We are interested in how accurate the MTurk annotations are with respect to gold-standard data. We are also interested in how the accuracy of each group differs from the others. We evaluate each group itself separately on the gold-standard data. Additionally, we evaluate each worker's performance on the gold-standard data and inspect their distribution in various groups.

6.1 Group Evaluation

As mentioned in the previous section, we collect three annotations for each HIT. They are assigned to respective trials in the order submitted by the workers. The results are summarized in Table 3. Trials are labeled as T_X and MV is the majority vote annotation among the three trials. The final column contains the baseline agreement where a worker labels each instance of a word with the most frequent label of that word in the gold-standard data. It is clear from this table that, since worker accuracy always exceeds the baseline agreement, subjectivity word sense annotation can be done reliably by MTurk workers. This is very promising. Considering the low cost and low time required to obtain MTurk annotations, a large scale SWSD is realistic. For example, (Akkaya et al., 2009) shows that the most frequent 80 lexicon keywords are responsible for almost half of the false hits in the MPQA Corpus[3] (Wiebe et al., 2005; Wilson, 2008), a corpus annotated for subjective expressions. Utilizing MTurk to collect training data for these 80 lexicon keywords will be quick and cheap and most importantly reliable.

When we compare groups with each other, we see that the best trial result is achieved in Group3. However, according to McNemar's test (Dietterich, 1998), there is no statistically significant difference between any trial of any group. On the other hand, the best majority vote annotation is achieved in Group2, but again there is no statistically significant difference between any majority vote annotation of any group. These results are surprising to us, since we do not see any significant difference in the quality of the data throughout different groups.

6.2 Worker Evaluation

In this section, we evaluate all 26 workers and group them as either spammers or well-meaning workers. All workers who deviate from the gold-standard by a

[3] http://www.cs.pitt.edu/mpqa/

	Group3				Group2				Group1				baseline
	T_1	T_2	T_3	MV	T_1	T_2	T_3	MV	T_1	T_2	T_3	MV	
Accuracy	89.7	86.9	86.6	88.4	87.2	86.3	88.1	90.3	84.4	87.5	87.5	88.4	62.2
Kappa	.79	.74	.73	.77	.74	.73	.76	.81	.69	.75	.75	.77	

Table 3: Accuracy and kappa scores for each group of workers.

Threshold		0.40	0.45	0.50	0.55	0.60	0.65	0.70	0.75
Spammer Count	G1	2	2	2	2	2	4	7	9
	G2	1	2	2	2	2	3	5	8
	G3	0	0	0	0	0	0	2	2
Spammer Percentage	G1	12%	12%	12%	12%	12%	24%	41%	53%
	G2	6%	12%	12%	12%	12%	12%	29%	42%
	G3	0%	0%	0%	0%	0%	0%	25%	25%

Table 4: Spammer representation in groups.

large margin beyond a certain threshold will be considered to be spammers. As discussed in Section 5, we require all participating workers to pass a qualification test before answering HITs. Thus, we know that they are competent to do subjectivity sense annotations, and providing consistently erroneous annotations means that they are probably spammers. We think a kappa score of 0.6 is a good threshold to distinguish spammers from well-meaning workers. For this threshold, we had 2 spammers participating in Group1, 2 spammers in Group2 and 0 spammers in Group3. Table 4 presents spammer count and spammer percentage in each group for various threshold values. We see that Group3 has consistently fewer spammers and a smaller spammer percentage. The lowest kappa scores for Group1, Group2, and Group3 are .35, .40, and .69, respectively. The mean kappa scores for Group1, Group2, and Group3 are .73, .75, and .77, respectively.

These results indicate that Group3 is less prone to spammers, apparently contradicting Section 6.1. We see the reason when we inspect the data more closely. It turns out that spammers contributed in Group1 and Group2 only minimally. On the other hand there are two mediocre workers (Kappa of 0.69) who submit around 1/3 of the HITs in Group3. This behavior might be a coincidence. In the face of contradicting results, we think that we need a more extensive study to derive conclusions about the relation between spammer distribution and built-in qualification.

6.3 Learning Effect

Expert annotators can learn to provide more accurate annotations over time. (Passonneau et al., 2006) reports a learning effect early in the annotation process. This might be due to the formal and informal interaction between annotators. Another possibility is that the annotators might get used to the annotation task over time. This is to be expected if there is not an extensive training process before the annotation takes place.

On the other hand, the MTurk workers have no interaction among themselves. They do not receive any formal training and do not have access to true annotations except a few examples if provided by the requester. These properties make MTurk workers a unique annotation workforce. We are interested if the learning effect common to expert annotators holds in this unique workforce in the absence of any interaction and feedback. That may justify working with the same set of workers over a long time by creating private groups of workers.

We sort annotations of a worker after the submission date. This way, we get for each worker an ordered list of annotations. We split the list into bins of size 40 and we test for an increasing trend in the proportion of successes over time. We use the Chi-squared Test for binomial proportions (Rosner, 2006). Using this test, we find that all of the p-values are substantially larger than 0.05. Thus, there is no increasing trend in the proportion of successes and no learning effect. This is true for both mediocre workers and very reliable workers. We think that the results may differ for harder annotation tasks where the input is more complex and requires some adjustment.

7 Related Work

There has been recently an increasing interest in Amazon Mechanical Turk. Many researchers have utilized MTurk as a source of non-expert natural language annotation to create labeled datasets. In (Mrozinski et al., 2008), MTurk workers are used to create a corpus of why-questions and corresponding answers on which QA systems may be developed. (Kaisser and Lowe, 2008) work on a similar task. They make use of MTurk workers to identify sentences in documents as answers and create a corpus of question-answer sentence pairs. MTurk is also considered in other fields than natural language processing. For example, (Sorokin and Forsyth, 2008) utilizes MTurk for image labeling. Our ultimate goal is similar; namely, to build training data (in our case for SWSD).

Several studies have concentrated specifically on the quality aspect of the MTurk annotations. They investigated methods to assess annotation quality and to aggregate multiple noisy annotations for high reliability. (Snow et al., 2008) report MTurk annotation quality on various NLP tasks (e.g. WSD, Textual Entailment, Word Similarity) and define a bias correction method for non-expert annotators. (Callison-Burch, 2009) uses MTurk workers for manual evaluation of automatic translation quality and experiments with weighed voting to combine multiple annotations. (Hsueh et al., 2009) define various annotation quality measures and show that they are useful for selecting annotations leading to more accurate classifiers. Our work investigates the effect of built-in qualifications on the quality of MTurk annotations.

(Hsueh et al., 2009) applies MTurk to get sentiment annotations on political blog snippets. (Snow et al., 2008) utilizes MTurk for affective text annotation task. In both works, MTurk workers annotated larger entities but on a more detailed scale than we do. (Snow et al., 2008) also provides a WSD annotation task which is similar to our annotation task. The difference is the MTurk workers are choosing an exact sense not a sense set.

8 Conclusion and Future Work

In this paper, we address the question of whether built-in qualifications are enough to avoid spammers. The investigation of worker performances indicates that the lesser constrained a group is the more spammers it attracts. On the other hand, we did not find any significant difference between the quality of the annotations for each group. It turns out that workers considered as spammers contributed only minimally. We do not know if it is just a coincidence or if it is correlated to the task definition. We did not get conclusive results. We need to do more extensive experiments before arriving at conclusions.

Another aspect we investigated is the learning effect. Our results show that there is no improvement in annotator reliability over time. We should not expect MTurk workers to provide more consistent annotations over time. This will probably be the case in similar annotation tasks. For harder annotation tasks (e.g. parse tree annotation) things may be different. An interesting follow-up would be whether showing the answers of other workers on the same HIT will promote learning.

We presented our subjectivity sense annotation task to the worker in a very simple way. The annotation results prove that subjectivity word sense annotation can be done reliably by MTurk workers. This is very promising since the MTurk annotations can be collected for low costs in a short time period. This implies that a large scale general SWSD component, which can help with various subjectivity and sentiment analysis tasks, is feasible. We plan to work with selected workers to collect new annotated data for SWSD and use this data to train a SWSD system.

Acknowledgments

This material is based in part upon work supported by National Science Foundation awards IIS-0916046 and IIS-0917170 and by Department of Homeland Security award N000140710152. The authors are grateful to the three paper reviewers for their helpful suggestions.

References

Cem Akkaya, Janyce Wiebe, and Rada Mihalcea. 2009. Subjectivity word sense disambiguation. In *Conference on Empirical Methods in Natural Language Processing (EMNLP 2009)*.

Chris Callison-Burch. 2009. Fast, cheap, and creative: evaluating translation quality using amazon's mechanical turk. In *EMNLP '09: Proceedings of the 2009 Conference on Empirical Methods in Natural Language Processing*, pages 286–295, Morristown, NJ, USA. Association for Computational Linguistics.

Thomas G. Dietterich. 1998. Approximate statistical tests for comparing supervised classification learning algorithms. *Neural Computation*, 10:1895–1923.

Pei-Yun Hsueh, Prem Melville, and Vikas Sindhwani. 2009. Data quality from crowdsourcing: a study of annotation selection criteria. In *HLT '09: Proceedings of the NAACL HLT 2009 Workshop on Active Learning for Natural Language Processing*, pages 27–35, Morristown, NJ, USA. Association for Computational Linguistics.

Michael Kaisser and John Lowe. 2008. Creating a research collection of question answer sentence pairs with amazons mechanical turk. In *Proceedings of the Sixth International Language Resources and Evaluation (LREC'08)*. http://www.lrec-conf.org/proceedings/lrec2008/.

Joanna Mrozinski, Edward Whittaker, and Sadaoki Furui. 2008. Collecting a why-question corpus for development and evaluation of an automatic QA-system. In *Proceedings of ACL-08: HLT*, pages 443–451, Columbus, Ohio, June. Association for Computational Linguistics.

Hwee Tou Ng. 1997. Getting serious about word sense disambiguation. In *Proceedings of the ACL SIGLEX Workshop on Tagging Text with Lexical Semantics: Why, What, and How?*

Rebecca Passonneau, Nizar Habash, and Owen Rambow. 2006. Inter-annotator agreement on a multilingual semantic annotation task. In *Proceedings of the Fifth International Conference on Language Resources and Evaluation (LREC)*.

Bernard Rosner. 2006. *Fundamentals of Biostatistics*. Thompson Brooks/Cole.

Rion Snow, Brendan O'Connor, Daniel Jurafsky, and Andrew Y. Ng. 2008. Cheap and fast—but is it good?: evaluating non-expert annotations for natural language tasks. In *EMNLP '08: Proceedings of the Conference on Empirical Methods in Natural Language Processing*, pages 254–263, Morristown, NJ, USA. Association for Computational Linguistics.

A. Sorokin and D. Forsyth. 2008. Utility data annotation with amazon mechanical turk. pages 1 –8, june.

J. Wiebe and R. Mihalcea. 2006. Word sense and subjectivity. In *(ACL-06)*, Sydney, Australia.

Janyce Wiebe, Theresa Wilson, and Claire Cardie. 2005. Annotating expressions of opinions and emotions in language. *Language Resources and Evaluation (formerly Computers and the Humanities)*, 39(2/3):164–210.

Theresa Wilson. 2008. *Fine-grained Subjectivity and Sentiment Analysis: Recognizing the Intensity, Polarity, and Attitudes of private states*. Ph.D. thesis, Intelligent Systems Program, University of Pittsburgh.

Non-Expert Correction of Automatically Generated Relation Annotations

Matthew R. Gormley[⋆†] and **Adam Gerber**[⋆†] and **Mary Harper**[⋆‡] and **Mark Dredze** [⋆†]
[⋆]Human Language Technology Center of Excellence
[†]Center for Language and Speech Processing
Johns Hopkins University, Baltimore, MD 21211, USA
[‡]Laboratory for Computational Linguistics and Information Processing
University of Maryland, College Park, MD 20742 USA
mrg@cs.jhu.edu,adam.gerber@jhu.edu,mharper@umd.edu,mdredze@cs.jhu.edu

Abstract

We explore a new way to collect human annotated relations in text using Amazon Mechanical Turk. Given a knowledge base of relations and a corpus, we identify sentences which mention both an entity and an attribute that have some relation in the knowledge base. Each noisy sentence/relation pair is presented to multiple turkers, who are asked whether the sentence expresses the relation. We describe a design which encourages user efficiency and aids discovery of cheating. We also present results on inter-annotator agreement.

1 Introduction

Relation extraction (RE) is the task of determining the existence and type of relation between two textual entity mentions. Slot filling, a general form of relation extraction, includes relations between non-entities, such as a person and an occupation, age, or cause of death (McNamee and Dang, 2009).

RE annotated data, such as ACE (2008), is expensive to produce so systems take different approaches to minimizing data needs. For example, tree kernels can reduce feature sparsity and generalize across many examples (GuoDong et al., 2007; Zhou et al., 2009). Distant supervision automatically generates noisy training examples from a knowledge base (KB) without needing annotations (Bunescu and Mooney, 2007; Mintz et al., 2009). While this method can quickly generate training data, it also generates many false examples. We reduce the noise in such examples by using Amazon Mechanical Turk (MTurk), which has been shown to produce high quality annotations for a variety of natural language processing tasks (Snow et al., 2008).

We use MTurk for annotation of textual relations to establish an inexpensive and rapid method of creating data for slot filling. We present a two step annotation process: (1) automatic creation of noisy examples, and (2) human validation of examples.

2 Method

2.1 Automatic generation of noisy examples

To create noisy examples we use a similar approach to Mintz et al. (2009). We extract relations from a KB in the form of tuples, (e, r, v), where e is an entity, v is a value, and r is a relation that holds between them; for example (J.R.R. Tolkien, occupation, author). Our KB is Freebase[1], an online database of structured information, and our corpus is from the TAC KBP task (McNamee and Dang, 2009)[2]. For each tuple, we find sentences in a corpus that contain both an exact mention of the entity e and of the value v. Of course, such sentences may not attest to the relation r, so the process produces many incorrect examples.

2.2 Human Intelligence Tasks

A Human Intelligence Task (HIT) is a short paid task on MTurk. In our HITs, we present the turker with ten relation examples as sentence/relation pairs. For each example, the user is asked to select from three annotation options: the sentence (1) expresses the relation, (2) does not express the relation, or (3) the

[1]http://www.freebase.com
[2]http://projects.ldc.upenn.edu/kbp/

Proceedings of the NAACL HLT 2010 Workshop on Creating Speech and Language Data with Amazon's Mechanical Turk, pages 204–207,

1.	The sentence expresses the relation. *Sentence*: For the past eleven years, James has lived in Tucson. *Relation*: "Tucson" is the residence of "James"
2.	The sentence does not express the relation. *Sentence*: Samuel first met Divya in 1990, while she was still a student. *Relation*: "Divya" is a spouse of "Samuel"
3.	The relation does not make sense. *Sentence*: Soojin was born in January. *Relation*: "January" is the birth place of "Soojin"

Figure 1: The three annotation options with examples.

relation does not make sense (figure 1.)

Of the ten examples that comprise each HIT, seven are automatically generated by the method above. The correct answer is known for the three remaining examples; these are included for quality assurance (control examples.) The three control examples are a positive example (expresses the relation,) a negative example (contradicts the true relation,) and a nonsense example (relation is nonsensical.)

All control examples derive from a subset of the automatically generated person examples. Positive examples were randomly sampled and hand annotated. Negative examples are familial relations in which we change the relation type so that it would not be expressed in the sentence. For example, the relation "Barack Obama is the parent of Malia Obama" would be changed to "Barack Obama is a sibling of Malia Obama." To generate nonsense examples we employ the same method for a different mapping of relations, which produces relations like "New Zealand is the gender of John Key."

2.3 HIT Design

MTurk is a marketplace so users have total freedom in choosing which HITs to complete. As such, HIT design should maximize its appeal. We assume that users find appealing those HITs through which they may maximize their own monetary gain, while minimizing moment-to-moment frustrations. We emphasized clarity and ease of use.

The layout consists of three sections (figure 2). The leftmost section is a progress list, which shows the user's answers and current position; the middle section contains the current relation example and annotation options; the rightmost section (not pictured) contains instructions. All sections and all UI elements remain visible and in the same position for the duration of the HIT, with only the text of the sentence and relation changing according to question number. Because only a single question is displayed at a time, we are able to minimize user actions such as scrolling, clicking small targets, or making large mouse movements. Additionally, we can monitor how much time a user spends on each question.

At all times the user is able to consult the instructions for the task, which include examples of each annotation option. The user is also reminded of the technical requirements for the HIT and expectations for honesty and accuracy. A comment box provides users with the opportunity to ask questions, make suggestions, or clarify their responses.

	# HITs	*Cost*	*Time (hours)*
Trial	50	\$2.75	27
Batch 1	500	\$27.50	34
Batch 2	765	\$42.08	25
Batch 3	500	\$27.50	22
Total	1815	\$99.83	108

Table 1: Size, cost and time to complete each HITs batch.

3 Results

We submitted a trial run and three full batches of HITs. Table 1 summarizes the costs and completion times for all HITs. The HITs were labeled rapidly and for a low cost (\$0.05 per HIT, i.e., .5¢ per annotation). Each HIT was assigned to five unique workers. We found that 50% of the 352 different workers completed 2 or more HITs (figure 3.) Our results exclude a trial run of 50 hits. Across the 17,650 examples the mean time spent was 20.77 seconds, with a standard deviation of 99.96 seconds. The median time per example was 10.0 seconds.

3.1 Analysis

To evaluate the annotations, two of the authors annotated a random sample of 247 (10%) of the 2471 noisy examples. In addition, we analyzed the workers agreement with the control examples.

We used two metrics to assess agreement. The first metric is pairwise percent agreement (*Pairwise*): the average of the example agreement scores, where the example agreement score is the percent of

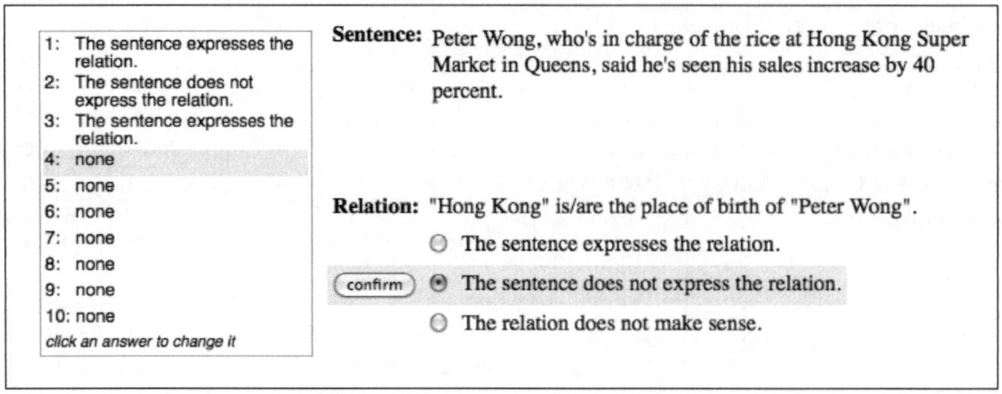

Figure 2: An example HIT with instructions excluded.

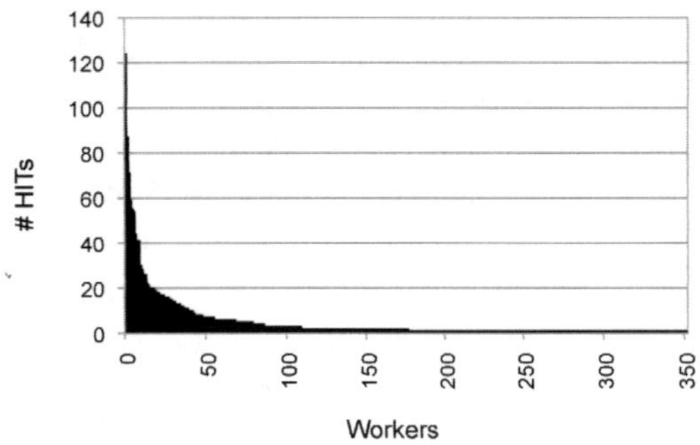

Figure 3: The number of HITs per worker, with columns sorted left to right.

	# Ex.	R	Exact-κ	Pairwise
E1/E2	247	2	0.64	0.81
E1/M	247	2	0.29	0.60
E2/M	247	2	0.39	0.70
C/M	1059	2	0.90	0.93
T(sample)	247	5	0.31	0.69
T(control)	1059	5	0.52	0.68
T(all)	3530	5	0.45	0.68

Table 2: Inter-annotator agreement

pairs of annotators that agreed for a particular example. The second metric is the exact kappa coefficient (*Exact-κ*) (Conger, 1980), which takes into account that agreement can occur by chance. The number of annotators (R) varies with the test scenario.

Table 2 presents the inter-annotator agreement scores for various subsets of the examples and combinations of annotators. On a sample of examples, we evaluated agreement between the first and second expert annotators (*E1/E2*) and also the agreement between each expert and the majority vote of the workers (*E1/M* and *E2/M*). The agreement between the two experts is substantially higher than their individual agreements with the majority. Yet, we achieve our goal of reducing noise.

We also analyzed the agreement between the known control answer and the majority vote of the workers (*C/M*). This high level of agreement supports our belief that the automatically generated negative and nonsense examples were easier to identify than noisy negative and nonsense examples. Finally, we evaluated the agreement between the five workers for different subsets of the data: the sample of noisy examples (*T(sample)*), the control examples only (*T(control)*), and all examples (*T(all)*). Table 3 lists the number of examples collected and the agreement scores for all workers for each relation type.

Table 4 shows the divergence of the workers' annotations from those of an expert. The high level of confusability for those examples which the expert annotated as *Not Expressed* suggests their inherent difficulty. The workers labeled more examples as *Expressed* than the expert, but both labeled few examples as *Nonsense*.

4 Quality Control

We identify spurious responses and unreliable users in two ways. First, worker responses are compared to control examples; greater agreement with controls should indicate greater confidence in the user. We filtered any worker whose agreement with the controls was less than 0.85 (*Control Filtered*). The second approach uses behavioral data. Because only a single example is visible at any time, we can mea-

Relation	*# Ex.*	*Exact-κ*	*Pairwise*
siblings	13	0.67	0.82
children	12	0.57	0.83
gender	80	0.46	0.70
place_of_death	40	0.43	0.68
parent	12	0.40	0.64
spouse	54	0.37	0.65
title	71	0.30	0.78
residences	228	0.29	0.60
ethnicity	38	0.28	0.54
occupation	551	0.26	0.77
activism	4	0.26	0.55
religion	22	0.23	0.55
place_of_birth	160	0.20	0.64
nationality	1044	0.19	0.67
schools_attended	8	0.16	0.55
employee_of	132	0.16	0.70
charges	2	0.14	0.70
Total	2471	0.35	0.69

Table 3: Inter-annotator agreement across relation type. *# Ex.* is the number of noisy examples. *Exact-κ* and *Pairwise* agreement are among the five workers.

		Worker			
		E	NE	Nn	Total
Expert-1	E	561	89	20	670
	NE	284	248	28	560
	Nn	1	1	3	5
	Total	846	338	51	1235

Table 4: Confusion matrix of expert-1 and user's annotations on the sample of noisy examples, for the choices Expressed (E), Not Expressed (NE), and Nonsense (Nn)

sure how much time a user spends on each example. The UI is designed to allow for the extremely rapid completion of examples and of the HIT in general. Thus, a user could complete the HIT in only a few seconds without even reading any of the examples. Still other users spend only a moment on all-but-one question, and then several minutes on the remaining question. Here, we filter a user answering three or more questions each in under three seconds (*Time Filtered*). We combine these two approaches (*Control and Time*), which yields the highest expert-agreement levels (table 5.)

5 Conclusion

Using non-expert annotators from Amazon Mechanical Turk for the correction of noisy, automatically generated examples is inexpensive and fast. We achieve good inter-annotator agreement using quality assurance measures to detect cheating. The result is thousands of new annotated slot filling example sentences for 17 person relations.

	E1/M	*E2/M*
Unfiltered	0.28	0.38
Time Filtered	0.32	0.43
Control Filtered	0.34	0.47
Control and Time	0.37	0.48

Table 5: Exact-κ scores for three levels of quality control and a baseline, between each expert and the majority vote on 231 sampled examples. For a fair comparison, we reduced the sample size to include only examples for which each level of quality control had at least one worker annotation remaining.

Acknowledgments

We would like to thank the 352 turkers who made this work possible.

References

ACE. 2008. Automatic content extraction. http://projects.ldc.upenn.edu/ace/.

R. Bunescu and R. Mooney. 2007. Learning to extract relations from the web using minimal supervision. In *Association for Computational Linguistics (ACL).*

A.J. Conger. 1980. Integration and generalization of kappas for multiple raters. *Psychological Bulletin*, 88(2):322–328.

Z. GuoDong, M. Zhang, D. H Ji, and Z. H. U. QiaoMing. 2007. Tree kernel-based relation extraction with context-sensitive structured parse tree information. In *Empirical Methods in Natural Language Processing (EMNLP).*

Paul McNamee and Hoa Dang. 2009. Overview of the TAC 2009 knowledge base population track. In *Text Analysis Conference (TAC).*

M. Mintz, S. Bills, R. Snow, and D. Jurafsky. 2009. Distant supervision for relation extraction without labeled data. In *Association for Computational Linguistics (ACL).*

R. Snow, B. O'Connor, D. Jurafsky, and A.Y. Ng. 2008. Cheap and fast—but is it good?: evaluating non-expert annotations for natural language tasks. In *Empirical Methods in Natural Language Processing (EMNLP).*

G. Zhou, L. Qian, and J. Fan. 2009. Tree kernel-based semantic relation extraction with rich syntactic and semantic information. *Information Sciences.*

Using Mechanical Turk to Build Machine Translation Evaluation Sets

Michael Bloodgood
Human Language Technology
Center of Excellence
Johns Hopkins University
bloodgood@jhu.edu

Chris Callison-Burch
Center for Language and
Speech Processing
Johns Hopkins University
ccb@cs.jhu.edu

Abstract

Building machine translation (MT) test sets is a relatively expensive task. As MT becomes increasingly desired for more and more language pairs and more and more domains, it becomes necessary to build test sets for each case. In this paper, we investigate using Amazon's Mechanical Turk (MTurk) to make MT test sets cheaply. We find that MTurk can be used to make test sets much cheaper than professionally-produced test sets. More importantly, in experiments with multiple MT systems, we find that the MTurk-produced test sets yield essentially the same conclusions regarding system performance as the professionally-produced test sets yield.

1 Introduction

Machine translation (MT) research is empirically evaluated by comparing system output against reference human translations, typically using automatic evaluation metrics. One method for establishing a translation test set is to hold out part of the training set to be used for testing. However, this practice typically overestimates system quality when compared to evaluating on a test set drawn from a different domain. Therefore, it's necessary to make new test sets not only for new language pairs but also for new domains.

Creating reasonable sized test sets for new domains can be expensive. For example, the Workshop on Statistical Machine Translation (WMT) uses a mix of non-professional and professional translators to create the test sets for its annual shared translation tasks (Callison-Burch et al., 2008; Callison-Burch et al., 2009). For WMT09, the total cost of creating the test sets consisting of roughly 80,000 words across 3027 sentences in seven European languages was approximately $39,800 USD, or slightly more than $0.08 USD/word. For WMT08, creating test sets consisting of 2,051 sentences in six languages was approximately $26,500 USD or slightly more than $0.10 USD/word.

In this paper we examine the use of Amazon's Mechanical Turk (MTurk) to create translation test sets for statistical machine translation research. Snow et al. (2008) showed that MTurk can be useful for creating data for a variety of NLP tasks, and that a combination of judgments from non-experts can attain expert-level quality in many cases. Callison-Burch (2009) showed that MTurk could be used for low-cost manual evaluation of machine translation quality, and suggested that it might be possible to use MTurk to create MT test sets after an initial pilot study where turkers (the people who complete the work assignments posted on MTurk) produced translations of 50 sentences in five languages.

This paper explores this in more detail by asking turkers to translate the Urdu sentences of the Urdu-English test set used in the 2009 NIST Machine Translation Evaluation Workshop. We evaluate multiple MT systems on both the professionally-produced NIST2009 test set and our MTurk-produced test set and find that the MTurk-produced test set yields essentially the same conclusions about system performance as the NIST2009 set yields.

Proceedings of the NAACL HLT 2010 Workshop on Creating Speech and Language Data with Amazon's Mechanical Turk, pages 208–211,
Los Angeles, California, June 2010.

2 Gathering the Translations via Mechanical Turk

The NIST2009 Urdu-English test set[1] is a professionally produced machine translation evaluation set, containing four human-produced reference translations for each of 1792 Urdu sentences. We posted the 1792 Urdu sentences on MTurk and asked for translations into English. We charged $0.10 USD per translation, giving us a total translation cost of $179.20 USD. A challenge we encountered during this data collection was that many turkers would cheat, giving us fake translations. We noticed that many turkers were pasting the Urdu into an online machine translation system and giving us the output as their response even though our instructions said not to do this. We manually monitored for this and rejected these responses and blocked these workers from computing any of our future work assignments. In the future, we plan to combat this in a more principled manner by converting our Urdu sentences into an image and posting the images. This way, the cheating turkers will not be able to cut and paste into a machine translation system.

We also noticed that many of the translations had simple mistakes such as misspellings and typos. We wanted to investigate whether these would decrease the value of our test set so we did a second phase of data collection where we posted the translations we gathered and asked turkers (likely to be completely different people than the ones who provided the initial translations) to correct simple grammar mistakes, misspellings, and typos. For this post-editing phase, we paid $0.25 USD per ten sentences, giving a total post-editing cost of $44.80 USD.

In summary, we built two sets of reference translations, one with no editing, and one with post-editing. In the next section, we present the results of experiments that test how effective these test sets are for evaluating MT systems.

3 Experimental Results

A main purpose of an MT test set is to evaluate various MT systems' performances relative to each other and assist in drawing conclusions about the relative quality of the translations produced by the systems.[2] Therefore, if a given system, say System A, outperforms another given system, say System B, on a high-quality professionally-produced test set, then we would want to see that System A also outperforms System B on our MTurk-produced test set. It is also desirable that the magnitudes of the differences in performance between systems also be maintained.

In order to measure the differences in performance, using the differences in the absolute magnitudes of the BLEU scores will not work well because the magnitudes of the BLEU scores are affected by many factors of the test set being used, such as the number of reference translations per foreign sentence. For determining performance differences between systems and especially for comparing them *across different test sets*, we use percentage of baseline performance. To compute percentage of baseline performance, we designate one system as the baseline system and use percentage of that baseline system's performance. For example, Table 1 shows both absolute BLEU scores and percentage performance for three MT systems when tested on five different test sets. The first test set in the table is the NIST-2009 set with all four reference translations per Urdu sentence. The next four test sets use only a single reference translation per Urdu sentence (ref 1 uses the first reference translation only, ref 2 the second only, etc.). Note that the BLEU scores for the single-reference translation test sets are much lower than for the test set with all four reference translations and the difference in the absolute magnitudes of the BLEU scores between the three different systems are different for the different test sets. However, the percentage performance of the MT systems is maintained (both the ordering of the systems and the amount of the difference between them) across the different test sets.

We evaluated three different MT systems on the NIST2009 test set and on our two MTurk-produced test sets (MTurk-NoEditing and MTurk-Edited). Two of the MT systems (ISI Syntax (Galley et al.,

[1] http://www.itl.nist.gov/iad/894.01/tests/mt/2009/ResultsRelease/currentUrdu.html

[2] Another useful purpose would be to get some absolute sense of the quality of the translations but that seems out of reach currently as the values of BLEU scores (the defacto standard evaluation metric) are difficult to map to precise levels of translation quality.

Eval Set	ISI (Syntax)	JHU (Syntax)	Joshua (Hier.)
NIST-2009 (4 refs)	33.10	32.77	26.65
	100%	99.00%	80.51%
NIST-2009 (ref 1)	17.22	16.98	14.25
	100%	98.61%	82.75%
NIST-2009 (ref 2)	17.76	17.14	14.69
	100%	96.51%	82.71%
NIST-2009 (ref 3)	16.94	16.54	13.80
	100%	97.64%	81.46%
NIST-2009 (ref 4)	13.63	13.67	11.05
	100%	100.29%	81.07%

Table 1: This table shows three MT systems evaluated on five different test sets. For each system-test set pair, two numbers are displayed. The top number is the BLEU score for that system when using that test set. For example, ISI-Syntax tested on the NIST-2009 test set has a BLEU score of 33.10. The bottom number is the percentage of baseline system performance that is achieved. ISI-Syntax (the highest-performing system on NIST2009 to our knowledge) is used as the baseline. Thus, it will always have 100% as the percentage performance for all of the test sets. To illustrate computing the percentage performance for the other systems, consider for JHU-Syntax tested on NIST2009, that its BLEU score of 32.77 divided by the BLEU score of the baseline system is $32.77/33.10 \approx 99.00\%$

2004; Galley et al., 2006) and JHU Syntax (Li et al., 2009) augmented with (Zollmann and Venugopal, 2006)) were chosen because they represent state-of-the-art performance, having achieved the highest scores on NIST2009 to our knowledge. They also have very similar performance on NIST2009 so we want to see if that similar performance is maintained as we evaluate on our MTurk-produced test sets. The third MT system (Joshua-Hierarchical) (Li et al., 2009), an open source implementation of (Chiang, 2007), was chosen because though it is a competitive system, it had clear, markedly lower performance on NIST2009 than the other two systems and we want to see if that difference in performance is also maintained if we were to shift evaluation to our MTurk-produced test sets.

Table 2 shows the results. There are a number of observations to make. One is that the absolute magnitude of the BLEU scores is much lower for all systems on the MTurk-produced test sets than on the NIST2009 test set. This is primarily because the NIST2009 set had four translations per foreign sentence whereas the MTurk-produced sets only have one translation per foreign sentence. Due to this different scale of BLEU scores, we compare performances using percentage of baseline performance. We use the ISI Syntax system as the baseline since it achieved the highest results on NIST2009. The main observation of the results in Table 2 is that both the relative performance of the various MT systems and the amount of the differences in performance (in terms of percentage performance of the baseline) are maintained when we use the MTurk-produced test sets as when we use the NIST2009 test set. In particular, we can see that whether using the NIST2009 test set or the MTurk-produced test sets, one would conclude that ISI Syntax and JHU Syntax perform about the same and Joshua-Hierarchical delivers about 80% of the performance of the two syntax systems. The post-edited test set did not yield different conclusions than the non-edited test set yielded so the value of post-editing for test set creation remains an open question.

Eval Set	ISI (Syntax)	JHU (Syntax)	Joshua (Hier.)
NIST-2009	33.10	32.77	26.65
	100%	99.00%	80.51%
MTurk-NoEditing	13.81	13.93	11.10
	100%	100.87%	80.38%
MTurk-Edited	14.16	14.23	11.68
	100%	100.49%	82.49%

Table 2: This table shows three MT systems evaluated using the official NIST2009 test set and the two test sets we constructed (MTurk-NoEditing and MTurk-Edited). For each system-test set pair, two numbers are displayed. The top number is the BLEU score for that system when using that test set. For example, ISI-Syntax tested on the NIST-2009 test set has a BLEU score of 33.10. The bottom number is the percentage of baseline system performance that is achieved. ISI-Syntax (the highest-performing system on NIST2009 to our knowledge) is used as the baseline.

4 Conclusions and Future Work

In conclusion, we have shown that it is feasible to use MTurk to build MT evaluation sets at a significantly reduced cost. But the large cost savings does not hamper the utility of the test set for evaluating systems' translation quality. In experiments, MTurk-produced test sets lead to essentially the same conclusions about multiple MT systems' translation quality as much more expensive professionally-produced MT test sets.

It's important to be able to build MT test sets quickly and cheaply because we need new ones for new domains (as discussed in Section 1). Now that we have shown the feasibility of using MTurk to build MT test sets, in the future we plan to build new MT test sets for specific domains (e.g., entertainment, science, etc.) and release them to the community to spur work on domain-adaptation for MT.

We also envision using MTurk to collect additional training data to tune an MT system for a new domain. It's been shown that active learning can be used to reduce training data annotation burdens for a variety of NLP tasks (see, e.g., (Bloodgood and Vijay-Shanker, 2009)). Therefore, in future work, we plan to use MTurk combined with an active learning approach to gather new data in the new domain to investigate improving MT performance for specialized domains. But we'll need new test sets in the specialized domains to be able to evaluate the effectiveness of this line of research and therefore, we will need to be able to build new test sets. In light of the findings we presented in this paper, it seems we can build those test sets using MTurk for relatively low costs without sacrificing much in their utility for evaluating MT systems.

Acknowledgements

This research was supported by the EuroMatrix-Plus project funded by the European Commission, by the DARPA GALE program under Contract No. HR0011-06-2-0001, and the NSF under grant IIS-0713448. Thanks to Amazon Mechanical Turk for providing a $100 credit.

References

Michael Bloodgood and K Vijay-Shanker. 2009. Taking into account the differences between actively and passively acquired data: The case of active learning with support vector machines for imbalanced datasets. In *Proceedings of Human Language Technologies: The 2009 Annual Conference of the North American Chapter of the Association for Computational Linguistics*, pages 137–140, Boulder, Colorado, June. Association for Computational Linguistics.

Chris Callison-Burch, Cameron Fordyce, Philipp Koehn, Christof Monz, and Josh Schroeder. 2008. Further meta-evaluation of machine translation. In *Proceedings of the Third Workshop on Statistical Machine Translation (WMT08)*, Colmbus, Ohio.

Chris Callison-Burch, Philipp Koehn, Christof Monz, and Josh Schroeder. 2009. Findings of the 2009 Workshop on Statistical Machine Translation. In *Proceedings of the Fourth Workshop on Statistical Machine Translation (WMT09)*, March.

Chris Callison-Burch. 2009. Fast, cheap, and creative: Evaluating translation quality using Amazon's Mechanical Turk. In *Proceedings of the 2009 Conference on Empirical Methods in Natural Language Processing*, pages 286–295, Singapore, August. Association for Computational Linguistics.

David Chiang. 2007. Hierarchical phrase-based translation. *Computational Linguistics*, 33(2):201–228.

Michel Galley, Mark Hopkins, Kevin Knight, and Daniel Marcu. 2004. What's in a translation rule? In *Proceedings of the Human Language Technology Conference of the North American chapter of the Association for Computational Linguistics (HLT/NAACL-2004)*, Boston, Massachusetts.

Michel Galley, Jonathan Graehl, Kevin Knight, Daniel Marcu, Steve DeNeefe, Wei Wang, and Ignacio Thayer. 2006. Scalable inference and training of context-rich syntactic translation models. In *Proceedings of the 21st International Conference on Computational Linguistics and 44th Annual Meeting of the Association for Computational Linguistics (ACL-CoLing-2006)*, Sydney, Australia.

Zhifei Li, Chris Callison-Burch, Chris Dyer, Juri Ganitkevitch, Sanjeev Khudanpur, Lane Schwartz, Wren Thornton, Jonathan Weese, and Omar Zaidan. 2009. Joshua: An open source toolkit for parsing-based machine translation. In *Proceedings of the Fourth Workshop on Statistical Machine Translation*, pages 135–139, Athens, Greece, March. Association for Computational Linguistics.

Rion Snow, Brendan O'Connor, Daniel Jurafsky, and Andrew Y. Ng. 2008. Cheap and fast - but is it good? Evaluating non-expert annotations for natural language tasks. In *Proceedings of EMNLP-2008*, Honolulu, Hawaii.

Andreas Zollmann and Ashish Venugopal. 2006. Syntax augmented machine translation via chart parsing. In *Proceedings of the NAACL-2006 Workshop on Statistical Machine Translation (WMT-06)*, New York, New York.

Creating a Bi-lingual Entailment Corpus through Translations with Mechanical Turk: $100 for a 10-day Rush

Matteo Negri[1] and **Yashar Mehdad**[1,2]
FBK-Irst[1], University of Trento[2]
Trento, Italy
{negri,mehdad}@fbk.eu

Abstract

This paper reports on experiments in the creation of a bi-lingual Textual Entailment corpus, using non-experts' workforce under strict cost and time limitations ($100, 10 days). To this aim workers have been hired for translation and validation tasks, through the CrowdFlower channel to Amazon Mechanical Turk. As a result, an accurate and reliable corpus of 426 English/Spanish entailment pairs has been produced in a more cost-effective way compared to other methods for the acquisition of translations based on crowdsourcing. Focusing on two orthogonal dimensions (*i.e. reliability* of annotations made by non experts, and overall corpus creation *costs*), we summarize the methodology we adopted, the achieved results, the main problems encountered, and the lessons learned.

1 Introduction

Textual Entailment (TE) (Dagan and Glickman, 2004) has been proposed as a generic framework for modelling language variability. Given a *text* T and an *hypothesis* H, the task consists in deciding if the meaning of H can be inferred from the meaning of T. At the monolingual level, the great potential of integrating TE recognition (RTE) components into NLP architectures has been demonstrated in several areas, including question answering, information retrieval, information extraction, and document summarization. In contrast, mainly due to the absence of cross-lingual TE (CLTE) recognition components, similar improvements have not been achieved yet in any cross-lingual application. Along such direction, focusing on feasibility and architectural issues, (Mehdad et al., 2010) recently proposed baseline results demonstrating the potential of a simple approach that integrates Machine Translation and monolingual TE components.

As a complementary research problem, this paper addresses the data collection issue, focusing on the definition of a fast, cheap, and reliable methodology to create CLTE corpora. The main motivation is that, as in many other NLP areas, the availability of large quantities of annotated data represents a critical bottleneck in the systems' development/evaluation cycle. Our first step in this direction takes advantage of an already available monolingual corpus, casting the problem as a translation one. The challenge consists in taking a publicly available RTE dataset of English T-H pairs (*i.e.* the PASCAL-RTE3 dataset[1]), and create its English-Spanish CLTE equivalent by translating the hypotheses into Spanish. To this aim non-expert workers have been hired through the CrowdFlower[2] channel to Amazon Mechanical Turk[3] (MTurk), a crowdsourcing marketplace recently used with success for a variety of NLP tasks (Snow et al., 2008; Callison-Burch, 2009; Mihalcea and Strapparava, 2009; Marge et al., 2010; Ambati et al., 2010).

The following sections overview our experiments, carried out under strict time (10 days) and cost ($100) limitations. In particular, Section 2 describes our data acquisition process; Section 3 summarizes

[1]Available at: http://www.nist.gov/tac/data/RTE/index.html
[2]http://crowdflower.com/
[3]https://www.mturk.com/mturk/

Proceedings of the NAACL HLT 2010 Workshop on Creating Speech and Language Data with Amazon's Mechanical Turk, pages 212–216,
Los Angeles, California, June 2010.

the successive approximations that led to the definition of our methodology, and the lessons learned at each step; Section 4 concludes the paper and provides directions for future work.

2 Corpus creation cycles

Starting from the RTE3 Development set (800 English T-H pairs), our corpus creation process has been organized in sentence *translation-validation* cycles, defined as separate "jobs" routed to CrowdFower's workforce. At the first stage of each cycle, the original English hypotheses are used to create a *translation* job for collecting their Spanish equivalents. At the second stage, the collected translations are used to create a *validation* job, where multiple judges are asked to check the correctness of each translation, given the English source. Translated hypotheses that are positively evaluated by the majority of trustful validators (*i.e.* those judged correct with a confidence above 0.8) are retained, and directly stored in our CLTE corpus together with the corresponding English texts. The remaining ones are used to create a new translation job. The procedure is iterated until substantial agreement for each translated hypothesis is reached.

As regards the first phase of the cycle, we defined our **translation HIT** as follows:

In this task you are asked to:

- *First, judge if the Spanish sentence is a correct translation of the English sentence. If the English sentence and its Spanish translation are blank (marked as -), you can skip this step.*
- *Then, translate the English sentence above the text box into Spanish.*

Please make sure that your translation is:

1. *Faithful to the original phrase in both meaning and style.*
2. *Grammatically correct.*
3. *Free of spelling errors and typos.*

Don't use any automatic (machine) translation tool! You can have a look at any on-line dictionary or reference for the meaning of a word.

This HIT asks workers to first check the quality of an English-Spanish translation (used as a gold unit), and then write the Spanish translation of a new English sentence. The quality check allows to collect accurate translations, by filtering out judgments made by workers missing more than 20% of the gold units.

As regards the second phase of the cycle, our **validation HIT** has been defined as follows:

Su tarea es verificar si la traducción dada de una frase del Inglés al espaol es correcta o no. La traducción es correcta si:

1. *El estilo y sentido de la frase son fieles a los de la original.*
2. *Es gramaticalmente correcta.*
3. *Carece de errores ortográficos y tipográficos.*

Nota: el uso de herramientas de traducción automática (máquina) no está permitido!

This HIT asks workers to take binary decisions (Yes/No) for a set of English-Spanish translations including gold units. The title and the description are written in Spanish in order to weed out untrusted workers (*i.e.* those speaking only English), and attract the attention of Spanish speakers.

In our experiments, both the translation and validation jobs have been defined in several ways, trying to explore different strategies to quickly collect reliable data in a cost effective way. Such cost reduction effort led to the following differences between our work and similar related approaches documented in literature (Callison-Burch, 2009; Snow et al., 2008):

- Previous works built on redundancy of the collected translations (up to 5 for each source sentence), thus resulting in more costly jobs. For instance, adopting a redundancy-based approach to collect 5 translations per sentence at the cost of \$0.01 each, and 5 validations per translation at the cost of \$0.002 each, would result in \$80 for 800 sentences.

  Assuming that the translation process is complex and expensive, our cycle-based technique builds on simple and cheap validation mechanisms that drastically reduce the amount of translations required. In our case, 1 translation per sentence at the cost of \$0.01, and 5 validations per translation at the cost of \$0.002 each, would result in $32 for 800 sentences, making a conservative assumption of up to 8 iterations with 50% wrong translations at each cycle (*i.e.* 800 sentences in the first cycle, 400 in the second, 200 in the third, etc.).

- Previous works involving validation of the collected data are based on ranking/voting mechanisms, where workers are asked to order a number of translations, or select the best one given the source. Our approach to validation is based on asking workers to take binary decisions over source-target pairs. This results in an easier, faster, and eventually cheaper task.

- Previous works did not use any specific method to qualify the workers' knowledge, apart from *post-hoc* agreement computation. Our approach systematically includes gold units to filter out untrusted workers during the process. As a result we pay only for qualified judgments.

3 Experiments and lessons learned

The overall methodology, and the definition of the HITs described in Section 2, are the result of successive approximations that took into account two correlated aspects: the quality of the collected translations, and the current limitations of the CrowdFlower service. On one side, simpler, cheaper, and faster jobs launched in the beginning of our experiments had to be refined to improve the quality of the retained translations. On the other side, *ad-hoc* solutions had to be found to cope with the limited quality control functionalities provided by CrowdFlower. In particular, the lack of regional qualifications of the workers, and of any qualification tests mechanism (useful features of MTurk) raised the need of defining more controlled, but also more expensive jobs.

Table 1 and the rest of this section summarize the progress of our work in defining the methodology adopted, the main improvements experimented at each step, the overall costs, and the lessons learned.

Step 1: a naïve approach. Initially, translation/validation jobs were defined without using qualification mechanisms, giving permission to any worker to complete our HITs. In this phase, our goal was to estimate the trade-off between the required development time, the overall costs, and the quality of translations collected in the most naïve conditions.

As expected, the job accomplishment time was negligible, and the overall cost very low. More specifically, it took about 1 hour for translating the 800 hypotheses at the cost of $12, and less than 6 hours to obtain 5 validations per each translation at the same cost of $12.

Nevertheless, as revealed by further experiments with the introduction of gold units, the quality of the collected translations was poor. In particular, 61% of them should have been rejected, often due to gross mistakes. As an example, among the collected material several translations in languages other than English revealed a massive and defective use of on-line translation tools by untrusted workers, as also observed by (Callison-Burch, 2009).

Step 2: reducing *validation* errors. A first improvement addressed the validation phase, where we introduced *gold units* as a mechanism to qualify the workers, and consequently prune the untrusted ones. To this aim, we launched the validation HIT described in Section 2, adding around 50 English-Spanish control pairs. The pairs (equally distributed into positive and negative samples) have been extracted from the collected data, and manually checked by a Spanish native speaker.

The positive effect of using gold units has been verified in two ways. First, we checked the quality of the translations collected in the first naïve translation job, by counting the number of rejections (61%) after running the improved validation job. Then, we manually checked the quality of the translations retained with the new job. A manual check on 20% of the retained translations was carried out by a Spanish native speaker, resulting in 97% Accuracy. The 3% errors encountered are equally divided into minor translation errors, and controversial (but substantially acceptable) cases due to regional Spanish variations.

The considerable quality improvement observed has been obtained with a small increase of 25% in the cost (less than $3). However, as regards the accomplishment time, adding the gold units to qualify workers led to a considerable increase in duration (about 4 days for the first iteration). This is mainly due to the high number of automatically rejected judgments, obtained from untrusted workers missing the gold units. Because of the discrepancy between trusted and untrusted judgments, we faced another limitation of the CrowdFlower service, which further delayed our experiments. Often, in fact, the rapid growth of untrusted judgments activates automatic pausing mechanisms, based on the assumption that gold units are not accurate. This, however, is a strong assumption which does not take into account the huge amount of non-qualified workers accepting (or even just playing with) the HITs. For instance, in our case the vast majority of errors came from workers located in specific regions where the native language is not Spanish nor English.

Step 3: reducing *translation* errors. The observed improvement obtained by introducing gold units in the validation phase, led us to the definition of a new translation task, also involving a similar qualification mechanism. To this aim, due to language variability, it was clearly impossible to use reference translations as gold units. Taking into account the limitations of the CrowdFlower interface, which does not allow to set qualification tests or split the jobs into sequential subtasks (other effective and widely used features of MTurk), we solved the problem by defining the translation HITs as described in Section 2. This solution combines a validity check and a translation task, and proved to be effective with a decrease in the translations eventually rejected (45%).

Step 4: reducing *time*. Considering the extra time required by using gold units, we decided to spend more money on each HIT to boost the speed of our jobs. In addition, to overcome the delays caused by the automatic pausing mechanism, we obtained from CrowdFlower the possibility to pose regional qualification, as commonly used in MTurk.

As expected, both solutions proved to be effective, and contributed to the final definition of our methodology. On one side, doubling the payment for each task (from $0.01 to $0.02 for each translation and from from $0.002 to $0.005 for each validation), we halved the required time to finish each job. On the other side, by imposing the regional qualification, we eventually avoided unexpected automatic pauses.

4 Conclusion and future work

We presented a set of experiments targeting the creation of bi-lingual Textual Entailment corpora by means of non experts' workforce (*i.e.* the CrowdFlower channel to Amazon Mechanical Turk).

As a first step in this direction, we took advantage of an already existing monolingual English RTE corpus, casting the problem as a translation task where Spanish translations of the hypotheses are collected and validated by the workers. Strict time and cost limitations on one side, and the current limitations of the CrowdFlower service on the other side, led us to the definition of an effective corpus creation methodology. As a result, less than $100 were spent in 10 days to define such methodology, leading to collect 426 pairs as a by-product. However, it's worth remarking that applying this technique to create the full corpus would cost about $30.

The limited costs, together with the short time required to acquire reliable results, demonstrate the effectiveness of crowdsourcing services for simple sentence translation tasks. However, while MTurk is already a well tested, stable, and rich of functionalities platform, some limitations emerged during our experience with the more recent CrowdFlower service (currently the only one accessible to non-US citizens). Some of these limitations, such as the regional qualification mechanism, have been overcome right after the end of our experimentation with the introduction of new functionalities provided as "Advanced Options". Others (such as the lack of other qualification mechanisms, and the automatic pausing of the HITs in case of high workers' error rates on the gold units) at the moment still represent a possible complication, and have to be carefully considered when designing experiments and interpreting the results[4].

In light of this positive experience, next steps in our research will further explore crowdsourcing-based data acquisition methods to address the complementary problem of collecting new entailment pairs from scratch. This will allow to drastically reduce data collection bottlenecks, and boost research both on cross-lingual and mono-lingual Textual En-

[4]However, when asked through the provided support service, the CrowdFlower team proved to be quite reactive in providing *ad-hoc* solutions to specific problems.

Elapsed time	Running cost	Focus	Lessons learned
1 day	$24	Approaching CrowdFlower, defining a naïve methodology	Need of qualification mechanism, task definition in Spanish.
7 days	$58	Improving validation	Qualification mechanisms (gold units and regional) are effective, need of payment increase to boost speed.
9 days	$99.75	Improving translation	Combined HIT for qualification, payment increase worked!
10 days	$99.75	Obtaining bi-lingual RTE corpus	Fast, cheap, and reliable method.

Table 1: $100 for a 10-day rush (summary and lessons learned)

tailment.

Acknowledgments

We would like to thank MTurk and CrowdFlower for providing the $100 credit used for the experiments, and our colleague Silvana Bernaola Biggio, who kindly accepted to validate our results.

The research leading to these results has received funding from the European Community's Seventh Framework Programme (FP7/2007-2013) under Grant Agreement n. 248531.

References

V. Ambati, S. Vogel and J. Carbonell 2010. *Active Learning and Crowd-Sourcing for Machine Translation.* To appear in Proceedings of LREC 2010.

C. Callison-Burch 2009. *Fast, Cheap, and Creative: Evaluating Translation Quality Using Amazon's Mechanical Turk.* In Proceedings of EMNLP 2009.

I. Dagan and O. Glickman 2004. *Probabilistic Textual Entailment: Generic Applied Modeling of Language Variability.* In Proceedings of the PASCAL Workshop of Learning Methods for Text Understanding and Mining.

M. Marge, S. Banerjee and A. Rudnicky 2010. *Using the Amazon Mechanical Turk for Transcription of Spoken Language.* In Proceedings of the 2010 IEEE International Conference on Acoustics, Speech and Spoken Language (ICASSP 2010).

Y. Mehdad, M. Negri, and M. Federico 2010. *Towards Cross-Lingual Textual Entailment.* To appear in Proceedings of NAACL HLT 2010.

R. Mihalcea and C. Strapparava 2009. *The Lie Detector: Explorations in the Automatic Recognition of Deceptive Language.* In Proceedings of ACL 2009.

R. Snow, B. O'Connor, D. Jurafsky, and A. Y. Ng 2008. *Cheap and Fast - but is it Good? Evaluating Non-expert Annotations for Natural Language Tasks.* In Proceedings of EMNLP 2008.

Error Driven Paraphrase Annotation using Mechanical Turk

Olivia Buzek
Computer Science and Linguistics
University of Maryland
College Park, MD 20742, USA
olivia.buzek@gmail.com

Philip Resnik
Linguistics and UMIACS
University of Maryland
College Park, MD 20742, USA
resnik@umd.edu

Benjamin B. Bederson
Computer Science and HCIL
University of Maryland
College Park, MD 20742, USA
bederson@cs.umd.edu

Abstract

The source text provided to a machine translation system is typically only one of many ways the input sentence could have been expressed, and alternative forms of expression can often produce a better translation. We introduce here error driven paraphrasing of source sentences: instead of paraphrasing a source sentence exhaustively, we obtain paraphrases for only the parts that are predicted to be problematic for the translation system. We report on an Amazon Mechanical Turk study that explores this idea, and establishes via an oracle evaluation that it holds the potential to substantially improve translation quality.

1 Introduction

The source text provided to a translation system is typically only one of many ways the input sentence could have been expressed, and alternative forms of expression can often produce better translation. This observation is familiar to most statistical MT researchers in the form of preprocessing choices — for example, one segmentation of a Chinese sentence might yield better translations than another.[1] Over the past several years, MT frameworks have been developed that permit *all* the alternatives to be used as input, represented efficiently as a confusion network, lattice, or forest, rather than forcing selection of a single input representation. This has improved performance when applied to phenomena including segmentation, morphological analysis, and more recently source langage word order (Dyer, 2007; Dyer et al., 2008; Dyer and Resnik, to appear).

We have begun to explore the application of the same key idea beyond low-level processing phenomena such as segmentation, instead looking at alternative expressions of meaning. For example, consider translating *The Democratic candidates stepped up their attacks during the debate*. The same basic meaning could have been expressed in many different ways, e.g.:

- During the debate the Democratic candidates stepped up their attacks.
- The Democratic contenders ratcheted up their attacks during the debate.
- The Democratic candidates attacked more aggressively during the debate.
- The candidates in the Democratic debate attacked more vigorously.

These examples illustrate lexical variation, as well as syntactic differences, e.g. whether the attacking or the increasing serves as the main verb. We hypothesize that variation of this kind holds a potential advantage for translation systems, namely that some variations may be more easily translated than others depending on the training data that was given to the system, and we can improve translation quality by allowing a system to take best advantage of the variations it knows about, at the subsentential level, just as the systems described above can take advantage of alternative segmentations.

Paraphrase lattices provide a way to make this hypothesis operational. This idea is a variation on the uses of paraphrase in translation introduced by Callison-Burch and explored by others, as well (Callison-Burch et al., 2006; Madnani et al., 2007; Callison-Burch, 2008; Marton et al., 2009). These authors have shown that performance improvements can be gained by exploiting paraphrases using phrase pivoting. We have investigated using pivoting to create exhaustive paraphrase lattices, and we have also investigated defining upper bounds by eliciting human sub-sentential paraphrases using Mechanical Turk. Unfortunately, in both cases, we have found the size of the paraphrase lattice prohibitive: there are

[1] Chinese is written without spaces, so most MT systems need to segment the input into words as a preprocessing step.

Proceedings of the NAACL HLT 2010 Workshop on Creating Speech and Language Data with Amazon's Mechanical Turk, pages 217–221,
Los Angeles, California, June 2010.

too many spans to paraphrase to make using Turk cost-effective, and automatically generated paraphrase lattices turn out to be too noisy to produce improved translations.

A potential solution to this problem comes from a different line of work we are pursuing, in which translation is viewed as a collaborative process involving people and machines (Bederson et al., 2010). Here, the idea is that in translating from a source to a target language, source- and target-language speakers who are *not bilingual* can collaborate to improve the quality of automatic translation, via an iterative protocol involving translation, back translation, and the use of a very rich user interface. For example, consider the following translation from English to French by an automatic MT system:

- **Source:** Polls indicate Brown, a state senator, and Coakley, Massachusetts' Attorney General, are locked in a virtual tie to fill the late Sen. Ted Kennedy's Senate seat.
- **System:** Les sondages indiquent Brown, un sénateur d'état, et Coakley, Massachusetts' Procureur général, sont enfermés dans une cravate virtuel à remplir le regretté sénateur Ted Kennedy's siège au Sénat.

Someone with only a semester of college French (one of the authors) can look at this automatic translation, and see that the underlined parts are probably wrong. Changing the source sentence to rephrase the underlined pieces (e.g. changing *Massachusetts' Attorney General* to *the Attorney General of Massachusetts*), we obtain a translation that is still imperfect but is more acceptable:

- **System:** Les sondages indiquent que Brown, un sénateur d'état, et Coakley, le procureur général du Massachusetts, sont enfermés dans une cravate virtuel pourvoir le sige au Sénat de Sen. Ted Kennedy, qui est décédé récemment.

One could imagine (and, indeed, we are building) a visual interface that allows a human participant on the target side to communicate back to a source-side collaborator, in effect saying, "These underlined pieces look like they were translated poorly; can you rephrase the relevant parts of your sentence, and perhaps that will lead to a better translation?"[2]

Putting these ideas together — source paraphrase and identification of difficult regions of input for translation — we arrive at the idea of *error driven paraphrasing* of source sentences: instead of paraphrasing to introduce as much variation as possible everywhere in the sentence, we suggest that instead it makes sense to paraphrase only the parts of a source sentence that are problematic for the translation system. In Section 2 we give a first-pass algorithm for error driven paraphrasing, in Section 3 we describe how this was realized using MTurk, and Sections 4 and 5 provide an oracle evaluation, discussion, and conclusions.

2 Identifying source spans with errors

In error driven paraphrasing, the key idea is to focus on source spans that are likely to be problematic for translation. Although in principle one could use human feedback from the target side to identify relevant spans, in this paper we begin with an automatic approach, automatically identifying that are likely to be incorrect via a novel algorithm. Briefly, we automatically translate source F to target E, then back-translate to produce F' in the source language. We compare F and F' using TERp (Snover et al., 2009), a form of string-edit distance that identifies various categories of differences between two sentences, and when at least two consecutive non-P (non-paraphrase) edits are found, we flag their smallest containing syntactic constituent.

In more detail, we posit that areas of F' where there were many edits from F will correspond to areas in where the target translation did not match the English very well. Specifically, deletions (D), insertions (I), and shifts (S) are likely to represent errors, while matches (M) and paraphrases (P) probably represent a fairly accurate translation. Furthermore, we assume that while a single D, S, or I edit might be fairly meaningless, a string of at least 2 of those types of edits is likely to represent a substantive problem in the translation.

In order to identify reasonably meaningful paraphrase units based on potential errors, we rely on a source language constituency parser. Using the parse, we find the smallest constituent of the sentence containing all of the tokens in a particular error string. At times, these constituents can be quite large, even the entire sentence. To weed out these cases, we restrict constituent length to no more than 7 tokens.

For example, given

F **The most recent probe to visit Jupiter** was the Pluto-bound New Horizons spacecraft in late February 2007.

E La investigación más reciente fue la visita de Júpiter a Plutón de la envolvente sonda New Horizons a fines de febrero de 2007.

F' The latest research visit Jupiter was the Pluto-bound New Horizons spacecraft in late February 2007.

spans in the the bolded phrase in F would be identified, based on the TERp alignment and smallest containing constituent as shown in Figure 1.

[2]Communicating which parts of the sentence are relevant across languages is being done via projection across languages using word alignments; cf. (Hwa et al., 2001).

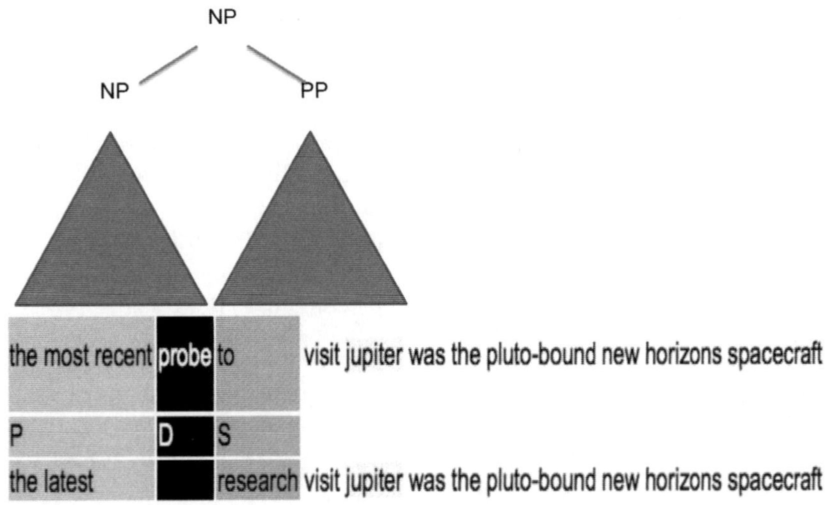

Figure 1: *TERp alignment of a source sentence and its back-translation in order to identify a problematic source span.*

3 Error driven paraphrasing on MTurk

We chose to use translation from English to Chinese in this first foray into Mechanical Turk for error driven paraphrase. This made sense for a number of reasons: first, because we expected to have a much easier time finding Turkers; second, because we could make use of a high quality English parser (in this case the Stanford parser); and, third, because it meant that we as researchers could easily read and judge the quality of Turkers' paraphrases.

To create an English-to-Chinese data set, we used the Chinese-to-English data from the MT08 NIST machine translation evaluation. We used English reference 0 as the source sentence, and the original Chinese sentence as the target. We chose reference 0 because on inspection these references seemed most reflective of native English grammar and usage. The data set comprises 1357 sentence pairs. Using the the above described algorithm to identify possible problem areas in the translation, with the Google Translate API providing both the translation and back-translation, we generated 1780 potential error regions in 1006 of the sentences. Then we created HITs both to obtain paraphrases, and to validate the quality of paraphrase responses. Costs were $117.48 for obtaining multiple paraphrases, and $44.06 for verification.

3.1 Obtaining paraphrases

Based on the phrases marked as problematic by our algorithm, we created HITs asking for paraphrases within 5 sentences, as illustrated in Figure 2. Workers were given 60 minutes to come up with a single paraphrase for each of the five indicated problematic regions, for a reward of $0.10. If a worker felt they could not come up with an alternate phrasing for the marked phrase, they had the option of marking an "Unable to paraphrase" checkbox. We assigned each task to 3 workers, resulting in 3 paraphrases for every marked phrase. From the 1780 errors, we got 5340 responses. Of these, 4821 contained actual paraphrase data, while the rest of the responses indicated an inability to paraphrase, via the checkbox response. All paraphrases were passed on to the verification phase.

3.2 Paraphrase Verification

In the verification phase, we generated alternative full sentences based on the 4821 paraphrases. Workers were shown an original sentence F and asked to compare it to at most 5 alternatives, with a maximum of 20 comparisons made in a HIT. (Recall that although F is the conventional notation for source sentences in machine translation, in this study the F sentences are in English.) Responses were given in the form of radio buttons, marking "Yes" for an alternate sentence if workers felt it was grammatical and accurately reflected the content of the original sentence, or "No" if it did not meet both of those criteria. Workers were given 30 minutes to make their decisions, for a reward of $0.05. This task was also assigned to 3 workers, resulting in 3 judgments for every paraphrase.

4 Evaluating Results

Using the paraphrase results from Mechanical Turk, we constructed rephrased full sentences for every combination of paraphrase alternatives. For example, if a sentence had 2 sub-spans paraphrased, and the two sub-spans had 2 and 3 unique paraphrasings, respectively, we would construct $2 \times 3 = 6$ alternative full sentences. From the 1780 predicted problematic phrases (within the 1006 automatically identified sentences with possible translation errors), we generated 14,934 rephrased sentences. Each rephrased English sentence was translated into a Chinese sentence, again via the Google Translate API. We then evaluated results for translation of the original sentences, and of all their paraphrase alternatives, via the TER metric, using the MT08 original Chinese sentence as the target-language reference translation. The evaluation set includes the 1000 sentence where at least one paraphrase was provided.[3]

Our evaluation takes the form of an *oracle study*: if we knew with perfect accuracy which variant of a sentence to translate, i.e. among the original and all its paraphrases, based on knowledge of the reference translation, how well could we do? An "oracle" telling us which variant is best is not available in the real world, of course, but in situations like this one, oracle studies are often used to establish the magnitude of the potential gain (Och et al., 2004). In this case, the baseline is the average TER score for the 1000 original sentences, 84.4. If an oracle were permitted to choose which variant was the best to translate, the average TER score would drop to 80.6.[4] Drilling down a bit further, we find that a better-translated paraphrase sentence is available in 313 of the 1000 cases, or31.3%, and for those 313 cases, TER for the best paraphrase alternative improves on the TER for the original sentence by 12.16 TER points.

5 Conclusions

This annotation effort has produced gold standard sub-sentential paraphrases and paraphrase quality ratings for spans in a large number of sentences, where the choice of spans to paraphrase is specifically focused on regions of the sentence that are difficult to translate. In addition, we have performed an initial analysis, using human-generated paraphrases to provide an oracle evaluation of how much could be gained in translation by translating paraphrases of problematic regions in the source sentence. The results suggest if paraphrasing is automatically targeted to problematic source spans using a back-translation comparison, good paraphrases of the problematic spans could improve translation performance quite substantially.

In future work, we will use a translation system supporting lattice input (Dyer et al., 2008), rather than the Google Translation API, in order to take advantage of fully automatic error-driven paraphrasing, using pivot-based approaches (e.g. (Callison-Burch et al., 2006)) to complete the automation of the error-driven paraphrase process. We will also investigate the use of human rather than machine identification of likely translation problems, in the context of collaborative translation (Bederson et al., 2010).

[3]For the other 6 sentences, all problematic spans were marked "Unable to paraphrase" by all 3 MTurkers.

[4]TER measures errors, so lower is better. A reduction in TER of 3.8 for an MT evaluation dataset would be considered quite substantial; a reduction of 1 point would typically be a publishable result.

References

Benjamin B. Bederson, Chang Hu, and Philip Resnik. 2010. Translation by iterative collaboration between monolingual users. In *Graphics Interface (GI) conference*.

Chris Callison-Burch, Philipp Koehn, and Miles Osborne. 2006. Improved statistical machine translation using paraphrases. In Robert C. Moore, Jeff A. Bilmes, Jennifer Chu-Carroll, and Mark Sanderson, editors, *HLT-NAACL*. The Association for Computational Linguistics.

Chris Callison-Burch. 2008. Syntactic constraints on paraphrases extracted from parallel corpora. In *EMNLP*, pages 196–205. ACL.

Chris Dyer and Philip Resnik. to appear. Forest translation. In *NAACL'10*.

C. Dyer, S. Muresan, and P. Resnik. 2008. Generalizing word lattice translation. In *Proceedings of HLT-ACL*, Columbus, OH.

C. Dyer. 2007. Noisier channel translation: translation from morphologically complex languages. In *Proceedings of the Second Workshop on Statistical Machine Translation*, Prague, June.

Rebecca Hwa, Philip Resnik, Amy Weinberg, and Okan Kolak. 2001. Evaluating translational correspondence using annotation projection. In *ACL '02: Proceedings of the 40th Annual Meeting on Association for Computational Linguistics*, pages 392–399, Morristown, NJ, USA. Association for Computational Linguistics.

Nitin Madnani, Necip Fazil Ayan, Philip Resnik, and Bonnie Dorr. 2007. Using paraphrases for parameter tuning in statistical machine translation. In *Proceedings of the Second Workshop on Statistical Machine Translation*, pages 120–127, Prague, Czech Republic, June. Association for Computational Linguistics.

Yuval Marton, Chris Callison-Burch, and Philip Resnik. 2009. Improved statistical machine translation using monolingually-derived paraphrases. In *Proceedings of the 2009 Conference on Empirical Methods in Natural Language Processing*, pages 381–390, Singapore, August. Association for Computational Linguistics.

Franz Josef Och, Daniel Gildea, Sanjeev Khudanpur, Anoop Sarkar, Kenji Yamada, Alexander Fraser, Shankar Kumar, Libin Shen, David Smith, Katherine Eng, Viren Jain, Zhen Jin, and Dragomir R. Radev. 2004. A smorgasbord of features for statistical machine translation. In *HLT-NAACL*, pages 161–168.

Matt Snover, Nitin Madnani, Bonnie Dorr, and Richard Schwartz. 2009. TER-Plus: Paraphrases, Semantic, and Alignment Enhancements to Translation Edit Rate. *Machine Translation*.

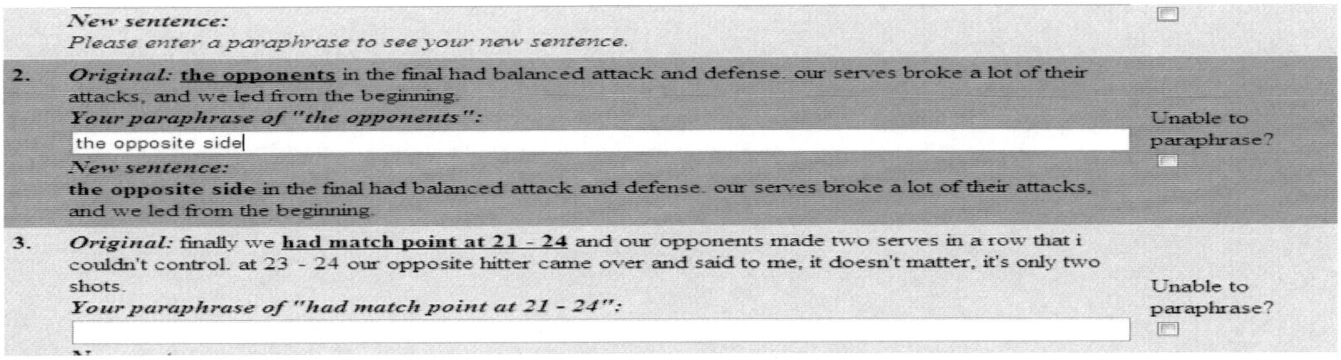

Figure 2: *HIT format 1: Obtaining sub-sentential paraphrases. Note that as the MTurker types a paraphrase into the box,what is typed appears immediately (character by character) in the full-sentence context under "New sentence", so that they can see immediately how the entire sentence looks with their paraphrase.*

the press trust of india quoted

the government minister for relief and rehabilitation kadam

> kadam, the governments relief and rehabilitation minister (2/3)
> the government minister concerned with relief and rehabiliation kadam (1/3)

as revealing today that in the last week, the monsoon has started in

all of indias states one

> every one of indias state, one (3/3)
> each of Indias states one (2/3)
> all states of india one (1/3)

after another, and that the financial losses and casualties have been serious in all areas. just in maharashtra, the state which includes

mumbai, indias largest city,

> india's largest city, mumbai (3/3)
> the largest city in India, Mumbai, (3/3)
> mumbai, the largest city of india, (3/3)

the number of people

known to have died

> who died (3/3)
> identified to have died (2/3)
> known to have passed away (2/3)

has now reached 358.

Figure 3: *Example of error-driven paraphrases produced via HIT format 1, above, for a single sentence. The paraphrase spans (indented) are shown with the number of MTurkers, out of 3, who labeled that paraphrase in context as acceptable using a "validation" HIT.*

Author Index